Effective Physical Security

Effective Physical Security: Design, Equipment, and Operations

Lawrence J. Fennelly
Editor

Butterworth–Heinemann
Boston   London   Oxford   Singapore   Sydney   Toronto   Wellington

Library of Congress Cataloging-in-Publication Data
Effective physical security : design, equipment, and operations /
    Lawrence J. Fennelly, editor.
        p.   cm.
    Includes bibliographical references and index.
    ISBN 0-7506-9390-8 (case bound)
    1. Burglary protection.   2. Crime prevention and architec-
tural design.   3. Crime prevention.
I. Fennelly, Lawrence J., 1940-
TH9705.E34   1992
658.4'7—dc20

British Library Cataloguing in Publication Data
Effective physical security.
    I. Fennelly, Lawrence J. *1940–*
    658.473   91-42942
    ISBN 0750693908   CIP

Butterworth Publishers
80 Montvale Avenue
Stoneham, MA 02180

10 9 8 7 6 5 4 3 2 1

Printed in the United States of America

Contributors

Effective Physical Security

Dan M. Bowers, Consulting Engineer, Randallstown, MD

Don T. Cherry, CPP, Director, Facility Control Design, Columbus, OH

Kenneth Dunckel, Safecracker, Pacifica, CA

James M. Edgar, J.D., Phoenix, AZ

Lawrence J. Fennelly, Sgt., Crime Prevention Specialist, Harvard University Police Department, Cambridge, MA

Richard Gigliotti, Corporate Security Director, UNC Naval Products, Montville, CT

Charles M. Girard, Ph.D., President, International Training, Research and Evaluation Council, Fairfax, VA

Ronald C. Jason, Security Training Officer, UNC Naval Products, Montville, CT

Herman Kruegle, Vice-President, Visual Methods Inc., Westwood, NJ

William P. McInerney, AHC, CPP, McInerney Consulting, Port Hueneme, CA

Robert L. O'Block, Ph.D., CPP, Department of Political Science/Criminal Justice, Appalachian State University, Boone, NC

Mike Rolf, President, Mirosystems Services, Harrison, OH

Joseph Wyllie, Joe Wyllie & Associates, Hicksville, NY

Contents

Preface and Acknowledgments

Crime prevention and loss prevention are closely allied fields differing primarily in their forms of management and sources of authority. A crime prevention officer is a public servant who possesses police powers. A loss prevention manager or security director works in the private sector and receives whatever authority he possesses from his employer, but he is not granted the powers of a public law enforcement officer. The job descriptions of these two positions, however, are quite similar and the skills required are identical. Prevention is the focus in both cases. The crime prevention officer and the loss prevention manager are expected to assess crime vulnerability—no matter whether it is of a residential area, small business, college campus, hospital, or a corporation—and recommend cost-effective security measures. Security problems are common to both the public sector and the private sector and so, too, are solutions.

Vulnerability assessment and target hardening encompass very important components of the crime and loss prevention field. For this reason, this book is devoted to security design, equipment, and operations. Effective Physical Security encompasses the latest technology in physical security, including information on environmental design, use of locks, security lighting, and guard force operations.

The 13 chapters in this book were culled from an earlier Butterworths publication, *Handbook of Loss Prevention and Crime Prevention, Second Edition*. This practical, pared-down volume will better serve crime prevention and loss prevention practitioners as well as students of police science.

A special thanks goes to those individuals and groups who aided and supported publication: Stephen Allen, Thomas Chuda, John Hunter, Albert Janjigian, American Society for Industrial Security, Door and Hardware Institute, National Crime Prevention Institute, Texas Crime Prevention Institute, and Assets Protection.

Thanks, also, to Joseph Barry, CPP, Fred Buck, Dennis Devlin, and M. Yee, who reviewed various chapters.

PART ONE
DESIGN

Chapter 1

Approaches to Physical Security*

RICHARD GIGLIOTTI and RONALD JASON

Protection of one's person and possessions is natural and universally accepted. Unfortunately, there are those who have made it their objective to deprive some of us of one or both of these. In the battle against the criminal element, our resourcefulness in designing and developing more and better methods of protecting our life, property, and livelihood has been unbounded. No system, however, can be made completely secure. Any system conceived can be defeated.

In other words, no physical protection system is 100 percent defeat-proof. It can be designed to eliminate most threats, but it will have its weak links; for example, the perimeter fence or the alarm system. In any event, if a system cannot fully protect against a threat, it must at a minimum offer enough protection so as to delay the threat until the system can be upgraded, at least temporarily, to the point at which the threat can be defeated (e.g., the arrival of local law enforcement authorities or on-site guard response force, the implementation of contingency measures such as additional physical barriers, the release of noxious gases, etc.).

Maximum security is a concept. Physical barriers, alarm systems, guard forces, and all the other components of a security system do not individually achieve maximum security. The parts of the system cannot realize the ultimate aim unless they are combined in the right proportions.

Levels of Physical Security

How would one categorize a particular security system? Would one consider protection minimum, medium, or maximum, and what criteria would be used in making this determination? Would a facility be compared to a prison, nuclear reactor, department store, or the average American home? While the initial question may appear to be answered easily, arriving at an intelligent and impartial assessment becomes much more difficult simply because there are no known universally accepted standards by which the security professional may evaluate a security system.

This lack of standards often serves to delude responsible individuals into believing that the protection they provide (or are paying for) is of a higher level than is actually the case. Because of the confusion and lack of cohesive opinion on the subject, this chapter considers the following five levels of security systems (also see Figure 1–1)[1]:

Level 1—minimum security
Level 2—low level security
Level 3—medium security
Level 4—high level security
Level 5—maximum security

Minimum Security

Such a system would be designed to *impede* some unauthorized external activity. Unauthorized external activity is defined as originating outside the scope of the security system, and could range from

*From *Security Design for Maximum Protection*, by Richard Gigliotti and Ronald Jason (Stoneham, MA: Butterworths, 1984).

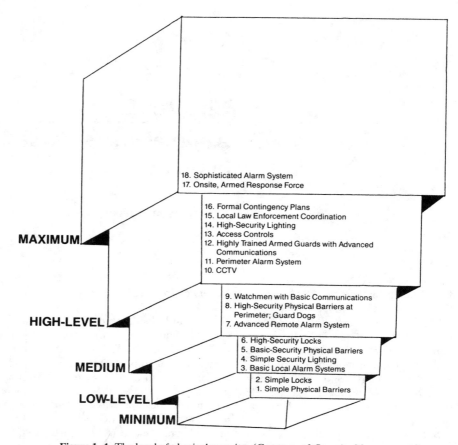

Figure 1–1. The level of physical security. (Courtesy of *Security Management*.)

simple intrusion to armed attack. By virtue of this definition, a minimum security system would consist of simple physical barriers such as regular doors and windows equipped with ordinary locks. The average American home is the best example of a site protected by a minimum security system.

Low-Level Security

This refers to a system designed to *impede and detect* some unauthorized external activity. Once simple physical barriers and locks are in place, they can be supplemented with other barriers such as reinforced doors, window bars and grates, high-security locks, a simple lighting system that could be nothing more elaborate than normal lighting over doors and windows, and a basic alarm system that would be an unmonitored device at the site of the intrusion that provides detection capability and local annunciation. Small retail stores, storage warehouses, and even

older police stations are examples of sites that could be protected by low-level security systems.

Medium Security

A system of this type would be designed to *impede, detect, and assess* most unauthorized external activity and *some* unauthorized internal activity. Such activity could range from simple shoplifting to conspiracy to commit sabotage. When a system is upgraded to the medium level, those minimum and low-level measures previously incorporated are augmented with impediment and detection capability as well as assessment capability. To reach the medium level of security, it is necessary to:

1. Incorporate an advanced intrusion alarm system that annunciates at a staffed remote location.
2. Establish a perimeter beyond the confines of the area being protected and provide high-security

physical barriers such as penetration-resistant fences at least eight feet high and topped with multiple strands of barbed wire or barbed tape at that perimeter, or use guard dogs in lieu of perimeter protection.
3. Use an unarmed guard (with basic training), equipped with the means for basic communication (e.g., commercial telephone) to off-site agencies.

Medium-security facilities might include bonded warehouses, large industrial manufacturing plants, some large retail outlets, and National Guard armories.

High-Level Security

A system of this sort would be designed to *impede, detect, and assess* most unauthorized *external and internal activity*. After those measures previously mentioned have been incorporated into the system, high-level security is realized with the addition of the following:

1. Closed-circuit television (CCTV).
2. A perimeter alarm system, remotely monitored, at or near the high-security physical barriers.
3. High-security lighting, which at a minimum provides at least 0.02 foot-candles of light around the entire facility.
4. Highly trained armed guards or unarmed watch-people who have been screened for employment and who are equipped with advanced means of communications such as dedicated telephone lines, two-way radio links to police, duress alarms, etc.
5. Controls designed to restrict access to or within a facility to authorized personnel.
6. Formal plans prepared with the knowledge and cooperation of police dealing with their response and assistance in the event of specific contingencies at the protected site.
7. Varying degrees of coordination with local law enforcement authorities.

Examples of high-level security sites include certain prisons, defense contractors, pharmaceutical companies, and sophisticated electronics manufacturers.

Maximum Security

Such a system is designed to *impede, detect, assess, and neutralize* all unauthorized *external and internal activity*. In addition to those measures already cited, it is characterized by:

1. A sophisticated alarm system too strong for defeat by a lone individual; remotely monitored in one or more protected locations; tamper-indicating with backup source of power.
2. On-site response force of highly screened and trained individuals armed 24 hours a day and equipped for contingency operations; and dedicated to neutralizing or containing any threat against the protected facility until the arrival of off-site assistance.

The highest level of physical security protection will be found at nuclear facilities, some prisons, certain military bases, and government special research sites, and some foreign embassies.

In order to upgrade a security system to the next highest level, all criteria for that level must be met (see Figure 1–1). Remember that individual criteria from a higher level can be met without the total system being upgraded. For example, if a medium-security facility institutes access controls and installs a closed-circuit television (CCTV) system, the overall level of security has not been upgraded to high-level. In reality, what results is a medium-security system with some high-level characteristics.[2] Depending on its capabilities, a high-level system could achieve maximum security by the addition of a neutralizing capability. By using modern methods, materials, and technology, a maximum-security system can be developed or an existing system upgraded.

This chapter will focus on several examples of components that could result in maximum security. When the term maximum security is used, it denotes the high level of physical security offered by the total system. There is little discussion of less than high-security components such as wooden doors, local alarm systems, and simple fences, because their presence in a maximum-security environment is incidental and does not significantly contribute to the maximum-security concept.

Maximum security is security in depth—a system designed with sufficient diversity and redundancy so as to allow the strength of one particular component to offset the weakness of another. There is no set rule regarding the number of protective layers; again, it depends on the material being protected. As a general rule, however, the more layers, the more difficult it is to defeat the total system. The Nuclear Regulatory Commission has for years inspected nuclear facilities on a component-specific basis. While such evaluation certainly can point out weaknesses in any component, it by no means attests to the effectiveness of the total system. Maximum security depends on the total system, not on its individual components.

The Psychology of Maximum Security

The concept of maximum security is as much psychological as it is physical. To the casual criminal, a maximum security facility is a target to be given up in favor of a minimum (or zero) security facility. To the security director, maximum security accurately describes the system of protection designed to allow him or her to go home at night with the conviction, real or imagined, that the assets entrusted for protection will still be there in the morning. To the average citizen, maximum security is a state of mind more than physical components.

When designing a protection system, one can capitalize on the psychological aspects of maximum security. If a system can create the appearance of being next to impenetrable, then it has succeeded in deterring some lesser adversaries. The same principle can be seen when one compares a threat dog to an attack dog. The former has been trained to put on a show of aggression while the latter has been trained to carry out his threat—a case of bite being worse than bark.

While the concept of maximum security may deter those who are not up to the challenge, it will not turn aside those who are. Whenever the value of the protected assets exceeds the degree of perceived risk, there will always be takers. For a criminal to act and, for that matter, a crime to be committed, there must be desire and opportunity; the criminal must want to commit the act and must have the opportunity. The effectiveness of the system can be measured in terms of eliminating the opportunity; the psychology of the system can be measured in terms of eliminating the desire.

Desire to commit a crime can be eliminated or reduced in a variety of ways. The end result is that the criminal feels the risk outweighs the treasure and moves on to another target. The strongest reason for a criminal to lose desire is the threat of getting caught. The possibility of apprehending the criminal may be increased by the use of lighting for observation capabilities, barriers that delay intrusion, alarms that signal an intrusion, and a security force that can neutralize intrusion. For the maximum psychological effect to be achieved, the capabilities of the protection system must be known to the criminal, that is, they must convince the criminal that the odds of getting caught are high. This can be accomplished by posting signs in and around the facility advertising its protection. While the capabilities of the system should be announced, details should be considered proprietary information and safeguarded accordingly. This is the primary reason that certain details of maximum security (e.g., radio codes, access controls, locks, etc.) are changed whenever key personnel terminate their employment. It is far simpler and cheaper to attempt to eliminate a criminal's desire than it is to eliminate opportunity.

There are those who disagree on the value of advertising a security system's capabilities. They feel that maintaining a low profile somehow will contribute to the overall effectiveness of the system, and criminals will not know that an attractive target exists. This philosophy can be called the ostrich syndrome; it may have been true before the advent of mass and multimedia, but it certainly is not today. A security director who plans to maintain a low enough profile that a criminal will be fooled is merely risking the assets he has been entrusted to protect. Rather, anyone surveilling a protected facility, passively or actively, will understand that she or he will have to plan it carefully and more than likely enlist additional help.

It is important, therefore, that consideration be given to the psychological aspects of maximum security when designing or maintaining a system. An implied presence can do wonders in dissuading criminals from targeting a facility.

The Value of Planning

When setting up a maximum security system, the best results come from a careful and detailed plan. Two basic questions must first be answered:

1. What is being protected?
2. How important is it? (This is measured in terms of political and economic impact, corporate commitment to its protection, and health and safety of the public.)

A third question is sometimes asked: Do the costs of protecting it outweigh its value? While this may be a consideration when planning for a security system less than maximum, it is tacitly implied that something calling for maximum security is worth the cost to someone. Once these questions have been answered, planning can commence.

One of the best approaches to take is to list the basic prerequisites of the security system. As was previously stated, maximum security is designed to *impede, detect, assess, and neutralize* all unauthorized *external and internal activity*. Under each prerequisite are listed those components that would accomplish it. If the system includes a capability to neutralize, this is stated and provided for accordingly:

Security force
Response force
Coordination with local law enforcement authorities (LLEA)

Next, decide which components are going to be used to impede (Table 1–1) detect (Table 1–2), assess (Table 1–3), and (if necessary) neutralize (Table 1–4).

Once the decision is made on the components that will be used to make up the maximum-security system, attention should be directed to developing a design-reference threat.

Table 1–1. Components to Impede

Physical Barriers	Locks
Perimeter fence	Perimeter fence
High-security doors	Openings
High-security windows	Designated doors
Vault	
Security Force	Access Controls
Manning levels	Protected areas
Training	Vital areas
Equipment	

Table 1–2. Components to Detect

Alarm Systems
Doors
Perimeter
Protected areas
Vital areas

Table 1–3. Components to Assess

Lighting	Communications	CCTV
Perimeter	On site	Perimeter
Protected areas	Off site	Protected areas
Vital areas		Vital areas

Table 12–4. Components to Neutralize

Security Force	Response Force	LLEA Coordination
Manning levels	Manning levels	Contingency planning
Training	Training	Training drills
Equipment	Equipment	

Design-Reference Threat

The design-reference threat defines the level of threat with which the facility's physical protection system could contend (or is designed to defeat). This is a most important consideration when designing or upgrading a system and is essential for cost-effective planning.

The security director should list all possible threats to a particular facility. For example, a hospital's security director might list the following as conditions or situations the system should be able to defeat:

Disorderly conduct
Internal theft or diversion
Assaults on employees or visitors
Armed attack on facility
Burglary
Robbery
Kidnapping
Auto theft from parking lot
Hostage incident

The next step is to evaluate these threats in descending order of credibility, that is, which are the most credible based on past experience, loss rates, crime statistics, and so on. The hospital in this example could list as follows, going from the most credible to the least:

1. Internal theft or diversion
2. Auto theft from parking lot
3. Disorderly conduct
4. Assaults on employees or visitors
5. Burglary
6. Robbery
7. Hostage incident
8. Kidnapping
9. Armed attack

In this example, internal theft or diversion is considered a very real possibility (probably based on past experience), followed by theft of automobiles from the hospital's parking lot. Although possible, the threat of armed attack carries low credibility and therefore is of far less concern when deciding on the design of and money to be invested in the security system. Once the credible, realistic threats have been identified and given priority, this information can be used to arrive at the design-reference threat.

The types of adversaries that would likely be encountered by the security system is another area of consideration when determining the design-reference threat. The Nuclear Regulatory Commission[3] describes six generic categories of adversaries and the characteristics of each:

1. Terrorist groups
2. Organized sophisticated criminal groups
3. Extremist protest groups
4. Disoriented persons (psychotic, neurotic)
5. Disgruntled employees
6. Miscellaneous criminals

The security director should now assess these potential adversary groups in terms of likelihood of encounter, from most likely to least. The hospital's list would probably look like this:

1. Miscellaneous criminals
2. Disgruntled employees
3. Disoriented persons
4. Organized sophisticated criminal groups
5. Extremist protest groups
6. Terrorist groups

The most likely threat group would include petty thieves from within the hospital's workforce.

Time, location, and circumstance influence the likelihood of a threat from a particular group. For example, labor disputes could lead to threats by disgruntled employees; hospitalizing an unpopular political figure could lead to threats by terrorists. In any case, extraordinary circumstances should not influence the determination of likely adversaries, but should be considered during contingency planning.

Once the likely threats and adversaries have been determined, it becomes necessary to correlate the two and establish a specific design-reference threat. The process begins by comparing the most credible threats with the most likely adversaries for a particular facility (in this case, the hospital).

1. *Internal theft or diversion*
   Miscellaneous criminals
   Disgruntled employees
   Organized sophisticated criminals
2. *Auto theft*
   Miscellaneous criminals
   Organized sophisticated criminals
3. *Disorderly conduct*
   Disoriented persons
   Miscellaneous criminals
4. *Assaults*
   Miscellaneous criminals
   Disoriented persons
   Organized sophisticated criminals
5. *Burglary*
   Organized sophisticated criminals
   Miscellaneous criminals
6. *Robbery*
   Disoriented persons
   Miscellaneous criminals
7. *Hostage incidents*
   Disoriented persons
   Miscellaneous criminals
   Disgruntled employees
   Extremist protesters
8. *Kidnapping*
   Organized sophisticated criminals
   Terrorists
   Extremist protestors
   Miscellaneous criminals
9. *Armed attack*
   Terrorists
   Extremist protestors

There is always overlap among adversary groups, and this fact must be kept in mind when preparing a threat-versus-adversary analysis. In our example, the hospital's security director has defined the primary threat to facility as being internal theft or diversion, and most likely adversaries in this area as miscellanous criminals followed by disgruntled employees and organized sophisticated criminals. The protection system must be designed or upgraded to counter the most real threat. The most worthy adversary, however, appears to be an organized sophisticated criminal, probably because of the hospital's drug supply. While is the least likely adversary in this threat, this is the most capable (in terms of desire, resources, and capabilities), and therefore the system must be designed to defeat her or him. Thus, at the same time, adversaries of lesser capability will also be defeated. A very simple analogy illustrates this principle: a screened door will, if properly installed, keep out flies; it will also keep out wasps, butterflies, and birds.

Continuing the process of determining the adversary most capable of carrying out the most credible threats, the hospital's security director will probably come up with the following results:

1. Internal theft—organized sophisticated criminals
2. Auto theft—organized sophisticated criminals
3. Disorderly conduct—disoriented persons
4. Assaults—organized sophisticated criminals
5. Burglary—organized sophisticated criminals
6. Robbery—miscellaneous criminals
7. Hostage incident—terrorists
8. Kidnapping—terrorists
9. Armed attack—terrorists

Planning a system to address a realistic security concern as well as the adversary most capable of causing that concern allows the system's architect to prepare for the worst possible case and least capable adversary alike.

Establishing the design-reference threat, therefore, is contingent on determining the groups to which the specific threats or adversaries belong:

1. *Internal Theft (crimes against property)*
   Auto
   Burglary
2. *Violent conduct (crimes against persons)*
   Robbery
   Disorderly conduct
   Assaults
   Hostage incidents
   Kidnapping
   Armed attack

On this basis the hospital's security director knows where to channel resources and the degree of protection needed. Since internal theft or diversion has been defined as the most credible threat, the system should be designed to counter this crime as it would be perpetrated by an organized sophisticated criminal. This is where much of budget money will be used. The next most credible threat is auto theft from the parking lot. Again, resources will have to be directed so as to counter auto theft perpetrated by an organized sophisticated criminal. At the other end of the scale, an armed attack on the facility is a very remote possibility: If it were to happen, chances are the act would be perpetrated by terrorists. Since the possibility is quite low, attention and resources (and budget money) will be minimal if any in this area, and more than likely will consist of contingency planning and/or local law enforcement coordination.

The design-reference threat and its supporting analysis become the basis for planning the measures that will be instituted to preclude its occurrence or counter its effects.

Example: A Nuclear Fuel Cycle Facility

Determining the design-reference threat for a nuclear fuel cycle facility, for example, would follow the same process.

1. *Possible threats*
   Internal theft or diversion
   Armed attack
   Hostage incident
   Burglary
   Civil disturbance
   Auto theft
   Sabotage
   Employee pilferage
   Kidnapping
   Robbery
   Assaults
2. *Credible threats (most to least)*
   Internal theft or diversion of nuclear material
   Sabotage (including threats)
   Armed attack (as a prelude to other action)
   Civil disturbance (including antinuclear demonstrations)
   Employee pilferage (of nonnuclear material)
   Assaults
   Auto theft (from parking lot)
   Kidnapping
   Hostage incident
   Burglary
   Robbery
3. *Potential adversaries (most to least)*
   Terrorist groups
   Disoriented persons
   Disgruntled employees
   Extremists or protesters
   Miscellaneous criminals
   Organized sophisticated criminals
4. *Match-up of threats and adversaries*
   a. Internal theft or diversion
      Disgruntled employees
      Disoriented persons
      Terrorists
   b. Sabotage
      Terrorists
      Disoriented persons
      Disgruntled employees
   c. Armed attack
      Terrorists
   d. Civil disturbance
      Extremists or protesters
   e. Pilferage
      Miscellaneous criminals
   f. Assaults
      Disoriented persons
   g. Auto theft
      Miscellaneous criminals
   h. Kidnapping
      Terrorists
      Disoriented persons
   i. Hostage incident
      Terrorists
      Disoriented persons
      Disgruntled employees
   j. Burglary
      Miscellaneous criminals
   k. Robbery
      Miscellaneous criminals
5. *Most credible threat, most capable adversary*
   a. Internal theft or diversion—terrorists

b. Sabotage—terrorists
c. Armed attack—terrorists
d. Civil disturbance—extremists or protesters
e. Pilferage—disgruntled employees
f. Assault—disoriented persons
g. Auto theft—miscellaneous criminals
h. Kidnapping—terrorists
i. Hostage incident—terrorists
j. Burglary—miscellaneous criminals
k. Robbery—miscellaneous criminals
6. *Basic generic threat groups*
   a. Theft
      Internal
      Pilferage
      Auto
      Burglary
   b. Violence
      Sabotage
      Armed attack
      Civil disturbance
      Assault
      Kidnapping
      Hostage incident
      Robbery

We can see that a nuclear fuel cycle facility's number one security concern is the theft or diversion of nuclear material. The most capable adversary (although the least likely) is a terrorist group. While theft may be the most serious concern, other violent actions, including sabotage and armed attack, are very real possibilities. The chance of a fuel cycle facility being burglarized or robbed (in the traditional sense) is negligible due to the heavy protection provided. The security director must therefore base this system on a design-reference threat that reflects the most serious concerns. The *Code of Federal Regulations* requires that nuclear fuel cycle facilities "must establish and maintain ... a physical protection system. ... designed to protect against ... theft or diversion of strategic special nuclear material and radiological sabotage."[4] The *Code* describes the threats the system must be able to defeat[5]:

1. Radiological sabotage. (i) A determined violent external assault, attack by stealth, or deceptive actions, of several persons with the following attributes, assistance, and equipment: (A) well trained, (B) inside assistance, which may include a knowledgeable individual who attempts to participate in a passive role, an active role, or both, (C) suitable weapons, up to and including hand-held automatic weapons, equipped with silencers and having effective long-range accuracy, (D) hand-carried equipment, including incapacitating

agents and explosives; (ii) an internal threat of an insider, including an employee (in any position).
2. Theft or diversion of formula quantities of strategic special nuclear material. (i) A determined, violent, external assault, attack by stealth, or deceptive actions by a small group with the following attributes, assistance, and equipment: (A) well trained, (B) inside assistance, which may include a knowledgeable individual who attempts to participate in a passive role, an active role, or both, (C) suitable weapons, up to and including hand-held automatic weapons, equipped with silencers and having effective long-range accuracy, (D) hand-carried equipment, including incapacitating agents and explosives, (E) the ability to operate as two or more teams; (ii) an individual, including an employee (in any position), and (iii) conspiracy between individuals in any position.

In summary, a design-reference threat is a systematic analysis of all possible threats and adversaries so that credible threats and adversaries can be identified and this information used as a basis for planning and implementing a physical protection system.

Layering for Protection

The designer must remember the principle of security-in-depth. Protection must be layered so as to provide diversity and redundancy (Figure 1–2). Whenever and wherever possible, layer components. Conduct a walk-through of the facility and likely threat routes. Start either at a point outside and

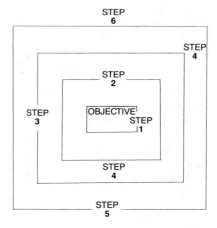

Figure 1–2. Layering. (Courtesy of *Security Management.*)

work in, or start at the most sensitive point within the facility and work out.

Physical Barriers

Physical barriers should be checked at the area considered the most sensitive, such as the vault, cell block, tool crib, shipping department. This area will be called the objective.

1. Provide a high-security barrier around the objective.
2. Enclose a high-security barrier within another high-security barrier.
3. Surround the outer barrier with a penetration-resistant fence.
4. Establish isolation zones on either side of the penetration-resistant fence.
5. Surround the outer isolation zone with yet another penetration-resistant fence and isolation zone.
6. Establish an isolation zone on the outside of the outermost fence.

Entry and exit points should be identified and determination should be made of which ones are vital to the effectiveness of the total system. High-security doors and windows must be installed or upgraded where appropriate. As a general rule, if a window is not needed at a particular location, it should be eliminated. The area containing the objective should be a vault or other such strong room, depending on cost considerations and the effectiveness of the total system. It is important to evaluate the structural components of the facility including walls, ceilings, and floors and determine their ability to withstand a threat equivalent to the design-reference threat.

Physical barriers are not exclusively for keeping someone out; they can also be used to keep someone in.

Locks

After deciding which openings require locks (high-security and otherwise), the types of locks are selected.

Access Controls

Protected and vital areas are designated and decision is made as to who will be admitted to the facility and who will be allowed unrestricted access within it. Generally, the protected area will include the facility itself and the outside area around it up to the first penetration-resistant fence. Vital areas would include the vault or strong room, and could include the alarm stations, emergency generator buildings, or other areas that could be considered vital to the protection of the objective and the facility. (One must not overlook the possibility that the facility itself, rather than its contents, could be the target of an action.)

Security Force

Appropriate staffing levels of the security force for each shift are established, with the amount of training necessary and desirable. (Some states have mandated training levels for security officers.) The force is equipped with resources to handle the design-reference threat.

Alarm Systems

A maximum security system should have a perimeter alarm system capable of detecting an intrusion anywhere on the perimeter. Additionally, all vital areas should be equipped with alarms capable of detecting the presence of an intruder. All doors that contribute to the protection system should be alarmed and all alarms continuously monitored by a person in a remote location on-site. Alarm circuits should be supervised so that tampering with the system or its components will cause an alarm.

Lighting

The value of lighting should be considered for impeding as well as for assessing. In deciding where security lighting should be directed; it should be kept in mind that proper placement will avoid silhouetting security personnel. High-intensity glare lighting, positioned so as to illuminate the isolation zone outside of the protected area, is always appropriate in a maximum-security environment. Also, inside areas can be illuminated so as to facilitate the use of normal CCTV, thus saving money on expensive low-light cameras, energy costs notwithstanding.

Communications

The ability to communicate on-site is of vital importance to the security force. Consider the alternatives for communications. In addition to commercial telephones, the security force should be equipped with at least one dedicated and supervised hot line to local law enforcement authorities (LLEA) and a two-way radio network. Each officer should have a two-way radio and the system should have at least a two-channel capability. Additionally, the facility should be able to communicate with LLEA by means of two-way radio.

CCTV

The CCTV cameras should be placed to ensure proper surveillance and assessment. Depending on the type and quality of equipment, the perimeter and protected and vital areas can be effectively monitored. The use of CCTV instead of personnel to serve this function can save money.

Response Force

If the nature of the security system requires it to neutralize a threat, attention must be directed toward establishing a response force of security personnel that is properly trained and equipped for that purpose. The number of personnel constituting a response force should be sufficient to counter the design-reference threat.

LLEA Coordination

When a system has been designed or upgraded to safeguard something that requires protection of this magnitude, local law enforcement authorities should be brought into the picture. It always helps to establish liaison very early in the game. Once the cooperation of LLEA is secured, it is helpful to consult with them on contingency planning to meet the design-reference threat, and if possible, to schedule joint training sessions and drills to exercise the plans.

Once the process of analysis has been completed, it is time to plan the security system. It is much easier to incorporate security features when a facility is constructed. In this respect, corporate support is essential. The security director should work with the architects and contractors throughout the construction. When this is not possible and an upgrade to an existing facility is necessary, the security director will more often than not become the chief architect of the upgrade. Whenever this happens, the value of planning as discussed will become evident, as it is the basis for the formal security setup.

The Security Plan

The security plan is frequently contracted out to a consultant who will work with the security director. Before system implementation, it is a necessary building document; after implementation, it becomes a necessary reference document. Needless to say, the plan should be treated as proprietary, and access to it should be restricted to those who have a *need to know.*

The plan can take many forms and contain much information. In its basic sense, it is a description of the protection system and its components. Detail can be as much or as little as desired by the security director. For use as a building document, however, it should be quite detailed. Much information can be deleted after implementation, but if the facility is regulated by an agency that requires safeguards, the plan may require many details. If this is the case, the document should be treated as sensitive.

The security plan should contain, but not necessarily be limited to, the following information:

1. A description of the facility and its organizational structure
2. The security organization of the facility
3. A discussion of the physical barriers used in the system
4. A discussion of the alarm system used
5. A description of access controls used to restrict access to or within the facility
6. A discussion of security lighting at the facility
7. A description of the communications capability
8. A description of the CCTV capability and its use
9. A breakdown of the security force; its organization, training, equipment, capabilities, resources, and procedures
10. A discussion of outside resources including LLEA and others as appropriate

Depending on the nature of the facility and its commitments to regulatory agencies, or if the security director so desires, certain other plans can be developed, such as contingency, training, and qualifications plans.

Justification

When it finally comes down to selling a security design or upgrade to the people who will have to pay for it, the job can be made somewhat easier by following a few basic principles.

There aren't many security directors who have not heard that, "Security contributes nothing to production, is an overhead item, and a necessary evil." Dealing with the "Necessary Evil Syndrome" has been the subject of much discussion since the business of assets protection started. Good security holds losses at a minimum and keeps costs down, thus resulting in increased profits. Fulfillment of the security mission can be called *negative profit*, compared with the *positive profit* generated by production. Accordingly, security management personnel must justify many, if not all, systems, expenditures, programs, personnel, approaches, and, at times, their own existence.

Most facilities cut costs for security before anything else; therefore a planned, systematic approach is necessary to keep this practice to a minimum and to secure the resources necessary for efficient security operation. Justification should be based on the following steps:

1. Convincing oneself that a proposal is justified
2. Convincing others that it is justified
3. Formulating the approach
4. Presenting the approach

Convincing Oneself That a Proposal Is Justified

It has been said that a good salesperson believes in the product. So too, must the security director believe in the proposal. Before it can be justified to anyone, it has to be justified in her or his mind. In some cases, this takes only a few minutes and consists of a mental evaluation of the issue. In others, it is a lengthy and detailed examination of alternatives.

As a first step, it is necessary to define the issue— just what it is that is wanted—personnel, equipment, policy, and the like. Then, consider the pros and cons: Do the results justify the expense; is there a cheaper way to accomplish the same thing; is it really necessary, and what happens if it isn't done? Is there enough money available to finance it?

Next, consider the benefit to the company: Will this increase profits? Not likely. Will this reduce overhead? Possibly. Will this make the job easier? Probably.

Turnaround time must be considered, that is, the time it will take to gain a return or realize a benefit from the expenditure or approach.

The security director must rely somewhat on gut feeling. If it is felt that the proposal is logical and rational but there is a negative gut feeling, set the proposal aside and reconsider it at a later date. Circumstances could change and the whole proposal could become moot.

Convincing Others That It Is Justified

Once the proposal is sound, it has to be sold to others who may see everything involving security printed in red ink. Generally, any money that can be saved, no matter what the percentage, is a plus when justifying a proposal. Money saved is negative profit and it should be sold as such.

Before an attempt is made to convince others of the soundness of an approach, the security director must research the whole issue, investing amounts of time and effort proportional to the expense and importance of the issue. Research is based on the company's past experience, personal experience, supporting documentation, and others' perceptions.

Company's Experience

The company may have encountered problems in this area in the past and therefore could be receptive to the idea. There may be a policy that could support the proposal or eliminate it from the start.

The security director should consider any adverse publicity that could result from implementation of, or failure to implement, the approach. Tarnished company image is perhaps one of the most overlooked areas of corporate concern. If a company is in the midst of a problem that threatens its image, its executives and public relations officers often will go to great lengths to preserve its image; however, the inclination to spend money to counter bad press diminishes as time goes by. The tendency to prevent reoccurrence of an unfavorable situation diminishes as more time elapses. An idea is best promoted hard on the heels of a situation in which it would have prevented the occurrence.

Personal Experience

A security director has probably dealt with the same issue before or is familiar with others' handling of a similar issue. Draw on previous experience to define and analyze possible short- and long-term ramifications and positive and negative results.

It is advisable to pay particular attention to idiosyncrasies that could provide necessary direction to the approach, and if possible, capitalize on them. For example, if the approving authority has a liking for gadgets and the approach calls for the use of gadgetry, this affinity could be parlayed into a successful acquisition.

Formulating the Approach

Armed with the raw data that have been accumulated up to this point, it is necessary to adopt a strategy for communicating arguments in a convincing manner.

Formulation of the approach is based on personal knowledge of and experience with the approving authority. If charts and transparencies are generally well received, they should be used; however, the amount of time that should be spent is in proportion to the magnitude of the project.

If personal experience shows that a concise approach is best, the security director should formulate accordingly. Decide on the format, written or verbal, and prepare for both. Consistency is important; the odds increase in favor of subsequent approvals if credibility has been established. Make a list of areas to be covered by priority (Figure 1–3). Certain basic information must be communicated regardless of the format:

1. Definition of the problem
2. Ramifications
3. Alternatives
4. Elimination of each alternative (except the one proposed)
5. The solution
6. Support for the solution

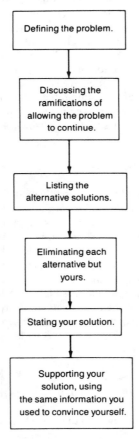

Figure 1–3. The justification process. (Courtesy of *Security Management*.)

Presenting the Approach

Once the issue has been researched and an approach formulated, it must be presented. (It is always a good idea to send a memo regarding the issue beforehand.) If a formal presentation is required, it is recommended that the presentation be tested on affected individuals who should be encouraged to offer their critiques.

The first consideration in this respect should be timing. Once the presentation commences, the approach should be presented as formulated and include the basic information already discussed. The security director must be concise and consistent; and anticipate any questions and be prepared to answer them. Depending on time and importance, audiovisual aids can be effective, as can handouts; it may be no more than a single page outline but it helps to leave something for later reference. Above all, you must not oversell.

If after this effort the proposal is not approved, and if you wish to protect yourself, do so with memos-to-file and other such correspondence so that if problems result from the proposal's disapproval, it can be shown that you tried.[6]

References

1. Richard J. Gigliotti, Ronald C. Jason, and Nancy J. Cogan, "What Is Your Level of Physical Security?" *Security Management*:46. © 1980. Copyright by the American Society for Industrial Security, 1655 N. Fort Drive, Suite 1200, Arlington, VA 22209. Reprinted with permission from the August 1980 issue of *Security Management* magazine.
2. Ibid., pp. 46–50.
3. "U.S. Nuclear Regulatory Commission," *Generic Adversary Characteristics Summary Report* (Washington, D.C.: The Commission, 1979), pp. 11–12.
4. *The Code of Federal Regulations*, title 10, part 73.1, Washington, D.C., 1982.
5. Ibid.
6. Richard J. Gigliotti, "The Fine Art of Justification," *Security Management*, © 1980. Copyright by the American Society for Industrial Security, 1655 N. Fort Drive, Suite 1200, Arlington, VA 22209. Reprinted with permission from the November 1980 issue of *Security Management* magazine, pp. 30–34.

Chapter 2
Environmental Design*

ROBERT L. O'BLOCK

Environmental design, or physical planning, is another approach to preventing crime. Its objective is to improve security in residential and commercial areas by limiting criminal opportunity through the use of physical barriers. It encompasses the consideration of building sites, quality of materials used in construction (particularly doors, windows, locks, and roofs), architectural design of structures, and the role of trees, shrubbery, lighting, and fencing in preventing crime. Environmental factors that are also relevant include careful planning of streets, walkways, and other arteries, as well as increased police technology through computerized dispatching and tracking of patrol cars.

The importance of manipulating one's environment to prevent crimes or attack was recognized long ago. Caves with only one entrance/exit and no windows provided good security for early people, and some caves were even located on high cliffs in which the tribes could isolate themselves with removable ladders. As civilization advanced, many other barriers, such as moats around castles and great walls surrounding cities, were utilized. The classic example is the Great Wall erected to protect China from the Mongols. Although providing a greater degree of protection, these barriers were not impervious to penetration, as exemplified by the Trojan Horse. According to legend, several thousand years ago the citizens of Troy developed a highly advanced system of environmental design, but determined Greeks managed to break their system by using a large hollow horse.

Throughout American history, the role of environmental design was not readily recognized as a significant factor in preventing crime. In fact, the

recognition of crime prevention through environmental design (CPTED) did not really begin to take root until the early 1960s. (See Table 2-1 for a brief synopsis of CPTED.) Elizabeth Wood, with experience in Chicago's public housing, developed a "social design theory," which stresses the importance of physical design considerations in achieving social objectives. She recommended that public housing facilities be designed both interiorly and exteriorly with areas for exercise, play, and loitering that would be private and yet allow for observation by occupants. Jane Jacobs, a contemporary of Wood, was interested in making the streets a safe part of the environment and in 1961 published *The Death and Life of Great American Cities*. She advocated street play for children, hypothesizing that mothers watching the street provided added protection for the streets and that passersby would increase safety for the children. She outlined positive effects of short blocks and the need for clear delineation between public, semipublic, and private areas. In 1964 Oscar Newman and Roger Montgomery, two architects, met with members of the St. Louis Police Department and two sociologists, Lee Rainwater and Roger Walker, to discuss a housing project. From this meeting arose the concept of defensible space. This concept fosters territorial recognition through design, maximizes surveillance through hardware, design, and routing, reduces fear and crime, enhances safety of adjoining areas, and reduces the stigma of public housing. The defensible space concept was studied in 1970 when the Law Enforcement Assistance Administration (LEAA) funded a project to revitalize two New York housing projects. Since that time various LEAA-funded studies have resulted in specific recommendations for increasing security in existing structures and for design considerations for new structures. The result has been a

* From *Security and Crime Prevention*, by Robert L. O'Block (Stoneham, MA: Butterworths, 1981).

Table 2–1. Crime Prevention through Environmental Design (CPTED)*

I.   What Is the Need for CPTED?
    a. Crime
    b. Fear of crime
    c. Improve the quality of life in the neighborhoods and the workplace
II.   Society's Response to Crime
    a. Public sector
    b. Private sector
    c. Criminal justice system
    d. Self-help type programs
III. Crime Concepts
    a. *"Urban Fortress Model"*
        This model represents a view of crime prevention which places sole reliance on securing buildings and areas so outsiders cannot gain access without approval.
        — Isolate the resident from an environment which is perceived to be hostile.
        — Designed to be effective against burglary and other crimes against residences.
    b. *"Defensible Space Model"*
        This model promotes that the design of the physical environment has the capacity to either deter or facilitate crime by enhancing the resident's ability to monitor and control has own environment.
        — Based on the public housing projects conducted by Oscar Newman, he identified the following variables:
        — *Territoriality*
        The capacity of the physical environment to create for each individual perceived zones of territorial influence that results in a proprietary interest and felt responsibility.
        — Design elements such as building placement, height, and size limitations.
        — *Natural surveillance*
        The capacity of physical design to provide surveillance opportunities or residents.
        — The defensible space concept proposed that if territoriality is achieved, it will help to eliminate or reduce the vulnerability to crime and, therefore, aid in deterring possible offenders.
    c. *"Urban Village Model"*
        It identifies social disorganization as a primary cause of crime, defining it as the breakdown in the mechanism that fosters personal relationships, cooperation, recognition, and morale.
        — The urban village model depends primarily on social homogeneity.
IV.   Crime Prevention through Environmental Design CPTED advocated that with the proper design and effective use of the building environment it will lead to a reduction in the incidence of crime and the fear of crime.
        — For several thousand years, an awareness of how the environment shapes behavior has been used by architects, city planners, and residential dwellers to elicit desired behaviors.
    — CPTED promotes a positive change in the attitude of the citizens.
    — There are *three Basic CPTED Strategies*:
    a. *Access control*
        This is a design concept directed at decreasing crime opportunity. Access control strategies are typically classified as:
        — Organized (guards, receptionists, etc.)
        — Mechanical (locks, physical security)
        — Natural (spatial definition)
    — An objective of access control is to deny access to a crime target and to create a perception of risk in offenders.
    b. *Surveillance*
        This is a design concept directed primarily at keeping intruders under observation. Therefore, the primary thrust of a surveillance is to facilitate observation.
        Surveillance strategies include:
        — Patrol (security, police, citizens)
        — Mechanical (lighting, CCTV)
        — Natural (windows, street observations)
    c. *Territoriality*
        This concept suggests that physical design can contribute to a sense of territoriality. Thus, the physical design can create or extend a sphere of influence so that users develop a sense of proprietorship, and potential offenders perceive that territorial influence.
        — At the same time, it was recognized that natural access control and surveillance contributed to a sense of territoriality, making it effective for crime prevention.
    d. *"Three-D" Approach*
        "Three-D" approach to space assessment provides a simple guide in determining how the space is designed and used.
    — All human space has some *designated* purpose.
    — All human space has social, cultural, legal or physical *definitions* that prescribe the desired and acceptable behaviors.
    — All human space is *designed* to support and control the desired behaviors.
    e. *CPTED planning*
        — Crime analysis
        — Demographics
        — Land use
        — Observations
        — Interviews
        — Coordination and communication
    — *Crime analysis*
        — Police
        — Reported crime
        — Trends and patterns

Table 2-1. Continued

- — M.O.
- — *Demographics*
  - — City planning, census bureau
  - — Nature of the population
- — *Land use*
  - — City planning, zoning, engineering
  - — Describe the physical allocations and use of land
- — *Observations*
  - — Go out into the neighborhoods
  - — What is happening, where, when, how, why
- — *Interviews*
  - — People's perceptions
  - — Survey
- — *Coordination and communication*
  - — Between police, security, planners, architects, engineers.
- f. *How police and security can use CPTED*
  - — *Police*

- • Organize neighborhoods and businesses
- • Neighborhood watch, business watch, citizen patrols, security surveys
- • Community and business organizing
- • Enabling legislation
- — *Private*
  - • Problem identification
  - • Building construction with CPTED
  - • Crime prevention programs
  - • Employee and citizen participation
- g. *Optimizing CPTED*
  - — Communications
  - — Security, architects, planners, engineers, and community
  - — What is the "State-of-the-Art"
  - — Evaluation and maintenance
  - — Reduce liability and improve the quality of life

*Prepared by James L. Humphrey.

growing body of knowledge on the effects of combined architectural and crime prevention concepts in preventing crime. In 1972 Newman published his classic book, *Defensible Space*, in which he presented ideas and applied strategies from the New York public housing project to aid in reducing the risk of being victimized and reducing fear of crime when on the streets. Although Wood and Jacobs recognized the need for changes in environmental design in the early 1960s, it was Newman's work that brought an awareness of the relationship between environmental design and crime. C. Ray Jeffery was also very instrumental in bringing the concept of environmental security through its embryonic stage of development to a well-defined science.[1] The efforts of researchers during the 1960s and early 1970s eventually culminated in the development of a conceptual model of environmental security, which is discussed below in greater detail.

Environmental Security (E/S) Conceptual Model

Gardiner has defined environmental security (E/S) as an urban planning and design process that integrates crime prevention with neighborhood design and urban development.[2] This approach combines traditional techniques of crime prevention with newly developed theories and techniques. It encompasses techniques and theories not only to reduce crime, but also to reduce fear of crime since this is equally serious and is a major contributor to the urban decay process. The basic premise of E/S,

then, is that deterioration in the quality of urban life can be prevented or at least minimized through designing and redesigning urban environments so that opportunities for crime are reduced while correspondingly reducing the fear of crime.

Types of crimes that E/S is effective against are those generally referred to as street crimes, crimes of fear, or predatory crimes. The Federal Bureau of Investigation classifies them as violent crimes, or crimes against persons such as murder, rape, assault, and robbery, and crimes against property such as burglary, larceny, and automobile theft. With this in mind, the reader should be able to recognize a significant limitation of E/S in preventing crime: The environmental approach will have little or no effect on offenses that are classified as white collar crimes such as embezzlement, computer-assisted crimes, gambling, loansharking, and various types of frauds. Nevertheless, the positive benefits of E/S as a deterrent of violent crime and salvation of urban areas are overwhelming. Gardiner's analysis of E/S is that it:

is a comprehensive planning process which attempts to redirect that part of the neighborhood decay process that is caused by crime and fear of crime. The goals of E/S which initiate the positive process of preserving neighborhoods are straightforward: to reorganize and structure the larger environments (city districts and communities), to reduce competition, conflict, and opportunities for crime and fear of crime, which undermine the fabric of a neighborhood, and to design the neighborhood environment to allow residents to use, control and develop a sense of responsibility for it—resulting in territoriality.[3]

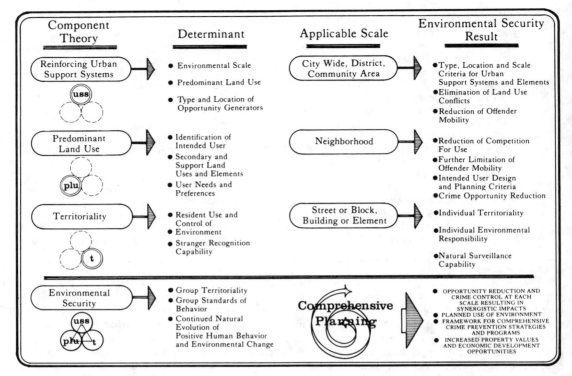

Figure 2–1. The environmental security concept diagram. (From Gardiner, Richard A., *Design for Safe Neighborhoods*. Washington, D.C.: National Institute of Law Enforcement and Criminal Justice, Law Enforcement Assistance Administration, U.S. Department of Justice, 1978.)

A diagram of the environmental security concept is presented in Figure 2-1, illustrating the various components, applications, and results that can be anticipated when the environmental security concept module is employed in designing or redesigning particular environments.

Reduction of Crime through E/S

Environmental security has as its primary goals the prevention of crime and reduction of fear of crime. The concept of environmental security provides several means by which these goals can be accomplished. The first of these is to maximize opportunities for apprehension. This is based on the theory that crime is at least partially deterred through a fear of apprehension rather than punishment, and that the greater the chance of apprehension, the less likely a criminal is to commit a crime. In this approach, the police attempt to maximize something known as omnipresence, that is, to project to the community the sense that the police are around every corner and that they may show up at any time.

The detective force attempts to aid in this by apprehending offenders after crimes occur, thereby adding to the sense of certainty of apprehension. It is not known to what extent the apprehension strategy deters crime, since, for example, only a small percentage of burglars are arrested. It is known, however, that since a real or perceived risk of apprehension is not always a deterrent, an actual ability to apprehend and arrest must be present. The effectiveness of the apprehension strategy is boosted through E/S in four ways. Environmental security serves to: (1) increase perpetration time, (2) increase detection time, (3) decrease reporting time, and (4) decrease police response time.

Perpetration time can be increased by making it more difficult for a crime to occur, which in turn also increases the time in which the criminal can be detected. Detection is enhanced by lighting, careful planning of buildings, entrances, landscaping, etc., which decrease reporting time since there is better observation of crimes in progress. A decrease in police response time is accomplished through better planning of streets, well-defined traffic paths inside buildings, and clearly marked entrances and exits.

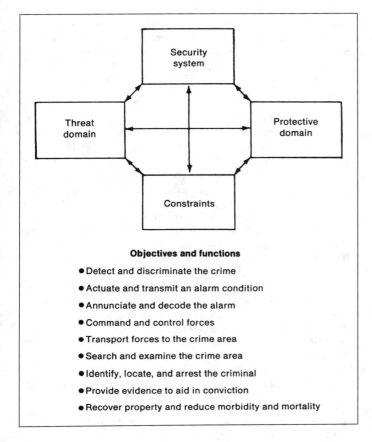

Figure 2–2. Security system interaction and objectives. (From *Decision Aids and CPTED Evaluation Criteria*. Washington, D.C.: Law Enforcement Assistance Administration, U.S. Department of Justice, 1978.)

Many of these factors are related to what is known as *opportunity minimizing*. This encompasses all aspects of target hardening, site inspection, liaison with builders, and design of model security codes. It also includes working with victims, educating citizens, and delving into the possibility of identifying victim-prone individuals, just as industry has long recognized the existence of accident-prone individuals and has made concessions for them.

Specifically, environmental design, used in opportunity-minimizing strategies, includes making:

- access to the offender's target impossible, too difficult, or too time-consuming
- detection or exposure on the premises too great by eliminating places where the criminal could conceal his presence
- arrival of the police or armed guards likely while the offender is still on the premises or before he can make a clean getaway
- the risk of armed resistance by others, with possible death or injury to himself, too great
- successful escape with stolen merchandise improbable because of poor escape routes and probable police interception
- it likely the offender will be identified through increased observation opportunities

The main crime-reducing potential of E/S lies in various methods of reducing opportunities, which is also related to increasing the risk of detection and apprehension. Figure 2-2 expresses the objectives of crime prevention through environmental design.

Influence of Architecture

As has been stated previously in this chapter, architects are of extreme importance in designing and redesigning structures. However, they are also influential from the beginning of a project in co-ordinating building permits and codes between police and public housing authorities. Mutual influence among these three sources must occur early enough so that drawings and specifications are not too fixed to permit needed or recommended changes.

The demand for a safer environment has resulted in a call for schools of architecture and urban design to include courses in crime prevention techniques in their curricula. The National Institute of Law Enforcement and Criminal Justice has recommended six points that should be included in the course of study[4]:

1. Promoting opportunities for surveillance
2. Strengthening the differentiation of private from public space
3. Fostering territoriality
4. Controlling access
5. Separating incompatible activities
6. Providing alternate outlets for potentially delinquent and criminal energies

Courses should also include a study of the effect of architecture on deterrence and displacement of crime. Course content for the study of crime deterrence should include aspects of target hardening such as fencing, alarm systems, lighting, and security patrols. However, crime displacement should be recognized as a possible adverse result of environmental security, since prevention of crime in one location may cause the same or a more serious crime to be committed in another. Will neighborhoods using E/S export crimes to other neighborhoods that do not effectively utilize E/S? Traditionally, this question has been left to criminologists, sociologists, and law enforcement officers to answer, but now it must also be faced by architects and urban planners.

Identification of Potential Targets

Identification of potential targets is a very important aspect of crime prevention. Any security program must be adapted and designed to the specific needs and special constraints of the target. After identifying potential targets, it must be determined whether personnel or physical structures are the most likely target, whether the potential attack is likely to arise from external or internal activities, and whether the probable method of attack (burglary, robbery, kidnapping, arson, etc.) can be recognized. Persons, places, and organizations associated with controversial social and political issues, or organizations in which there are a high number of dissatisfied employees, for example, should be considered high-risk targets, as should persons of real or perceived wealth and influence.

Once this initial assessment of target risk has been undertaken, the individual, organization, or establishment can use environmental security as another approach in strengthening security measures. Through E/S, incorporation of security features in offices, plants, or residences can be accomplished. Factors to be considered should include:

- An evaluation of the locale or proposed locale of the structure
- Physical barriers to control access, including barriers for infrequently used entrances
- Determining the necessity, placement, and type of mechanical security devices (alarm systems, electronic surveillance instruments, locking systems) and incorporating them into the design and construction of the structure
- Utilization of door and window designs that provide maximum security while still allowing for observation of exteriors and the maintenance of privacy interiorly
- Design characteristics that promote quick searches of building interiors and the identification of unusual or suspicious persons, objects, or situations
- Design characteristics that foster observation of the structures, inhibit concealment, and cause the offender to spend an increased amount of time and effort in order to commit an offense, so that the possibility of reporting the crime and apprehending the offender is increased

It can be seen that in order to make the most of the potential benefits of E/S, many factors must be taken into consideration. Advance planning is perhaps one of the most important of these, as are early cooperation among architects, law enforcement personnel, and public housing authorities, and the identification of targets. All of these factors should result in successful site selection, incorporation of physical security measures to protect both property and personnel, an established crime prevention attitude among occupants of the structure, and maintenance of security precautions once the building is complete.

Defensible Space

The chief proponent of the concept of defensible space, as previously mentioned, is Oscar Newman. His book of the same title clearly illustrates this concept.[5] Newman defines defensible space as a "surrogate term for the range of mechanisms— real and symbolic barriers, strongly defined areas of influence, and improved opportunities for surveillance that combine to bring an environment under the control of its residents."[6] It is argued that the complexity of most large cities and the apathy of their citizens make this dream impossible by definition. However, in theory there is much to be said for the community action approach as a form of group cohesiveness. Newman further states, "A defensible space is a living residential environment which can be employed by inhabitants for the enhancement of their lives, while providing security for their families, neighbors, and friends." Areas lacking such characteristics increase both risk and fear of crime, which leads to a gradual deterioration of the general environment. When uncertainty of one's safety exists, even to the extent of being insecure when traveling to and from the housing unit, there is neither a cohesive neighborhood nor a sense of territoriality, and the result is further decay of the moral, spiritual, and physical conditions of the area. Recognition of these negative attributes of socially and physically dissolving environments brought to light the means by which combined efforts of law enforcement and architects could foster the development of the positive attributes of territoriality, cohesiveness, and effective policing measures that act as major deterrents to future offenders. Newman has demonstrated, through his work with New York housing projects, that the means to accomplish these positive results include grouping dwelling units to reinforce associations of mutual benefit, delineating paths of movement, defining areas of activity for particular users through their juxtaposition with internal living areas, and providing for natural opportunities for visual surveillance.[7]

Within the area of environmental design, Newman suggests that the concept of defensible space be divided into four major categories: (1) territoriality, (2) natural surveillance, (3) image and milieu, and (4) safe areas.

Territoriality refers to an attitude of maintaining perceived boundaries. The residents of a given area feel a degree of closeness or cohesiveness; they unite in orientating themselves toward protection of their territory, which they feel is theirs. Outsiders are readily recognized, observed, and approached if their actions indicate hostility or suspicious behavior. This principle can be likened to the behavior of a barking dog when another dog enters his territory.

Natural surveillance refers to the ability of the inhabitants of a particular territory to casually and continually observe public areas of their living area. Physical design of structures should promote optimum surveillance opportunities for the residents in order to reach maximum E/S potential.

Image and milieu involve the ability of design to counteract perceptions of a housing project being isolated and its occupants vulnerable to crime. Physical design of a housing project should strive to project uniqueness in an attempt to offset the stigma of living in public housing projects.

Safe areas are locales that allow for a high degree of observation and random surveillance by the police, in which one could expect to be reasonably safe from crime. Location is one of the most important factors to consider when implementing the concept of environmental security.

Role of Barriers

A significant amount of environmental security is accomplished through the creation of barriers. Hall defines a barrier as a system of devices or characteristics constructed to withstand attack for a specified period of time.[8] The objective of barriers is to prevent or delay the unauthorized access to property. Hall further describes a barrier as being comprised of living and material elements. The living elements include watch or sentry dogs and guards who may be stationed on the premises, and local law enforcement officers and private security forces who are off-premises. Material components of barriers may be psychologic in nature, which are basically deterrent factors resulting from the material barriers, or they may be physical barriers that protect the premises against actual physical attacks. Doors, windows, walls, roofs, and locks are all examples of physical barriers. The effectiveness of material barriers primarily depends upon the amount of time they can withstand attack. The longer a barrier remains intact, the greater the chances of apprehension of the offender and prevention of the crime. All barriers can be defeated in time; therefore, logically the most successful barrier would be the one that could resist a threat for a sufficient amount of time until appropriate action could be taken by law enforcement officers after being notified by an alarm, a resident, or a passerby. The importance of apprehension in deterring crime has previously been alluded to, but it should be recognized that the critical factors in increasing apprehension are increasing perpetration time and reducing response time of authorities.

There are many types of barriers, and the type used depends on the environment and the property that is to be protected. The various barriers are discussed below and illustrated in Figure 2–3.

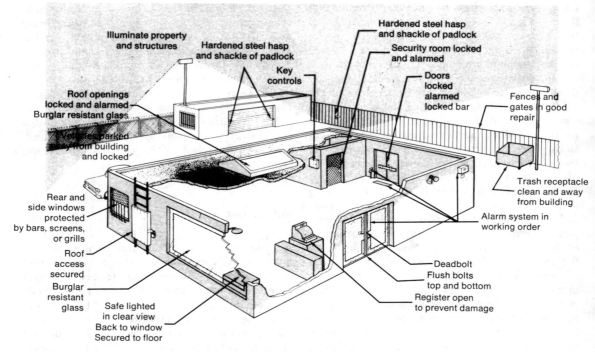

Figure 2–3. Barriers for environmental security.

Fences

One of the most commonly used barriers is fencing. Fencing, or perimeter security, is considered the first line of defense. It is very important to the establishment of territoriality. Many fences are inconspicuous if properly constructed and installed, are fairly reasonable in cost, and are easy to maintain.

Landscaping

Landscaping should be given particular attention when the grounds are checked for security. Large bushy plants or shrubs should be avoided as much as possible, particularly near entryways. Although attractive, removing them will eliminate ideal hiding places for potential intruders, rapists, or voyeurs. Large trees or plants that obstruct viewing of the structure from the street should also be avoided if feasible. Tall shrubbery and trees can provide camouflage for an intruder and, in many cases, it is best to eliminate or significantly reduce large amounts of foliage located near a structure. On the whole, foliage should be no more than two feet high,

and trees and telephone poles ideally should be placed forty to fifty feet from the structure. Of course, this is not always possible.

Landscaping can also be used advantageously in that dense, thorny hedges and bushes serve as natural barriers and can add privacy if planted close to basement or ground-floor windows. Landscaping can also help cover an unsightly fence, but concern with aesthetics should never sacrifice security. Strict upkeep of the landscaping should be maintained year round, and inspections should be made to check for any attempts at breaking in behind the foliage-covered area.

Windows and Doors

The most frequent mode of criminal entry into a residence is forcing, breaking, or opening windows or doors that are inadequately protected. Windows and doors accessible to an intruder should be a primary concern for the security of any structure, since a majority of burglaries occur via these modes. Even though door and window security is an effective and simple method of increasing the security of a structure, builders continue to use low-quality, low-security hardware and materials, and manufacturers continue to produce locks that can be easily and quickly compromised.

Window Security

Any window located less than eighteen feet above ground level or within ten feet of a fire escape should be considered accessible and therefore vulnerable. However, windows high off the ground should not be considered secure, just less vulnerable, since some high windows can be reached from adjacent buildings or from the roof using a grappling hook and rope. A number of precautions can be taken to protect such windows. Several options should be considered regarding the design, construction, and installation of windows, including specific requirements for window frames and glazing materials. Each window constructed and installed, for example, should be able to withstand a force of at least 300 pounds of pressure applied in any direction upon the nonglazed portions (in the locked position) without disengaging the lock or allowing the window to be opened or removed from its frame. Window frames should be constructed so that windows can be opened only from the inside. Frames should be solid so that glass, in resisting impacts of a sledgehammer, does not pop out of the frame. In addition, the frames should receive periodic painting, repair, replacement, or other maintenance as needed.

Considering hardware for windows is also a must in assuring security. Intruders prefer to enter windows by overcoming hardware, rather than by breaking glass, since the noise of breaking glass and the appearance of a broken window are likely to attract unwanted attention. When glass is broken, illegal entry is most often accomplished by reaching through a relatively small opening to release the window's lock or latch. Therefore, a quality key-operated window lock that cannot be released by reaching through a hole in the glass can offer substantial security against unauthorized entry.

A key-operated lock device should prevent the window from being opened or removed from its frame, while withstanding a force of 300 pounds applied in any direction to a nonglazed portion of the window. The key that operates the cylinder on a window lock should not be permanently kept in either the cylinder keyway or any location within three feet of any portion of the window. This strategy will prevent a criminal from breaking a small hole in the glass, reaching in, and using the key to unlock the window. It should be noted that for emergency exit purposes, the key should be placed in the general vicinity of the window and its location be known to all persons who use the room.

If a window is protected by metal bars (a gird or other configuration of sturdy metal permanently installed across a window in order to prevent entry), metal mesh grille (a sturdy grille of expanded metal or welded wires permanently installed across a window or other opening to prevent entry), or sliding metal gate (an assembly of sturdy metal bars joined together so that it can be moved to a locked position across a window to prevent entry), no additional construction or hardware is necessary. Metal bars should be at least one-half inch in diameter and placed no more than five inches apart. Further, the bars should be secured in three inches of masonry or one-eighth inch steel wire mesh.

Various methods are available to make the glass itself more secure. Depending upon the amount of security desired, different materials can be utilized. Traditionally, the types of glass recommended by architects (sheet, plate, tempered, and wire) are relatively vulnerable to breakage. For highest resistance (unbreakable glass), vinyl-bonded laminated glass, one-half inch thickness or more, can be used. Acrylic plastic sheets of three-eighths inch thickness or more than also be used. The most important feature of vandal-resistant glazing materials is that although they eventually can be broken, the breaking process requires so much time, trouble, and noise that it provides substantial security in most instances. Display windows susceptible to hit-and-run tactics should be of burglary-resistant material and plainly labeled as such.

In order to increase surveillance of windows by neighbors, police officers, and other persons using public streets or sidewalks, plants and shrubs should not obstruct the view of any window visible from public areas. Natural obstructions or constructed visual barriers, such as fences, walls, and screens may promote concealment of intruders during a forcible entry of a private or commercial structure. Each publicly visible and accessible window should also be illuminated to allow for observation of the interior of the structure.

Door Security

As with windows, there are many factors to consider if one wishes to install secure doors. Inadequate doors permit easy access to the premises by intruders. Fragile doors, improperly fitting doors, and inadequate locking mechanisms all contribute to the problem.

All exterior doors should be metal or solid hardwood, not hollow core. If solid wood, they should be at least two inches thick. Added security for solid or metal doors can be provided by the inclusion of an optical viewer; such a device should be mandatory. Double doors should be flush-locked with a long bolt. Other vulnerable points on a door that must be considered include the frame, hinges, door panels, and the lock.

Door frames should be sufficiently strong to withstand spreading under pressure. Two-inch thick wood or metal with a rabbeted jamb or hollow metal with a rabbeted jamb filled with solid material should assist in meeting this criterion. Burglars have been known to employ automobile bumper jacks between door frames to spread them enough to release door locks, thus easily opening the door. Certainly this is quite a tax placed upon the door frame; therefore, this is one area in which quality materials and construction cannot be overlooked. Crowbars are also used to pry the door out of the frame, usually placed at the level of the lock and pressure exerted to spread the frame. Frames not of sufficient strength, coupled with incorrect locks, usually will give enough to release the bolt in the lock. Hinges should be placed inside the doorway and all pins welded into place.

Glass panels on doors should be avoided if they are within reaching distance of the inside door handle. Glass panels in general invite intruders, thereby decreasing overall security of the door. Panels of any kind should be protected against being kicked in or knocked out. This can be accomplished by installing bars or sheet metal on the inside of the door, which reinforces the panels.

Door locks should consist of deadbolts or deadlatches with a one-inch throw. Chain locks should not be relied upon as they offer very minimal security.

In general, it is best to limit exterior doors to the minimum while still complying with fire and building codes. Every door creates another possibility for unauthorized entry and, therefore, should be controlled as much as possible. Other varieties of doors such as sliding glass, garage, and loading dock doors must also be appropriately secured.

Wall and Hallway Security

Walls are generally not considered to be points of entry because of their usual solid construction. However, for some years, the trend has been toward the construction of less secure curtain walls because of the increased costs of more secure materials. Intruders do break through walls using various methods. One method is to back a truck into an alley wall until it crumbles. A more sophisticated technique is using an instrument to burn through walls of almost any construction. Such an instrument is available for use in legitimate construction, primarily for burning holes in cement. (One can see the consequences when a legitimate tool gets in the hands of criminals.) Another problem in wall security is that cheap plaster wall separations are used in the construction of many shopping centers. Once any exterior openings or walls are illegally penetrated, the intruder can go from shop to shop through the cheap interior plaster walls. This is also true of insecure basement walls and floors; once inside, the intruder can work his way to the desired area. To counteract these problems, thick, solid walls should become a part of any construction and/or backup protective devices such as the various alarm systems, guards, or closed circuit surveillance systems should be utilized.

Hallways should always be considered early in the planning stage since many problems can arise when sensitive areas are placed in the path of high traffic areas. A frequent mistake is to locate restrooms in the stockrooms, which substantially increases the likelihood of pilferage. Therefore, it is essential that businesses determine which personnel will need to be in what location, and who will be using which access points. Management should see that needed security measures will not be ignored in the planning stages of building or remodeling solely because of objections of inconvenience on the part of employees. Although a compromise is often needed between security and convenience, neglecting security measures completely will only result in further loss to the business in the form of internal and external security problems, and increased costs of installing security measures after the fact.

Other Openings

Roof hatchways, skylights, manholes, coal delivery chutes, and ventilating ducts all can serve as potential entry points for an intruder, and may be overlooked when planning for security. They generally are not used and may be difficult to reach, but they should be locked, barred, bolted, and/or alarmed and continually inspected for signs of tampering. Roof openings, especially those not open to observation from occupied buildings, are particularly attractive to potential burglars since once on the roof, they are generally out of view from the ground level and can take their time in breaking in. Some imaginative intruders have been known to enter structures such as flat-roofed warehouses by cutting holes through the roof and ceiling, obviously neutralizing sophisticated perimeter alarm systems located at more obvious points of entry such as doors and windows. Entrances of this type are facilitated by roofing construction of light-weight, thin materials.

Skylights also present security problems in that their presence provides another source of entry. Skylights must be protected in much the same way as windows, preferably with bars and mesh installed on the inside of the opening so that it is not easily removed. The roofs of structures adjacent to accessible buildings can be additionally protected by chain link fences topped with barbed-wire, alarming, and/or surveying the roof.

Lighting

Illumination is most important in discouraging criminal activity and enhancing public safety. Ample documentation of the effect of lighting on criminal activity is provided by a comparison of day and night crime rates and by the effects of an electrical black-out in a city. Lighting is one of the most effective deterrents to certain types of crime, such as vandalism, burglary, and muggings. Two ways that lighting can be used to prevent crime are: (1) to increase the probability of criminal activity being observed, and (2) to give an empty structure the semblance of being occupied. A person intending to commit a crime naturally desires to minimize the probability of being observed by either law enforcement officers or private citizens. This aversion to being seen includes the approach to and departure from the crime scene as well as the time required to commit the crime.

An increase in lighting levels, like most crime prevention methods, has costs. Lighting equipment, the labor to install and maintain it, and the electrical power to operate it, have become significantly more expensive in recent years, and costs probably will continue to increase. Of the light sources suitable for exterior use, the common incandescent type is the least expensive to purchase and install. However, both the amount of light per watt of electrical energy used and bulb life are lower than for other types. Bulb life is of considerable importance, particularly in those areas where access to the fixture is difficult.

Exterior lighting is especially important in illuminating shrubbery, particularly that located at strategic points such as entryways and sidewalks. It is generally not necessary to illuminate each and every tree, shrub, or bush to have adequate lighting, but in addition to entrances and sidewalks, dark alleys and parking lots should be well lit. At least a 60-watt light shining at every point of potential entry (doors, windows, exhaust fans) should be considered for high-risk areas. Pathways from the house to a detached garage should also be illuminated. Placing of lights should result in bringing the security of a structure close to that which can be expected during the day.

Each facility or residence will have varying factors that will require special attention when determining lighting requirements. However, it is generally recognized that major security problems in lighting concern exterior lighting requirements. Many plans for lighting call for lighting boundaries and approaches while others call for lighting certain areas and structures within the property boundaries. A combination of both is perhaps the best solution in deterring attempts at entry by intruders. In addition to providing security, lighting should also be used as a safety precaution to avoid accidents and possible lawsuits. This is an important consideration for both home-owners and business personnel.

Exterior lighting is generally divided into four broad categories: (1) standby lighting, (2) movable lighting, (3) continuous lighting, and (4) emergency lighting. Standby lighting is automatically or manually switched on and off as desired. Movable lighting is manually operated, can be moved from place to place, and is generally used as supplemental lighting. Continuous lighting is used for glare projection, which deters crime since security personnel can see out, but intruders cannot see in. It also is used when the width of the lighting strip is limited by adjoining property or buildings. Emergency lighting can be comprised of any of the other three types and used when the normal lighting system fails.

Floodlights and street lights are common examples of exterior lighting systems. Floodlights can provide adequate illumination for most exterior security lighting requirements. A floodlight forms a beam that can be projected to a distant point or used to illuminate a particular area. The beam widths of floodlights vary and are differentiated into narrow, medium, and wide beams. Floodlights located in high crime rate areas should be protected by a vandal-resistant plastic cover. The placement of floodlights should be done with planning and skill so that maximum potential of their effectiveness can be realized. When properly used, floodlights have proved to be invaluable in the illumination of property that is vulnerable to vandalism.

Although statistical data on the effectiveness of street lights in reducing crime are inconclusive, if given a choice the average intruder usually will choose a darkened street over a well-lighted one. Perhaps for this reason, street lighting has been blamed for displacing crime rather than reducing the overall level of crime. However, street lighting does serve to reduce the fear of crime, which is an essential factor in the survival of many urban neighborhoods. Street lighting makes an environment less strange, thereby reducing fear; but it cannot completely eliminate the fear of being victimized, since crimes frequently occur during the day. Whether or not it prevents or deters crime, street lighting has many other positive functions. It serves to: prevent or reduce vehicular and pedestrian accidents, provide visual information for vehicular and pedestrian traffic, facilitate and direct vehicular and pedestrian flow traffic, promote social interaction, promote business and industry, contribute to a positive nighttime visual image, provide a pleasing daytime appearance, and provide inspiration for community spirit and growth.[9]

Burned out or broken street lights should be reported to the appropriate public safety department as soon as possible. Residents of neighborhoods in which there are not enough street lights should organize and petition for needed improvements. Businesses also can take advantage of municipal lighting, although it should not be solely relied upon for providing adequate lighting.

Private residences as well as businesses should be equipped with an auxiliary lighting system. This consists of battery operated lights, which are normally kept plugged into an electrical outlet, and the battery is kept charged by the household current. If power is halted, the device automatically turns on the light using battery power. Exterior lighting cables should also be encased to prevent cutting, and the lighting system should be connected to an alarm system so that if lights are turned off or if tampering occurs, authorities can be notified. Another highly recommended security measure for homeowners is to have a master switch for the entire property installed in the main bedroom. This allows for all lights to be quickly switched on if a suspicious noise is heard outside the house or if an intruder is suspected.

The importance of automatic light, in creating a deception of occupancy and averting a burglary, should not be underestimated. This is perhaps the most important aspect of interior lighting in providing security. Timers with twenty-four hour dials allow users to set an on and off schedule of lighting that coincides with their normal light usage. Lamps turned on and off by the timers should be varied, and for maximum security several lamps should be used. Timers can also be used to turn appliances on and off.

Warning Signs

Antiburglary devices should be advertised to the general public. Warning signs can be effectively displayed at the perimeter of such defenses so that would-be burglars possibly will be deterred after finding out what they are up against. These warning signs serve mainly to indicate to the criminal that there are security measures in existence, that criminals will be prosecuted, and that the property is being watched after. Most warning signs will not deter the "hard-core" or professional burglar, but will serve to turn away vandals, mischievous juveniles, and some amateur burglars.

Messages provided through the use of signs vary. Commonly used ones include: "Property Protected by Alarm Systems," "Night Watchman on Duty," "No Loitering Allowed," "Beware of Police Dog," or "No Trespassing." Signs should strategically be placed at entryways and other vulnerable locations on the outside grounds. Signs also can be used on the inside of structures to promote security and, in effect, to control access.

Parking Security

Parking for visitors, personnel, and residents must be given careful consideration in the design of a business, public facility, or housing complex. A well-designed parking area should provide safe, easy, and convenient parking to all motorists while efficiently utilizing available space. Individual factors that must be considered are entrances, exits, physical design of aisles, paving, lighting, and pedestrian walks.

The aisles should be large enough to accommodate automobiles, yet maximize the potential use that can be made of the area. Entrances and exits must be clearly differentiated, and as few in number as necessary to provide efficient operation. Also, adequate signs and directional arrows should be provided. Ninety-degree parking, where feasible, seems to be the most space-efficient, but if not feasible, sixty-degree parking angles should be used. The parking site should be located outside the inner perimeter of the facility so that guard control is facilitated. In this way, employees and visitors must all walk through a guarded gate, provided a guard is employed. If outer perimeter parking cannot be provided, some method of physical division separating the building from parked automobiles should be constructed. Chain link fences often can be used for this purpose while at the same time increasing security for the vehicles. Lighting is very important in the parking area. It helps to deter vandalism, pilfering, and attacks on personnel, and reduce the fear of victimization. Generally, floodlights or street lights are employed for this purpose.

Security of Public Facilities

It is the responsibility of civil authorities to oversee the establishment or improvement of security of public buildings. This responsibility includes antiterrorist measures, preventing destruction of the premises, and protecting personnel working in such structures, since public buildings are very often targets of terrorist attacks. Prime targets or high-risk public buildings include courthouses, administrative buildings, civic centers, and buildings of architectural merit or historic value. Each facility should have tailored anticrime measures incorporated into the design and construction of the facility, according to indications of security assessments. In addition to individual necessities for security, other measures that should be taken include:

1. Access restrictions and identification requirements for personnel and/or visitors requesting access to certain areas
2. Electronic screening of individuals and property within or near the facility
3. Installation of surveillance devices and sensors combined with special alarm systems
4. Emergency barrier doors and special locks activated manually or by remote control
5. Removal of dangerous objects or obstructions that could conceal or interfere with rapid and effective emergency responses
6. Provision of special lighting[10]

Interagency cooperation is again of prime importance in the execution of these requirements. Appropriate law enforcement agencies and fire departments should have opportunities to approve all design and construction plans well in advance of construction.

Routine inspections also should be conducted and security systems evaluated, particularly before special events likely to attract large public gatherings or gatherings of persons likely to demonstrate militant behavior. In addition, it should be realized that security systems are only as good as the people who implement and maintain them. For this reason, inspections should include checks on security personnel as well as equipment and overall security procedures. Searches should be conducted by properly trained and alert personnel capable of foreseeing unusual circumstances that might contribute to vulnerabilities. All possible steps within reasonable cost-effectiveness should be taken to protect the safety of persons using the building and the physical structure itself. Consequences of neglecting such responsibilities could be grave.

Parks

Parks as public facilities deserve special consideration since they must be designed not only with security but also recreation and pleasant environmental characteristics in mind. Parks have proved to be fertile grounds for criminals in the past and to counteract such situations, parks must be planned to promote easy accessibility for police patrol, observation by the private sector, and, very importantly, an attitude of territoriality. Parks should be located in "safe areas" and possess other desirable environmental characteristics, such as adequate lighting and methods to quickly report criminal activity.

Physical Security for Antiterrorism

Many incidents of terrorism depend upon the existence of architectural structures that encourage or do not resist terrorist behavior. Examples of such structures are those with multiple uncontrollable access doors, or those with floor plans that do not foster searches of the interior. In the case of serious bomb threats this could prove to be a real detriment. The responsibility for preventing such design errors is often left to public law enforcement officials. In many cases, public law enforcement agencies constitute the sole source of expertise regarding matters of security, not only for public facilities but also for many businesses and organizations. Therefore, the effectiveness of police countermeasures against incidents of terrorism can correspond directly to the incidence of such crimes within the community. This situation results in the necessity of police developing a high degree of expertise in this area of crime prevention. Authorities involved in such advisory capacities should be capable of distinguishing currently needed security designs or equipment and security devices that may be needed or desired in the future. This requires an individual with foresight, knowledge of sophisticated criminal tactics, and the ability to anticipate future vulnerabilities of a particular organization. In addition, law enforcement agencies should request the assistance of architects, contractors, and local fire departments when developing recommendations.

Structures that minimize opportunities for terrorist attacks have limited points of public access while still allowing for nonpublic access and exit routes enabling police to be quickly dispatched in an emergency and occupants to be quickly evacuated. Limiting access points allows for better identification procedures and better inspection procedures of bags and packages. Maximizing window space also lessens the potential for terrorist attacks. Visibility is increased, which reduces the desirability of the structure for occupation since authorities can more easily observe what takes place inside. Other extreme physical security measures, such as portal metal detectors, should be used only when the threat of violence becomes reasonably certain and the expense of employing them can be justified.

Site Selection

When constructing a facility for security, the first factor that must be considered is the building site itself. The main criterion that should guide the selection process is a maximum security site at a minimum or reasonable cost. A decision to build at a particular site should be made only after an in-depth study of the proposed locations. The study of the proposed locale should include interviews with security executives of other facilities in the area concerning their experience and rate of crime problems in each area. Area crime statistics should also be obtained from local law enforcement agencies, coupled with an on-site evaluation by persons with expertise in determining the area's crime potential. When deciding to locate at a particular site one should also consider requirements of the company or business, in which case there may have to be some degree of compromise. If, for example, a certain location is desired because of the potential manpower available but the site is also in an area prone to civil disturbances, both priorities must be evaluated. Of course, if there are no overbearing company priorities, then a site with a low potential for crime can be chosen without conflict.

After a decision has been made regarding the selection of a particular site, the security consultant can then recommend specific perimeter barriers and internal security measures based on the present and potential vulnerabilities of the locale. Specific factors (in addition to crime statistics) that will be useful in making an informed and intelligent decision of site selection include:

- Distance from public transportation facilities (the closer the better)
- Distance from public safety agencies
- Status of municipal lighting systems in the general area
- Amount of travel on streets, including nighttime travel
- Presence of other businesses in the area
- Store hours of other businesses in the neighborhood
- Sophistication or intensity of security measures taken by adjacent businesses
- Location of the proposed site within a block; for example, corner lots increase security compared to lots in the middle of a block
- Existence of potential fire hazards near the proposed site
- Labor relations in the general area
- General economic conditions of surrounding neighborhoods as evidenced by housing conditions, unemployment ratios, etc.
- Likelihood of natural disasters or "acts of God," such as floods, hurricanes, etc.

Planning the Facility

Site selection is perhaps the single most important factor in determining the relative security of a structure. After the building site has been selected, the next step in assuring maximum security is conferring with the architect and designing the overall plan for the structure. Early communication with the architect is essential if he or she is to be provided with advance security requirements to be incorporated into the design. This will prevent the need for more expensive measures after construction is complete and will also prevent undesirable revisions of the design as a result of after-the-fact changes. Clients cannot assume that architects will automatically include the necessary security controls since, at the present time, security training is neither mandatory nor always included in the curricula of schools of architecture. In fact, most architects expect their clients to be aware of security problems and bring them to their attention when drafting the original plan of the structure.

Factors to consider in planning include recommendations made as a result of on-site evaluations, provisions for basic exterior security measures, provisions for internal security measures, and special provisions for high-risk merchandise handled by the business. As Strobl points out, the planner must attempt to anticipate problems and find means to incorporate the program into the overall operational procedures of the facility so that it is reasonably acceptable to the majority of the population affected by it.[11] Changes or measures likely to cause inconvenience to a majority of persons are not likely to be acceptable and must be minimized as much as possible during the planning stage. If security requirements are not incorporated in the initial plans and subsequent measures cause undue inconvenience to the occupants of the building, crime and the fear of crime will remain potential threats.

Model Security Codes

Although physical and architectural features of residential and commercial structures have been recognized as important variables affecting crime rates, all too frequently insufficient consideration is given to security factors before and during construction; security protection is too often added as an afterthought, if at all. The basic nature of our present society seems to be that people want things done for them and crime prevention is no different. If it were left up to the general public to make their homes and businesses more crime resistant, a large percentage of them would neglect this responsibility. There appear to be only a few rugged individualists left who will take care of problems themselves. That is why model security codes must be established and built into all new construction. Otherwise, it simply will not get done and we shall continue to have excessively high crime rates for homes and businesses and a continued demand for police attention that could be directed toward other types of criminal activity. Insurance premiums will also continue to soar, resulting in unnecessary expenses for everyone.

For this reason, many states either are conducting studies or have already enacted laws to improve building security standards for the purpose of inhibiting criminal activity. Building codes for this purpose have arrived rather late on the scene considering that for many years there have been building codes to assure electrical and plumbing standards, zoning ordinances, and fire prevention regulations. Therefore, the establishment of a set of uniform security building codes to promote crime prevention will be a substantial step forward for the field of criminal justice and related sciences. The objective of such codes should be to provide minimum standards to safeguard property and public welfare

through the regulation and control of the design, construction, materials, use, location, and maintenance of all new or remodeled structures within a municipality. The National Institute of Law Enforcement and Criminal Justice of the LEAA has recommended security codes for commercial buildings that should be followed. The security codes developed by this agency include guidelines for the use and installation of doors, locks, windows, roof openings, and alarm systems.

Security codes have also been established for residential dwellings. The use of metal or solid hardwood doors, deadbolt locks, sturdy door frames, adequate window security, lighting, and landscaping are all essential factors that must be included in security codes for residences. At this time mandatory alarm systems should be avoided. Requiring alarms would only invite the misuse of these devices. Law enforcement agencies, municipal planning and building code enforcement officials, builders, realtors, and consumer protection groups should all work together in instituting appropriate security codes for residences. Special attention should be given to the exterior doors and locks, sliding doors, and window locking devices a builder proposes to use. In addition, all exterior doors should have an outside light.

It is important that all neighborhoods and municipalities institute model security codes for both residential and commercial establishments so that crime is actually reduced rather than displaced. Additional information can be obtained from the National Criminal Justice Reference Service or the National Sheriffs Association.

It should be mentioned also that the recommendations for security codes are a result of extensive research and laboratory testing of materials by the Law Enforcement Standards Laboratory (LESL) at the National Bureau of Standards. This agency has conducted research that has assisted law enforcement and criminal justice agencies in the selection and procurement of quality equipment. In addition to subjecting existing equipment to laboratory testing, a priority of LESL is to conduct research that will lead to the development of several series of documents, national voluntary equipment standards, user guidelines, and surveys. One such document is the NILECJ Standard for the Physical Security of Door Assemblies and Components.[12]

Environmental Factors in Rural Crime

Up to this point the concept of E/S has been directed mainly at urban areas. However, rural areas, becoming increasingly victimized by crime, may also need to experiment with E/S concepts. Many questions have been raised regarding the problem of rural crimes. Such variables as low visibility and relative isolation of farm property, decreased police patrols in rural areas, and vulnerability of farm equipment and outbuildings have all been assumed to contribute to an overall vulnerability of rural residents and property to crime. One study, however, found that many of these physical and spatial aspects of rural areas were not related to property crime victimization.[13] The size of the tract in acres, distance one lives from the nearest town, distance from one's neighbors, visibility of one's buildings to the neighbors, the number and condition of buildings, and fencing on one's property were not found to be related to property crimes. This might be explained by the fact that most properties are accessible to potential criminals. Results of the study did seem to suggest that property located behind the residence rather than between the residence and the public road was less vulnerable in that this location increased the risk to perpetrators.

This is clearly an area that requires more research, since the effects of applications of E/S concepts to rural areas are yet unclear. It may be that rural crime will not be as receptive to the E/S concepts, but perhaps there are some aspects of rural crime that can be dramatically affected through physical design.

Conclusion

The concept of environmental security is becoming a well-defined science that demands attention from architects, law enforcement authorities, city planners, business owners, and private citizens, all of whom should be concerned with measures to control crime. Clearly, E/S has been shown by several researchers and studies to effectively reduce crime and the fear of crime by reducing opportunities for crime and increasing the risk for the perpetrator. E/S should be a part of comprehensive planning from the design phase to the completion of construction projects. At the present time, however, model security codes are only encouraged, not mandatory, in most locales, as is true for the inclusion of E/S courses in architectural schools. It is important, therefore, to see that steps are taken to implement E/S measures as mandatory requirements so that all municipalities will benefit from the concept. This also will reduce the possibility of crime displacement.

Crime prevention through environmental security has most effectively been applied to high density urban areas and much research must be done on the applications of its concepts to rural areas. The most important factor in utilizing it effectively is to evaluate existing and planned structures, determine how they relate to present and potential crime patterns, and then recommend the inclusion of design measures in cooperation with architects, fire departments, and zoning and planning agencies to counteract criminal opportunities. This new area of crime prevention promises to be a most challenging and rewarding field for criminal justice, architecture, and urban planning.

References

1. Jeffery, C. Ray, *Crime Prevention Through Environmental Design*. Beverly Hills: Sage Publications, Inc., 1977.
2. Gardiner, Richard A., *Design for Safe Neighborhoods*. Washington, D.C.: National Institute of Law Enforcement and Criminal Justice, Law Enforcement Assistance Administration, U.S. Department of Justice, 1978.
3. Ibid.
4. "Crime Prevention Courses in Schools of Architecture and Urban Planning," *Private Security*. Washington, D.C.: National Advisory Committee on Criminal Justice Standards and Goals, Dec. 1976, p. 195.
5. Newman, Oscar, *Defensible Space*. New York: The Macmillan Co., 1972, p. 3.
6. Ibid.
7. Ibid.
8. Hall, Gerald, *How to Completely Secure Your Home*. Blue Ridge Summit, Pa.: Tab Books, 1978, p. 12.
9. *Street Lighting Projects*, National Evaluation Program, Phase 1 Report, Series A, No. 21. Washington, D.C.: National Institute of Law Enforcement and Criminal Justice, Law Enforcement Assistance Administration, U.S. Department of Justice.
10. *Report on the Task Force on Disorders and Terrorism*. Washington, D.C.: National Advisory Committee on Criminal Justice Standards and Goals, U.S. Government Printing Office, 1976, p. 58.
11. Strobl, Walter M., *Crime Prevention Through Physical Security*. New York: Marcel Dekker, Inc., 1978, p. 1.
12. NILECJ Standard for the Physical Security of Door Assemblies and Components, National Institute of Law Enforcement and Criminal Justice, Washington, D.C.: U.S. Department of Justice, Dec. 1974.
13. Phillips, Howard, et al., *Environmental Factors in Rural Crime*. Wooster, Ohio: Ohio Agricultural Research and Development Center, Research Circular 224, Nov. 1976, p. 5.

Chapter 3

Designing Security with the Architects

LAWRENCE J. FENNELLY

Too often when a building complex was built, the contractor turned over the keys to the owner and that was it. During the 1970s, management was saying: "Hold it, we want some say as to what type of locks, lighting, and alarms you are going to install and exactly what kind of hardware you are going to put on my exit doors."

Security was being neglected because the security personnel did not have a chance for input. Yes, it is a great building and the contractor can be proud; his cement, plumbing, and electrical work is perfect, but as a means of cutting costs deadbolt locks, eye viewers in the doors, chains, and non-removable hinges were omitted. Key-in knob locks were installed. A pipe wrench will open this type of door lock or the expansion of the doorframe will pop the door open.

The crime/loss prevention officer is not concerned just with locks. His concern is the overall vulnerability of the site. If you believe that most crimes can be prevented, then you must be involved in the early stages of designing security.

We have, from the 1970s, seen a new approach, namely Building Security Codes (see Appendix 3a, which follows). Buildings should be constructed with a level of security in mind. Law enforcement has the knowledge of crime trends and of burglary; therefore, they should be involved with state and local planning boards.

Designing Security with the Architects

Crime prevention and security officers throughout the country today are working with various architects for the sole purpose of improving the state of security within the community. Crime is not always predictable because it is the work of human scheming. In our efforts to combat this threat, it is essential that we all attempt to reduce the opportunity so often given to the criminal to commit crime. Every building, large or small, creates a potential crime risk and planners and architects owe it to their clients to devise and implement effective security measures.

The subject of designing security with architects is another way of conducting a security survey, but in this case, it is before construction. It extends far beyond the protection of doors and windows. It even deals with the quality of one vendor's products versus another of a lesser quality. The following checklist is prepared to be used as an initial guide to assist you with the architects to obtain better security.

Anticipation of Crime Risk Checklist

1. As you do with any security survey, your first step is to consult with the occupants of the complex.
2. Identify areas which will house items of a sensitive nature or items of value like safes, audiovisual equipment, etc.
3. Identify the main crime targets.
4. Assess the level of protection required.
5. Examine the facilities that the company currently occupies. From that survey, the building characteristics and personality can tell you how the structure has been used or abused.
6. Is there cash being handled within the building which will have to get to a bank?
7. Is there a concentration or an even distribution

of valuables within the complex? Decide on the area most vulnerable to criminal attack and make your recommendation to harden that target.

8. Reduce entrances to a minimum thereby reducing movement of staff and visitors.
9. What is the crime risk in the area?
10. What is the level of police patrol and police activity in the area?
11. What are the distances from the complex to the local police and fire stations?
12. Have the materials being used met state and national standards?
13. Who will clean and secure the complex day and night? Are they dependable, intelligent, and reliable?
14. Make note of employee behavior.

Designing Security and Layout of Site

Designing security into a new complex should begin with interior security. Work your way to the exterior and then to the outer perimeter. Keep in mind these six points before you sit down with the architects:

1. Elimination of all but essential doors and windows
2. Specification of fire-resistant material throughout the interior
3. Installation of fire, intrusion, and environmental control systems
4. Separation of shipping and receiving areas
5. Provisions for the handicapped
6. Adequate lighting around the perimeter, before and during construction

Building Site Security and Contractors

It is safe to say that all contractors will experience a theft of stocks or material before completion of the site. They should be made aware of this fact and be security-conscious at the beginning of construction before theft gets too costly. Thefts which appear to be of an internal nature should be analyzed in relation to previous such thefts at other sites.

Checklist

1. The contractor should appoint security officers or a liaison staff person to work with police on matters of theft and vandalism.

2. Perimeter protection:
   a. Gate strength
   b. Hinges
   c. Locks and chains
   d. Lighting
   e. Crime rate in the neighborhood
   f. Construct a 10- or 12-foot fence topped with three rows of barbed wire.
3. Location of contractor's building on site:
   a. Inspect security of this building.
   b. Review their security procedures and controls.
   c. Light building inside and out.
4. No employees should be permitted to park private cars on site.
5. Materials and tools on site should be protected in a secured yard area.
6. Facilities for storage and security of workmen's tools and clothes should be kept in a locked area.
7. The sub-contractor is responsible to the main contractor.
8. Security officers should patrol at night and on weekends.
9. Use temporary alarm protection for the site.
10. Payment of wages to employees should be with checks.
11. Deliveries of valuable material to site and the storage of such items should be placed in a secured area.
12. Establish a method to check fraudulent deliveries using authorized persons only.
13. Check for proper posting of signs around the perimeter.
14. Identify transportable material and property. Operation identification should be available.
15. Method used to report theft:
   a. Local police
   b. Office
   c. Insurance company
   d. Security company

If guards are needed to protect the site, determine:

1. Hours of coverage
2. Do they answer to the general contractor or the owner of the complex? (They should be answering to the general contractor.)
3. Are they employed by the general contractor or are they a contract guard company?
4. What are their police powers?
5. How are they supervised?
6. What type of special training do they receive?
7. Have local police been advised of their presence on site?

8. What is the uniform of the guard on duty, flash-light (size), firearms, night sticks or chemical agents?
9. How are promotions in the guard company obtained?
10. What keys to the complex does the guard have?
11. What are the guard's exact duties? Does guard have a fixed post or a roving patrol?
12. Review the guard's patrol.
13. Are the guards carrying a time clock?
14. Should they write a report on each shift?
15. Who reviews these reports?
16. Be sure each guard has sufficient responsibilities and is active during tour of duty.
17. Does the guard have an up-to-date list of who to call in case of emergency?

Building Design: Interior Checklist

1. Where is the payroll office?
2. Examine security as it pertains to cash and the storage of cash overnight.
3. Be familiar with cars parking within the complex.
4. Employ staff supervision of entryways.
5. Avoid complex corridor systems.
6. Visitors:
   a. Are they restricted as to how far they can maneuver?
   b. Are there special elevators?
   c. Is there limited access?
7. What are the provisions and placement of the reception desk?
8. Where will vulnerable equipment and stock be housed?
9. Custodial quarters:
   a. Where will they be housed?
   b. Will there be a phone?
   c. What other security devices will be installed?
   d. Can this area be secured when the staff leaves at night?
10. Can staff quarters be secured properly?
11. Industrial plants should be designed and laid out to combat internal vandalism.
12. Electric, water and gas meters should be built into the outside wall for service access.
13. Department stores and other buildings accessible to public use, in addition to shape and layout, should be designed with deterrents to prevent crime:
    a. Access for handicapped and disabled persons:
       i. Guard rails

ii. Telephones
iii. Toilets
b. Provisions for one-way mirrors throughout the store
c. Closed circuit television:
   i. Who will monitor it?
   ii. Is it hooked up to the alarm system with a recorder?
d. Beeper or signal system
e. Zoned intrusion alarm panel on street floor for quick police response
f. Zoned fire alarm panel on street floor for quick fire department response
g. Lighting 24 hours a day
h. Display area vulnerable?
i. Freight elevator access to the street
14. Apartments
a. Avoid overdensity
b. Avoid neurosis
c. Plan on reduction of vandalism
d. Trash chutes and storage areas kept clear
e. Basement access reduced
f. Security in tenants' storage area
g. Key security implemented
h. Foyer should also be locked
i. Vandal-proof mailboxes
j. Who will occupy the complex?
   i. Upper, midddle, or lower class people
   ii. All white or all non-white families
   iii. Combination of i and ii
   iv. Senior citizens

Building Design: Exterior Access Checklist

1. External doors
   a. Choice of final exit doors
   b. Design and strength of door and frame
   c. Choice and strength of panels: glass and wood
   d. Be sure hinges cannot be removed from the outside
   e. Minimum number of entrances
   f. Fire doors are secure
   g. Tools and ladders are accessible (garage doors)
   h. Lights over entrances
   i. Choice of locks and hardware
   j. Use only steel doors and frames
   k. Eliminate exterior hardware on egress doors wherever possible
2. Building line
   a. Lines of vision
   b. Hidden entrances
3. Architectural defects affecting security

4. Roof
    a. Access to
    b. Skylights
    c. Pitch angle
5. External pipes
    a. Flush or concealed?
6. Podium blocks
    a. Access to upper windows
7. Basement
    a. Access points inside and out
    b. Storage areas
    c. Lighting
    d. Fuel storage areas
    e. Number of entries to basement, stairs, and elevators
    f. Grills on windows
8. False ceilings
    a. Access to and through
9. Service entrances
    a. Service hatches
    b. Ventilation ducts
    c. Air vent openings
    d. Service elevators
    e. Grills on all ducts, vents, and openings over 12 inches

Building Access: Windows and Glass

The purpose of the window, aside from aesthetics, is to let in sunlight, to allow visibility, and to provide ventilation. The following types of windows provide 100 percent ventilation: casement, pivoting, jalousie, awning, and hopper. The following provide 50 to 65 percent ventilation: double-hung and sliding.

Factors to consider in the selection of type and size of a window are:

1. Amount of light, ventilation, and view requirements
2. Material and desired finish
    a. Wood
    b. Metal, aluminum steel, stainless steel
3. Window hardware
    a. Durability
    b. Function
4. Type of glazing available
5. Effectiveness of weatherstripping
6. Appearance, unit size, and proportion
7. Method opening—hinge/slider, choice of line of hinges
8. Security lock fittings
9. No accessible louvre windows
10. Ground floor—recommend lower windows, large fixed glazing and high windows, small openings
11. Consider size and shape to prevent access
12. Consider size because of cost due to vandalism
13. Use of bars or grilles on inside
14. Glass
    a. Double glazing deterrent
    b. Type of glass
    c. Vision requirements
    d. Thickness
    e. Secure fixing to frame
    f. Laminated barrier glass—uses
    g. Use of plastic against vandalism
    h. Fixed, obscure glazings for dwellinghouse garages
    i. Shutters, grilles, and louvres can serve as sun control and visual barriers as well as security barrier

Ironmongery

The Lock and Its Installation

By definition, a lock is a mechanical, electrical, hydraulic, or electronic device designed to prevent entry to a building, room, container, or hiding place to prevent the removal of items without the consent of the owner. A lock acts to temporarily foster two separate objects together, such as a door to its frame or a lid to a container. The objects are held together until the position of the internal structure of the lock is altered—for example, by a key—so that the objects are released.

1. Perimeter entrance gates
    a. Design
    b. Locking devices and hardware
    c. Aesthetics
2. Door ironmongery
    a. Theft-resistant locks
        i. Choice of manufacturer
        ii. Design
    b. Electrically operated
    c. Access control
    d. Mortise security locks
    e. Sliding bolts
    f. Flush bolts
    g. Dead bolts
    h. Hinge bolts
    i. Non-removable hinges on all outside doors
    j. Key control system
    k. Door viewers
    l. Safety chains

m. Choice of panic bolts
n. Fire doors
o. Sliding doors
p. Additional locks and padlocks
q. Quality of locks to be used
r. Sheet metal lining protection of door
3. Window ironmongery
   a. Security window locks built-in during manufacture
   b. Security window locks fitted after manufacture
   c. Transom window locks
   d. Locking casement stays
   e. Remote controlled flexible locks
4. Additional ironmongery
   a. Hardware should be of the highest quality
   b. Control of keys
   c. High grade steel hasps
   d. Strong lock for strong door or window needs strong frame.

Our objective is the prevention of defeating locks through force. When stress is applied to a door in the form of bodily force, pry bars or jacks, something has to give. Every mechanical device has its fatigue and breaking point although no one, to our knowledge, has properly defined this point for doors, locks and frames in terms of pounds of pressure or force.

Doors

There are four types of door operation: swinging, by-pass sliding, surface sliding, and slide-hinged folding.

Physical door types are wood, metal, aluminum, flush, paneled, french, glass, sash, jalousie, louvered, shutter, screen, dutch, hollow-core doors, solid core doors, batten doors, pressed wood doors, hollow metal framed doors, and revolving doors.

Garage and overhead doors can be constructed in a panel type, flush, or webbed.

Each of the above doors has a need for a specific type of security hardware. I am not going to go into these specifics but I want to mention some additional factors to consider in the selection of hardware:

1. Function and ease of door operation
2. Material, form, surface texture, finish, and color
3. Durability in terms of
   a. Anticipated frequency of use
   b. Exposure to weather and climatic conditions in the selection of hardware material. Finish aluminum and stainless steel recommended

in humid climates and where corrosive conditions exist (i.e., sea air).

Finish door hardware should include:

1. Locks, latches, bolts, cylinders, and stop works, operating trim
2. Non-removable hinges
3. Panic hardware
4. Push and pull bars and plates
5. Kick plates
6. Stops, closers, and holders
7. Thresholds
8. Weatherstrippings
9. Door tracks and hangers

Standards have yet to be adjusted to determine the minimum lock requirements necessary for security, but various considerations are evident from the variety of provisions which currently exist. A dead bolt and/or dead latch is essential. The standard latch which functions primarily to keep the door in a closed position can easily be pushed back with such instruments as a credit card or thin metal objects.

Door should be of solid construction. If wood is used, the door should have a solid wood core. Doors should be installed so that hinges are located on the inside. If this is not possible, hinges should be installed in a manner which will prohibit their being removed and/or the pins being tampered with.

Rolling overhead doors not controlled or locked by electric power can be protected by slide bolts on the bottom bar. With crank-operated doors, the operating shaft should be secured. Chain-operated doors can be secured in a manner which allows a steel or cast iron keeper and pin to be attached to the hand chain.

Intrusion Alarm Systems Checklist

1. Quality of products being used. Are they listed in Underwriters Laboratories?
2. Plan for vulnerable materials to be in protected areas.
3. Determine smallest area to be protected.
4. Audible alarm termination type of horn.
5. Instant or delayed audible warning.
6. Silent alarms, connected to police or central station.
7. Choice of detection equipment—motion, infrared magnetic contacts, etc.
8. Degree of protection—building perimeter, site perimeter, target protection, internal traps, overall construction.

9. Sufficient alarm zones (plus extras) to fit the lifestyle of the complex.
10. If it is a union contractor, then the alarm company will have to be a union company or permission must be obtained for a nonunion alarm vendor.
11. Environmental aspect influences the architects in selecting alarm components.
12. Electric outlets will have to be placed for areas where power will be needed.
13. Methods of monitoring a supervised line.
14. Who will service in the event of breakdown?

CCTV Checklist

1. Quality of products to be used.
2. Type and style of lens and monitors to be used.
3. Who is going to monitor the monitors?
4. Electric outlets needed at each camera location.
5. Who will service in the event of breakdown?
6. Size of control room to determine the amount of controls and panel which will be able to be monitored.
7. Who will install and repair system?

Card Access Control Checklist

1. Credit card size, capable of having your private post office box number printed on it, so lost cards can be returned back to you.
2. Comes in various types, magnetic, electric circuit continuity, magnetic stripe, passive electronic, IR optical, differential optics and capacities.
3. Site location will determine:
   a. Number of entry control points
   b. Number of badges needed
   c. Rate at which persons must be passed through entry—control points
   d. The number of levels of access that need to be accommodated
   e. Procedures that are used to issue badges
4. Equipment should have:
   a. Tamper alarm to detect tampering with the electrical circuits
   b. Battery backup supply
   c. Capability to detect tampering with line circuits
5. Card access control provides control over lifestyle of building
6. Applications are many, aside from security
   a. Controlled access
      i. Buildings

ii. Parking areas
   b. Alarms, ultrasonic motion detectors
   c. CCTV
   d. Watchmen tours
   e. Heating system
   f. Smoke and fire detection
   g. Temperature and humidity controls
   h. Refrigeration and air conditioning controls
   i. Time and attendance
   j. Elevator control
   k. Gas pump control
   l. Xerox copy control

Storage Rooms, Safes, and Vaults Checklist

Storage Rooms

1. Consider
   a. Vulnerabilities
   b. Contents
   c. Risk management principles
   d. Type of storage area
   e. Period of complex occupancy
   f. Underwriters Laboratory listing
2. Placement—can it be seen from outside?
3. Construction and type of material
4. Restrictions on open area around storage room
5. Installation factors in design stage
6. Intrusion protection
7. Fire protection
8. Ventilation of storage room
9. Water and fireproofing
10. Emergency exit

Safes

1. Correct type of safe required for needs; money versus document type of safe
2. Wheels removed and bolted down
3. Placement of safe—visibility
4. Weight factor and floor weight capacity
5. Security of safe to fabric of building
6. Provisions of area in concrete for installation of floor safe

Vaults

1. A U.S. Government Class 5 Security Vault Door, which has been tested and approved by the Government under Fed. Spec. AA-D-600B (GSA-FSS) and affords the following security

protection which applies only to the door and not to the vault proper
   a. 30 man-minutes against surreptitious entry
   b. 10 man-minutes against forced entry
   c. 20 man-hours against lock manipulation
   d. 20 man-hours against radiology techniques
2. Door options
   a. Right or left hand door swing
   b. Hand or key change combination lock
   c. Optical device
   d. Time-delay lock
3. Weight of vault versus floor strength
4. Wall thickness
5. What you want to protect will determine the degree of protection

Exterior Lighting Checklist

1. Is the lighting adequate to illuminate critical areas (alleys, fire escapes, ground level windows)?
2. Are the foot candles on horizontal at ground level? (A minimum of five foot candles)
3. Is there sufficient illumination over entrances?
4. Are the perimeter areas lighted to assist police surveillance of the area?
5. Are the protective lighting system and the working lighting system on the same line?
6. Is there an auxiliary system designed to go into operation automatically when needed?
7. Is there an auxiliary power source for protective lighting?
8. How often is the auxiliary system tested?
9. Are the protective lights controlled by automatic timer or photo cells, or manually operated?
10. What hours is this lighting used?
11. Is the switch box(es) and/or automatic timer secured?
12. Can protective lights be compromised easily (i.e., unscrewing of bulbs)?
13. What type of lights are installed around the property?
14. Are they cost effective?
15. Are the fixtures vandal-proof?
16. Is there a glare factor?
17. Is there an even distribution of light?
18. Are the lights mounted on the building versus pole fixtures?

Crime Prevention Awareness Points

1. Has the general contractor made arrangements to secure the perimeter and to provide adequate lighting of the complex before starting work?
2. Has the general contractor been advised to secure equipment and work area from internal theft and to also so advise all subcontractors? Be sure to inspect the area and make immediate recommendations.
3. Observe entrance gate security.
4. Check for vehicles parking close to the construction site.
5. Is the building too close to adjoining property?
6. Vandalism: Is the site subject to attack before completion?
7. Will cars be parking around the complex after completion?
8. Landscape coverage: Could it be a crime risk?
9. External lights—on the building versus on the grounds.
10. What security is given to main utilities, transformers, etc., preferably underground?
11. Temporary construction locks should be installed throughout the building during the construction process and later replaced with the permanent hardware after all exterior and interior work has been completed and the site is ready for occupancy.
12. Times when site is most vulnerable: Between the time construction has ended and when the new occupants have completely moved in, there tends to be confusion. Movers and decorators shouldn't be allowed uncontrolled access to the site. While something can be carried in, something else can be carried out. Identification badges should be used during this period.
13. Size of the complex and the amount of occupancy can give you an idea for the complex's crime rate.
14. The time period our society is going through has an effect on the conditions the architects are working under in planning a building for construction.

Appendix 3a

Model Residential and Commercial Building Security Ordinance

Any builder, contractor or owner desiring to have a decal awarded to any single or multi-family dwelling currently existing, under construction, or to be constructed may voluntarily meet the following specifications dealing with building security.

Residential Buildings

I. Doors
  A. Exterior Doors
    1. All exterior doors, except sliding glass doors or metal doors, with or without decorative mouldings, shall be either solid core wood doors or stave or solid wood flake doors and shall be a minimum of one and three-eights inch (1⅜″) in thickness.
      a) Hollow Core Doors
        No hollow core door or hollow core door filled with a second composition material, other than mentioned above, will be considered a solid core door.
    2. Hinges
      All exterior door hinges shall be mounted with the hinge on the interior of the building. Except where a non-removable pin hinge or stud bolt is used, such hinges may be installed with the hinge facing the exterior of the building.
    3. Hinge and Strike Plate Lock Area
      The shim space between the door buck and door frame shall have a solid wood filler 12 inches above and below the strike plate area to resist spreading by force applied to the door frame.
      a) Screws securing the strike plate area shall pass through the strike plate, door frame and enter the solid wood filler a minimum of ¼ inch.
    4. Glass in Exterior Doors
      No glass may be used on any exterior door or window within forty (40) inches of any lock except:
      a) That glass shall be replaced with the same thickness of polycarbonate sheeting of an approved type.
        (1) Plexiglass shall not be used to replace glass.
      b) That door locks shall be a double cylinder keyed lock with mortised dead bolt that extends into the strike plate a minimum of one inch.
      c) *French doors* shall have a concealed header and threshold bolt in the stationary, or first/closed door, on the door edge facing.
      d) *Dutch doors* shall have a concealed header type securing device interlocking the upper and lower portions of the door in the door edge on the door strike side provided:
        (1) That a double cylinder lock with a one-inch dead bolt be provided on the upper and lower sections of the door and the header device be omitted.
      e) Sliding Glass Doors
        (1) Sliding glass doors shall be installed so as to prevent the lifting and removal of either glass door from the frame from the exterior of the building.
        (2) Fixed panel glass door (non-sliding) shall be installed so that the securing hardware cannot be removed or circumvented from the exterior of the building.

(3) Each sliding panel shall have a secondary locking or securing device in addition to the original lock built into the panel.
  (a) Second device shall consist of:
      i) A charlie bar type device.
      ii) A track lock, wooden or metal dowel.
      iii) Inside removable pins or locks securing the panel to the frame.
(4) All "glass" used in exterior sliding glass doors and fixed glass panels to be of laminated safety glass or polycarbonate sheeting. Plexiglass or single strength glass will not qualify for this program.

5. Locks and Keying Requirements
  a) Except as provided in Section A-4-b (Glass in Exterior Doors), all exterior doors, where the lock is not within 40 inches of breakable glass, shall incorporate a single cylinder mortised or bored locking device with a one-inch dead bolt.
  b) Locking Materials
     (1) No locking device on an exterior door shall be used that depends on extruded plastics for security or strength feature of the locking or securing mounts. Plastics and nylon materials may be used to a minimum degree in lubricant or wear-resistant features.
     (2) Cylinders used in locking devices must resist pulling from the exterior of the building.
     (3) Cylinder rings shall be compression-resistant and may or may not be free-turning to resist circumvention from the exterior.
     (4) Dead bolts shall be case-hardened steel or contain a case-hardened steel rod, fixed or movable, inside the dead bolt feature. The dead bolt is to be dead locked against reasonable end pressure.
  c) Keying Requirements
     (1) During construction
        Each contractor or party building a home or apartment for occupancy by another shall, during the construction period, use a keying system that incorporates either:
        a) The original cylinders used during the construction period may be re-pinned and new keys furnished to the owner or occupant.
        b) Reasonable key control shall be exercised and all full-cut keys fitting the exterior doors upon occupancy shall be given to the renter or owner. In cases of rental property master keys and grant master keys shall be kept under security.

II. Windows
  A. Double Hung Wood
     1. All locking devices to be secured with ¾ inch full-threader screws.
     2. All window latches must be key locked or a manual (non-spring loaded or flip type) window latch. When a non-key-locked latch is used, a secondary securing device must be installed. Such secondary securing device may consist of:
        a) Each window drilled with holes at two intersecting points of inner and outer windows and appropriate sized dowels inserted in the holes. Dowels to be cut to provide minimum grasp from inside the window.
        b) A metal sash security hardware device of approved type may be installed in lieu of doweling.
        Note: Doweling is less costly and of a higher security value than more expensive hardware.
  B. Sliding Glass Windows
     1. Same requirements as sliding glass doors.
  C. Awning Type Wood and Metal Windows
     1. No secondary device is required on awning type windows but crank handle may be removed by owner as security feature after residence establishment.
     2. Double hung metal windows are secured similar to the double hung wood window using metal dowels.

III. Miscellaneous
  A. Door Viewers
     All front entrance doors without other means of external visibility shall be equipped with a door viewer that shall cover at least 160 degrees of viewing. Such viewer

to be installed with the securing portion on the inside and non-removable from the outside.

Commercial Buildings

I. Doors
   A. Exterior Doors
      All exterior doors shall meet the requirements as set forth for residential buildings. Should glass doors be installed, they shall be of laminated safety glass or polycarbonated sheeting.
   B. Rolling Overhead or Cargo Doors
      Doors not controlled or locked by electric power operation shall be equipped with locking bars that pass through guide rails on each side. The locking bars shall have holes drilled in each end and a padlock placed in each end once the bar is in the locked position. The padlock shall have a case hardened shackle with locking lugs on the heel and toe of the shackle and a minimum of four-pin tumbler operation.
II. Other Exterior Openings
   A. Windows
      Fixed glass panels, sliding glass and double hung windows, awning type and metal windows, must meet or exceed the requirements set forth for residential buildings.
   B. Roof Openings
      Skylights shall be constructed of laminated safety glass or polycarbonated sheeting.
   C. Hatchways
      Hatchways shall be of metal construction or wood with a minimum of 16-gauge sheet metal attached with screws. Unless prohibited by local fire ordinances, the hatchways shall be secured by case hardened steel hasps and padlocks meeting the requirements set forth in cargo doors.
   D. Air Ducts
      Air ducts or air vent openings exceeding 8 inches by 12 inches shall be secured by installing a steel grille of at least ⅛ inch material of two-inch mesh or iron bars of at least ½ inch round or one inch by ¼ inch flat steel material spaced no more than five inches apart and securely fastened with round headed flush bolts or welded.
   E. Air Conditioners
      Single unit air conditioners mounted in windows or through the wall shall be secured by flat steel material two inches by ¼ inch formed to fit snugly over the air conditioning case on the outside and secured with round headed flush bolts through the walls.
   F. Alarm Systems
      All commercial establishments maintaining an inventory and assets of $5000 or more, or having a high incident rate of housebreaking in the past, shall have an intrusion detection system installed. The system shall cover all possible points of entry to include entry through the walls and roof. The system shall be a silent type with a hookup to the servicing police agency and shall have a backup energizing source.

Chapter 4
Security Surveys

LAWRENCE J. FENNELLY

A security survey is a critical on-site examination and analysis of an industrial plant, business, home, or public or private institution, to ascertain the present security status, to identify deficiencies or excesses, to determine the protection needed, and to make recommendations to improve the overall security.[1]

It is interesting to note that a definition of crime prevention as outlined by the British Home Office Crime Prevention Program—"the anticipation, recognition and appraisal of a crime risk and the initiation of action to remove or reduce it"—could, in fact, be an excellent definition of a security survey. The only difference, of course, is that a survey generally does not become the "action" as such but rather a basis for recommendations for action.

This definition can be divided into five component parts and analyzed so that its implications can be applied to the development of a working foundation for the security surveyor.

1. *The Anticipation*. How does the anticipation of a crime risk become important to the security or crime prevention surveyor? Obviously, one of the primary objectives to a survey is the anticipation or prevention aspects of a given situation—the pre- or before concept. Thus, an individual who keeps anticipation in the proper perspective would be maintaining a proper balance in the total spectrum of security surveying. In other words, the anticipatory stage could be considered a prognosis of further action.

2. *Recognition*. What means will provide an individual who is conducting a survey of the relationships between anticipation and appraisal? Primarily, the ability to recognize and interpret what seems to be a crime risk becomes one of the important skills a security surveyor acquires and develops.

3. *Appraisal*. The responsibility to develop, suggest, and communicate recommendations is certainly a hallmark of any security survey.

4. *Crime Risk*. This, as defined in this text, is the opportunity gained from crime. The total elimination of opportunity is most difficult, if not most improbable. Thus, the cost of protection is measured in:

1. Protection of depth
2. Delay time

Obviously, the implementation of the recommendation should not exceed the total (original/ replacement) cost of the item(s) to be protected. An exception to this rule would be human life.

5. *The Initiation of Action to Remove or Reduce a Crime Risk*. This section indicates the phase of a survey in which the recipient of the recommendations will make a decision to act, based on the suggestions (recommendations) set forth by the surveyor. In some cases the identification of security risk is made early in a survey and it is advisable to act upon the recommendation prior to the completion of the survey.

The responsibility to initiate action based on recommendations is the sole duty of the recipient of the survey. This is to suggest that the individual who receives the final evaluation and survey will be the individual who has commensurate responsibility and authority to act.[2]

There are basically three types of surveys:

1. *Building Inspection* is advising a tenant in a large complex of his vulnerabilities as they pertain to the physical characteristics of the dwelling.
2. *A Security Survey* on the other hand would be conducted on the whole complex versus doing only a portion of the site.

3. *A Security Analysis* is more of an in-depth study including risk management, analyzing risk factors, environmental and physiological security measures, analyzing crime patterns, and fraud and internal theft.

The Best Time to Conduct the Survey

Most crime prevention officers and security directors agree that a survey is most effective:

1. After a crisis within the cooperation.
2. After a breaking and entering or major larceny.
3. Upon request.

There are times when a merchant hears he can get something for nothing and thereby calls the crime prevention officer in the town to conduct such a survey, but in reality has no intention of spending a dime for improvement. A close friend of mine conducted a detailed security survey on a factory warehouse and office building. The recipient of the survey followed only one of his recommendations which was to leave a light on over the safe in the back room of his warehouse. The owner had completely disregarded other recommendations such as hardware improvements on doors, windows, and skylights. Unfortunately, thieves returned and almost put him out of business.

Classifications of Survey Recommendations

The various classifications of recommendations can be best explained through an example. The classifications are maximum, medium, and minimum. The example selected is a museum that contains $25 million in various art treasures; the complex has no security.

Maximum Security

Obviously, the museum needs an alarm system; therefore, to apply our maximum security classification recommendation, it should read:

> Alarm the perimeter (all exterior and interior doors, all windows and skylights). Four panic alarms to be installed at various locations, and six paintings which are worth twelve million dollars should be alarmed—each on a separate 24-hour zone.

I specifically did not mention ultra-maximum security because this term applies to an armed camp —machine guns, men in full battle dress (guards) armed with semi-automatic rifles, grenades, flame throwers, mines, and locking devices equipped with dynamite which will blow up when the intruder attempts picking the lock. It is dramatic and it is ultra-maximum. It is not ridiculous for Fort Knox to provide ultra-maximum security to protect its billions in gold bullion.

Medium Security

A medium security classification recommendation would read:

> Alarm all basement windows and all ground floor windows which are at the rear of the building. Install one panic alarm by the main entrance. Alarm the six paintings worth $12 million each alarmed on a separate 24-hour zone.

Minimum Security

Finally, a minimum security classification recommendation would read:

> From a risk management point of view, alarm the six paintings which are worth $12 million, each painting to be alarmed on a separate 24-hour zone.

First Step

These three examples clearly show the degree of security one can obtain by trying to plan a security package. I have stated these examples because your first step in conducting a security survey is the interview you have with the individual to whom you turn over your report. It is during this interview that you form an appraisal on the degree of protection which is required and needed.

There are times when you may have to state all three recommendations in a report. There are also times when you must be conscious of the fact that you may force the receiver of your report to accept less security than you suggested because you did not thoroughly and clearly explain your security points.

Developing Your Security Points

Like most professionals, we need tools to do an effective job. The following are suggested to assist you when conducting your surveys: tape measure, floor plans, magnifying glass, flashlight, camera with flash, small tape recorder, screwdriver, penknife, pencil and paper.

Your survey is to be conducted systematically so the recipient can follow your recommendations in some kind of order. Start with the perimeter of the building. Once inside the building, start at the basement and work your way to the attic. Do not be afraid to be critical of the area that you are in. This is what the recipient wants.

After you have done several surveys you will develop a style of putting them together and they become easy.

Dos and Don'ts in Developing Your Report

Dos

1. Be honest in your recommendations. You are the expert.
2. Call the shots as you see it.
3. Be critical—physically tear the property apart.

Don'ts

1. Don't overexaggerate your reports. They are too important.
2. Don't inflate the report with maps and floor plans.
3. Don't repeat your statements.

The written report should include the following:

Page One: Introduction or sample covering letter.
Page Two: A. Identification of building.
         B. Specific statement of the major problem.
         C. Alternative recommendations to the problems.
         D. List of your further recommendations.

General statements such as the following can be included in the report:

1. Physically inventory all property at least once a year. Your inventory should have listed the name of the item, the manufacturer model serial value, color, and date purchased.
2. Engrave all property in accordance with the established operation identification program.
3. All typewriters should be bolted down and all files, cabinets and rooms containing valuable information or equipment should be locked when not in use.

Other Keys to Being an Effective Surveyor

Only when you have developed the ability to visualize the potential for criminal activity will you become an effective crime scene surveyor. This ability is the part of the process that is referred to as an art. Nonetheless, it is important that when you arrive on a survey site, you are prepared to give a property owner sound advice on the type of security precautions to consider.

In summary, to be a good crime prevention surveyor, you will have to be a good investigator. You must understand criminal methods of operation and the limitations of standard security devices. In addition, you must be knowledgeable about the type of security hardware necessary to provide various degrees of protection.[3]

Nine Points of Security Concern

1. General purpose of the building, i.e., residence, classroom, office. Consider the hours of use, people who use the building, general hours of use, people who have access, key control, maintenance schedule. Who is responsible for maintenance? Is the building used for public events? If so, what type and how often? Is the building normally opened to the public? Identify the significant factors and make recommendations.
2. Hazards involving the building or its occupants. List and prioritize, i.e., theft of office equipment, wallet theft, theft from stockrooms. Identify potential hazards which might exist in the future.
3. Police or guard security applications. What can they do to improve the response to the building and occupants from a patrol, investigation, or crime prevention standpoint? Would the application of guards be operationally and/or cost effective?
4. Physical recommendation. Inspect doors, windows, lighting, access points. Recommend physical changes which would make the building more secure such as pinning hinges on doors and fences.
5. Locks, equipment to be bolted down, potential application of card control and key control. Make specific recommendations.
6. Alarms. Would an alarm system be cost effective? Would the use of the building preclude the use of an alarm? Are the potential benefits of an alarm such that the building use should be changed to facilitate the use of an alarm? Consider all types of alarms, building-wide or specific

offices. Consider closed circuit television application and applications for portable or temporary alarm devices.

7. Storage. Are there specific storage problems in the building, i.e., expensive items which should be given special attention, petty cash, stamps, calculators, microscopes? Make specific recommendations.

8. Are there adequate "No Trespassing" signs posted? Are other signs needed?

9. Custodians. Can they be used in a manner which would be better from a security standpoint?

Personality of the Complex You Are Surveying

Each complex that you survey will have a distinctive personality. Let us take an average building which is opened from 9 A.M. to 5 P.M. The traffic flow is heaviest during this period. During the span from 5 P.M. to 1 A.M., the building is closed to the public. Some staff members may work late. Who secures the building? At 1 A.M., the cleaning crew arrives and prepares the building for another day. The whole personality of the complex must be taken under consideration before your report is completed.

Let's take a further example of building personality. The complex is 100 feet by 100 feet and it has two solid core doors, one large window at the front of the building and is air conditioned.

Case # 1: The complex is a credit union on the main street directly next door to the local police department versus the same credit union on the edge of town.

Case # 2: This is a large doctor's office. The doctor is an art buff and has half a million dollars in art in the office versus a doctor who has no art but has a small safe that has about $200 worth of Class A narcotics inside.

Case # 3: This building houses a variety store which closes at 6 P.M. versus a liquor store which is open until 2 A.M.

In the above three cases, I have given six examples of the personality of a complex. As I have stated, your recommendations must be tailored to fit the lifestyle and vulnerabilities of these buildings.

Positive and Negative Aspects of Making Recommendations

In making your recommendations for security improvements, you must consider the consequences of your suggestion in the event the property owner implements it. There are negative as well as positive aspects involved.

Take for example a housing complex that has a high crime rate from outsiders and within. Your recommendation is, "Build a 10-foot high fence around the complex."

Positive Aspects

The reduction of crime—the environment can be designed so that the individual considering the criminal act feels that there is a good chance for him to be seen by someone who will take action on his own to call the police.

Vandalism will be less—the target of attack can be made to appear so formidable that the person does not feel able to reach the target. It will add to the physical aesthetics of the area through environmental design.

Visual negative impact—this insures the property of the residents adding to their secure environment. Limiting the number of points of entry and establishing access control will primarily direct the decreasing of crime opportunity and operate to keep unauthorized persons out.

Negative Aspect

A fortress environment may create more of a psychological barrier than a physical one. It is socially undesirable and yet is being replicated throughout our country at an increasing rate.

Community Reaction

This cannot be disregarded. Furthermore, vandalism at the time of early installation should be considered.

Consciousness of fear may develop by those tenants whose apartments face the fence; but as the tenants come and go, it will eventually be accepted.

Like all fences, they are subject to being painted by groups with a cause.

Crime Analysis

It is not necessary for you to be a statistician, but the more you know about and understand the local crime problems, the better equipped you will be to analyze the potential crime risk loss in surveying a business or a home.

Crime analysis collection is simply the gathering of raw data concerning reported crimes and known offenders. Generally, such information comes from crime reports, arrest reports, and police contact cards. This is not to say that these are the only sources available to collect crime data.

The analysis process as applied to criminal activity is a specific step-by-step sequence of five interconnected functions:

1. Crime data collection
2. Crime data collation
3. Data analysis
4. Dissemination of analysis reports
5. Feedback and evaluation of crime data

Crime analysis of the site that you are surveying will supply you with specific information, which will enable you to further harden the target in specific areas where losses have occurred. It is a means of responding "after the fact" when a crime was committed.

Key Control

Key control is a very important factor in conducting a survey. Check to find out if they are in the habit of picking up keys from employees at their termination or if they have an accurate record of who has which keys. Within a few short minutes, you should realize whether or not the recipient of your survey has a problem.

Almost every company has some sort of master key system. The reason being that many people must have access to the building without the inconvenience of carrying two dozen keys around every day. Master keys are required for company executives, middle managers, security department, as well as the maintenance department.

Guidelines for Key Control

- Purchase a large key cabinet to store and control the many keys which are in your possession.
- Two sets of key tags should be furnished or obtained with the new key cabinet.
    A. One tag should read "file-key, must not be loaned out."
    B. Second tag should read "Duplicate."
  The key cabinet should be equipped with *loan tags* which will identify the person to whom a key

is loaned. This tag is then to be used and hung in the numbered peg corresponding to the key that was used.

- Establish accurate records and files, listing the key codes, date key was issued, and who received it.
- Have each employee sign a receipt when he/she receives a key.
- All alarm keys should be marked and coded.
- A check should be made of what keys are in the possession of watchmen and staff.
- Do not issue keys to any employee unless absolutely necessary.
- Only one person should order and issue keys for the complex.
- Change the key cylinder when an authorized key holder is discharged for cause. Furthermore, terminated or retired employees should produce keys previously issued at the time of termination.
- Periodic inspections should be made to assure that possession of keys conforms to the record of issuance. These periodic inspections should be utilized to remind key holders that they should be immediately notified of any key loss.
- The original issue of keys and subsequent fabrication and reissuance of keys should assure that their identity is coded on the keys so the lock for which they were manufactured cannot be identified in plain language.

Closed Circuit Television

Closed circuit television (CCTV) is a valuable asset to any security package and an even more valuable tool if hooked up to a recorder. CCTV is a surveillance tool which provides an added set of eyes. If this equipment is on the site you are surveying, it is your job to evaluate its operation and effectiveness.

1. Is it working properly?
2. How is it being monitored?
3. Is it statistically placed where it will be most beneficial?
4. What are the type and quality of the lens and components?

Intrusion Alarms

If the site which you are surveying already has an alarm system, check it out completely. Physically walk through every motion detector unit. Evaluate the quality of the existing alarm products versus what is available to meet the needs of the client:

I surveyed a warehouse recently which was only five years old. It was interesting to note that the warehouse had a two-zone alarm system. The control panel was to the right of the front door which was about fifteen feet from the receptionist. Both alarm keys were in the key cylinders and, according to the president of the company, "The keys have been there since the system was installed." My point is, for a dollar, another key could be duplicated and now the area is vulnerable to attack.

Another time, while doing a survey of an art gallery in New York, the security director stated that he had not had a service call on his alarm system in two years. We then proceeded to physically check every motion detection unit and magnetic contact. You can imagine his reaction when he found out that 12 out of the 18 motion detection units were not working.

In conclusion, intrusion alarms come in all shapes and sizes using a variety of electronic equipment. It is advisable to be familiar with the state of art of electronics so you can produce an effective report.

Lighting and Security

What would happen if we shut off all the lights at night? Stop and think about it!

The results of such a foolish act would create an unsafe environment. Senior citizens would never go out and communities would have an immediate outbreak of thefts and vandalism. Commercial areas would be burglarized at an uncontrollable rate. Therefore, lighting and security go hand in hand.

The above example may seem to be far-fetched, but in fact, installation of improved lighting in a number of cities has resulted in the following:

1. Decrease in vandalism
2. Decrease in street crimes
3. Decrease in suspicious persons
4. Decrease in commercial burglaries
5. In general, a reduction in crime

Street Lights

Street lights have received most widespread notoriety for their value in reducing crime. Generally, street lights are rated by the size of the lamp and the characteristics of the light dispersed. More specifically, there are four types of lighting units that are utilized in street lighting. The most common, and oldest, is the incandescent lamp. It is the least expensive in terms of energy consumed and the number needed. As such, incandescent lighting is generally recognized as the least efficient and economical type of street lighting for use today.

The second type of lighting unit that, as a recently developed system, has been acclaimed by some police officials as "the best source available," is the high intensity sodium vapor lamp. This lamp produces more lumens per watt than most other types. It is brighter, cheaper to maintain, and the color rendition is close to that of natural daylight.

The third and fourth types of devices commonly used for street lighting are the mercury vapor and metal halide lamps. Both are bright and emit a good color rendition. However, the trend now is to use metal halide because it is more efficient than mercury vapor.

Other Security Aspects

Depending upon the type of facility that you are surveying, the following should be reviewed:

1. Communications network, walkie-talkies, and locations of interior and exterior phones.
2. Guard force and security personnel, their training, police powers, uniforms, use of badges, and method of operation.

Your objectives are to identify vulnerabilities, evaluate the site, and provide critical assessment. Methodology and style is purely that of the surveyor, but do not forget it also represents a document from you and your department.

Security Survey Follow-up

The follow-up to your security survey takes many forms, from actually sitting down with the recipient to going by the site and seeing if any changes have actually taken place. Some police departments produce five to seven surveys a day. They do not evaluate their performance because of the time and manpower involved. In this way, they are failing to examine their own effectiveness. The reason for the follow-up is to encourage increased compliance and to ensure that recommendations are understood. Without this step you will not know if the recipient has taken any action.

The basic security survey framework consists of five steps:

1. Generating the survey request
2. Conducting the physical inspection

3. Delivering survey recommendations
4. Following up after the report is completed
5. Evaluating the program

For every crime that is committed, there is a crime prevention or loss reduction defense or procedure that, if followed, could delay or deny a criminal from committing that act.

Physical security is implementing those measures which could delay or deny unauthorized entry, larceny, sabotage, fire, and vandalism. This chapter of security surveys is geared to assist both private security and public law enforcement to harden a target, and to provide assistance to the community to further reduce losses.

For purposes of further assisting your security survey, several checklists have been included at the end of this chapter.

Residential Security

A large percentage of home robberies occur by way of a door or a window. In most cases the front, rear, bulkhead or garage door is unlocked. Front and rear doors often have inadequate locks or they are built in such a way that the breaking of glass to the side of the door or on the door itself will then require the thief to simply reach inside and unlock the door. Windows on the first floor level are the crook's next choice for entry. Basement windows are the least desirable because it may require the unlawful individual to get dirty and, like executives, he is a man concerned about his appearance.

Defensive Measures

Doors (Front, Rear, Basement, and Garage)

The first important item is to install deadbolts on all entry doors. It should be a cylinder deadbolt with a one-inch projecting bolt, and made of hardened steel. This lock should be used in conjunction with your standard entry knob lock. Using viewing devices on entry doors with a wide angle lens is also standard for your door to prevent any unwanted intrusions of your home.

1. Doors with glass in them. The back door is one of the burglar's favorite entryways. Most rear doors are made partly of glass and this is an open invitation to a burglar. For this type of door, you must have a double cylinder deadbolt for protection.

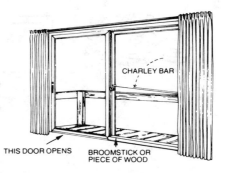

Figure 4–1. To prevent force sliding of aluminum sliding doors, you can mount a Charley bar which folds down from the side.

This type of lock requires a key to open it from the inside as well as the outside because most burglars break the glass and try to gain entry by opening the locked door from inside.

2. Sliding Glass Doors. These entries should be secured so they cannot be pried out of their track. Also, you can prevent jimmying of your door by putting a "Charley bar" made from wood and cut to size and placed in the track when closed (see Figure 4–1).

Bulkheads should also be included as part of your overall security package, and secured with square bolt or deadbolt locks.

Windows

Windows come in a variety of shapes, sizes and types, each of which presents a different type of security problem. Windows provide an inviting entryway for a burglar. He does not like to break glass because the noise may alert someone. On double-hung sash-type windows, drill a hole through the top corner of the bottom window into the bottom of the top window. Place a solid pin into the hole to prevent the window from being opened (see Figure 4–2). Keyed window latches may also be installed to prevent the window from being opened. Grilles and grates may also be installed over extremely vulnerable accesses.

Entrances

Any opening through which a human body can pass is an entrance. Front doors, basements, patio doors, garages that have access to the house, and windows on the second floor are all entryways to burglars. No one way is more important to protect than the other

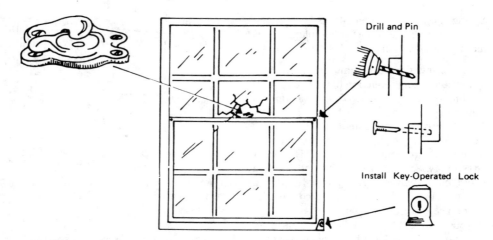

Figure 4–2. A double-hung window can be easily jimmied open with a screwdriver. Glass can be broken adjacent to the crescent latch, or by prying against hardware, and the screws can be popped out. To prevent this, you should drill a hole through the top corner of the bottom window and place a solid pin in the hole. You should also install a key-operated lock.

entryway as your defense is only as good as the weakest link in your security chain.

Setting up Inner Defenses

Even with the precautions already mentioned, a burglar may still get into your home. Once there, you should try to slow him down on his spree as time is the one element working against him. One successful method is to convert a closet into a vault, by installing a dead bolt lock to the door. You have now considerably strengthened your inner defenses. Restricting access from one part of your home to another via deadbolts, etc., will give the burglar yet another obstacle to overcome, if he should break into your home.

Having a burglar alarm stand watch for you is like an insurance policy. You hope you never need it, but it is comforting to know it's there. They very best system is a perimeter system that stops an intruder before he enters your dwelling but it is also costly. Less expensive methods involve using pads under rugs and also motion detectors.

Remember, no home can be made 100 percent burglar-proof, but in most instances, by making it extremely difficult for the burglar to enter your home, you will discourage him. He will move on to a home where the pickings are easier.

Residential security is more important to us than we realize. Just ask the victim of a home that has been burglarized. The mother and wife responds "I felt personally threatened and upset over the losses but more upset over the fact that our home was violated." The father and husband responds "I'm happy my wife and daughter weren't home or they could have been hurt. Now I've got to call the police, my insurance agent, the repairman and *maybe* an alarm company."

Too often people say, "It won't happen to me," "Our neighborhood never had a theft," "I sleep with a small gun by my bed," "I have a dog for protection," or "I don't need an alarm system." These are before-the-incident types of excuses. The cause of residential crime can be found in the individual's environment and lifestyle. Crime can be controlled and losses reduced by corrective human behavior. Physical security measures play an important role in preventing many crimes, but these measures are only effective if they are installed and used properly.

Alarms

Residential intrusion alarms are becoming more popular and installed more frequently. The control panel (UL listed) also handles the fire alarm system. An audible horn will distinguish which system has gone off. The control panel should have an entrance/exit delay feature which will aid in the overall reduction of false alarms. Depending on the style of the home, any number of components can be used. However, keep in mind that only a total coverage type of system should be recommended and installed.

Lighting

Improved lighting provides another residential security measure. Although some studies have documented crime reduction after improved lighting systems have been installed, these studies typically have not accounted for displacement effects. Even if individuals living in a residence reduce the likelihood of a burglary by better lighting, they may only be displacing the burglary to another, less lit area.

Home Security Checklist

Massachusetts Crime Watch[4] put together the following Home Security Checklist, which deals with thirty-five (35) security check points.

Entrances

1. Are the doors of metal or solid wood construction?
2. Are door hinges protected from removal from outside?
3. Are there windows in the door or within 40 inches of the lock?
4. Are there auxiliary locks on the doors?
5. Are strikes and strike plates securely fastened?
6. If there are no windows in the door, is there a wide angle viewer or voice intercommunications device?
7. Can the lock mechanism be reached through a mail slot, delivery port, or pet entrance at the doorway?
8. Is there a screen or storm door with an adequate lock?
9. Are all exterior entrances lighted?
10. Can entrances be observed from the street or public areas?
11. Does the porch or landscaping offer concealment from view from the street or public area?
12. If door is sliding glass door, is the sliding panel secured from being lifted out of the track?
13. Is charley bar or key operated auxiliary lock used on sliding glass door?
14. Is sliding door mounted on the inside of the stationary panel?

Entrances from Garage and Basement

15. Are all entrances to living quarters from garage and basement of metal or solid wood construction?

16. Does door from garage to living quarters have auxiliary locks for exterior entrance?
17. Does door from basement to living quarters have an auxiliary lock operated from living quarters side?

Ground Floor Windows

18. Do all windows have key operated locks or a method of pinning in addition to regular lock?
19. Do all windows have screens or storm windows that lock from inside?
20. Do any windows open onto areas that may be hazardous or offer special risk to burglary?
21. Are exterior areas of windows free from concealing structure or landscaping?

Upper Floor and Windows

22. Do any upper floor windows open onto porch or garage roofs or roofs of adjoining buildings?
23. If so, are they secured as adequately as if they were at ground level?
24. Are trees and shrubbery kept trimmed back from upper floor windows?
25. Are ladders kept outside the house where they are accessible?

Basement Doors and Windows

26. Is there a door from the outside to the basement?
27. If so, is that door adequately secure for an exterior door?
28. Is the outside basement entrance lighted by exterior light?
29. Is the basement door concealed from street or neighbors?
30. Are all basement windows secured against entrance?

Garage Doors and Windows

31. Is automobile entrance door to garage equipped with a locking device?
32. Is garage door kept closed and locked at all times?
33. Are garage windows secured adequately for ground floor windows?
34. Is outside utility entrance to garage as secure as required for any ground floor entrance?
35. Are all garage doors lighted on the outside?

Protecting Personal Property

A number of programs have been developed throughout the country which are geared to aid the citizen to reduce losses in the community. A number of these programs are listed below:

1. *Operation Identification* is a program which started in 1963 in Monterey Park, California. This program encourages citizens to engrave their personal property with a State Driver's License Number.
2. *Bicycle Registration and Anti-Theft Program:* Some communities have started a mandatory registration of bicycles as well as an educational program. The educational program identifies poor quality locks which are used to secure 10-speed bikes as well as providing instructions to properly secure a bike.
3. *Auto Theft Prevention* is another educational type of program which is generally implemented by the distribution of printed material and is covered at community meetings. How many times have you seen a person keep the engine running while going into the store to buy a quart of milk? An example of giving the criminal an opportunity to commit a crime.
4. *Neighborhood Watch:* This program, initiated in 1971, encourages people to report suspicious circumstances in their neighborhoods to the police, as well as familiarizing the citizens with crime prevention techniques which may be employed to reduce criminal opportunity. *Be alert for these suspicious signs*[5]:

    - A stranger entering your neighbor's house when the neighbor isn't home
    - Unusual noises, like a scream, breaking glass, or explosion
    - People, male or female, in your neighborhood who don't live there
    - Someone going door-to-door in your neighborhood, if he tries to open the doors or goes into the backyard, especially if a companion waits out front or a car follows close behind
    - Someone trying to force entry into a home, even if he's wearing a repairman's uniform
    - A person running, especially if carrying something of value
    - If you see anything suspicious, call the police immediately. Give them a physical description of the person and license plate number of the car. Even if nothing is wrong, they'll thank you for your alertness.

5. *Security Surveys:* Many police departments today have trained crime prevention officers who can provide security survey assistance to residents, enabling the citizen to better protect family, home and environment.
6. *Citizen Patrols:* The citizen patrol can be viewed as part of the long historical tradition of vigilantism in this country, with all the ambivalence present in that term. Presently, where their numbers are reported to be increasing in a number of suburban communities and cities across the country, citizen patrols are seen ideally as performing a relatively simple and narrowly defined role—to deter criminal activity by their presence. Their function should be that of a passive guard—to watch for criminal or suspicious activity and to alert the police when they see it.

    Drawing on information that exists about current citizen groups, what are the advantages over other protective measures?

    - Patrols are relatively inexpensive.
    - Patrols can perform a surveillance function effectively.
    - Patrols take advantage of existing behavior patterns.
    - Patrols can improve an individual's ability to deal with crime.
    - Patrols contribute to other desirable social goals related to neighborhood cohesiveness and the provision of a desirable alternative to less acceptable activity. In practice, however, patrols exhibit serious shortcomings:
    - The typical patrol is formed in response to a serious incident or heightened level of fear about crime. The ensuing pattern is cyclic: increased membership, success in reducing criminal activity at least in a specific area, boredom, decreasing membership, dissolution. As a result, patrols tend to be short-lived.
    - The passive role of a patrol is difficult to maintain.
    - The police will be reluctant to cooperate with a patrol, and may even oppose it.
    - The patrol may aggravate community tensions.

The principal problems of patrols relate to their inability to sustain the narrow, anticrime role they initially stress. They may be an effective temporary measure to deal with criminal contagion in a particular area. Over the longer term, however, the inherent risks may outweigh the continued benefits.

The proliferation of patrols in recent years is evidence that they fill a need, but it should be recognized that patrols are no substitute for adequate police protection.

In conclusion, residential security can best be obtained by (1) getting the facts on what you can do to secure your home; (2) analyzing these facts; and (3) arriving at a decision and implementing security measures.

References

1. Raymond M. Momboisse, *Industrial Security for Strikes, Riots and Disasters*, Springfield: Charles C. Thomas, Publisher, 1968, p. 13.
2. Arthur A. Kingsbury, *Introduction to Security and Crime Prevention Surveys* (Charles C. Thomas, Publishers), pp. 6, 7.
3. Washington Crime Watch, Crime Prevention Training Manual, Security Survey Section, p. 8.
4. Massachusetts Crime Watch, Home Security Test Booklet, LEAA, 1980.
5. Dick LaFaver, *The Home Security Book*, #16, (Shell Oil Company) p. 6.

Appendix 4a

Site Survey and Risk Assessment*

VICTOR HAROLD

Crime prevention, or lessening the potential for crime, begins with a major in-depth security analysis of the business or facility. A survey of the interior and exterior will point out security deficiencies and potential for intrusion or the probability that a crime will occur at that spot.

After the survey, an appraisal and recommendation for action should be immediately undertaken. A timetable for implementing the recommendations should be originated and strictly followed.

It is possible the site survey is beyond the ability of most business managements. If it is you are advised to obtain the services of a qualified security professional.

You are also urged to have this service performed immediately. Consider the vulnerability of your business to imminent criminal intrusion. Many burglarized companies as well as those which were victimized by white collar crime have suffered irreversible losses, slowdown, and even shutdown.

This appendix broadly points out the external and internal geographical areas which may require immediate and long-term consideration to help prevent criminal breach of the premises.

1. Can you obtain a neighborhood crime statistics report from the local police?
2. Can you determine if there has been any labor unrest in the area?
3. Can you obtain a report which details the extent of damage a labor unrest may have had on a firm in the area?
4. What is the prevalent type of damage done to

---

*Reprinted with permission of Victor Harold from *How to Stop Theft in Your Business*.

companies during a labor unrest in the area?

5. Has your company ever been victimized by the labor unrests of other companies in the area?

6. Have prior tenants or owners of your facility ever reported a criminal incident?

7. What types of crimes are the most prevalent in the area? List by percentage and frequency.

8. Is your facility very visible from the local roads?

9. Is there easy access by emergency vehicles to your building from the local roads?

10. Have you a chart showing the frequency of police patrols in the area?

11. Do you know how long it would take an emergency or police vehicle to reach your facility?

12. Have you an evaluation of your building's roof and doors which details the length of time it will take for a break-in to be successful?

13. Have you an evaluation of the safes, locks, and other devices to ascertain how long they can delay being opened?

14. If you require separate storage of high-risk or valuable items, are they placed in a high security area which may discourage intrusion?

15. Is personnel movement within the building controlled?

16. Have the door and window hardware been evaluated for ease of entry?

17. Have window openings been secured? (Check with local fire department codes.)

18. Are important files and computer operations secured in an area that prohibits unauthorized entry?

19. Is the lighting sufficient throughout all work areas?

20. Are vent and roof access panels and doors wired and latched to prevent intrusion?

21. Have you prevented external access to the locker rooms, vending and lounge areas?

22. Are the financial handling areas separate and secure?

23. Do you keep confidential your safe's contents, the combinations and the controls needed to maintain security?

24. Are the removable panels and grates in which a person or inventory may be concealed periodically removed and checked?

25. Can these panels and grates be more securely fastened without compromising the item to which they are installed?

26. Will you require police, fire department, or building department approval to more securely fasten those panels and grates?

27. Are the incoming electrical lines well secured and vandal free?

28. Are the panels on all electrical items fastened?

29. Are the electrical power grids, panels, backup, power supplies, etc., kept in a separate locked area?

30. Have you conducted a walk around the property to see if trees, hedges, walls, and fences can hide a person or goods?

31. Have you considered immediate action to correct?

32. If some visibility obstructions exist, are you taking steps to correct?

33. To prevent inventory from going out with the trash, are you keeping a secure trash collection area?

34. To prevent roof access, are trees and their branches next to buildings removed?

35. Are ladders kept secure?

36. Are you aware that noisy equipment can mask unauthorized entry?

37. Are all exterior building entry points alarmed?

38. Are you aware that certain internal and external conditions may affect the alarm?

39. Is there a log of alarm malfunctions and their causes?

40. Have all the causes of alarm malfunction been remedied?

41. Is there an alarm listing and maintenance schedule?

42. Has the police or security company's response to an alarm been tested?

43. Are key management personnel frequently tested on alarm use?

44. Have key personnel been given specific alarm control assignments to include alarm opening, closing, checkout procedures and accountability?

45. Are there clearly established money handling procedures to follow for safeguarding cash, deposits, etc.?

46. Do you have a policy for reporting a theft other than security breaches? (Anonymously, if you think it is best.)

47. Are office machines, shop equipment, and other easily movable items marked for identification purposes?

48. Are vendors, sales people, and repair persons logged in and out, and when necessary, given visitor's passes?

49. Are the employees frequently updated on security procedures?

50. Are you keeping a file of security deficiencies and a schedule for correction?

Appendix 4b

Physical Security Survey*

VICTOR HAROLD

Exterior Physical Characteristics

Perimeter

A. Grounds
1. Is the fence strong and in good repair?
2. Fence height—Is it designed so that an intruder cannot climb over it?
3. Distance of fence from building—Is it designed so that an intruder cannot crawl under it?
4. Are boxes or other materials placed at a safe distance from the fence?
5. Are there weeds or trash adjoining the building that should be removed?
6. Are stock, crates or merchandise allowed to be piled near building?
7. Is there a cleared area on both sides of the fence?
8. Are unsecured overpasses or subterranean passageways near fence?
9. Are fence gates solid and in good condition?
10. Are fence gates properly locked?
11. Are fence gates' hinges secure and non-removable?
12. What types of lock and chain are used to secure gate?
13. Have unnecessary gates been eliminated?
14. Do you check regularly those gates that you've locked?
15. Are blind alleys near buildings protected?
16. Are fire escapes and exits designed for quick exit but difficult entry?
17. Is the perimeter reinforced by protective lighting?
18. Has shrubbery near windows, doors, gates, garage, and access roads been kept to a minimum?
19. What are the physical boundaries of the residence's grounds?
20. Does lighting illuminate all roads?
21. Is there a procedure to identify vendors, sub-contractors, and visitors before entrance to the gate?

B. Exterior Doors
1. Are all doors strong and formidable?
2. Are all door hinge pins located on the inside?
3. Are all door hinges installed so that it would be impossible to remove the closed door(s) without seriously damaging the door or jam?
4. Are all door frames well constructed and in good condition?
5. Are the exterior locks double cylinder, deadbolts, or jimmy-proof type of locks?
6. Can the breaking of glass or a door panel then allow the person to open the door?
7. Are all locks working properly?
8. Are all doors properly secured or reinforced?
9. Are all unused doors secured?
10. Are your keys in possession of authorized personnel?
11. Are keys issued to personnel who actually need them?
12. Are the padlocks, chains, and hasps heavy enough?
13. Are the hasps installed so that the screws cannot be removed?
14. Are all hasps, padlocks, and chains case-hardened?

C. Exterior Windows
1. Are nonessential windows either bricked-up or protected with steel mesh or iron bars?

2. Are all windows within 14 feet of the ground equipped with protective coverings?
3. Are the bars or screens mounted securely?
4. Do those windows with locks have locks that are designed and located so that they cannot be reached and/or opened by breaking the glass?
5. Are small and/or expensive items left in windows overnight?
6. Is there security type glass used in any of the above windows?
7. Are windows located under loading docks or similar structures protected?
8. Can windows be removed without breaking them?
9. Are all vents and similar openings having a gross area of one square foot or more secured with protective coverings?
10. Are windows connected to an alarm system adequately protected?
11. Are windows which aren't secured by bars or alarms kept locked or otherwise protected?
12. Have windows (doors) been reinforced with Lexan?
13. Are all windows properly equipped with locks or reinforced glass and/or decorative protective bars or sturdy shutters?
14. Are unused windows permanently closed?

D. Other Openings
1. Do you have a lock or manholes that give direct access to your building or to a door that a burglar could easily open?
2. Have you permanently closed manholes or similar openings that are no longer used?
3. Are your sidewalk doors or grates locked properly and secured?
4. Are your sidewalk doors or grates securely in place so that the entire frame cannot be pried open?
5. Are your accessible skylights protected with bars or intrusion alarm?
6. Eliminate unused skylights that are only an invitation to burglary.
7. Are exposed roof hatches properly secured?
8. Are fan openings or ventilator shafts protected?
9. Is there a service tunnel or sewer connected to building?
10. Do fire escapes comply with city and state fire regulations?
11. Are your fire exits or escapes so designed that a person can leave easily but would have difficulty in entering?

12. Do fire exit doors have a portable alarm mounted, to communicate if door is opened, or is it hooked up to the intrusion alarm?
13. Can entrance be gained from an adjoining building?

E. Exterior Lighting
1. Is the lighting adequate to illuminate critical areas (alleys, fire escapes, ground level windows)?
2. Foot candles on horizontal at ground level? (Estimation: _____.)
3. Is there sufficient illumination over entrances?
4. Are the perimeter areas lighted to assist police surveillance of the area?
5. Are the protective lighting system and the working lighting system on the same line?
6. Is there an auxiliary system that has been tested?
7. Is there an auxiliary power source for protective lighting?
8. Is the auxiliary system designed to go into operation automatically when needed?
9. Are the protective lights controlled by automatic timer or photo cells, or manually operated?
10. What hours is this lighting used?
11. Is the switch box(es) and/or automatic timer secured?
12. Can protective lights be compromised easily (i.e., unscrewing of bulbs)?
13. What type of lights are installed around the property?
14. Are they cost effective?
15. Are the fixtures vandal proof?
16. Is there a glare factor?
17. Is there an even distribution of light?

Interior Physical Characteristics

1. What is the name of the site?
2. What is the address?
3. Give the full name and exact title of the administrative officer.
4. Provide telephone number.
5. List the name of the surveying officer.
6. Give the full name and exact title of the security liaison.
7. Describe the security problem at this site.
8. What is the general purpose of site?
9. What is the range of hours in use?
10. Which hours and days represent high activity use?

11. How many people have access to site?
12. Is site normally open to the public?
13. List number of rooms occupied by the various departments and offices.
14. Who does maintenance?
15. On what schedule does maintenance operate?
16. List the estimated dollar value of equipment and property in each department/office.
17. What area has the highest dollar value?
18. What area contains the most sensitive material?

A. Interior Lighting
   1. Is there a back-up system for emergency lights?
   2. Is the lighting provided during the day adequate for security purposes?
   3. Is the lighting at night adequate for security purposes?
   4. Is the night lighting sufficient for surveillance by the local police department?
B. Doors
   1. Are doors constructed of a sturdy and solid material?
   2. Are doors limited to essential minimum?
   3. Are outside door hinge pins spot welded or bradded to prevent removal?
   4. Are those hinges installed on the inward side of the door?
   5. Is there at least one lock on each outer door?
   6. Is each door equipped with a locking device?
C. Offices
   1. Can entrances be reduced without loss of efficiency?
   2. Are office doors locked when unattended for a long period of time?
   3. Is there a clear view from receptionist's desk of entrance, stairs, and elevators?
   4. Are maintenance people, visitors, etc., required to show identification to receptionist?
   5. Are desks and files locked when office is left unattended?
   6. Are items of value left on desks or in an unsecure manner?
   7. Are all typewriters bolted down?
   8. Are floors free of projections, cracks and debris?
   9. During normal working hours, is the storage facility kept locked when not in use?
   10. How many people have keys to this door?
D. Keys
   1. Total keys issued? Total masters?
   2. Is there a key control system?

3. What is the basis of issuance of keys?
4. Is an adequate log maintained of all keys that are issued?
5. Are key holders ever allowed to duplicate keys?
6. Are keys marked "Do Not Duplicate"?
7. If master key(s) are used, are they devoid of markings identifying them as such?
8. Are losses or thefts of key(s) promptly reported to security officer or police?
9. Whose responsibility is it for issuing and replacement of keys? (Name and Title)
10. When was the last visual key audit made? (to ensure they hadn't been loaned, lost or stolen)
11. Were all the keys accounted for? (If no, how many were missing? How often do you conduct visual audits?)
12. Are your duplicate keys stored in a secure place? Where?
13. Are keys returned when an employee resigns, is discharged or suspended? (If not, why not?)

E. Locks
   1. Are all entrances equipped with secure locking devices?
   2. Are they always locked when not in active use? (If no, why not?)
   3. Is the lock designed or the frame built so that the door cannot be forced by spreading the frame?
   4. Are all locks in working order?
   5. Are the screws holding the locks firmly in place?
   6. Is the bolt protected or constructed so that it cannot be cut?
   7. Are locks' combinations changed or rotated immediately upon resignation, discharge, suspension of an employee having possession of a master key(s)? If no, why not?
   8. Are your locks changed once a year regardless of transfers, or known violations of security? If no, why not?
   9. When was the last time the locks were changed?
F. Petty Cash
   1. The amount of petty cash kept
   2. Are funds kept to a minimum?
   3. Where is petty cash secured?
   4. Are blank checks also stored there?
   5. Are checks pre-signed?
   6. Is the accounting system adequate to prevent loss or pilferaging of funds accessible to unauthorized persons at any time?

7. Are funds kept overnight in a safe, locked desk or file cabinet?
8. Is this storage area secure?
9. Are locks in storage area replaced when keys are lost, missing or stolen?
10. Number of people who handle petty cash

G. Safes
1. What methods do you use for protecting your safe combination?
2. Are combinations changed or rotated immediately upon resignation, discharge, suspension, etc., of an employee having possession of the combination? If no, why not?
3. Is your safe approved by Underwriters Laboratories?
4. Is your safe designed for burglary protection as well as fire protection?
5. Where is safe(s) located?
6. Is it well lit at night?
7. Can it be seen from outside?
8. Do you keep money in your safe?
9. Do you keep cash at a minimum by banking regularly?
10. Do you use care in working the combination so that it isn't observed?
11. Do you spin the dial rather than leaving it on "day lock"?
12. Do you have a policy making certain the safe is properly secured and the room, door(s), windows are locked, night light(s) on and that no one has hidden inside?
13. Is your safe secured to the floor or wall?
14. Are combinations changed at least every six months? If not, when was the last time?
15. Do you have a protective theft alarm? If yes, is it local or central?
16. When was system last tested?

H. Inventory Control
1. When was the last time an inventory of business equipment was made, listing serial numbers and descriptions?
2. Were any items missing or unaccounted for?
3. Have all typewriters, etc., been bolted down or otherwise secured?
4. Has the site marked all of their business equipment?
5. Is all expensive business equipment stored in a security cabinet or room?

Appendix 4c
Plant Security Checkist*

VICTOR HAROLD

1. Have your obtained a list of certified protection professionals from the American Society for Industrial Security (Arlington, Virginia)?
2. Have you assigned a senior executive to act as liaison with the security consultant?
3. Have you assessed overall plant vulnerability to a variety of risks?
4. Have you checked with local police agencies about the incidence of vandalism, damage, reported internal losses, burglaries, and other crimes in the vicinity?
5. Have you checked with fire officials about the local incidence and type of fires and extent of losses?
6. Do you have periodic reviews of the plant security system, especially with a view toward effectiveness?
7. Do you periodically review the efficiency of the assigned security executive's willingness to carry out the function?

* Reprinted with permission of Victor Harold.

8. In many situations, the cost of security is far greater than actual or expected loss. Have your circumstances been analyzed for cost effectiveness?
9. Do you maintain a list of security regulations?—properly posted?—periodically reviewed?
10. Are you certain that there has not been any negligence in the guard force?
11. How often do you review the methods used to screen new employees, and are you certain screening is done?
12. Is there a policy to prevent laxity and indiscriminate use of badges and passes?
13. Upon termination of a senior executive, are locks, codes, and passwords changed?
14. Have you trained line supervisors to daily check the plant's physical condition, both interior and exterior?
15. Do you tell your plant engineers to daily check critical utility areas for damage; i.e., sewers, telephone, water, electric?
16. If security equipment is to be installed, has the installation plan been approved by a qualified group; i.e., fire department, architect, police department, or engineer?
17. Has there been a recent security evaluation of hardware, containers, fire control equipment, safety items, locks, and bars?
18. Do you have a daily inspection of interior and exterior intrusion detection systems, fire systems, and sprinkler systems?
19. Do you daily test and examine your alarm system for jumpers and proper operation?
20. Is your alarm system of the divided type, that is, small segments can be disconnected from the still operational main system?
21. Do you have a security communication network? Are all parts operating?
22. If you use closed circuit television and cameras, are all stations functioning well?
23. When purchasing new equipment, is the suitability and reliability of the items checked out by a dependable group?
24. Have you a study showing that your security measures can generate a return on investment because losses are avoided and assets are recovered?
25. Has a thorough security survey identified various probable events; i.e., pilferage, white collar crime, etc., to which the company is vulnerable?
26. Can an approximate dollar amount be placed on each factor?
27. Will the survey estimate the cost versus benefit ratio of attempting to correct any security infringement?
28. Does the security survey answer the following:
    (a) What is the possibility of a specific occurrence?
    (b) What is the probability of a specific occurrence?
    (c) What set of circumstances has to be in place for a situation to happen?
    (d) If a problem occurs, how much will it cost to correct and restore?
    (e) Is there any personal risk for my people?
    (f) If we do not install a security system, can we handle most situations on our own?
    (g) What is the correct security level required to accomplish the mission?
29. Do you minimize contact between employees and nonemployees (as much as possible)?
30. Do you keep a record of which employee has keys to specific areas?
31. Are locks changed regularly?
32. Are doors double or triple locked?
33. Are external signs posted stating that alarm systems are in operation?
34. Because the roof is a weak spot, has it been properly protected from intrusion; i.e., sensitive sonic alarms or microwave?
35. Have perimeter entrances been minimized to prevent accessability by key?
36. Have you determined if you need a badge or employee pass identification system?
37. Are your employees trained to challenge an unrecognized visitor or non-pass–wearing person?
38. Are outside service vendors escorted to the job site? Periodically checked? Or stayed with? And escorted out?
39. Do you retain a security consultant to annually review your physical security needs and update security devices?
40. Do your employees know you will prosecute theft offenders?
41. Have you requested that your alarm agency notify you if the premises have been visited during unusual hours by an employee with a key?
42. Are office keys given only to those who need access?
43. Have you a record of which key was given to whom?
44. Do you collect keys immediately from terminated employees?
45. Do you change the locks of areas in which terminated employees had access?

46. Are keys marked with "do not duplicate" logos?
47. Are serial numbers ground off from keys to prevent duplication by number?
48. Is a responsible executive in charge of key distribution?
49. Are spare keys kept in a secure cabinet?
50. Are duplicate records kept indicating key distribution? Date and time issued?
51. Can your telephones be locked to prevent unauthorized after-hours use?
52. Have you a locksmith who periodically checks all lock operations?
53. Can personal items be secured in a locked desk drawer?
54. Are important papers kept in a double locked and fireproofed file?
55. When filing cabinets are unlocked for use, are keys removed and secured?
56. Are office machines bolted down and locked?
57. Are your office machines and plant equipment marked for identification?
58. Are the serial numbers of office and plant equipment recorded, duplicated, and secured?
59. Are briefcases with important documents left in a locked cabinet?
60. Are important papers removed from desks and locked when the area is not staffed?
61. When the building shuts down for the evening or weekend, are doors and windows checked by a manager?
62. Do service personnel from outside vendors have proper identification?
63. When shutting down for the evening, are potential hiding places checked?
64. Are the police and fire department numbers posted near each telephone?
65. Are safe combinations changed very frequently?
66. Are the guards' watchclock tapes checked every evening?
67. Have you determined if a shredder is necessary?
68. Do you avoid keeping large sums of cash overnight?
69. Do visitors sign in?
70. If the employees wear passes, do your security people check them even if the wearers are familiar?
71. If you have a facility which requires constant security, do you escort your visitors?
72. Is a vigil kept on outside maintenance people, especially communications workers?
73. If you have a sensitive security area, is access to it kept limited?
74. Is the security area marked with signs and color coded?
75. Do you have a need for an area where sensitive talks need to take place?
76. Do you periodically check offices for signs of tamperings; i.e., moved desks, paint marks, putty and other fillers used to seal holes, dust and scratch marks, and more?
77. Do you avoid discussing on the phone what you are going to do about your security situation?
78. Do you avoid ordering security sweeps and changes in security structure over the phone?
79. Do you test the integrity of the security service by ascertaining if they will plant a device?
80. Do your security officers observe the counter-surveillance people at work?
81. Are the items prone to tapping or targets for security intrusion sealed? Are the seals checked regularly?
82. If a bug is found, do you continue to search for more?
83. Are all entry places alarmed?
84. Do you have a locker area for employees' personal use? Is the facility kept secure?
85. Are your security guards routinely polygraphed?

Appendix 4d

Guard Security Checklist*

VICTOR HAROLD

1. Have you determined whether or not you have limited security requirements?
2. If you have determined that your security needs are complex, have you talked about your needs to a select group of trustworthy agencies?
3. If your security needs are simple, are you aware that it is time consuming and a waste of productivity to obtain a wide variety of competitive bids?
4. Have you checked with a local law enforcement official for recommendations?
5. Have you checked with colleagues who are using security services for recommendations?
6. If you are analyzing a security agency, have you requested information on the amount, type, and stipulations of their insurance coverage?
7. Have you requested information on the security agency's clients, the names of current customers, and the length of time the account has been with the agency?
8. Have you requested information on the agency's financial status?
9. Is the agency willing to reveal guard training techniques?
10. Does the agency have guard incentive programs?
11. Does the agency have a career program for their guards?
12. Do the guards meet educational and medical checks?
13. Has the agency a set of standards to which guards are held? What are they?
14. Have you reviewed the credentials of the senior executives of the guard company?
15. Will your account have a representative assigned who is from the highest level of management?

16. Will the agency you select have the capabilities to offer other services such as investigations, disaster planning, executive protection, employee screening, and polygraph testing?
17. Have you determined if the agency you are selecting has a union affiliation? Which one?
18. Will there be a union conflict if your employees go on strike?
19. Have you visited the agency's local office?
20. Have you discussed prior clients and why they are no longer clients?
21. Have you visited current accounts and talked to management?
22. In the contractual arrangement with the guard company, have you avoided too much control over their employees?
23. Have you double checked the insurance liability of the agency?
24. Does the contract with the guard company assure that they are an independent contractor, thereby relieving your firm of joint employer liability?
25. Have you reviewed the contract's provisions for replacing unsatisfactory guards and for terminating the contract?
26. Does the contract guarantee costs?
27. Does the contract contain penalties for non or poor performance?
28. Is there an agreement by the guard company to refrain from doing business with a competitive company?
29. Have you assigned a senior person to monitor security services to determine that standards are being met, and that the agency's contractual obligations are being fulfilled?
30. If your plant is paying for guard services, have you discussed wages and job related expenses; i.e., travel, holidays, supervisors, etc.?
31. Have you discussed any special training

* Reprinted with permission of Victor Harold.

required to accomplish the assignment; i.e., firearms, CPR, fire safety, first aid, etc.?

32. If your situation requires a formal presentation and contract, have the documents been reviewed by your legal counsel and insurance company?

33. Have you reviewed provisions for contract terminations?

34. Does the contract have self-imposed penalties for nonperformance?

Appendix 4e
Office Security Checklist

In 1979 the UCLA Campus Police Department put together the following Office Security Checklist, which deals with thirty security points pertaining to operational procedures, as well as physical characteristics:

1. Do you restrict office keys to those who actually need them?

2. Do you keep complete up-to-date records of the disposition of all office keys?

3. Do you have adequate procedures for collecting keys from former employees?

4. Do you secure all typewriters, adding machines, calculators, photocopiers, etc., with maximum security locks?

5. Do you restrict duplication of office keys, except for those specifically ordered by you in writing?

6. Do you require that all keys be marked "Do Not Duplicate" to prevent legitimate locksmiths from making copies without your knowledge?

7. Have you established a rule that keys must not be left unguarded on desks or cabinets, and do you enforce that rule?

8. Do you require that filing cabinet keys be removed from locks and placed in a secure location after opening of cabinets in the morning?

9. Do you have procedures which prevent unauthorized personnel from reporting a "lost key" and receiving a "replacement"?

10. Do you have a responsible person in charge of issuing all keys?

11. Are all keys systematically stored in a secured wall cabinet of either your own design or from a commercial key control system?

12. Do you keep a record showing issuance and return of every key, including name of person, date and time?

13. Do you use telephone locks to prevent unauthorized calls when the office is unattended?

14. Do you provide at least one lockable drawer in every secretary's desk to protect purses and other personal effects?

15. Do you have at least one filing cabinet secured with an auxiliary locking bar so that you can keep business secrets under better protection?

16. Do you record all equipment serial numbers and file them in a safe place to maintain correct identification in the event of theft or destruction by fire?

17. Do you shred all important papers before discarding in wastebaskets?

18. Do you lock briefcases and attache cases containing important papers in closets or lockers when not in use?

19. Do you insist on identification from repair personnel who come to do work in your office?

20. Do you deposit incoming checks and cash each day so that you do not keep large sums in the office overnight?

21. Do you clear all desks of important papers every night and place them in locked fireproof safes or cabinets?

22. Do you frequently change the combination of your safe to prevent anyone from memorizing it or passing it on to a confederate?

23. When working alone in the office at night, do you set the front door lock to prevent anyone else from getting in?

24. Do you have the police and fire department

telephone numbers posted/handy?

25. Do you check to see that no one remains hiding behind you at night if you are the last to leave the office?

26. Are all windows, transoms, and ventilators properly protected?

27. Do you double check to see that all windows and doors are securely locked before you leave?

28. Are all doors leading to the office secured by heavy duty, double cylinder deadbolt locks?

29. If your office is equipped with a burglar alarm system or protected by a guard service, do you make sure the alarm equipment is set properly each night?

30. Do you have a periodic security review made by a qualified security expert or locksmith?

Appendix 4f
Home Security Checklist

VICTOR HAROLD

Exterior

1. Do you have a burglar alarm?
2. Are there stickers on your windows and doors, stating that the property is under surveillance?
3. Are bicycles, garden equipment, and other items kept indoors and locked?
4. Is your mailbox locked?
5. Are front and back doors kept lighted in evening?
6. Are shrubs and trees trimmed low, below window level?
7. Do you arrange for mail and newspaper pickup, or stop deliveries, if you are not at home?
8. Is your grass kept mowed while you are away?
9. Is there a neighborhood watch program?
10. Have you placed lights on timers or photocells if you go away?
11. Are police notified of your extended absence?

Doors

1. Do all doors, especially the garage, close tightly?
2. Are all doors double locked?
3. Are overhead doors locked when not in use? Is there a track lock?

4. If padlocks are used, are they of high quality?
5. If hinges and hasps show, are the screws and hinge pins of the type which cannot easily be removed?
6. If your car is in the garage, are the doors locked and the keys removed?
7. Are the entrance doors solid core?
8. Is there a security plate in the lock area to prevent jimmying?
9. Are there peepholes in the entrance doors?
10. If the entry doors have glass, is the glass 40 or more inches from the lock?
11. Are sliding doors locked, and has an antislide bar on the lower track, as well as bars on top of the doors, been installed to prevent lifting of the door off the track?

Windows

1. Are the window air conditions bolted to prevent removal from the outside?
2. Can the basement windows be locked?
3. Do you use auxiliary pins and other locks on all windows?
4. If windows are kept open for ventilation, can they be locked in the open position?

General Home Security

1. Can all exterior doors be locked from the inside?
2. Are the locks on all exterior doors of the deadbolt type?
3. If a door or window is opened while you are home, will there be a warning sound or light?
4. When you retire or leave, do you check doors and windows to be certain they are locked?
5. When repairmen and utility company representatives come to your door, do you request identification?
6. Can your basement door be locked to prevent entry into the house?
7. Are extra house keys kept isolated or hidden?
8. Do you avoid indiscriminate handing out of duplicate keys?
9. If you park your car in a public lot, do you separate the car keys from the house keys?
10. Have you an outside light which remains on all night?
11. Are all low level windows which are easily accessible kept doubly secure with latches and bolts?
12. Have you installed window and door devices which audibly and visually indicate a break-in is in effect or has occurred?
13. Are your skylights well secured, that is, not easily removed from the roof?
14. Are window air conditioners well installed and not removable from the outside?
15. Are your portable fire extinguishers kept in good condition?
16. Are they kept in easily accessible areas?
17. Are smoke and heat detectors installed near sleeping areas and on every level of the house?
18. Are the detectors tested frequently?
19. Are fire drills a regular routine with your family?
20. Do you have an emergency notification system which will enable other households to know that a situation (medical, panic, robbery) is occurring?
21. If a suspicious vehicle is in the area, is a description and the license number noted?
22. If you go away, can you get a neighbor to park a spare car in your driveway?
23. Do you have a home safe for valuable items?
24. Shouldn't you have an alarm system survey to help determine your security and safety needs?

Miscellaneous

1. Is valuable property inventoried, periodically updated, and the list secured?
2. Is the list of serial numbers of those items which have been recorded kept off the premises?
3. Are valuable items marked with a scriber and an identifying number?
4. Are emergency telephone numbers memorized and also prominently displayed near the telephone?
5. Do you avoid keeping cash in the house?
6. If you have weapons, are they secured?

PART TWO
EQUIPMENT

Chapter 5
Physical Barriers*

RICHARD GIGLIOTTI and RONALD JASON

When we speak of physical barriers, most people tend to think in terms of reinforced concrete walls, chain link fences topped with barbed wire, modern bank vaults, and other such apparent applications of maximum security. We can think back, however, to the Roman Empire, whose power and influence extended over what was then almost all of the known world. The continuance of this power was guaranteed by the establishment of outposts throughout the conquered territories controlled by powerful Roman legions. These outposts were actually fortified garrisons—an example of using physical barriers for protection of a base of operations.

This same principle has been used throughout recorded history: the British and Colonial fortresses during the Revolutionary War; the U.S. Army forts in the Indian territories during the last half of the nineteenth century; the French Maginot Line in World War II; and even the protected base camps established by American forces in Viet Nam. It is interesting to note that the last were actually a variation of the system of forts used during the Revolutionary War to which forces could retire with a relative degree of safety for rest and reequipping.

The concept of physical barriers is not unique to homo sapiens. When a monkey climbs a tree, it is taking advantage of a natural barrier in its environment, which provides a form of physical security. While in the tree, it is out of danger from the carnivores that prowl the jungle floor, though not completely safe from attack by other natural enemies.

People have used barriers to enhance physical security throughout history. Our earliest forebears had the instinctive need for physical security in its

most primitive form—the cave and the tree. Certainly, the need for some edge in the game of survival was crucial to our continued existence. We could not outrun the saber-toothed tiger and giant wolf; we had no protective shell like that of the giant tortoise; we could not intimidate our enemies by sheer size as could the mastodon; and our reproductive capacity was limited. Only by using the security provided by climbing the nearest tree or taking shelter in a handy cave were we allowed the necessary time to continue progress along the evolutionary path.

As intelligence increased over the centuries, we understood that certain changes and improvements could be made to the natural shelter available. There was not much to do to a tree, but by dragging rocks, boulders, and fallen trees across the mouth of his cave, a person could erect rudimentary walls and fences, physical barriers that enhanced the natural protection. The eventual addition of animal skins to cover the openings in cave dwellings was another sign of the march toward civilization and was another component in developing physical security.

Doors

The modern equivalent to the caveman's animal skin is the door. The function of a door in physical security is to provide a barrier at a point of entry or exit. The function of a door in maximum security is still to provide such a barrier; however, the barrier must also be impenetrable by ordinary means, and offer the maximum delay time before penetration by extraordinary means (i.e., by the use of cutting tools, hand-carried tools, and some explosives).

During construction of a maximum-security facility, it is necessary to define the function of all doors and their relationship to the total protection system.

*From *Security Design for Maximum Protection*, by Richard Gigliotti and Ronald Jason (Stoneham, MA: Butterworths, 1984).

When an existing door is evaluated, the function must again be defined and must include the area or material protected.

It is not necessary to make all doors maximum security—only those that are essential to the effective functioning of the total security system. Once a particular door is designated to be incorporated into the overall system, it must be upgraded to provide maximum security. There are two options in this respect: one can replace the door with a commercially available, penetration-resistant model, or upgrade it to provide the necessary resistance. Obvious areas of concern when dealing with maximum-security doors are door hinges and hardware. This chapter discusses hinges and other door hardware, and locks and locking mechanisms are covered in detail in the next chapter.

Personnel Doors

The average industrial personnel door is a hollow steel composite door with 18-gauge metal facing. It is usually hung on butt hinges with nonremovable pins, and may open in either direction. It may have ventilation louvers or glass panels. According to the *Barrier Penetration Database*,[1] the hollow steel door can be penetrated in one minute or less by various methods, including:

1. Defeat of the locking mechanism, if a knob is accessible, by using a half-pound pipe wrench to break it (0.4 ± 0.08 minutes)
2. Prying the door open using a 15-pound pry bar (0.2 ± 0.04 minutes)
3. Penetration using a 10-pound fire axe (3.8 ± 0.08 minutes)

Hollow steel doors can be made more penetration-resistant by a variety of methods:

1. Bolting or welding a steel plate to the inside and/or outside of the door (especially if louvers or glass are present)
2. Installation of several dead bolts that go into all four sides of the door frame[2]
3. After removing the metal back, welding quarter-inch steel louvers on the inside of the front panel of the door, three to four inches apart from top to bottom and replacing the back door panel (Figure 5–1)
4. Replacing hardware with more penetration-resistant types or upgrading existing hardware[3]

By upgrading the hollow steel door, additional weight is added and will be a consideration when

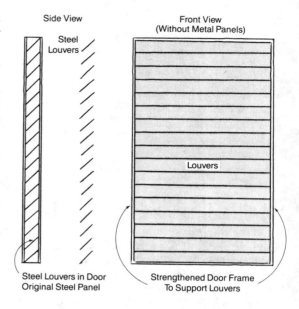

Penetration Resistance Time
Approximately 10–15 Minutes To
Penetrate Through Door

Figure 5–1. Hardened door. (Courtesy of U.S. Army Material Systems Analysis Activity.)

evaluating hinges and hardware. In most cases, hinges will have to be reinforced to compensate for the added weight.

Substantial steel doors or security-class doors are commercially available and are made of three-quarter-inch steel on one side and eighth-inch steel on the other, and filled with 3 inches of fiberglass or similar material. Ten pounds of bulk explosives take 1.5 ± 0.3 minutes to penetrate this type of door.[4]

In addition to the door-hardening techniques mentioned above, there are ready-made security panels that have been marketed under the name DELIGNIT® by Blomberger Holzindustrie of Blomberg, West Germany. This product is highly tempered plate material consisting mainly of hardwood veneers (primarily beech) cross-laminated and bonded under pressure with phenolic resins. The material is available in thicknesses of 20, 30, 40 and 50mm in a variety of standard sizes, as well as specially ordered sizes and thicknesses, and is suitable for construction of bullet-resistant and burglar-impeding doors, partition walls, and so on.

Tests conducted by official agencies in West Germany and in Britain indicate successful resistance of a sample 30-mm panel to a limited variety of small-arms fire up to and including .357-caliber magnum and 12-gauge shot-gun. In addition, a test was conducted wherein two 30-mm sections of DELIGNIT® panel were spaced 150mm apart and subjected to fire from a military rifle firing the 7.62 NATO standard round. The result of a series of five shots was that no bullet penetrated the inner of the two panels.

While the manufacturer does not provide a finished door, it can provide the names of door fabricators who have had experience with their material. The manufactuer claims it can be worked by any carpentry shop equipped to handle hardwood veneers, although use of carbide-tipped cutting tools is recommended.

Frames for maximum-security doors should be anchored to the wall in such a manner that penetration resistance is at least equal to that of the door itself. If at all possible, hinges should be inaccessible from the side of the door that would face the likely threat. As an alternative, individual hinges should be case-hardened or replaced with a heavy-duty, case-hardened piano hinge and the hinge pins made unremovable by welding or pinning (Figure 5–2).

Additionally, some consideration should be given to installing quarter-inch steel plates over exposed hinges, which will offer an additional barrier to cutting and require somewhat more explosives to defeat. Another way to increase the resistance of hinges is to mortise them into the door jamb and door, thus exposing little if any of the hinge pin. The installation of a piano hinge on the outside of the door and jamb would provide a barrier to the support hinges.

A simple yet effective application of the dead bolt principle previously mentioned is to install half-inch steel rods, equidistant between support hinges, on the inside of the door. On the inside door jamb, install a quarter-inch steel plate that has been drilled to accept the rod. If the hinges are defeated, the arms will continue to hold the door secure.

An existing security-class door can be hardened to increase penetration time from 1 to 2 minutes to 20 to 30 minutes by "welding heavy angle iron or small structural I-beam to form a 14-inch or smaller grid on the inside of the front door panel (without interfering with the locking mechanism)"[5] (Figure 5–3).

No high-security door should have its hardware and hinges accessible from the side from which a threat is likely. Doors should open toward the likely threat direction.

In addition to the solid maximum-security doors discussed thus far, several companies make turnstile-type doors. These are useful for controlling access; however, they have no use as high-security barriers.

Retrofit Upgrading Existing Doors

To harden an existing door against tool attack, the customary practice is to clad the attack side with

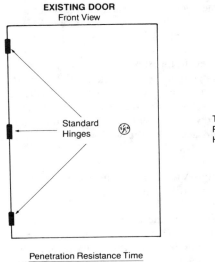

EXISTING DOOR
Front View

Standard Hinges

Penetration Resistance Time
Approximately 30 Seconds

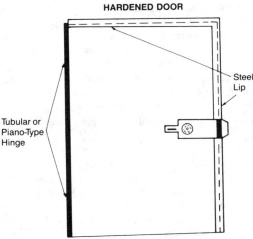

HARDENED DOOR

Steel Lip

Tubular or Piano-Type Hinge

Penetration Resistance Time
Approximately 5–10 Minutes
(Depending on Type of Door)

Figure 5–2. Hardening door jamb seam, hinges and locking devices. (Courtesy of U.S. Army Material Systems Analysis Activity.)

HARDENED DOOR
Back View with Rear Cover Removed

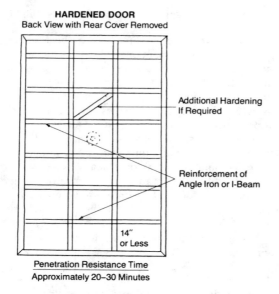

Additional Hardening
If Required

Reinforcement of
Angle Iron or I-Beam

14"
or Less

Penetration Resistance Time
Approximately 20–30 Minutes

Figure 5–3. Hardening fire class or improving security class doors. (Courtesy of U.S. Army Material Systems Analysis Activity.)

heavy-gauge sheet metal or steel plate. This solution has as its principal merit the fact that it can be implemented quickly with materials that can be purchased locally. Cladding should be applied only to solid or laminated wood or to substantial hollow metal doors. The thinnest recommended cladding material is 12-gauge steel sheet. It must be securely fastened to the door by using carriage bolts with The nuts applied from the protected side. The nuts should be tack-welded to the bolts to prevent removal or, alternatively, the ends of the bolts can be peened to serve the same function. Bolts should be not less than 5/16 inch in diameter and should be spaced from 6 to 10 inches apart and as close to the edge as the door frame will allow, preferably not more than 1 or 2 inches.

If the cladding is applied to an outward-opening door, it probably will be necessary to provide protection to the free edge of the cladding to prevent its being pried up and peeled off the substrate. This can be accomplished by forming the sheet metal cover so that it wraps around the door edges, or it may be practical to build up the outside face of the door frame with a steel guard that will deny access to the edge of the cladding.

Experiments were conducted at the Navy Construction Battalion Civil Engineering Laboratory[6] in the use of 9-gauge low-alloy, high-strength steel sheet and three-quarter inch plywood to build up

a laminated veneer for retrofit hardening. They showed that a two-inch laminated panel consisting of exterior steel layers, one central steel layer, and two plywood layers (S-P-S-P-S) was found to have the added merit of stopping all calibers of pistol fire and high-powered rifle fire up to and including .30-06 military ball rounds. A door constructed by this system would have the merits of both attack and bullet resistance.

With retrofit cladding, it is necessary to take into account the effects of the door fit due to the additional thickness and the problem of additional weight. To install this heavy door it is necessary to provide for mounting with heavy-duty hinges and protect against hinge-pin removal and hinge destruction if resistance against attack is to be accomplished.

The door recommended for this application is a hollow door with a skin of 12-gauge cold-rolled steel reinforced by internal channel stiffeners of 22-gauge or thicker steel. The hollow spaces between the stiffeners may be filled with suitable material as needed for thermal insulation.

Door Frames

The high-security door system will not present full resistance to attack and penetration unless the frame is hardened to a level similar to that of the door itself. Similarly, the attack resistance of the frame means little without commensurate strength of its attachment to the surrounding wall and the door. In fact, to be effective the doors, frames, and wall attachments must be designed as attack-resistant assemblies.

The frame should be fabricated of 16-gauge or thicker steel. To strengthen and support it against being spread apart or crushed by hydraulic jacks or other tools, the frame (jambs and head) must be filled with a suitable cement grouting, and bonded to and backed by the wall structure surrounding the door system.

Hinge Vulnerability and Common Countermeasures

Door installations in which the hinges are located on the exterior side of the frames are vulnerable to unauthorized entry through attack on the hinges. It is frequently possible to use a drift punch and hammer to drive out the hinge pin and then open the door from the hinge side. Alternatively, the hinge knuckle can be cut off with a hacksaw, cold chisel, or torch, and entry then made.

The most common countermeasures to that threat are to inhibit or prevent the removal of the hinge pins. This is most frequently done by peening over or tack-welding the ends of the pins. Another approach is to install a set screw in the knuckle so that it locks the pin in place. Peened and welded hinge pins can be freed by filing off their ends and then driving them out. Set screws are seldom effective in resisting an attack with a drift pin and hammer. Still another technique is the use of a continuously interlocking hinge system running the full length of the door (piano hinge).

Some manufacturers make hinges in which the knuckles completely cover the ends of the hinge pins and thus prevent their being driven out with a drift pin. Regardless of how the pin is protected, if the knuckle is exposed on the outside, it is generally possible to saw off or otherwise remove and/or destroy the assembly and thus gain entry by prying open the door from the hinge side.

Door and Frame Interlocking

Various countermeasures have been used to prevent entry through destruction or removal of the hinge pin and/or knuckle assembly. The most common of these is to install a substantial protruding steel dowel pin in the hinge edge of the door or frame and a mating socket or hole in the frame or door so that the pin engages in the socket when the door is closed. In this manner the door and frame are interlocked automatically whenever closed and the removal of the hinge will not allow opening of the hinge side. Using this basic approach, one can devise a variety of pin-in-socket, tongue-in-groove, or other similar devices to provide interlocking on the hinge side of the door. In the case of large fabricated steel doors, it is simple to orient the channel-iron-framing member (on the hinge side) so that it creates a cavity (groove) into which a corresponding angle iron (tongue), which is welded to the door frame, can engage. In view of the relatively simple nature of the design and installation of positive interlocking hardware (i.e., internal steel dowel pin-in-socket or tongue-in-groove) for coupling the hinge sides of the door to the frame, it is recommended that this practice be used wherever highly valuable, critical, or sensitive assets are secured. The following is quoted from the Sandia Laboratories' *Barrier Technology Handbook*:[7]

Doors, due to their functional requirements and associated hardware, impose design restrictions and are, in many cases, one of the weakest links in a structure. For barrier purposes, the principle of balanced design requires that doors with associated frames, hinges, bolts and locking mechanisms be strengthened to afford the same penetration delay as is provided by the floors, walls, and ceilings of the parent structure. Conversely, if the door structure cannot be enhanced, it may not be cost effective to upgrade the existing structure. No currently available standard or commercial doors or hardware provide significant resistance against determined adversaries.

Hinges Appropriate for Door Weight

In designing the hinge system, the weight of the door must be considered. For example, a door designed for resistance against tool attack only might weigh 10 to 15 pounds per square foot, and could be hung on butt hinges, particularly if the door is used infrequently.

Vehicle Doors

The standard security vehicle overhead door found in many facilities is usually of the corrugated steel, roll-up variety. These doors are ordinarily constructed of 16-gauge steel with a stiffness required to withstand 20 pounds per square foot of wind pressure and can be easily penetrated. Using a 6-foot pry bar and a 2×4 plank weighing 20 to 25 pounds, penetration time is 0.8 ± 0.2 minutes. Hardening this type of door is difficult; therefore its use in a maximum-security environment should be kept to a minimum. Specifically designed vehicle doors are usually constructed of at least quarter-inch steel plate and are more penetration resistant.[8] Table 5–1 shows estimated penetration times for standard vehicle doors. Corrugated roll-up and hollow steel panel doors offer little resistance to explosive attack; delay time is governed by the set-up, retreat, return, and crawl-through times. Thermal cutting by torch or oxy-lance (burn bar) affords the same delay as for a personnel door. The material thickness of the panel door requires more time than does the corrugated door material.[9]

Hand-carried tools, for example, jimmy bars and axes, can be used to penetrate a vehicle door. A vehicle itself may be used to effect penetration quickly when the noise associated with such an attack is not a major consideration. Where there is any large door opening, the threat of vehicular attack is always present.

Certain techniques exist for hardening and thus upgrading vehicle doors. Rubber tires could be installed directly behind the outer vehicular door (with

Table 5–1.   Estimated Penetration Times for Standard Vehicle Doors

Barrier	Countermeasure	Countermeasure Weight (pounds)	Penetration Time (minutes)
Corrugated steel	Jet Axe, JA-I	20	0.8 ± 0.2
	Pry bar and 2 × 4 plank	23	0.9 ± 0.2
Hollow steel	Pry bar	15	0.2 ± 0.4
	Fire axe	10	3.8 ± 0.8
	Bulk explosives	10	About 1

From the U.S. Nuclear Regulatory Commission.

a portion below ground level) for greater penetration resistance, or a door clad with sheet metal could be used to resist vehicular penetration. Redwood could be inserted into a panel door to increase resistance to penetration by thermal tools. In this case, however, increased weight necessitates the use of correspondingly upgraded hardware, which, as an added benefit, enhances protection of the door against tool and vehicular attack. Alternately laid steel channels welded together and covered by sheet metal could be used as a door and could provide significant penetration resistance.[10]

Where lateral wall space is not a consideration, the use of a manual or mechanically actuated sliding door should be considered. The door should be constructed (or hardened) to the same standards and by the same methods as specified for personnel doors. In addition, the top runner track must be reinforced and a substantial and well-anchored channel must be provided for the bottom of the door to travel in.

The sliding door presents definite security advantages over those offered by the corrugated steel roll-up door. For example, the structural steel members needed to support a roll-up door adequately are of greater bulk and complexity than those required by the sliding door. The joints necessary in the corrugated steel roll-up door present a weakness in overall structure and are vulnerable to attack. By its very nature, the sliding door is a single, solid entity. Because of its method of mounting, it is almost impervious to forced entry by use of a pry bar, especially when the top track rail is hardened.

Aside from being rammed with a vehicle, the main vulnerability of the sliding door would be to prying against its opening edge. This method of attack can be forestalled by installation of several manually activated drop-pins similar to the familiar barrel bolt, although of much larger and sturdier construction. These drop into receiver holes drilled into the inner rail of the bottom track or into the floor. An intruder attempting to cut through these drop-pins would have to make a lateral cut the entire width of the door (unless able to determine the approximate location of the pins by either spotting the heads of their mounting bolts that protrude through to the outer door surface, or by simply estimating that the pins have been situated on and equidistant from the door's center line). To prevent this, drop-pins must remain undetectable from the outside of the door and they should be spaced at random intervals along the lower door. While the upper track anchoring points would ordinarily be subject to tool attack, their protection by a steel plate or apron on the outside, or attack side of the door, would discourage anyone concerned with effecting a stealthy entry.

The third type of vehicle door that may be encountered in a high-security installation is very similar to that used in the average homeowner's garage. This consists of a series of rigid panels that are joined together along their horizontal edges by hinges so that when the door is raised, it rolls up along a track and usually stores itself under spring tension, parallel to, but approximately eight feet off the floor. There is similarity between these doors only in a generic sense. The home garage door usually has panels constructed of tempered Masonite® or similar product set into wooden framing, with each panel joined to those adjacent by three hinges and usually with a series of glass panes replacing one of the lateral panels. This door can be defeated with nothing more sophisticated than a rock or a shoe. Even without the glass, the panels can be quickly broken out of their support framing.

The high-security articulated vehicle door, however, is usually constructed of panels composed of a corrugated metal stiffener sandwiched between aluminium plate or special steel alloy panels. The hinges are often of the continuous or piano-type and the track has been reinforced to resist external force and to carry the door's extra weight when in the retracted or stored position. As previously stated, however, this type of door is susceptible to vehicle attack or forced entry by lifting with a pry bar.

Vault Doors

By their purely functional design and often massive construction, vault doors serve instantly to discourage attempts at forced entry by all but the most determined adversaries. This is probably the ultimate application of the psychology of maximum security as a deterrent. Prior to opting for the construction of a vault, however, careful consideration must be given to the following questions:

1. What is the expected maximum period that vault protection will be required?
2. Are there federal, state or local government regulations that require vault protection of these assets?
3. Are the assets being protected of a size and configuration that would make their unauthorized removal extremely difficult without the use of heavy or special equipment not generally available in the area?
4. Can the assets being protected be rendered unusable by removal of key components? (Separate storage of these components would be required; however, the size of the resultant security system could be reduced with appropriate corresponding dollar savings.)
5. Will movement of the assets being protected be kept at a minimum?
6. Are there large numbers of persons requiring daily access to these assets during the course of their duties?
7. Would theft of these assets have an adverse effect on:
   a. The company's continued ability to remain in business (a trade secret or nonpatented process, material, machine, etc.)?
   b. Health and welfare of the general public?
   c. The environment?
   d. National security?
8. Will construction of a vault lower insurance premiums?
9. Can a vault be constructed within the existing facility without extensive renovation and/or reinforcement?
10. In the event of company growth, would the present facilities be sufficient to accept this growth and provide the room for expansion, or would a move elsewhere be necessary?

Strong Room Doors

If, after considering the pros and cons of vault acquisition, it is decided that the cost of protection would be prohibitive in comparison to the benefits, serious consideration should be given to construction of a vault-type room or strong room.

A strong room is defined as an interior space enclosed by or separated from other similar spaces by walls, ceiling, and floor constructed of solid building materials, with no windows and only one entrance. Strong room doors should be of heavy-gauge metal construction or of solid hardwood reinforced with a metal plate on the inside. Door louvers and baffle plates (if used) should be reinforced with no. 9-gauge, two-inch-square wire mesh fastened on the interior side of the door. Heavy-duty hardware should be used in constructing a strong room door, and all screws, nuts, bolts, hasps, hinges, pins, and the like should be securely fastened. The door should be set into a suitable frame in the same manner as previously described for installation of personnel doors. Where air-conditioning or heating ducts pass over or through the strong room, or where sewers or tunnels may pass under this space (and they are of a size and shape large enough to accommodate a small person), they should be equipped with personnel barriers. Duct barriers should be constructed of heavy-gauge wire mesh securely fastened to the duct by welding. For sewers and utilities tunnels, effective barriers can be constructed of steel bars or rods, half-inch in diameter, extending across the width of the pipe or tunnel with a maximum spacing of six inches between the bars. The ends of these bars or rods should be firmly anchored to prevent removal and, where the vertical and horizontal bars or rods meet, they should be welded together. In effect this will form a very substantial grillwork that cannot be easily defeated.

Emergency Doors

While some may argue that emergency doors have no place in a maximum-security setting, their use is mandated most of the time. If a facility is of a certain size and/or employs a certain number of people, it must by statute provide a specific number of emergency exits. In the maximum-security environment these should be kept to the minimum required by law. Their number and location depend on many variables such as the type of work being performed in the building, and the work space configuration (or partitioning) within the building. To ensure that emergency exits do not diminish the effectiveness of the maximum-security measures in place, the following questions must be answered:

1. Where are the emergency exists located with respect to the assets being protected?
2. What type of emergency exit door (including hinges, locking mechanism, frame, anchoring, etc.) will be installed?
3. Into what areas will the emergency exits allow personnel to pass?
4. Will the doors be alarmed?

If particularly valuable or strategic material is processed or ordinarily handled near an emergency exit, the possibility of a diversion of this material through the door is very real. It would be relatively easy for a dishonest employee to hide quantities of the material during an emergency evacuation or drill and cache it outside the facility for later retrieval. The possibility must be considered.

There are no hard and fast rules relative to the construction of emergency doors and hinges and methods of mounting. The obvious choice would be doors, hinges, and frames of construction and quality equal to the other security doors in use at a facility. It naturally follows that if a high-security door is procured, the method of mounting should not negate the money spent on its purchase. The only element of an emergency exit over which there is little if any control is its locking mechanism. Most ordinances covering the use of emergency exits and devices are fairly specific in requiring the use of a panic bar locking mechanism. The type of panic bar usually encountered on emergency exit doors is most susceptible to defeat by an adversary using a simple wire hook or coat hanger. In order to maintain security of the exit, some people have chained or otherwise locked (from both sides) emergency exits. This can have disastrous consequences such as those experienced during the fire at the Coconut Grove nightclub in Boston, where nearly 500 lives were lost because the exit doors were locked.

Methods are available, however, to ensure that exit doors keep people out and also allow the safe exit of those inside. One system provides overlapping sections fastened to stiles that meet and overlap when the door closes. The stiles close the gaps around the door so that prying tools cannot be forced through to trip the panic bar. None of the equipment is exposed, so would-be intruders are not able to push it out of the way. When the panic bar is depressed, however, the barrier springs free and the door opens easily. As added security, the hinges are tamper-resistant, which makes defeat by removing them quite difficult.

Another type of panic-bar emergency device eliminates the bar that can be easily tripped and replaces it with a rim device that is not as likely to be snagged by a coat hanger.

At most facilities, emergency exits allow personnel to exit into parking lots, alleyways, or city streets. When evacuation is necessary, however, people should be channeled by physical barriers to a central assembly area that is under the control of the security department. Personnel should not be allowed to exit into a parking lot, alley, or street. To allow this could facilitate employee theft or diversion of the assets being protected, or could lead to a breach in the security system by an insider who would allow accomplices to enter the facility and plunder it. In addition to employing physical barriers to move evacuating employees to a controlled safe area, the security department should be organized to provide some sort of monitoring of the evacuation process and routes to ensure that stolen or diverted material is not passed through or thrown over a fence to an accomplice or for later retrieval.

Alarming of emergency exit doors should be mandatory. Not only should the door have a locally annunciating alarm, but it must be tied into the facility's central alarm station. In this way, each of the alarm systems serves to back up the other. To ensure positive performance, these alarm systems must be periodically checked. It is suggested that a check at least twice a day of both systems be implemented. In addition, each emergency exit door should have a tamper-indicating seal (or seals) affixed (Figure 5–4) and these should be checked each time the alarm system is checked.

Roofs

In arriving at a design for a maximum-security roof (or ceiling), the most obvious and simplest solution would appear to be to use the same specifications and technology employed in construction of the high-security walls in this space or building. There are, however, considerations that must be made that are not instrumental in wall design.

1. How much loading will this roof or ceiling be subjected to?
2. If this is a ceiling in a multistory facility, will the space directly above the protected area be covered by a trained suitably equipped member of the security force or by a sophisticated alarm system that annunciates locally and at a remote monitoring station that is staffed around the clock?
3. Will the integrity of the roof or ceiling be broken by piping, ductwork, or access hatches?

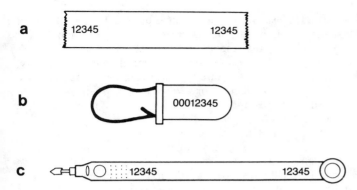

Figure 5–4. Tamper-indicating door seals: (a) Serially-numbered tape type. (b) Serially-numbered heavy wire and plastic type. (c) Serially-numbered plastic strap type.

4. Will any portion of the roof be accessible from outside the protected area, or conversely, grant access outside the protected area from inside it?
5. Will the roof or ceiling be alarmed; monitored by security officers or CCTV; equipped with adequate lighting to permit proper assessment; not provide places of concealment for instruders such as air-conditioning units, exhaust fan hoods, smoke pipes, etc.?

These and many more site-specific questions must be worked out between the building architect or room designer and the person responsible for ensuring that the degree of security necessary will be provided. Officials involved in the preliminary planning stages of the construction of a new facility or up-grading of an existing one into the maximum-security class must include the company security director. This individual should be prepared to discuss these matters with the staff and obtain input of the personnel who will have day-to-day responsibility for being sure that the system works. If the facility is part of a corporation that may have installations of this type in other locations, a visit to one or more of these sites by the security staff would pay handsome dividends in avoiding mistakes that may be plaguing others. Careful and imaginative planning will eliminate costly (and embarrassing) oversights that may require considerable time, effort, and expense to rectify.

The prime requisite of any roof in a maximum-security setting is its ability to withstand or defeat attempts at forced entry. The roof most commonly selected is usually constructed of poured concrete, approximately 5½ inches thick with steel reinforcing rods on 8 × 12-inch centers embedded in the center of the concrete slab. In tests of resistance to forced entry, it was found that 4 pounds of bulk explosives and 20-pound bolt cutters required only 2.8 ± 0.4 minutes to effect penetration.[11] Another type of

roof construction often found in industry and government buildings consists of 16-gauge sheet metal placed on ribbed steel decking, covered by 2 inches of insulation followed by a final covering of a half-inch of asphalt and gravel. Using a 10-pound fire axe and a five-pound shovel, penetration was achieved in 2.3 ± 0.7 minutes. In a test of this same type of roof construction, 20 pounds of Jet-Axe JA-I charge and equipment effect penetration in 0.8 ± 0.2 minutes.[12] The conclusion reached in the study from which these results are drawn is that while there are quite a few variations in the types of materials and the manner in which they may be assembled, they can all be defeated in about a minute with a few pounds of appropriate explosive. The obvious answer, therefore, is to construct the best roof possible, but to prevent anyone from reaching it by establishing a protected area around the building, then providing adequate assessment capabilities, alarms, and the like to detect anyone who may have managed to penetrate the protected area.

If the construction of a strong room is being considered within an existing maximum-security setting, there are several combinations of commonly available materials from which to fabricate a homogeneous roof or ceiling that will provide significant resistance to forcible entry.

The creation of this roof or ceiling is well within the capabilities of any commercial carpenter with assistance from a sheet metal shop. In tests conducted by the Civil Engineering Laboratory of the Navy Construction Battalion Center, the best composite material consisted of 0.10-inch sheets of 6061-T6 aluminum over half-inch plywood on both sides of an 18-gauge 304 stainless steel sheet. In laboratory tests[13] a panel constructed in this manner was subjected to attack by a 7¼-inch circular saw equipped with a metal cutting blade and an oxyactelylene torch; the average rate of linear progression was 3.06 inches per minute. Switching over to the circular saw with metal cutting blade, 22 seconds passed without complete penetration. In all cases, large quantities of smoke were generated, as the saw blades and stainless steel sheet became extremely hot. Subsequent tests indicated that an abrasive blade on the saw was ineffective.

To defeat attempts simply to disassemble the roof when the composite is assembled into standard-sized panels and then used as conventional building materials, the substrate should be laid in a random pattern to avoid the neat layering of edges through all the various materials. The components can be bonded together through the use of nuts and bolts, screws, tempered screw-nails, or ringed nails; however, the nuts and bolts should be peened to prevent removal and the heads of the screws should be ground for the same purpose. Although it would be possible for someone to shear off the nail heads, the holding action of the nail shanks would still present a formidable task to anyone inclined to attempt to peel the roof. If this type of composite is used, it must be remembered that it would be covered by insulation and probably several different layers of weatherproof roofing. This additional material would add substantially to the penetration resistance of such a roof. Its use is not recommended, however, in the construction of a roof that is not alarmed, not easily visible to the guard force or well lighted, or that is close to or part of the protected area perimeter. As previously indicated, this material would be suitable inside an already protected installation, or could be used in small low buildings located well within a protected area.

Upgrading Existing Roofs

When the company security department is faced with the task of upgrading an in-place facility, the task becomes many times harder. The installation of alarms, lights, doors, walls, gates, and many other security responsibilities must be considered.

Before upgrading the roof of an existing facility, the security director must climb up there and have a first-hand look. What can be seen? Are there fire escapes that allow access to the roof? Are there roof hatches, skylights, ducts, piping, air-conditioning units, strong and firmly attached downspouts, coamings (which could anchor a grappling hook)?

Once you have made an assessment of the roof's liabilities, you must consult the individual responsible for maintaining plant services (usually the chief of maintenance or of the physical plant), and ascertain which of these potential access points are essential to plant operations. If the plant site is an old building, many of these potential problems can be eliminated as the elements are nonfunctional, having been replaced by more modern equipment but remaining in place simply because they plug a hole that would be left in the roof by their removal. Once a decision is made as to which of these appurtenances can be removed, the subsequent hole should be rehabilitated so that the physical integrity and strength of the repair is not less than that of any other part of the original and undamaged roof structure.

Low, flat roofs that might be susceptible to scaling through use of a grappling hook should have shielding installed behind the coaming to prevent the hook from finding a secure anchoring point. This need not be anything more exotic than panels of heavy-gauge sheet metal. These can be anchored to the lip of the coaming and roof and angled back toward the roof to form an inclined plane up which the hook will ride, right back over the edge (Figure 5–5).

Another possibility that may be worthy of consideration, especially for facilities situated in remote areas, would be attack by helicopter. If the roof

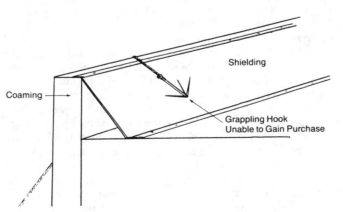

Figure 5–5. Grappling hook shielding.

Shielding

Coaming

Grappling Hook
Unable to Gain Purchase

of the main building, or the building that would be the attackers' objective, is flat and thus suitable for landing a helicopter, or even if it is not flat but is suitable for landing an attack force from a hovering helicopter, consideration should be given to installation of one or more tall lightweight metal light poles to the roof. These will prevent the helicopter from landing or coming close enough to the roof to discharge personnel. These poles could also support area floodlights that would light the protected area and rooftop. In addition, flagpoles, radio communications antennas, tall chimneys and exhaust stacks, or guy wires serve to prevent attack by such a stratagem.

Floors

In most buildings, the floor is probably the least thought of part of the total security package. It exists for the purpose of providing a smooth dry working surface and as a base on which the building may be erected floor by floor. True? Ordinarily, this would be a good thumbnail description of the purposes of flooring; however, in a maximum-security installation, the same amount of thought that has been devoted to design of the walls and roof must be alloted to the floor. A typical floor is usually constructed of poured concrete, 6 to 8 inches thick, reinforced with rebar steel rods or 6-inch square mesh of no. 10 wire. Floors constructed in this manner are adequate for most facilities; however, penetration time by one or two adversaries using explosives, sledgehammers, and bolt cutters in any combination averages two to four minutes.[14]

This penetration time does not take into account the time spent in arriving at the site, setting up for the penetration, retreat time (if explosives are to be used), and crawl-through. If the target is located in a multistory building, the attempted penetration may come from above or below, and therefore the floor in the space above the target site must provide an amount of resistance equivalent to that of the other security features.

How can existing floors similar to what is described be afforded an additional measure of penetration resistance? The most obvious answer would be to increase the floor's thickness by adding additional layers of rebar, reinforcing wire, and poured concrete. This simplistic solution should not be implemented lightly, as the addition of what may amount to quite a number of tons of weight to a structure that was not originally designed for this additional weight could present a very real per-

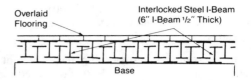

Figure 5–6. I-beam application to floors. (Courtesy of U.S. Army Material Systems Analysis Activity.)

sonnel safety hazard. If this is the only feasible solution, a competent engineering firm should analyze the situation and design the necessary additional supporting columns or beams to ensure an adequate margin of safety.

If the cost of accomplishing a complicated building redesign and renovation as briefly described above is not possible, an alternative may be to relocate the objective to a ground floor or perhaps even into a below-ground location. If the target is relocated to ground level, it should be placed away from exterior walls, preferably toward the center of the structure with several intervening walls between it and any exterior wall (that is, layered; see Figure 5–2). If there is a basement or utility space under the site selected for relocation, it should be sealed off or provided with sophisticated alarms to preclude entry from that point.

An interesting method of tremendously increasing the penetration resistance of a wall that would be adaptable to floors (and ceilings) would be to anchor steel I-beams into the concrete walls, interlocking as many additional beams as necessary across the width of the floor (or ceiling). These beams could then be covered with a simple overlaid wooden floor, which could be tiled or carpeted as required. The accompanying illustration shows how this hardening method would appear in cross-section (Figure 5–6).[15] Properly installed, these I-beams would increase the penetration resistance time to approximately two to four hours. The additional weight, however, restricts the use of such a hardening or protection method to new construction or to a facility in which the proper steps have been taken to ensure the total system has been properly engineered.

Fences

Fences are used to:

1. Define a particular area.
2. Preclude inadvertant or accidental entry into the area.

3. Prevent or delay unauthorized entry.
4. Control (or channel) pedestrian and vehicular traffic.

In a maximum security setting, fences are not the ideal barrier (Table 5–2); walls of solid construction should be used for the purposes described above. It is recognized, however, that walls are an often undesirable or impractical, and fences are the most viable alternative.

The type of fence used in a maximum security setting should be chosen after careful analysis of many factors. Based on determination of the objectives it will serve, additional questions should be answered:

1. Will one fence be enough, or will two or more in a series be required?
2. Will there be vehicle barriers in conjunction with the fence?
3. How far will the fence be from the area of chief concern?
4. What will be the closest area of concealment to the fence?
5. Will the fence be alarmed?

Environmental conditions will certainly affect the design of a fence system and should be considered; for example:

1. Will erosion under the fence be a problem?
2. Will corrosion of the fence be a problem?
3. What natural features or vegetation around the fence might interfere with detection or assessment of activity in the area?

Selection of the kind of fence will not stop at a choice of fabric; decisions must be made as to height,

the means of anchoring the posts and bottom, and the type of topping. If two or more fences are to be installed, what, if anything, will be placed between them, and what will be the distance between them? Finally, considering the kinds of tools likely to be required for penetration, what will be the total penetration time for all fences and obstacles? Once these questions are answered, planning can commence. The type most frequently encountered is no. 11 American wire gauge or heavier, with 2 inch mesh openings, 7 feet in height, topped by three strands of barbed wire or tape evenly spaced 6 inches apart and angled outward 30 to 45 degrees from the vertical.

This type of fence can be breached in 4.3 ± 0.3 seconds using no material aids, but with the assistance of one person not crossing.[16] To increase the penetration time of this fence to 8.4 ± 1 second, it is necessary to install V-shaped overhangs with concertina barbed wire or tape inside the V.[17] The types of fences described can be driven through in a light pickup truck in 2 ± 1 seconds with no significant damage to the truck.[18]

Less frequently encountered fences include the V-fence, which consists of 3-inch posts set at an angle of 60 degrees in 30-inch diameter by 24-inch high concrete footings 12 inches below grade. The posts are in 10-foot centers and staggered 5 feet front to back. The chain link mesh is 10 feet high with a cable installed at the top. Corrugated steel sheet is placed on the outside posts to prevent crawling under. Nine rolls of GPBTO (general purpose barbed tape obstacle) are used inside the V to delay crawl-through.

All rolls are secured to the chain link mesh with wire ties. Cutting through this fence takes about

Table 5–2. Penetration Aids

Item	Description	How Used
Canvas sheet	6' × 8' folded sheet	Thrown over top of fence to aid climbing
Cutters	Bolt cutters, wire cutters, tin snips	To cut fence fabric, barbed wire, or tape
Steps	18" iron rods bent into step form	Hooked into fence fabric and used as climbing aids
Wire hooks	6" to 12" lengths of stiff wire bent into hooks	Hold barbed tape to fence to aid climbing
Long hooks	3" rods bent into hooks	Pull down barbed tape toppings to aid climbing
Ladder	7' step ladder	To jump over fence
Extension ladder	20' ladder hinged in the middle to form an A	To cross over combination barbed tape-fence barriers
Pry bar	10' 2 × 4 or piece of 2" pipe	Lift fence fabric to aid crawling underneath fence
Plywood	4' × 8' sheet of ⅜" plywood	Put over barbed tape to aid crossing
Carpet	4' × 15' heavy carpet rolled up on a 5' 4 × 4	Throw over fence to aid climbing
Plank	Two 8' 2 × 2 planks with a nail in one end	To lift carpet roll over fence

From the U.S. Department of Commerce, National Bureau of Standards.

four minutes. Climb-over takes only 40 seconds, using ladders and bridges as breaching aids.[19] This same fence can be equipped with razor ribbon instead of GPBTO, with a second sheet of corrugated steel attached to the inside posts to form a V-shaped trough filled with 2- to 5-inch rocks and 9-inch diameter telephone poles, and with six rolls of barbed tape concertina. Thus outfitted, it offers penetration resistance of 10 minutes for digging and crawling under. Climb-over times are similar to those of the V-fence previously described. While personnel penetration cannot be prevented, breaching by a vehicle is almost impossible for the latter type of V-fence.[20]

Regardless of how elaborate fences may be, they still offer only a modicum of security. Fences are necessary, but investments in this area should be kept to a minimum as the money can be better used on other components of the total system.

In a maximum-security environment, there are certain things that must be kept in mind regarding the use of fences. Height should be a preliminary consideration. The higher the fence, the better the chances of defeating a climb-over by personnel using most simple breaching aids. Whenever a fence is used in a maximum-security system, the method of anchoring it is very important. No matter how sophisticated the fence may be, if the fabric can be pried up from ground level using a 2 × 4 or similar breaching aid, it is nearly useless.

According to *Barrier Technology Handbook*[21]:

> The time required to go under a fence is only slightly longer than the time required to climb a fence without a barbed tape topping but is significantly shorter than the time required to climb a fence with a barbed tape topping when only limited aids are used.

Penetration time can be doubled by the addition of a bottom rail (Figure 5–7).[22] Many fences are constructed so that the bottom of the fabric either touches the ground or is no more than two inches

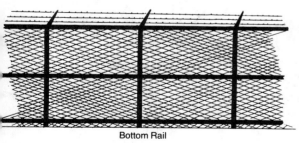

Bottom Rail

Figure 5–7. Bottom fence rail.

above ground level. Without some method of anchoring this fabric, crawl-under is quite simple. If cost is no obstacle, burying the lower portion of the fabric (about three to six inches) in concrete would virtually preclude crawl-under. Another alternative would be to anchor the bottom of the fence fabric with 3-inch reinforcing rods to precast concrete sills that are 8½ feet long, 10 inches high, and 3 inches wide. Each sill is buried under the fence fabric, between posts, with three inches of sill above ground and the reinforcing rods from the sill bent around the fence fabric. This method is effective in that it takes less time to cut through or climb over the fence than it does to separate the fabric from the reinforcing rods.[23]

Topping a fence with barbed wire or tape is another consideration. The U.S. Nuclear Regulatory Commission (NRC) requires protected area fences to be topped with at least three strands of barbed wire, angled outward at a 30- to 45-degree angle. As previously mentioned, this particular topping does very little to preclude climb-overs. A somewhat better topping is GPBTO, often called razor ribbon. It is intimidating in appearance and thus offers a psychological deterrent to less than determined adversaries. In actuality, however, the use of breaching aids generally improves penetration times for barbed-tape-topped fences. The *Handbook* states[24]:

> The fastest penetration times for barbed tape-topped fences were achieved when a piece of carpeting was thrown over the fence. The carpet was made by nailing the end of 4 feet wide by 15 feet long heavy carpet to a 5 feet long 4 × 4 and then rolling the carpet around the 4 × 4.

Generally, the addition of any barbed wire or barbed tape topping does not significantly increase penetration resistance. An intruder who is discoouraged from climbing over and crawling under will probably choose to go through the fence.

Cutting through the fence generally takes more time than climbing over and crawling under. Once again, the fact that the bottom portion of the fabric is securely anchored increases penetration time. If the bottom is not anchored, "it takes only a single row of approximately 12 to 15 cuts to make a man-sized opening. Anchoring the fence in concrete doubles the cutting time."[25] To double the cutting time through chain link fence, it is necessary to fasten another layer of fabric to the inside of the fence.[26]

Yet another way of increasing cut-through time would be to interlace metal or wood lattice in the fabric. This technique, however, significantly reduces visibility and should not be used when the fence is the single component of a perimeter protection system. (Fences should never be the single component of a perimeter protection system in a maximum-security environment.)

Entry and Exit Points

Entry and exit points must be considered when erecting a security fence. The first criterion should be that the integrity of all gates and doors be the same as or better than that of the fence in which they are installed. They should be kept to the minimum number necessary to maintain compliance with governmental and/or company mandates.

Gates should open out if at all possible. Many swing in and out and should be modified accordingly. They should be equipped with a jamb or frame to strengthen the integrity of the opening. The most common types are swing gates and sliding gates with variations.

Most vehicular gates have access roads aimed directly at them, thus facilitating vehicle intrusions. Penetration resistance of most fabric-type gates is equivalent to that of the fence in which they are installed. Vehicle drive-through is easier at a gate than at any other part of the fence. The use of metal doors set in jambs rather than gates offers a somewhat higher degree of penetration resistance but the coost is usually not worth it, although for emergency fence doors this should be mandatory. For any emergency door in a perimeter fence, opening should be facilitated by a panic bar on the inside. Emergency doors should be locked and the panic bars installed so that an intruder cannot use the bar to open the door from the outside. Although access controls are discussed in Chapter 6, it should be noted that any opening of perimeter fence doors or gates should be controlled and monitored.

Another method of controlling pedestrian traffic through fences is by use of turnstile gates. Penetration time (by deactivating electrical controls or forcible entry) is approximately one minute. When installed in a common chain link fence, an adversary would probably choose to breach the fence rather than the turnstile gate.

The weak link in a gate is usually the hardware—hinges and locks. Fence gate locks should be accessible only from the inside. Built-in locks depend on fence alignment for effectiveness and should be supplemented with a piece of case-hardened or stainless steel chain and padlock. The chain should be wrapped around the fencepost and gatepost until it is as tight as possible, and padlocked; there should

be no slack left in the chain. Where possible, stainless steel cable should be used, as it tends to flatten out when attacked with bolt cutters and is somewhat difficult to defeat. A bridle can be made from three-eighths- to half-inch stranded stainless steel cable, looped on both ends using NiccoPress fasteners (Figure 5–8). Bridles can be used in conjunction with case-hardened padlocks for a variety of purposes.

A double-leaf swing gate should be securely anchored where both leaves meet by a solid foot bolt, several feet long, on each leaf that is dropped into a steel anchoring hole in the ground (Figure 5–9). The addition of a chain or cable and padlock will also enhance the gate's security.

Because fences are not the ideal physical barriers in a maximum security environment, their usefulness is limited. Their primary function should be to simply define a particular area.

Walls and Moats

In designing a maximum security perimeter barrier system where cost is no object, the most penetration-resistant structure would be a thick, high wall. Walls, however, do not allow free visual access to the area outside. A possible alternative is the modern equivalent of the medieval moat. It completely surrounds the protected area, and all entry and exit points are bridged with either fixed or movable structures. These points can be kept to the absolute minimum and controlled around the clock. They can also be equipped with methods of preventing breach by ramming with a vehicle.

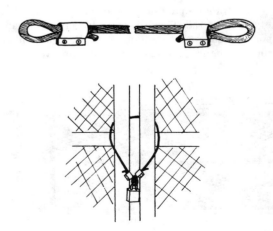

Figure 5–8. Bridle.

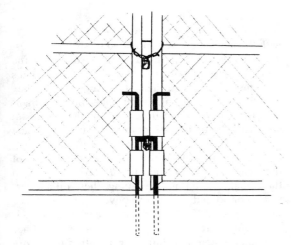

Figure 5–9. Double leaf gate drop bolts.

The moat would be of the dry type and equipped with a suitable drainage system. It would be at least 8 feet deep and measure a minimum of 10 feet from edge to edge. To increase protection, a standard chain link fence topped with an outrigger equipped with three strands of GPBTO would be positioned at the inner edge. This would be attached in such a way that there would be little or no lip that could be used to support a ladder or serve as a working platform for someone attempting to cut through the fence fabric. The fence posts would be a minimum of three inches in diameter and concrete filled. Top rails would not be used. The strong fence posts would maintain the longitudinal rigidity required, but by omitting the top rail stiffener, a degree of instability is introduced that would increase protection by making it difficult for someone to secure a good anchor point for a bridge or from which to work to penetrate the area.

The bottom edge of the fence fabric would be embedded in the concrete at the time the moat lining is poured to prevent entry by prying up the fabric and crawling under.

The specification of moat depth and width can only be reached when integrated into the total barrier design. A minimum depth of 8 feet is recommended as this would require a larger ladder to reach from the moat bottom to the top of the fence. Such a ladder would be bulky and difficult to maneuver and could not easily be hidden if it must be brought to the planned penetration site on foot. An 8-foot depth would also serve as a definite deterrent to anyone contemplating penetration by crashing through the fence with a vehicle. Any commonly

available tracked vehicle, including a bull-dozer, would be unable to climb out of the moat due to this depth and the 90-degree wall angle. A minimum width of 10 feet is recommended as this would preclude the use of uncomplicated bridges such as a 4 × 8-foot sheet of three-quarter-inch plywood. To prevent a ladder (modified by the addition of hooks or steel rods to one end) from being used as a bridge by hooking or inserting the modified end into the fence, an aluminum or galvanized steel sheet would be attached to the outside of the fence to a height of three feet. This ladder could still be used as a bridge by hooking it into the fence fabric above this plate, but the angle and the unsteadiness would provide a very unstable work platform. The easiest way to bridge this type of perimeter barrier would be with a 20-foot extension ladder modified so that the upper end has a hook attached to the end of each leg. To use, the ladder would be extended to its full height then allowed to fall across the moat so that the hooks would fall behind the top of the fence fabric. Once the hooks were in position, the ladder would form an inclined plane over which the adversaries could climb or crawl and drop to the ground inside the protected area.

This type of entry can, however, be defeated by a double moat system, which is nothing more than a second 8-foot × 10-foot (or larger) moat immediately adjacent to the first with the previously specified fence installed between on a 12- to 15-inch-thick reinforced concrete wall. The fence would be topped with a Y-type of barbed tape standoff with concertina tape installed in the center of the Y as well as on either side of the outrigger arms.

On either fence, a motion detection system would be required, as would a detection system located between 10 and 15 feet beyond and parallel to the second moat. To prevent the inadvertant entry of personnel and wildlife, an outer-perimeter chain link fence eight feet high and topped with three strands of GPBTO would be installed. Depending on the amount of property available, this fence would be located a minimum of 25 feet from the outer edge of the first moat.

In our example, cost *is not a factor;* the objective is to use fencing and other physical barriers as a first line of defense. As previously mentioned, our preference is the use of walls rather than fences.

Topography

The natural deterrence offered by topography, while of often limited value, should be taken into consideration when designing or upgrading a facility to the maximum-security level. Rivers and other large bodies of water, swamps, escarpments, deserts, and so forth are all examples of natural obstacles that may be used in various ways.

Probably the most famous examples of the optimal use of natural barriers were the prisons on Alcatraz Island in California and the French penal colony on Devil's Island located off the coast of (then) French Guiana. The physical barriers used to contain the prisoners in these facilities were usually enough to discourage escape attempts. Even if they might be defeated, however, the escapee was still left with no way off the island except by using materials at hand or (in the case of Alcatraz) attempting to swim to freedom. Although both of these prisons were in operation for many years, only a very few escapes were ever successful.

When a facility has a river or other large body of water as a boundary, the natural obstacle may be used in conjunction with more traditional fences as a deterrent. The clear view of the approach route across these areas would serve to discourage an adversary from attempting an approach from that direction, especially if faced with sophisticated alarms and barriers around the objective. In a remote or isolated area, a river or large body of water abutting the site could also serve as adversary approach or escape routes, thereby turning these nominal topographic barriers into liabilities against which additional protective means or procedures must be provided.

The advantage offered by a desert environment would be similar to that provided by a natural water barrier. As with water obstacles, the possibility of an unseen approach across a barren landscape would be very slim. The advantages of isolation and early detection could be outweighed by the fact that approach and/or escape might be accomplished across the very feature that seems to offer some degree of protection, from any direction.

Swamps, while not usually a consideration in a maximum-security setting, could conceivably be encountered. The principal advantage offered by marshy terrain is its impenetrability to usual forms of ground transportation. The most practical setting for a facility in a swampy area would be at the center of the swamp with only one access road. In the event of successful penetration of the facility, this access road could be blocked to contain the adversaries until outside assistance arrives at the scene.

The security offered by a deep forest should also be considered. When a facility is located in a remote area of dense forest, with very limited and con-trolled access routes, this remoteness serves to discourage all but the most determined adversaries. As with the natural barriers provided by swamps, forest locations would require adversaries to forego the usual methods of transportation when access routes are limited and controlled. This might mean they would have to walk in, carrying all the equipment and arms they believe necessary for the successful completion of their mission. In addition, their escape plan must be structured to require, as the last resort, escape by foot. Depending on the remoteness of the objectives, the terrain to be encountered, and the climatic conditions prevailing, these difficulties, when considered above and beyond the resistance to be expected from the on-site security personnel, could force the adversaries to choose another course of action and shift their attention to a more vulnerable target.

In summary, natural barriers may be efficiently incorporated into a total security system only when effective, round-the-clock monitoring of these approach areas by a security guard or CCTV system is provided.

References

1. *Barrier Penetration Database*, Revision 1 (Upton, N.Y.: Brookhaven National Laboratory, 1978), p. 17.
2. Ibid., p. 18.
3. *Hardening Existing SSNM Storage Facilities, Preliminary Report* (Aberdeen, Md.: U.S. Army Materiel Systems Analysis Activity, 1979), p. 33.
4. *Barrier Penetration Database*, p. 18.
5. *Hardening Existing SSNM Storage Facilities*, p. 31.
6. *Technical Memorandum No. 61-78-9*. (Port Hueneme, Calif.: Civil Engineering Laboratory, Naval Construction Battalion Center).
7. *Barrier Technology Handbook*, 77-0777 (Albuquerque, New Mexico: Sandia Laboratories, 1978).
8. *Barrier Penetration Database*, p. 17.
9. *Barrier Technology Handbook*.
10. Ibid.
11. Ibid.
12. Ibid.
13. *Technical Memorandum No. 51-78-04* (Port Hueneme, Calif.: Civil Engineering Laboratory, Naval Construction Battalion Center, 1977).
14. *Hardening Existing SSNM Storage Facilities*, p. A-6.
15. Ibid., diagram 5.
16. *Barrier Penetration Database*, p. 8.
17. Ibid., p. 9.
18. Ibid., p. 8.
19. *Barrier Technology Handbook*, paragraph 3.5.4.
20. Ibid., paragraph 3.7.4.3.

21. Ibid., pp. 78–79.
22. Ibid.
23. Ibid.

24. Ibid., p. 77.
25. Ibid., p. 79.
26. Ibid., p. 80.

Chapter 6

The Use of Locks in Physical Crime Prevention*

JAMES M. EDGAR and
WILLIAM D. MCINERNEY

Lock Terminology and Components

The effectiveness of any locking system depends on a combination of interrelated factors involved in the design, manufacture, installation, and maintenance of the system. A prevention specialist needs to understand the weaknesses and strengths of the various systems, and know how each must be used to achieve maximum benefit from its application. This requires a thorough understanding of the inner workings of the various types of locks. It is not sufficient to know what in someone's opinion is a good lock. A good lock today may not be as good tomorrow as technology improves and manufacturers alter their designs and production techniques. A lock that is excellent in some applications may be undesirable in others. A knowledge of the basic principles of locking systems will enable a preventions specialist to evaluate any lock and determine its quality and its effectiveness in a particular application.

Key-Operated Mechanisms

A key-operated mechanical lock uses some sort of arrangement of internal physical barriers (wards, tumblers) which prevent the lock from operating unless they are properly aligned. The key is the

device used to align these internal barriers so that the lock may be operated. The lock itself is ordinarily permanently installed. The key is a separate piece which is designed to be removed from the lock to prevent unauthorized use.

Three types of key-operated locks will be introduced in this section: disc or wafer tumbler, pin tumbler, and lever.

Tumbler Mechanisms

A tumbler mechanism is any lock mechanism having movable, variable elements *(the tumblers)* which depend on the proper key (or keys) to arrange these tumblers into a straight line permitting the lock to operate. The tumbler, which may be a disc, a level or a pin, is the lock barrier element which provides security against improper keys or manipulation. The specific key which operates the mechanism (which is called the *change key*) has a particular combination of cuts or bittings which match the arrangement of the tumblers in the lock. The combination of tumblers usually can be changed periodically by inserting a new tumbler arrangement in the lock and cutting a new key to fit this changed combination. This capability provides additional security by protecting against lost or stolen keys.

Tumbler mechanisms and the keys that operate them are produced to specifications which vary with each manufacturer and among the different models produced by each manufacturer. These specifications are known as the *code* of the lock mechanism. The coding for each mechanism provides specifica-

*Permission obtained from National Crime Prevention Institute, School of Justice Administration, University of Louisville.

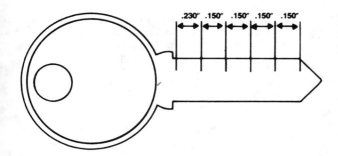

Figure 6–1. The spacing or position of each cut on the key is a fixed dimension corresponding to the position of each tumbler in the lock.

tions for both the fixed and variable elements of the lock assembly. Fixed specifications include:

- The dimensions of each of the component parts of the lock and the established clearances between each part (e.g., the size and length of the key must match the size and depth of the keyway)
- The spacing of each tumbler position and their relation to each other (Figure 6–1)
- The depth intervals or increments in the steps of each cut or bitting (Figure 6–2)

The relationship between the dimensions of the tumblers and the bitting on the key is shown for a typical pin tumbler mechanism in Figure 6–3. These codes provide a locksmith with dimensions and specifications to produce a specific key to operate a particular lock or to key additional locks to the combination of a particular key.

The different arrangements of the tumblers permitted in a lock series are its *combinations*. The theoretical or mathematical number of possible combinations available in a specific model or type of lock depends on the number of tumblers used and the number of depth intervals or steps possible for each tumbler. If the lock had only one tumbler which could be any of ten lengths, the lock would have a total of ten combinations. If it had two tumblers, it would have a possible total of 100 (10 × 10) combinations. With three tumblers, 1000 (10 × 10 × 10) combinations are possible. If all five tumblers were used, the lock would have a possible 100,000 combinations. The number of mathematically possible combinations for any lock can be determined by this method.

Due to a number of mechanical and design factors, however, not all of these theoretically possible (implied) combinations can actually be used. Some combinations allow the key to be removed from the lock before the tumblers are properly aligned (shedding combinations)—something that should not be possible with a properly combinated tumbler lock. Others, such as equal-depth combinations, are avoided by the manufacturers. Some combinations result in a weakened key which is prone to break off in the lock. Others are excluded because the space from one cut in the key erodes the space or positioning of adjacent cuts. The combinations which remain after all of these possibilities have been removed are called *useful combinations*. The useful combinations which are actually employed in the manufacture of the lock series are the basis for the *bitting chart* which lists the total combinations used in a particular type of model or lock. When other factors are equal, the more combinations that can actually be used in a lock, the greater its security. Total useful combinations range from one for certain types of warded locks to millions for a few high security tumbler key mechanisms.

Disc or Wafer Tumbler Mechanisms

Disc tumbler mechanisms consist of three separate parts: the keys, the cylinder plug, and the cylinder shell (or housing) (Figure 6–4). The plug contains the tumblers, which are usually spring-loaded flat plates that move up and down in slots cut through the diameter of the plug. Variably dimensioned key slots are cut into each tumbler. When no key is

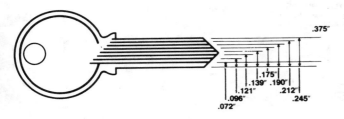

Figure 6–2. The depth interval (increment) of the steps of each cut or bitting is a fixed dimension.

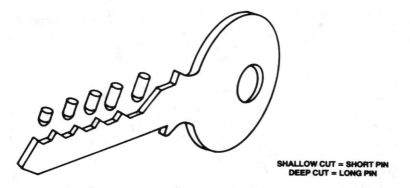

Figure 6–3. The depth of each cut corresponds to the length of each tumbler in the lock.

SHALLOW CUT = SHORT PIN
DEEP CUT = LONG PIN

inserted or an improper key is used, one or more tumblers will extend through the sides of the plug into either the top or bottom locking grooves cut into the cylinder shell, firmly locking the plug to the shell. This prevents the plug from rotating in the shell to operate the lock. The proper change key has cuts or bittings to match the variations of the tumblers. When inserted, the key aligns all of the tumblers in a straight line at the edge of the cylinder plug (the *shear line*) so that no tumbler extends into the shell. This permits the plug to rotate.

Disc mechanisms generally provide only moderate security with limited key changes or combinations. Depth intervals commonly used are from .015 to .030 inches which permit no more than four or five depths for each tumbler position. Some models used as many as six tumblers. The more commonly found

five-tumbler mechanism which allows five depth increments for each tumbler position would have a maximum of 3.125 implied combinations. The number of useful combinations would, of course, be considerably fewer for the reasons indicated earlier. Some added security is provided by the common, although not universal, use of warded and paracentric keyways which help protect against incorrect keys and manipulation. Nevertheless, most of these locks may be manipulated or picked fairly easily by a person with limited skills. In addition, the variations cut into the tumblers can be *sight read* with some practice while the lock is installed. Sight reading involves manipulating the tumblers with a thin wire and noting the relative positions of each tumbler in the keyway. Since each lock has only a limited number of possible tumbler increments, the correct

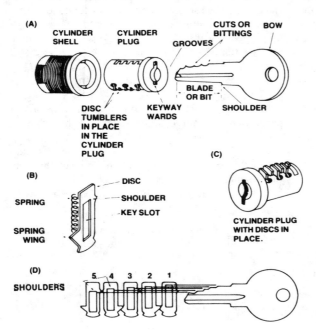

Figure 6–4. The key slots in the discs correspond to the cuts or bittings cut in the key. Note how each cut in the key will align its corresponding disc in a straight line with the others.

arrangement of these increments can be estimated with fair accuracy permitting a key to be filed or cut on the spot to operate the lock.

Pin Tumbler Mechanisms

The pin tumbler mechanism is the most common type of key-operated mechanism used in architectural or builders (dooor) hardware in the United States. The security afforded by this mechanism ranges ffrom fair in certain inexpensive cylinders with wide tolerances and a minimum of tumblers to excellent with several makes of high security cylinders, including those that are listed by Underwriters Laboratories as manipulation- and pick-resistant.

The lock operates very much like disc tumbler mechanisms (see Figure 6–5). The locking system itself consists of a key, a cylinder plug, and a cylinder shell or housing. Rather than using discs, the mechanism uses pins as the basic interior barrier. Each lock contains an equal number of upper tumbler pins *(drivers)* and lower tumbler pins *(key pins)*. The proper key has cuts or bittings to match the length of the lower pins. When it is inserted, the tops of the key pins are aligned flush with the top of the cylinder plug at the shear line. The plug may then rotate to lock or unlock the mechanism. When the key is withdrawn, the drivers are pushed by springs into the cylinder plug, pushing the key pins ahead of them until the key pins are seated at the bottom of the pin chamber. The drivers extending into the plug prevent it from rotating (Figure 6–6).

If an improper key is inserted, at least one key pin will be pushed into the shell, or one driver will extend into the plug. In either case, the pin extending past the shear line binds the plug to the shell. One or more key pins may be aligned at the shear line by an incorrect key, but all will be aligned only when the proper key is used.

Depth intervals commonly used for pin tumbler cylinders vary from .0125 to .020 inches. These intervals allow between five and ten depths for each tumbler position. The number of pins used ranges from three to eight—five or six being the most common number. Maximum useful combinations for most standard pin tumbler cylinders (assuming eight tumbler depth increments) are as follows:

3 pin tumblers =	approximately	130 combinations
4 pin tumblers =	approximately	1,025 combinations
5 pin tumblers =	approximately	8,200 combinations
6 pin tumblers =	approximately	65,500 combinations

These estimates assume that the useful combinations amount to no more than 25 percent of the mathematically possible combinations. Many common pin tumbler locks use less than eight increments, so the number of useful combinations for a specific lock may be much lower than the figures given above. Master keying will also greatly reduce the number of useful combinations.

Pin tumbler mechanisms vary greatly in their resistance to manipulation. Poorly constructed, inexpensive cylinders with wide tolerances, a minimum number of pins and poor pin chamber alignment may be manipulated quickly by persons of limited ability. Precision-made cylinders with close tolerances, a maximum number of pins, and accurate pin chamber alignment, may resist picking attempts even by experts for a considerable time.

Most pin tumbler lock mechanisms use warded keyways for additional security against incorrect keys and manipulation. The wards projecting into the keyway must correspond to grooves cut into

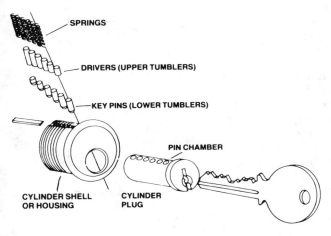

Figure 6–5. Basic pin tumbler cylinder lock mechanism.

SPRINGS

DRIVERS (UPPER TUMBLERS)

KEY PINS (LOWER TUMBLERS)

PIN CHAMBER

CYLINDER SHELL OR HOUSING

CYLINDER PLUG

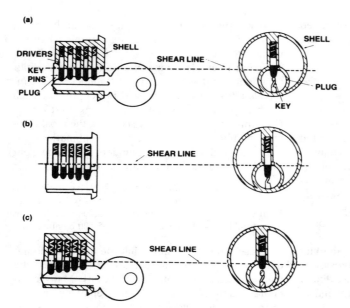

(a) DRIVERS, SHELL, SHEAR LINE, KEY PINS, PLUG, SHELL, PLUG, KEY

(b) SHEAR LINE

(c) SHEAR LINE

Figure 6–6. Operation of a pin tumbler cylinder mechanism. (a) When the correct key is inserted, the bittings in the key align the tops of the lower tumblers (key pins) with the top of the cylinder plug at the shear line. The plug may then be rotated in the shell to operate the lock. (b) When the key is withdrawn, the springs push the upper tumblers (drivers) into the cylinder plug. With the pins in this position, the plug obviously cannot be turned. (c) When an incorrect key is used, the bittings will not match the length of the key pins. The key will allow some of the drivers to extend into the plug, and some of the key pins will be pushed into the shell by high cuts. In either case, the plug cannot be rotated. With an improper key, some of the pins may align at the shear line, but only with the proper key will all five align so that the plug can turn.

the side of the key, or the key cannot enter the lock. When the wards on one side of the keyway extend past the center line of the key, and wards on the other side also extend past the center line, this is known as a *paracentric* keyway (Figure 6–7). While warded keyways are commonly used on most pin tumbler mechanisms, paracentric keyways are usually restricted to the better locks. They severely hinder the insertion of lockpicks into the mechanisms and the ability of the manipulator to maneuver the pick once it is inserted.

Modifications have been made to the drivers in better locks to provide increased security against picking (see Figure 6–8). The usual modified shapes are the *mushroom* and the *spool*. Both of these shapes have a tendency to bind in the pin chamber when picking is attempted, making it more difficult to maneuver them to the shear line. To be consistently successful in picking pin tumbler cylinders with either type of modified driver, special techniques must be used.

There are a number of variations of the pin tumbler cylinder on the market. One which is seeing increasingly widespread use is the *removable core cylinder* (Figure 6–9). These were originally produced by the Best Universal Lock Company whose initial patents have now expired. Most major architectural hardware manufacturers now have them available in their commercial lock lines. This type of cylinder uses a special key called the *control key* to remove the entire pin tumbler mechanism (called the *core*) from the shell. This makes it possible

to quickly replace one core with another having a different combination and requiring a different key to operate. Because of this feature, removable core cylinders are becoming increasingly popular for institutional use, and use in large commercial enterprises where locks must be changed often.

Removable core cylinders do not provide more than moderate security. Most systems operate on a common control key, and possession of this key will allow entry through any lock in the system. It is

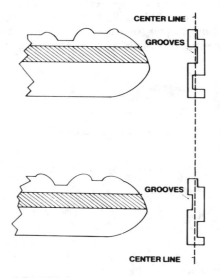

CENTER LINE
GROOVES
GROOVES
CENTER LINE

Figure 6–7. Milled, warded, and paracentric keys.

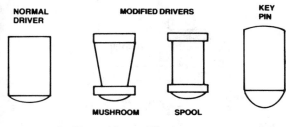

Figure 6–8. Pin tumbler modification.

not difficult to have an unauthorized duplicate of the control key made. If this is not possible, any lock, particularly a padlock, of the series may be borrowed and an unauthorized control key made. Once the core is removed from a lock, a screwdriver or other flat tool is all that is necessary to operate the mechanism. Additionally, the added control pins increase the number of shear points in each chamber, thus increasing the mechanism's vulnerability to manipulation.

Another variation that has been in widespread use for many years is *master keying*. Almost any pin tumbler cylinder can easily be master keyed. This involves merely the insertion of additional tumblers called *master pins* between the drivers and key pins. These master pins enable a second key, the *master key*, to operate the same lock   (see Figure 6–10). Generally, an entire series of locks is combinated to be operated by the same master key. There may also be levels of master keys including submasters which open a portion, but not all, of a series; master keys which open a larger part; and grand masters which open the entire series. In very involved installations, there may even be a fourth level (great grand master key).

There are a number of security problems with master keys. The most obvious one is that an unauthorized master key will permit access through any lock of the series. Less obvious is the fact that master keying reduces the number of useful combinations that can be employed since any combination used must not only be compatible with the change key, but with the second, master key. If a sub-master is used in the series, the number of combinations is further reduced to those which are compatible with all three keys. If four levels of master keys are used, it should be obvious that the number of useful combinations becomes extremely small. If a large number of locks are involved, the number of locks may exceed the number of available combinations. When this occurs, it may be necessary to use the same combination in several locks which permits one change key to operate more than one lock *(cross keying)*. This creates an additional security hazard.

One way of increasing the number of usable combinations and decreasing the risk of cross keying is to use a *master sleeve* or ring. This sleeve fits around the plug, providing an additional shear line similar to the slide shear line in a removable core system. Some of the keys can be cut to lift tumblers to sleeve shear line, and some to the plug shear line. This system, however, requires the use of more master pins. Any increase in master pins raises the susceptibility of the lock to manipulation, since the master pins create more than one shear point in each pin chamber, increasing the facility with which the lock can be picked.

Thus, while master-keyed and removable core systems are necessary for a number of very practical reasons, you should be aware that they create additional security problems of their own.

The basic pin tumbler mechanism has been extensively modified by a number of manufacturers to improve its security. The common features of high security pin tumbler cylinder mechanisms are that they are produced with extremely close tolerances and that they provide a very high number of usable combinations. Additional security features include the use of very hard metals in their construction to frustrate attacks by drilling and punching.

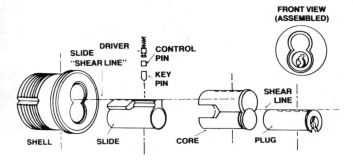

Figure 6–9. Removable core, pin tumbler, cylinder mechanism.

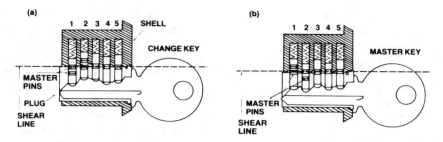

Figure 6–10. Master-keyed pin tumbler cylinder mechanism. (a) This is a simple master-keyed system using master pins in the first and second tumbler positions. When the change key is inserted, note that the top of the first master pin aligns with the top of the cylinder plug. The remaining positions show the key pins aligned with the top of the plug. This arrangement permits the plug to turn. (b) With the master key inserted, the first position aligns the top of the key pin with the cylinder plug. The master pin is pushed further up the pin cylinder. The second position shows the master pin aligning at the top of the plug. The master pin has dropped further down the pin hole in the plug. The remaining three positions are unchanged. This arrangement also allows the plug to rotate.

Lever Tumbler Mechanisms

Although the lever lock operates on the same principles as the pin or disc tumbler mechanism, its appearance is very different. Figure 6–11 illustrates a typical lever mechanism. Unlike pin or disc tumbler devices, the lever lock does not use a rotating core or plug, and the bolt is usually an integral part of the basic mechanism thrown directly by the key. The only other type of mechanism in which the key directly engages the bolt is the warded mechanism. You will recall that the bolt in pin or disc tumbler systems is usually directly operated by the *cylinder plug*, not the key. The key is used to rotate the plug, but never comes into direct contact with the bolt.

Despite these somewhat deceptive appearances, the lever lock operates very much like the other tumbler mechanisms. Each *lever* is hinged on one side by the *post* which is a fixed part of the *case*. The leaf *springs* attached to the levers hold them down in a position which overlaps the *bolt notch* as shown in Figure 6–12. In this position, the *bolt* is prevented from moving back into a retracted position by its *fence* which is trapped by the front edges (*shoulders*) of the levers. When the key is inserted and slightly rotated, the bittings on the key engage the *saddle* of the lever, raising it to a position where the fence aligns with the slot in the lever (called the *gate*). In this position, the fence no longer obstructs the movement of the bolt to the rear, and the bolt can be retracted.

The retraction is accomplished by the key engaging the shoulder of the bolt notch. While the bittings of the key are still holding the levers in an aligned position, the key contacts the rear shoulder of the bolt notch, forcing the bolt to retract as the key is rotated. As the bolt is retracted, the fence moves along the gate until the bolt is fully withdrawn. When the key has rotated fully, completely retracting the bolt, it can be withdrawn.

If an improperly cut key is inserted and rotated in the lock, either the levers will not be raised far enough to align all of the gates with the fence, or

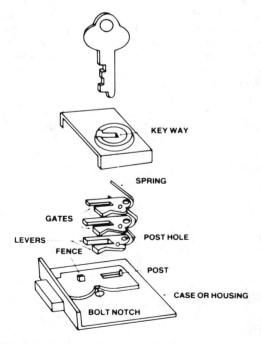

Figure 6–11. Lever tumbler mechanism.

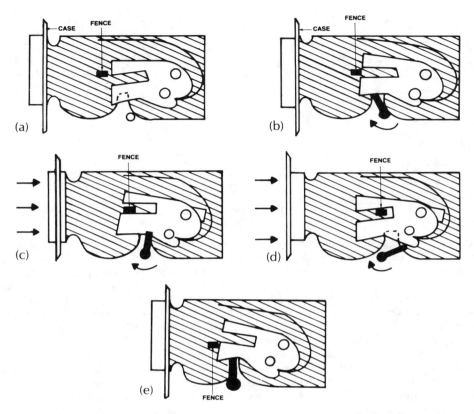

Figure 6–12. Operation of a typical lever tumbler mechanism. (a) The bolt is in the fully extended *locked* position and the key has been withdrawn from the keyway. In this position, the spring forces the lever down toward the bolt notch trapping the fence against the forward edge (shoulder) of the lever. This prevents the bolt from being forced back. (b) The key has been inserted and the bitting on the key has lifted the lever against the spring tension, aligning the gate with the fence. The bolt can now be moved back into the retracted position. (c) The key has begun to force the bolt back into a retracted position by engaging a shoulder of the bolt notch at the same time it is keeping the lever suspended at the correct height to allow the fence to pass into the gate. (d) The bolt is now fully retracted and the key can be withdrawn. (e) If an improper key is inserted, the bitting either will not lift the lever high enough for the fence to pass through the gate or the lever will be raised too high and the fence will be trapped in front of the lower forward shoulder of the lever. From this position, the bolt cannot be forced back into the retracted position.

one or more levers will be raised too high, so that the bottom edge of the lever obstructs the fence (as in Figure 6–12). In either case, the bolt is prevented from being forced to the rear, thus opening the lock.

Figure 6–13 a shows one version of the basic lever. A number of variations are on the market. Some levers are made with projections built into the gate designed to trap the fence in various position (Figure 6–13). The front and rear traps prevent the fence from being forced through the gate when the bolt is in either the fully extended or fully retracted position. Figure 6–13 shows another variation: serrated (saw-tooth) front edges. These serrations are designed to bind against the fence when an attempt is made to pick the lock. They are commonly found on high security lever tumbler mechanisms.

Lever mechanisms provide moderate to high security depending on the number of levers used, their configuration, and the degree of care used in the construction of the lock mechanism. Any mechanisms using six or more tumblers can safely be considered a high security lock. Some mechanisms use a

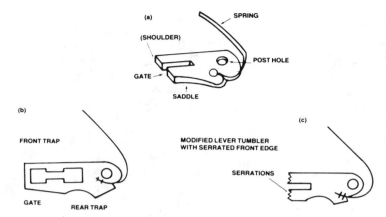

Figure 6–13. Lever tumblers. To operate the lock, the key contacts the lever at the saddle, lifting it until the fence is aligned with the gate. The saddles on the various tumblers are milled to different depths to correspond to different cuts on the key.

double set of levers, requiring a double bitted key. The levers are located on both sides of the keyway. This configuration makes the lock very difficult to pick or manipulate.

Lever locks are commonly found in applications where moderate to high security is a requirement, including: safe deposit boxes, strong boxes, post office boxes, and lockers. The lever mechanisms available in the United States, because of the integrated, short throw bolt are not ordinarily used as builders hardware. But they are commonly used in that application in Europe and some of these locks have found their way into the United States.

Combination Locks

In principle, a combination lock works in much the same way as a lever mechanism. When the tumblers are aligned, the slots in the tumblers permit a fence to retract which releases the bolt so that the bolt can be opened. The difference is that where the lever mechanism uses a key to align the tumblers, the combination mechanism uses numbers, letters, or other symbols as reference points which enable an operator to align them manually.   Figure 6–14 shows a simplified view of a typical three-tumbler combination lock mechanism. The tumblers are usually called *wheels*. Each wheel has a slot milled into its edge which is designed to engage the *fence* when the slot has been properly aligned. This slot is called a *gate*. The fence is part of the lever which retracts the bolt. The gates are aligned with the fence by referring to letters, numbers, or other symbols on the dial. The sequence of symbols which permits the lock to operate are its *combination*. A typical combination sequence using numbers is 10-35-75. The fact that three numbers are used in the combination indicates that the lock contains three tumblers. The number of tumblers in a lock always corresponds to the number of symbols used in its combination. Few modern combination locks use more than four tumblers because combinations of five or more symbols are unwieldy and hard to remember. Older models, however, used as many as six.

Both *drive cam* and dial are fixed to the *spindle* so that as the dial is rotated, the drive cam will also rotate in an identical fashion. The drive cam has two functions. It is the means by which motion of the dial is transferred to the wheels, and when all wheels are properly aligned and the fence retracted, it is the mechanism by which the bolt lever is pulled to retract the bolt.

The wheels are not fixed to the spindle, but ride on a *wheel post* which fits over the spindle. These wheels are free-floating and will not rotate when the dial is turned unless the *flies* are engaged. The flies are designed to engage pins on the wheels at predetermined points (determined by the combination of that particular lock). When the flies engage these pins, the wheels pick up the rotating motion of the dial. When the flies are not engaged, the wheels will remain in place when the dial is rotated.

To operate a typical three-wheel combination lock, the dial is first turned four times in one direction to allow all of the flies to engage their respective wheels so that as the dial is being turned, all of the wheels are rotating with it. At this point the wheels are said to be *nested*. The object is to disengage each wheel at the spot where its gate will be aligned with the fence. To do this, the operator stops the dial when the first number of the combination reaches the index mark on the dial ring. This first stop aligns the gate of wheel 1 with the fence.

The operator then reverses direction to disengage

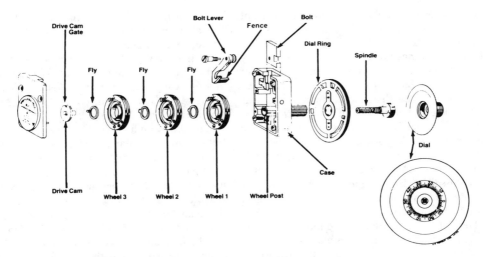

Figure 6–14. Three-tumbler combination.

wheel 1, which remains stationary, and rotates the dial three turns to the second number in the combination. When this number is under the index mark, wheel 2 is aligned. Again reversing direction to disengage wheel 2, the operator makes two turns to the last number of the combination. This aligns wheel 3. At this point all of the gates are aligned with the fence. The operator then reverses direction once again and turns the dial until it stops.

This last operation has two functions. It aligns the gate on the drive cam with the fence which permits the fence to retract into the space provided by the three gates in the wheels and the fourth gate in the drive cam. The bolt lever is now engaged with the wheels and drive cam. As the operator continues rotating the dial, the drive cam pulls the bolt lever to retract the bolt. When the dial will no longer rotate, the bolt is fully retracted, and the lock is open.

The security afforded by combination mechanisms varies widely. The critical elements are the number of tumblers used in the lock, the number of positions on the tumbler where the gate can be located, and the tolerances in the width of the gate and fence. Wide tolerances allow the fence to enter the gates even when they are not quite completely aligned. So that, although the proper combination may be 10-35-75, the lock may also operate at 11-37-77.

Until the 1940s it was often possible to open many combination locks by using the sound of the movement of the tumblers and feeling the friction of the fence moving over the tumblers as indicators of tumbler position. (Tumblers in combination locks

do not click despite Hollywood's contentions to the contrary). Skilled operators were often able to use sound and feel to determine when each tumbler came into alignment. Modern technology has all but eliminated these possibilities, however, through the introduction of sound baffling devices, nylon tumblers, improved lubricants to eliminate friction, false fences, and cams which suspend the fence over the tumblers so that they do not make contact until after the gates are already aligned (see Figure 6–14).

Another manipulation technique of recent vintage utilized the fact that the tumbler wheels with gates cut into them are unbalanced: more weight is on the uncut side than on the cut side. By oscillating the dial, these cut and uncut sides could be determined, and the location of the gates estimated. The introduction of counterbalanced tumblers has virtually eliminated this approach to the better mechanisms.

Radiology has also been used to defeat combination locks. A piece of radioactive material placed near the lock can produce ghost images of the tumblers on sensitive plates showing the location of the gates. Nylon and teflon tumblers and shielding material which are opaque to radiation are used to defeat this technique.

Lock Bodies

Most lever tumbler and warded mechanisms contain an integrated bolt as a part of the mechanism. The key operates directly to throw the bolt, thereby opening and locking the lock. This is not true of pin and disc tumbler locks. These consist of two major components. The cylinder plug, the shell, the tumblers, and springs are contained in an assembly known as the *cylinder*. The other major component is the *lock body* which consists of the *bolt assembly* and case or housing. The bolt assembly consists of the bolt itself, a *rollback*, and a *retractor*. This assembly translates the rotating motion of the cylinder plug to the back-and-forth motion that actually operates the bolt. When the cylinder is inserted into the lock body, it is typically connected to the bolt assembly by a *tail piece* or *cam*. A cylinder can be used in a number of different lock bodies. Here we will be primarily concerned with the types of bodies used on standard residential and light commercial doors. The pin tumbler is the usual mechanism used in these locks, although some manufacturers offer door locks using disc tumbler cylinders (such as the Schlage Cylindrical Lock introduced earlier).

Bolts

There are two types of bolts used for most door applications: the *latch bolt* and the *deadbolt*. Examples of these are illustrated in   Figure 6–15. They are easily distinguished from each other. A latch bolt always has a beveled face, while the face on a standard deadbolt is square.

Latch Bolt

This bolt, which is sometimes called simply a latch, a locking latch (to distinguish it from nonlocking latches), or a spring bolt is always spring-loaded. When the door on which it is mounted is in the process of closing, the latch bolt is designed to automatically retract when its beveled face contacts the lip of the strike. Once the door is fully closed, the latch springs back to extend into the hole of the strike, securing the door.

A latch bolt has the single advantage of convenience. A door equipped with a locking latch will automatically lock when it is closed. No additional effort with a key is required. It does not, however, provide very much security.

The throw on a latch bolt is usually three-eighths but seldom more than five-eighths inches. Because it must be able to retract into the door on contact with the lip of the strike, it is difficult to make the throw much longer. But, because there is always some space between the door and the frame, this means that a latch may project into the strike no more than one quarter inch (often as little as one eighth inch on poorly hung doors). Most door jambs can be spread at least one half inch with little effort, permitting an intruder to quickly circumvent the lock.

Another undesirable feature of the latch bolt is that it can easily be forced back by any thin shim (such as a plastic credit card or thin knife) inserted between the face plate of the lock and the strike. Antishim devices have been added to the basic latch bolt to defeat this type of attack. They are designed to prevent the latch bolt from being depressed once the door is closed.   Figure 6–16 shows a latch bolt with antishim device. These are often called *deadlocking latches*, a term which is mildly deceptive since these latches do not actually deadlock and they are not nearly as resistant to jimmying as deadlocks. Often a thin screwdriver blade can be inserted between the face plate and the strike, and pressure applied to break the antishim mechanism and force the latch to retract.

Another type of latch bolt is shown in Figure 6–16.   This is an *antifriction latch bolt*. The antifriction device is designed to reduce the closing pressure required to force the latch bolt to retract. This permits a heavier spring to be used in the mechanism.

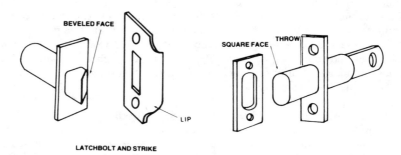

Figure 6–15. Basic types of bolts.

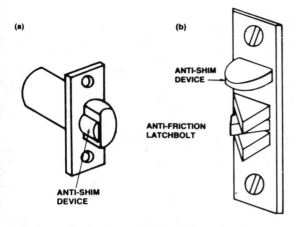

(a)   **(b)**

ANTI-SHIM
DEVICE

ANTI-FRICTION
LATCHBOLT

ANTI-SHIM
DEVICE

Figure 6–16. Modified latchbolts. (a) Latchbolt with antishim device. (b) Antifriction latchbolt with antishim device.

Most modern antifriction latches also incorporate an antishim device. Without it, the antifriction latch is extremely simple to shim.

Deadbolt

The deadbolt is a square-faced solid bolt which is not spring loaded and must be turned by hand into either the locked or unlocked position. When a deadbolt is incorporated into a locking mechanism, the result is usually known as *deadlock*. The throw on a standard deadbolt is also about one half inch, which provides only minimal protection against jamb spreading. A *long-throw deadbolt*, however, has a throw of one inch or longer. One inch is considered the minimum for adequate protection. Properly installed in a good door using a secure strike, this bolt provides reasonably good protection against efforts to spread or peel the jamb.

The ordinary deadbolt is thrown horizontally. On some narrow-stile doors, such as aluminum-framed glass doors, the space provided for the lock is too narrow to permit a long horizontal throw. The *pivoting deadbolt* is used in this situation to get the needed longer throw (Figure 6–17). The pivoting movement of the bolt allows it to project deeply into the frame—at least one inch, usually more. A minimum of one inch is recommended. When used with a reinforced strike, this bolt can provide good protection against efforts to spread or peel the frame.

Increased security against jamb spreading is provided by a number of different types of deadbolts that collectively are known as *interlocking deadbolts*. These are specifically designed to interlock the door

and the strike so that the door jamb cannot be spread. The most common of these is the *vertical-throw deadbolt* shown in Figure 6–17. This is usually a rim-mounted device. The other two devices shown in Figure 6–17 (*the expanding bolt deadbolt* and the *rotating deadbolt*) are meant to be mounted inside the door. These locks require a securely mounted strike or they are rendered ineffective.

Door Lock Types

Five basic lock types are used on most doors in the United States: rim-mounted, mortise, tubular, cylindrical, and unit. Each of these has a number of advantages and disadvantages from the point of view of the protection offered. Each, however, with the single exception of the cylindrical lockset, can offer sound security when a good lock is properly installed.

Mortise

It was but a few years ago that almost all residential and light commercial locks were mortise locks. A mortise lock, or lockset, is installed by hollowing out a portion of the door along the front or leading edge and inserting the mechanism into this cavity. Suitable holes are then drilled into the side of the door in the appropriate spot for the cylinders and door knob spindle (where the door knob is part of the unit, as is usually the case). Figure 6–18 shows a typical mortise lockset. These mechanisms require a door which is thick enough to be hollowed out without losing a great deal of its strength in the process. One of the major weaknesses of mortise locks is that the cylinder is usually held in the lock with a set screw which provides very little defense against pulling or twisting the cylinder out of the lock with a suitable tool. Cylinder guard plates can be used to strengthen this lock's resistance to this threat. On some mortise locks, the trim plate acts as a cylinder guard.

Rim-Mounted

A rim-mounted mechanism is very simply and lock which is installed on the surface (rim) of the door (Figure 6–18). Most are used on the inside surface, since outside installation requires a lock that is reinforced against direct attacks on the case itself. Commonly these are supplementary locks installed where the primary lock is not considered enough

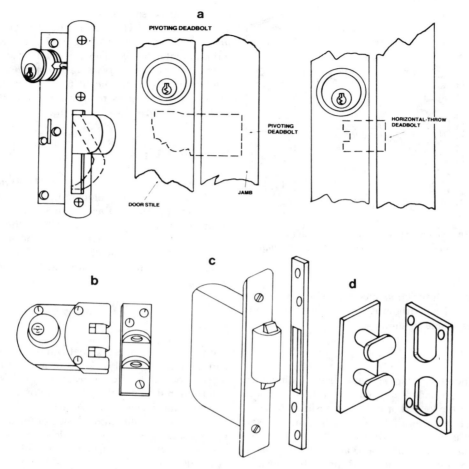

Figure 6–17. Modified deadbolts. Note the difference in penetration into the jamb. The deeper penetration afforded by the pivoting bolt increases protection against jamb spreading.

protection. These may or may not be designed for key operation from the outside. If they are, a cylinder extends through the door to the outside where it can be reached by a key.

Tubular

This lock (sometimes called a bore-in) is installed by drilling a hole through the door to accommodate the cylinder (or cylinders) and a hole drilled from the front edge of the door to the cylinder for the bolt assembly (Figure 6–18). This type of installation has virtually replaced the mortise lock in most residential and light commercial applications because it can be installed quickly and by persons of limited skill.

Cylindrical Lockset

The cylindrical lockset ordinarily uses a locking latch as its sole fastening element (Figure 6–18). It is installed like the tubular lock by drilling two holes in the door. The cylinders are mounted in the door knobs, rather than in a case or inside the door, which makes them vulnerable to just about any attack (hammering, wrenching, etc.) which can knock or twist the knob off the door. Unfortunately, because it is inexpensive and simple to install, about 85 percent of all residential locks currently being used in new construction in the United States are of this type. It provides virtually no security whatsoever. There is perhaps no harder or faster rule in lock security than the rule that all cylindrical locks should be supplemented by a secure, long-throw

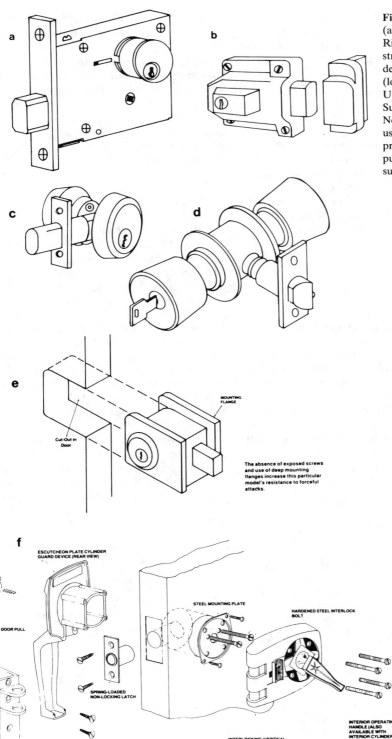

deadbolt. Or, better yet, they should be replaced. A number of more secure locks designed to replace the cylindrical lock are now on the market. One of these is illustrated in Figure 6–18.

Unit Locks

A unit lock is installed by making a U-shaped cutout in the front edge of the door and slipping the lock into this cutout. This type of lock usually has the advantage of having no exposed screws or bolts. It is ordinarily used in place of mortise locks where the door is too narrow to mortise without considerable loss of strength. A good unit lock properly installed on a solid door provides excellent protection against attempts to remove the cylinder, or to pry or twist the lock off the doors.

Cylinders

Cylinders are mounted in the lock body in a number of ways. Most mortise cylinders are threaded into the lock and secured with a small set screw (Figure 6–19). Tubular and rim locks use cylinder interlock screws inserted from the back of the lock. Better mechanisms use one-quarter inch or larger diameter hardened steel screws for maximum resistance to pulling and wrenching attacks. (Figure 6–19). Better cylinders incorporate hardened inserts to resist drilling.

Two basic cylinder configurations are available. *Single cylinder* locks use a key-operated cylinder on the outside, and a thumb-turn or blank plate on the inside (Figure 6–20). *Double cylinder* locks use a key-operated cylinder on both sides of the door. (Figure 6–20). This prevents an intruder from breaking a window near the door, or punching a hole through the door, reaching in, and turning the lock from the inside. The disadvantage of double cylinders is that rapid exit is made difficult since the key must first be located to operate the inside cylinder. If a fire or other emergency makes rapid evacuation necessary, a double cylinder lock could pose a considerable hazard.

Padlocks

The distinguishing feature of padlocks is that they use a shackle rather than a bolt as the device which fastens two or more objects together (Figure 6–21). The shackle is placed through a hasp which is permanently affixed to the items to be fastened. Three methods are commonly used to secure the shackle inside the lock body. The simplest and least secure method is to press a piece of flat spring steel against an indentation in the shackle. When the key is inserted, it rotates to spread the spring releasing the shackle (Figure 6–22). This is a locking method commonly found on warded padlocks. More rarely it is found on tumbler-type locks, but it is found occasionally on the less expensive models.

A slightly more secure method uses a locking dog. The dog is spring-loaded and fits into a notch cut into the shackle (Figure 6–22). The key is used to retract the dog, permitting the shackle to be withdrawn. Both of these spring-loaded mechanisms are vulnerable to attacks that take advantage of the fact

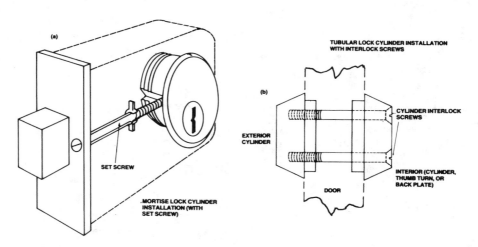

Figure 6–19. Mortise lock cylinder installation. (a) With set screw. (b) With interlock screws.

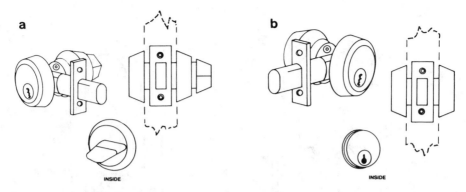

Figure 6–20. (a) Single cylinder deadlock with interior thumb turn. (b) Double cylinder deadlock with interior key cylinder.

that the locking device can be forced back against the spring by a suitable tool. Shimming and rapping are common techniques used to open them. Often a stiff wire can be pushed down the shackle hole to engage and force back the spring or locking dog. Spring-loaded padlocks should not be used where reasonable security is required.

Positive locking techniques do much to reduce the vulnerability of padlocks to these types of attacks. The most common positive locking method uses steel balls inserted between the cylinder and the shackle. In the locked position, the ball rests half in a groove in the cylinder, and half in a notch cut into the shackle. In this position the shackle cannot be forced past the steel ball. When the cylinder is turned to the unlocked position, the groove deepens, permitting the ball to retract into the cylinder when pressure is put on the shackle. This releases the shackle and opens the lock. These locks are designed so that the key cannot be removed unless the lock is in the locked position.

Padlocks are vulnerable to attacks at several points. The shackle can be pried out of the lock by a crowbar or jimmy, or it can be sawed or cut by bolt cutters. The casing can be crushed or distorted by hammering. Modifications have been incorporated into better padlocks to reduce their vulnerability to these approaches. Heavy, hardened steel cases and

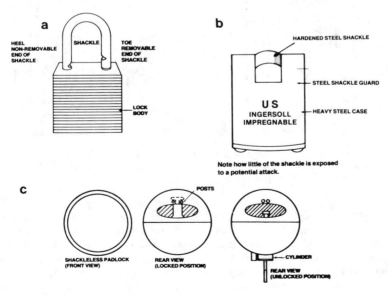

Figure 6–21. (a) Warded padlock. (b) High security padlock. (c) Shackle-less padlock.

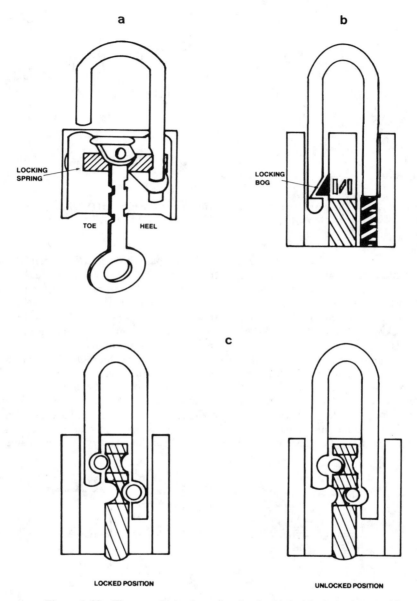

Figure 6–22. Three methods of securing the shackle inside the lock body. (a) Warded padlock with locking spring (heel locking). (b) Padlock with locking dog (toe locking). (c) Positive locking padlock (heel and toe locking).

shackles are used to defeat cutting and crushing. Rotating inserts and special hardened materials are used to prevent the sawing of shackles. Toe and heel locking is used to prevent prying (Figure 6–22).

High security padlocks are large and heavy, using hardened metals in the case, and a thick, hardened, and protected shackle. Positive locking methods are always used. As little of the shackle is exposed to attack as possible in the locked position. A typical high security padlock is shown in Figure 6–21. This is the shackleless padlock which is designed so that a locking bar which is contained entirely inside the case is used in the place of an exposed shackle. This is sometimes called a hasp lock rather than a padlock.

A padlock is, however, no better than the hasp

it engages. Hasps offering reasonable security are themselves made of hardened metals. They must be properly mounted on solid materials so that they cannot be pried off. In the locked position, no mounting screw or bolt should be accessible. Padlocks and hasps should always be considered as a unit. There is no point in mounting a high security padlock on an inferior hasp. The hasp and lock should always be of approximately the same quality. Where they are not, the complete device is only as good as its weakest member.

Strikes

Strikes are an often overlooked but essential part of a good lock. A deadbolt must engage a solid, correctly installed strike, or its effectiveness is significantly reduced. The ordinary strike for residential use is mounted with two or three short (usually less than one inch) wood screws on a soft wood door frame. It can be easily pried off with a screwdriver. High security strikes are wider, longer, and often incorporate a lip which wraps around the door for added protection against jimmying and shimming (Figure 6–23).   Three or more offset wood screws at least 3½ inches long are used to mount the strike. These screws must extend through the jamb and into the studs of the door frame. This provides added protection against prying attacks. Additionally, none of the fastening screws should be in line. In-line screws tend to split soft wood when they are screwed in. Strikes designed for installation on wood frames should always use offset screws as fasterners.

Reinforced steel should be used on metal framed doors, especially aluminum frames. Aluminum is extremely soft metal, and unless a reinforced strike is used, the jamb can be peeled away from the strike area exposing the bolt to a number of attacks, or allowing it to clear the jamb thereby freeing the door to open. Bolts should be used to mount strikes in metal frames. If the bolt does not penetrate a substantial steel framing member, then a steel plate should be used to back the bolt (very large steel washers may be an acceptable substitute). This prevents the strike from being pried out of aluminum or thin steel frames.

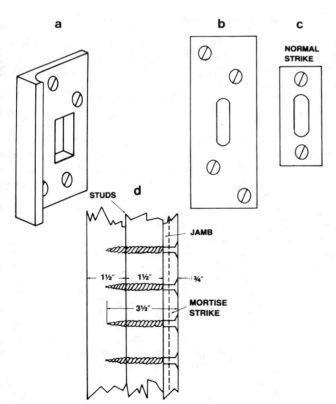

Figure 6–23.   security strikes. (a) Security strike with reinforced lip to prevent jimmying and shimming. (b) Security strike for wood frames with offset screws. (c) Normal strike. (d) Proper installation of a strike on a wood frame.

Attacks and Countermeasures

There are two basic methods of attacking locks themselves: surreptitious techniques and force. There are also a number of ways of circumventing a lock by assaulting the objects to which it is fastened. This chapter will be concerned only with techniques used to defeat locks themselves, and the measures that can be used to forestall those techniques.

No lock is completely invulnerable to attack. A lock's effectiveness is determined by how long it will resist the best effort of an intruder. An expert can pick an average pin tumbler cylinder in seconds, and no lock can survive strong force applied for a sufficient length of time. The sole object of using any lock at all is to *delay* an intruder. A good lock makes entry riskier or more trouble than it's worth, and that is the objective. Fortunately, most potential intruders are not experts, thus most moderately secure locks can survive for a reasonable amount of time against common attack techniques.

The proper use of countermeasures will significantly reduce a locking system's vulnerability to breaching by an unauthorized person. Not all of the countermeasures suggested in the following sections will be appropriate for every application, however. There is always the necessity of striking a suitable compromise position between the expense and inconvenience of a locking system and the value of the items it is designed to protect. Complex and expensive very high security systems are simply not appropriate for most residential applications. On the other hand, a cheap padlock on a warehouse containing valuable merchandise is an open invitation for someone to break in and steal it. The objective should always be to ensure reasonable protection in the circumstances surrounding a particular application. With locks, overprotection is often more harmful than insufficient protection. If the user is faced with a more complex security system than really necessary, she or he simply won't use it. A great many unlawful entries are still made through *unlocked* doors and windows. The temptation to avoid the inconvenience of constantly locking and unlocking barriers seems to be insurmountable in some people. Contributing to this temptation by insisting on more protection than the user actually needs simply aggravates the problem.

Surreptitious Attacks

Four basic surreptitious approaches are used to breach locking devices: illicit keys, circumvention of the internal barriers of the lock, manipulation of the internal barriers, and shimming. The susceptibility of any locking device to these approaches cannot be eliminated but can be minimized through the use of commonsense countermeasures.

Illicit Keys

The easiest way of gaining entry through any lock is by using the proper key for that lock. Thousands of keys are lost and stolen every year. A potential intruder who can determine which lock a lost or stolen key fits has a simple and quick means of illicit entry. If an intruder can't get hold of the owner's key, quite often he or she can make a duplicate. The casual habit of leaving house keys on the key-ring when a car is left in a commercial parking lot or for servicing provides a potential intruder with a golden opportunity to duplicate the house keys for later use. One can also find out the owner's address very quickly by examining the repair bill or tracing the automobile license number.

The risk of lost, stolen, or duplicated keys cannot be eliminated entirely, but certain steps can be taken to minimize it.

Maintain Reasonable Key Security

- Under some circumstances, it is almost impossible to avoid leaving at least the ignition key with a parked car, or one to be serviced. But all other keys should be removed.
- When keys are being duplicated, the owner should ensure that no extra duplicates are made.
- Many locks, particularly older locks, have their key code stamped on the front of the case or cylinder. This permits anyone to look up the code in a locksmith's manual and find the proper combination for that lock (or for that combination lock). Codebooks are readily available for most makes of lock, so if the code appears anywhere on the lock where it can be read after the lock is installed and locked, it should be removed by grinding or overstamping. If removal is not possible, the lock or its combination should be changed.
- Managers and owners of commercial enterprises should maintain strict control over master keys and control keys for removable core cylinders. The loss of these keys can compromise the entire system, necessitating an extensive and expensive, system-wide recombination. Too often in large institutions, just about everyone can justify a need

for a master key. This is nothing more than a demand for convenience that subverts the requirements of good security. The distribution of master keys should be restricted to those who literally cannot function without them.

Since it is impossible to prevent people from losing keys no matter how careful they are, the next precaution is to *ensure that the lost key cannot be linked to the lock it operates.*

- The owner's name, address, telephone number, or car license number should never appear anywhere on a key ring. This has become common practice to ensure the return of lost keys, but if they fall into the wrong hands, the address provides a quick link between the keys and the locks they fit. The proper protection against lost keys is to always have a duplicate set in a secure place.
- For the same reasons, keys which are stamped with information that identifies the location of the lock should not be carried around. This used to be a common practice on locker keys, safety deposit box keys, and some apartment building keys. It is no longer as common as it once was, but it still exists. If the keys must be carried, all identifying information should be obliterated, or they should be duplicated on a clean, unmarked key blank.

Recombinate or Replace Compromised Locks. If all these precautions fail and the owner reasonably believes that someone has obtained keys to her or his locks, the combinations of these locks should be changed immediately. Where this is not possible, the locks may have to be replaced. When only a few locks are involved, recombinating cylinders is a fairly quick and inexpensive operation well within the competence of any qualified locksmith.

Another common attack method using a key against which there is less direct protection is the *try-out key*. Try-out key sets are a common locksmith's tool and can be purchased through locksmith supply houses, often by mail. These sets replicate the common variations used in the combination of a particular lock series. In operation, they are inserted into the lock one at a time until one is found that will operate the lock.

Try-out keys are commercially available only for automotive locks. There is nothing, however, to prevent a would-be intruder from building a set for other locks. In areas where one contractor has built extensive residential and commercial developments, most of the buildings will often be fitted with the same lock series. If it is an inexpensive series with a limited number of useful combinations, a home-made try-out key set which replicates the common variations of this particular lock series could be very useful to the potential intruder.

The defense against try-out keys is simply to use a lock with a moderate to high number of available combinations. Any lock worth using has at least several thousand useful combinations. No intruder can carry that many try-out keys, so the risk that he or she will have the proper key is minimal.

Circumvention of the Internal Barriers of the Lock

This is a technique used to directly operate the bolt *completely bypassing* the locking mechanism which, generally, remains in the locked position throughout this operation. A long, thin, stiff tool is inserted into the keyway to bypass the internal barriers and reach the bolt assembly. The tool (often a piece of stiff wire) is then used to maneuver the bolt into the retracted, unlocked position. Warded locks are particularly vulnerable to this method (as was indicated earlier), but some tumbler mechanisms which have an open passageway from the keyway to the bolt assembly are also susceptible. Some older padlocks and cylindrical mechanisms had an open passageway of this sort. Few of these are manufactured anymore, but some of the older models are still in use. Any lock which has such an opening should be replaced with a better device if reasonable security is a requirement.

Manipulation

The term manipulation covers a large number of types of attacks. At least fifty discrete techniques of manipulating the mechanism of a lock without the proper key have been identified. Fortunately, however, they all fall rather neatly into four general categories: *Picking, impressioning, decoding,* and *rapping.* Regardless of the specific technique used, its purpose is to maneuver the internal barriers of a tumbler mechanism into a position where they will permit the bolt to be retracted. In a disc pin tumbler mechanism, this means that the cylinder plug must be freed to rotate; in a lever lock, the levers must be aligned with the fence.

The basic countermeasures against all forms of manipulation are the use of close tolerances in the manufacture of the mechanism, and increasing the number of pins, discs, or levers. Close tolerances and a large number of tumblers make manipulation a time-consuming process. A number of specific defenses to the various forms of manipulation also have been developed. These will be presented in some detail below.

Picking. Lock picking is undoubtedly the best known method of manipulation. It requires skill developed by dedicated practice, the proper tools, time, and often a small dose of good luck. No lock is proof against picking, but the high security locks are so difficult to pick that it takes even an expert a long time to open them. One definition of a high security mechanism, in fact, is one that cannot be picked by an expert in less than half a minute.

The techniques involved in picking the three basic types of tumbler mechanisms are very similar—so similar, in fact, that an example using the pin tumbler cylinder will serve to illustrate the rest.

All picking techniques depend on the slight clearances that must necessarily exist in a mechanism for it to function. The basic technique requires slight tension to be placed on the part of the mechanism that retracts the bolt (which is the cylinder plug in pin tumbler mechanisms) by a special tension tool designed for that purpose (Figure 6–24). The result of this tension is shown in Figure 6–25. The pin chamber in the plug has moved slightly out of alignment with the pin chamber in the cylinder shell creating two *lips* at points (A) and (B). When the key pin is pushed up by the pick, it tends to catch at the shear line because the lip at point (A) permits it to go no farther. This pushes the driver above the shear line where the lip at point (B) prevents it from falling down into the cylinder plug once more. As long as tension is maintained, it will stay above the shear line.

This operation is facilitated by the fact that, as shown in Figure 6–26, the pin chambers in a cylinder plug are seldom in a perfectly straight line. Consequently, the pin closest to the direction of

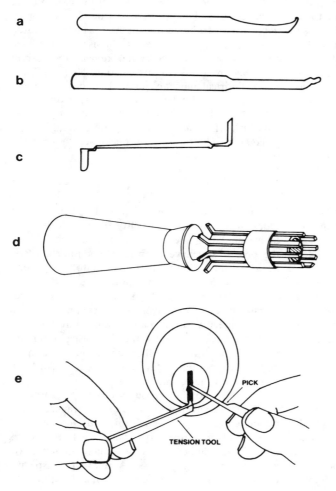

a

b

c

d

e

PICK

TENSION TOOL

Figure 6–24. Lock picks. (a) Standard pick. (b) Rake pick. (c) Tension tool. (d) Special pick for tubular mechanisms. (e) Pick and tension tool in use.

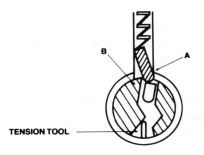

Figure 6–25. Illustration of the misalignment caused in a pin tumbler cylinder when tension is applied.

tension will be more tightly bound than the rest of the pins when tension is applied. It can easily be located because it will offer the most resistance to being maneuvered by the pick. Each pin is tested by lifting it with the pick. The pin that is most resistant is picked first. When this pin reaches the shear line, often the cylinder plug will move slightly. The picker receives two important benefits from this very small movement: first it indicates that the pin has indeed been lifted to the shear line, and second, the movement of the cylinder increases the misalignment between the pin chamber in the plug and the one in the shell making it even less likely that the driver will drop down into the plug (Figure 6–27). Once this pin has been picked, the pin next nearest the direction of tension will be the most tightly bound. It is located and picked next. The cylinder plug will again move a very small amount. This operation continues until all of the pins are picked above the shear line, and the cylinder plug is free to rotate.

There are endless variations of this basic picking technique. One of the most common is the use of a *rake pick*. When this pick is used, very slight tension is applied to the plug, then the rake is run along the tumblers lifting them slightly each time until all of them reach the shear line. Raking increases the chance that one or more key pins will inadvertently be pushed up into the cylinder shell—which will not allow the plug to rotate. It is often necessary to release the tension applied to the plug, and start over again several times. Nevertheless, it is a very fast technique, and very popular. With luck, an expert using a rake can pick an average pin tumbler in a few seconds.

Most of the improvements in lock technology made over the last few thousand years have been devoted to increasing the resistance of locks to lock-picking. The major defense is the use of very close tolerances in the mechanism during manufacture. This makes the forced misalignment between the

plug and shell necessary for successful picking more difficult to achieve. The addition of more tumblers is also some protection against picking, since it takes the operator more time to pick all of the tumblers in the mechanism. The Sargent Keso mechanism and the Duo disc tumbler use this basic approach. The twelve pins in the former, and fourteen (soon to be seventeen) discs in the high security (U.L.) Duo take a reasonably long time to successfully pick. In addition, the unusual configurations of these tumblers makes picking even more difficult.

The unusual arrangement of tumblers is also a basic security feature of Ace (tubular) mechanisms. These cannot be picked using ordinary picks. But there are special tools available which facilitate picking this lock. The Ace lock also requires special skills, but these are not too difficult to achieve once basic picking techniques have been mastered.

Modifications of pin design for increased resistance to picking (and other forms of manipulation) are becoming increasingly important as a basic means of precluding this form of attack. As shown in Figure 6–28, mushroom, spool and huck pins tend to bind in the pin chamber when tension is applied to the cylinder plug, preventing the key pin from reaching the shear line. The use of these pins does not provide an absolute defense against picking attempts, but a steady hand and a great deal of skill are required to pick them successfully.

Pins which must be rotated provide what is perhaps the maximum currently available protection against picking. The Medeco and the new Emhart interlocking mechanism both require pins to be lifted to the shear line *and* rotated to a certain position before the lock will operate. It is very, very difficult to consistently rotate these pins into the correct position. The interlocking pins on the Emhart also make it extremely difficult to pick the key pin to the

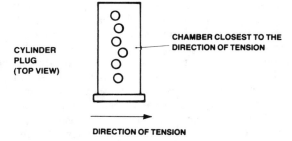

Figure 6–26. Pin chamber misalignment. Pin chambers on even the best cylinders are not in a perfectly straight line. The misalignment in this illustration is highly exaggerated for clarity.

Figure 6–27. Increased misalignment occurs as each pin is picked.

shear line, since when interlocked, the two pins act as if they were one solid pin. The key pin and driver will not split at the shear line unless the pins are first rotated to the correct position.

Fewer such embellishments are possible with discs and levers. Most high security lever locks, however, do use levers which have a front edge cut in a saw-tooth design (serrated). These serrations tend to catch on the fence as it is pushed back to provide pressure on the levers. This often makes it necessary for the operator to release tension and start over again, increasing the time spent picking the lock. The use of two sets of levers with two corresponding fences also increases a lever mechanism's resistance to picking attempts.

Impressioning. Impressioning is a technique used to make a key that will operate the lock. It cannot ordinarily be used against high security mechnisms, but against the average lock, it can be very successful.

To make a key by impressioning, a correct key blank is inserted into the lock. It is then securely gripped by a wrench or pliers (there are also special tools available for this purpose) and a strong rotational tension is applied to the plug. While this tension is applied, the key is moved up and down in the keyway. Since the tumblers are tightly bound in the lock by the tension applied to the plug, they will leave marks on the blank. The longest key pin will leave the strongest impression. The key is then removed and a slight cut is filed in the blank at this point. The top of the key is smoothed down with a file or abrasive paper, and the key is again inserted to pick up the impression of the next longest pin. As long as the pin leaves an impression, the cut is deepened. When the pin will no longer leave a mark, the cut is at the right depth. When all of the cuts are to the right depth, the key will operate the lock and permit entry.

Certain types of lock mechanisms are more susceptible to impressioning than others. Warded locks are easily defeated by this method since the fixed wards can be made to leave strong impressions, and, as previously stated, the depth of the cut on a warded key is not critical. Lever locks are probably the most immune to this technique, since it is difficult to bind the levers in such a manner that they will leave true impressions on the key blank. The use of serrated levers greatly increases this difficulty.

The average pin and disc tumbler mechanism is vulnerable to this approach, but some of the better high security mechanisms, because of their unusual keys, are not. The Medeco and Emhart interlocking mechanisms are highly resistant. The correct angles of the slant cuts necessary on these keys cannot be determined by impressioning. The special design of the pins in the BHI Huck-Pin cylinder makes the pins bind almost anywhere in the pin hole except at the shear line. All the impressions which appear on the key blank are, therefore, likely to be false impressions. So, although this mechanism uses a fairly standard paracentric key, it is still very difficult to defeat by impressioning. Modified spool and mushroom tumblers in any pin tumbler mechanism also tend to increase the difficulty of getting good impression marks.

Decoding. Another method of making a key for a particular lock is through decoding. It was mentioned earlier that most disc tumbler mechanisms can be sight read fairly easily. Sight reading involves the manipulation of the tumblers with a thin wire while noting their relative positions in the keyway. Since each mechanism has only a limited number of possible tumbler increments, the correct alignment of these increments can be estimated with fair accuracy, permitting a key to be filed or cut on the spot to rotate the lock. This is one method of decoding.

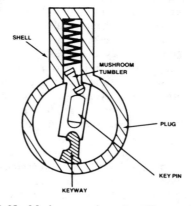

Figure 6–28. Mushroom and spool tumblers tend to bind in the pin hole when manipulation is attempted.

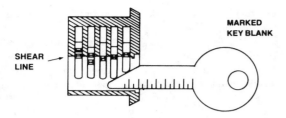

Figure 6–29. Decoding using a marked key blank.

A more common method is to insert a decoding tool or a specially marked key blank for a short distance into the keyway of a pin or disc tumbler mechanism. Using the key, rotational tension is applied to the plug which causes misalignment between the pin chambers in the plug and shell. The key is then slowly inserted into the keyway until it has forced the first tumbler to the shear line   (Figure 6–29). The length of this first key pin is determined by the distance the blank (or special tool) enters the keyway. The blank is then moved to the second tumbler, and so on until the length of all of the tumblers is determined and a key can be cut.

Pin tumbler cylinders having wide tolerances are the mechanisms which are most susceptible to this particular decoding method. Disc tumblers are less so, although most can be easily sight read. (The Duo, however, is very resistant to sight reading.) Lever locks require special equipment to decode.

The special features offered on some high security pin tumbler systems dramatically increase their resistance to this technique. Some are almost immune. The Ace can be decoded, but it usually requires special tools. The use of mushroom or spool tumblers in almost any mechanism increases its resistance to decoding. And, of course, the close tolerances of any of the better mechanisms are a basic defense against decoding as well as impressioning and picking.

Rapping. This approach relies on the fact that pins in a tumbler mechanism can move freely in the pin chambers. Tension is applied to the plug, resulting in the usual misalignment between the core and shell pin bores. The lock is then struck with a sharp tap just above the tumblers. This causes the pins to jump in their bores. As each key pin reaches its shear line, it pushes the driver before it into the shell where it tends to bind, unable to drop back down into the plug because of the lip caused by the misalignent. Not all of the drivers will be pushed over the shear line by one rap. Several may be required.

Theoretically, almost any lock may be defeated by rapping, but in practice it is a method that is used primarily on padlocks. Since padlocks are not encased in a door, they respond more freely to rapping. Modified, manipulation-resistant pins make rapping very difficult, but not impossible, it is, nevertheless, not a practical approach to high security padlocks which use close tolerances and modified pins.

Shimming

Any part of a locking mechanism which relies on spring pressure to hold it in place is vulnerable to shimming unless it is protected. Spring-loaded latch bolts can be shimmed by a thin plastic or metal tool unless they are protected by antishim devices. The locking dogs in padlocks are susceptible to a shim inserted into the shackle hole. The shim acts to force the dog back against the spring pressure releasing the shackle. Padlocks which use heel and toe locking are more difficult to shim, but the safest course to use is a nonsprung, positive locking system which cannot be threatened by shimming at all.

Forceful Attacks

If a potential intruder does not have the skills necessary to decode, impression, or pick a lock, the only course is to either find a key, or use force against the lock to disable and breach it. Comparatively few intruders have developed manipulative skills, so it is not surprising that the large majority of attacks on locks employ force of one kind or another. Locks can be punched, hammered, wrenched, twisted, burned, pulled, cut, exploded, and pried. Given the right tools and a sufficient amount of time, any lock can be defeated by force. But the nature of forceful attacks entails a number of real disadvantages to an intruder who is trying to gain entry without being discovered in the process. Large and cumbersome tools which are difficult to carry and conceal are often required. This is especially true if one of the better protected locks is being attacked. Secondly, forceful attacks usually make a considerable amount of noise. Noise, especially unusual noise, tends to prompt people to investigate. Third, it is always immediately evident to even a casual observer that the lock has been attacked. When surreptitious techniques are used, the lock can be opened without damage, and relocked, and no one will be able to tell that an unlawful entry has taken place. This often permits the intruder to thoroughly cover tracks even before an investigation is started.

The object of countermeasures against forceful

attacks is to increase these hazards. Generally more force will have to be applied to stronger, protected locks, requiring larger and more sophisticated tools, taking more time, making more noise, and leaving more evidence that the lock has been defeated.

While it is sometimes possible to wrench, pry, or pull an entire lock out of a door, most attacks are directed at either the bolt or the cylinder. If the bolt can be defeated, the door is open. If the cylinder can be defeated, the bolt can be maneuvered into an unlocked position. The more common of these attacks will be presented below, along with measures that can be taken to strengthen a lock against them. It bears repeating that no lock is absolutely immune to forceful attacks. The object is to make its defeat more difficult, noisier, and more time consuming, thereby increasing the chances that an intruder will be detected or simply give up before successfully breaching the lock.

Attacks on Bolts

Bolts can be pried, punched, and sawed. The object of these attacks is to disengage the bolt from the strike.

Jimmying and Prying. A jimmy is by definition a short prying tool used by burglars. It is a traditional and well known burglar tool. But other, more lawful, prying tools will work just as well if not better. These include: prybars, crowbars, nail pullers, and large screwdrivers.

The easiest prying attack is against latch bolts with antishim devices. A screwdriver or similar tool with a flat blade is inserted between the strike and latch bolt. Pressure is applied until the antishim mechanism inside the lock breaks. The latch is then easily pushed into the retracted position, and the door is open. A supplementary long-throw or interlocking deadbolt is the best defense against this attack. Noninterlocking, long-throw deadbolts are theoretically vulnerable to jimmying, but it takes a much larger tool, more time, and the destruction or spreading of part of the door jamb so that the end of the dead bolt can be reached with the prying tool. Even then, a great deal of force is required to push the bolt back into the lock and free the door. These combined disadvantages make direct jimmying attacks against long-throw deadbolts very impractical. They are even more impractical against interlocking deadbolts. If the lock and strike are properly installed, the whole strike would have to be pried loose. This would ordinarily entail the

destruction of a considerable portion of the jamb around the strike.

A deadbolt also can be attacked indirectly by prying. An attempt is made to spread the door frame so that the bolt is no longer engaging the strike (Figure 6–30). An average man can apply about 600 inches/pounds of force using a pry bar 30 inches long. This is usually more than enough to spread a door jamb to clear the normal one-half inch bolt, but a one inch (or longer) bolt is more difficult to clear. Interlocking bolts are almost impossible to defeat with this method since they, in effect, anchor the door to the door frame. In order to spread the frame, the entire strike would have to be pried out. A properly installed security strike is very difficult to remove. Interlocking deadbolts were designed to resist just this type of attack. By and large, they are successful. When properly installed, they are as a practical matter, virtually immune.

Automobile bumper jacks (or similar tools) can also be used to spread a door jamb and release the bolt (Figure 6–31). Most American jacks are rated at one ton. It is probably safe to say that most wooden door frames will succumb to that much force. Reinforced metal frames are more resistant. Long-throw and interlocking deadbolts provide some protection. They may even provide enough protection in most circumstances, since a jamb can only be spread so far by the jack before it buckles outward releasing the jack. The best defense against jamb spreading, however, is a properly constructed and reinforced door frame.

Fortunately, this type of attack is fairly rare. An

Figure 6–30. Jamb spreading by prying with two large screwdrivers.

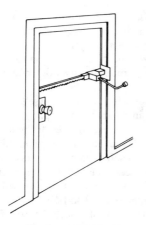

Figure 6–31. Use of an automobile bumper jack to spread the door frame. Standard bumper jacks are rated to 2000 pounds. The force of the jack can be applied between the two jambs of a door to spread them and overcome, by deflection, the length of the latch throw.

automobile jack is an awkward tool, hard to carry and conceal, and it requires some time to set up and operate.

Punching. The California Crime Technological Research Foundation (CCTRF) identified punching as a possible direct attack on a deadbolt   (Figure 6–32). The attacker would have to punch through the wall and framing members to reach the bolt. It would be fairly easy to miss the bolt on the first few tries. So several attempts may be necessary. In essence, the punch and hammer are used to force the bolt back into the body of the lock, allowing it to clear the strike. CCTRF determined that an average man can apply a force of 125 inches/pounds with a one-pound hammer.

Most bolts will probably succumb to a determined punching attack. But it is a noisy approach, and rather hit or miss since it is somewhat difficult to tell if the punch is actually engaging the bolt, and the punch has a tendency to be a serious disadvantage to an intruder, making this an attack of last resort.

Sawing. Bolts can be sawed by inserting a hacksaw or hacksaw blade between the face plate and the strike. (A portion of the jamb will usually be removed or the jamb spread to allow easy access.) Better locks now use hardened bolts or hardened inserts inside the bolt to resist sawing. An even better defense are free-wheeling rollers placed inside the bolt. When the saw reaches these rollers, the sawing action rolls them back and forth but will not cut

them. Modified bolts are present in almost all relatively secure locks. They are virtually immune to sawing attacks.

Peeling. Another way to expose the bolt in metal-framed doors is by peeling. Thin sheet steel and aluminum can be easily peeled. The normal counter measures against this attack is to use a reinforced strike. Peeling may also be used with prying in an attempt to force the bolt back into the lock.

Attacks on Cylinders

Like bolts, cylinders can be pried and punched. They also can be drilled, pulled, wrenched, or twisted. The usual objective of such attacks is to completely remove the cylinder from the lock. Once it has been removed, a tool can be inserted into the lock to quickly retract the bolt.

Cylinder Pulling. The tool usually used for cylinder pulling is a slam hammer or dent puller—a common automobile body shop tool ordinarily used to remove dents from car bodies. The hardened self-tapping screw at the and of the puller is screwed into the keyway as far as it will go. The hammer is then slammed back against the handle. More often than not, an unprotected cylinder will be yanked entirely out of the lock with one or two slams. CCTRF determined that 200 inches pounds of force could be applied to a cylinder by a dent puller, using a 2½ pound hammer having an 8 inch throw.

Many cylinders are vulnerable to this kind of

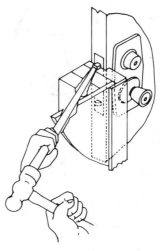

Figure 6–32. Forcing the deadbolt with a drift punch and hammer.

attack because they are poorly anchored in the lock. Mortise cylinders, for example, are ordinarily threaded into the housing and held in place with a small set screw. The threads are usually soft brass or cast iron. A good yank shears both these threads and the set screw.

Most tubular and rim cylinders are held in place by two (or more) bolts inserted from the rear of the lock. This is a much more secure method of retaining the cylinder and one which resists pulling. Retaining bolts of at least ¼ inch in diameter made of hardened steel are good protection against most pulling attempts.

The threat of pulling can be significantly reduced by the addition of a cylinder guard. Some better lock assemblies are offered with built-in guards. Locks that do not have a built-in guard can be protected with a bolt-on guard. These are bolted over the cylinder using carriage bolts that extend completely through the door (Figure 6–33). They offer the maximum available resistance to pulling. The cylinder guard when correctly mounted cannot be pried off without virtually destroying the entire door.

Cylindrical (lock-in-knob) locksets are extremely vulnerable to pulling. Often the door knob will be pulled off with the cylinder exposing the entire internal mechanism to manipulation. There is no method of reinforcing a cylindrical lockset against the threat of pulling. The best measure is to replace it or add a good supplementary deadlock with a cylinder guard.

Lug Pulling. If the cylinder itself is protected against pulling, an attacker may turn to the cylinder plug. The plug is much harder to pull, and requires a special tool that looks something like a gear puller. A hardened self-tapping screw is engaged in the keyway and pressure is slowly exerted on the plug until the tumblers snap and the plug can be pulled from the cylinder shell. The bolt mechanism can then be operated by a tool inserted through the shell. The ordinary cylinder guard is no protection against this attack. A special guard is available, however, which is designed to prevent the plug from being pulled (see Figure 6–34).

Wrenching, Twisting, and Nipping. Most cylinders project from the surface of the door sufficiently to be gripped by a pipe wrench or pliers. Twisting force is applied to the cylinder by the wrench which is often sufficient to snap or shear the set-screws or bolts that hold the cylinder in the lock. If the cylinder does not project enough for a wrench to be used, a ground down screwdriver can be inserted in the keyway and twisting force applied to the screwdriver with a wrench. CCTRF found that an 18-inch long pipe wrench could apply a maximum torque of 3,300 inches/pounds to a protruding cylinder housing, and a screwdriver turned with a wrench could produce 600 inches/pounds.

The proper protection against this threat once again is a cylinder guard. Some of the built-in guards are free-wheeling, which prevents a twisting force from being successfully applied. Those that are not free-wheeling are still made of hardened steel which does not allow the wrench to get a good bite, but more importantly, prevents the wrench from reaching the actual cylinder. If a screwdriver and wrench are used, the cylinder might be twisted loose, but it cannot be pulled out. So, although the lock might be damaged, it will not be defeated.

Bolt nippers also can be used to remove protruding cylinders by prying and pulling. Cylinder guards also forestall this type of attack.

Cylindrical locksets are very susceptible to wrenching, twisting, and nipping attacks. Some of the better cylindrical devices have free-wheeling door knobs which provide some protection against wrenching and twisting. Some incorporate break-

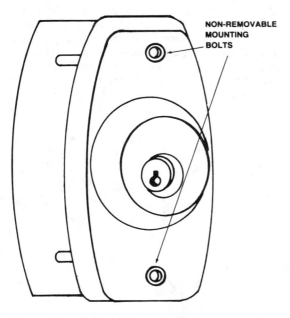

NON-REMOVABLE MOUNTING BOLTS

Figure 6–33. Bolt-on cylinder guard with backplate. This commercially available plate is of heavy aluminum and is mounted from the inside of the door with hardened steel bolts that enter threaded holes in the guard. It combines good protection with good appearance.

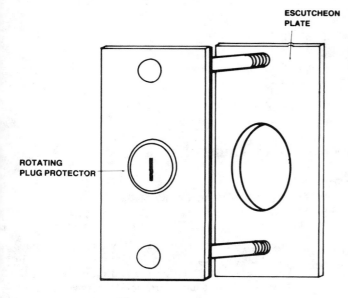

ESCUTCHEON PLATE

ROTATING PLUG PROTECTOR

Figure 6–34. Cylinder guard with rotating plug protector.

away knobs which do not expose the internal mechanism of the lock when the knob is twisted off. Nevertheless, combinations of twisting, pulling, and hammering attacks usually quickly defeat these devices. The best remedy is to replace cylindrical mechanisms or supplement them with guarded deadlocks.

Drilling. Cylinder plugs can be drilled out using a fairly large drill bit. But the most common drilling attack is centered on the shear line between the plug and shell (Figure 6–35). A smaller bit is used to drill through the pins, creating a new shear line and releasing the plug which can then be rotated using a screwdriver or key blank in the keyway. Most of the better locks incorporate hardened inserts to frustrate drilling. Any lock receiving Underwriter's Laboratory approval incorporates these features. Hardened materials do not prevent drilling, but drilling through tempered steel is a long and slow process which greatly increases the chances of detection.

BHI's Huck-Pin cylinder has an added protection against drilling. When most cylinders are drilled at the shear line, the drivers will fall out of the shell into the plug, releasing the plug to rotate. BHI's drivers are flanged which prevents them from falling out, so they still effectively lock the mechanism after it is drilled. This does not prevent the entire cylinder from being drilled out, but this is an even longer and slower process than drilling along the shear line.

Punching. Rim-mounted deadlocks are particularly vulnerable to punching. These are ordinarily mounted on the back of a door with wood screws. But, since most of the currently available doors are made with particle board cores under a thin veneer overlay, screws are seldom able to take much pressure. Several good blows with a hammer and punch on the face of the cylinder will often drive it through the door, pulling the screws out, so the entire lock body is dislodged.

Correctly mounting the lock using bolts which extend through the door and engage an escutcheon plate (or even large washers) on the front side generally frustrates punching attacks.

Cylindrical locksets are vulnerable to combination punching and hammering attacks. The knob is first broken off, then the spindle is punched through the lock, exposing the latch bolt assembly to manipulation.

Hammering. Hammering, as well as pulling, wrenching, and twisting, is a quick and very effective way of disabling cylindrical locksets. It is not as effective against cylinders, particularly those that are protected by cylinder guards. Ordinarily the knob on a cylindrical mechanism can be quickly broken off by one or two strong blows. There is no direct defense against this type of attack. Again, the only viable solution is a supplementary guarded deadlock, or replacement of the cylindrical lockset with a more secure lock.

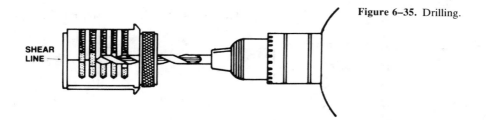

Figure 6–35. Drilling.

Locks and the Systems Approach to Security

Locks are an essential part of most security systems. They are, however, only one part. The effectiveness of a lock cannot be considered apart from the effectiveness of the entire system. A lock is no better than the door it is on, or the frame in which the door is mounted. The strongest lock available on a substandard door does not prevent the door from being defeated, even though the lock cannot be.

The degree of protection required from any security system reflects the value of the items to be protected. Most residences require only a modest degree of security—sufficient to thwart the casual or opportunistic intruder. Jewelry stores, banks, and other establishments which must necessarily keep valuable items on the premises attract a more determined attacker. The degree of protection for these places must, therefore, necessarily be greater. But whatever the degree of protection required, the actual protection offered by any system is no greater than the vulnerability of its weakest member. A good lock on a poor door provides no more protection than the strength of the door. A good lock on a solid door in a substandard wall is as vulnerable as the wall is weak.

The locks employed in any protection system must complement the system. If a moderate degree of security is required (as in a residential application), a good cylinder properly installed in a secure lock body must be correctly mounted on a good, solid door. The door itself must be correctly hung, using good hardware, on a properly constructed door frame. The frame must be strongly braced, and secured to the wall. The wall itself must be at least as strong as the door system installed in it. If the lock, the door, the frame or the wall is significantly weaker than the rest of the system, it is the point most likely to be successfully attacked.

A good lock is essential to a good security system. It is often the point at which an intruder will focus an attack. But good locks are not synonymous with good security. Always examine the system as a whole.

Key Control*

EUGENE D. FINNERAN

Before an effective key control system can be established, every key to every lock that is being used in the protection of the facility and property must be accounted for. Chances are good that it will not even be possible to account for the most critical keys or to be certain that they have not been copied or compromised. If this is the case, there is but one alternative—to rekey the entire facility.

Once an effective locking system has been installed, positive control of all keys must be gained and maintained. This can be accomplished only if an effective key record is kept. When not issued or used, keys must be adequately secured. A good, effective key control system is simple to initiate, particularly if it is established in conjunction with the installation of new locking devices. One of the methods which can be used to gain and maintain effective key control follows:

1. Key cabinet—a well-constructed cabinet will have to be procured. The cabinet will have to be of sufficient size to hold the original key to every lock in the system. It should also be capable of holding any additional keys which are in use in the facility but which are not a part of the security locking system. The cabinet should be installed in such a manner so as to be difficult, if not impossible, to remove from the property. It should be secured at all times when the person designated to control the keys is not actually issuing or replacing a key. The key to the key cabinet must receive special handling, and when not in use it should be maintained in a locked compartment inside a combination-type safe.

2. Key record—some administrative means must

*From *Security Supervision: A Handbook for Supervisors and Managers*, by Eugene D. Finneran (Stoneham, MA: Butterworths, 1981).

be set up to record key code numbers and indicate to whom keys to specific locks have been issued. This record may take the form of a ledger book or a card file.

3. Key blanks—blanks which are to be used to cut keys for issue to authorized personnel must be distinctively marked for identification to insure that no employees have cut their own keys. Blanks will be kept within a combination-type safe and issued only to the person authorized to cut keys and then only in the amount that has been authorized by the person responsible for key control. Such authorization should always be in writing, and records should be maintained on each issue which will be matched with the returned key. Keys which are damaged in the cutting process must be returned for accountability.

4. Inventories—periodic inventories will have to be made of all key blanks, original keys, and all duplicate keys in the hands of the employees to whom they have been issued. This cannot be permitted to take the form of a phone call to an employee, supervisor, or executive asking if they still have their key. It must be a personal inspection of each key made by the person who has been assigned responsibility for key control.

5. Audits—in addition to the periodic inventory, an unannounced audit should be made of all key control records and procedures by a member of management. During the course of these audits a joint inventory of all keys should be conducted.

6. Daily report—a daily report should be made to the person responsible for key control from the personnel department, indicating all persons who have left or will be leaving the employ of the company in the near future. A check should be made, upon receipt of this report, to determine if the person named has been issued a key to any lock in the system. In the event a key had been issued, steps should be initiated to insure that the key is recovered.

Security force personnel will normally be issued master keys, when such a system is in effect, or they will be issued a ring of keys permitting them to enter any part of the guarded facility. Keys issued to the security force should never be permitted to leave the facility. They should be passed from shift to shift and must be receipted for each time they change hands. The supervisor must insure that all security personnel understand the importance of not permitting keys to be compromised.

A lost master key compromises the entire system and results in the breakdown of the security screen. Such compromise will necessitate the rekeying of the entire complex, sometimes at a cost of thousands of dollars.

If rekeying becomes necessary, it can most economically be accomplished by installing new locking devices in the most critical points of the locking system and moving the locks removed from these points to less sensitive areas. Of course, it will be necessary to eventually replace all the locks in the system, but by using the manner just described the cost can be spread out over several budgeting periods.

Appendix 6a

Key Control and Lock Security Checklist*

JOHN E. HUNTER

1. Has a key control officer been appointed?
2. Are locks and keys to all buildings and entrances supervised and controlled by the key control officer?
3. Does the key control officer have overall authority and responsibility for issuance and replacement of locks and keys?
4. What is the basis for the issuance of keys, especially master keys?
5. Are keys issued only to authorized personnel? Who determines who is authorized? Is the authorization in writing?
6. Are keys issued to other than installation personnel? If so, on what basis? Is it out of necessity or merely for convenience?
7. Are keys not in use secured in a locked, fireproof cabinet? Are these keys tagged and accounted for?
8. Is the key cabinet for duplicate keys regarded as an area of high security?
9. Is the key or combination to this cabinet maintained under appropriate security or secrecy? If the combination is recorded, is it secured?
10. Are the key locker and record files in order and current?
11. Are issued keys cross-referenced?
12. Are current records maintained indicating:
    a. Buildings and/or entrances for which keys are issued?
    b. Number and identification of keys issued?
    c. Location and number of master keys?
    d. Location and number of duplicate keys?
    e. Issue and turn-in of keys?
    f. Location of locks and keys held in reverse?
13. Is an audit ever made, asking holders to actually produce keys, to ensure that they have not been loaned or lost?
14. Who is responsible for ascertaining the possession of keys?
15. Is a current key control directive in effect?
16. Are inventories and inspections conducted by the key control officer to ensure compliance with directives? How often?
17. Are keys turned in during vacation periods?
18. Are keys turned in when employees resign, are transferred, or are fired?
19. Is the removal of keys from the premises prohibited when they are not needed elsewhere?
20. Are locks and combinations changed immediately upon loss or theft of keys or transfer or resignation of employees?
21. Are locks changed or rotated within the installation at least annually regardless of transfers or known violations of key security?
22. Are current records kept of combinations to safes and the dates when these combinations are changed? Are these records adequately protected?
23. Has a system been set up to provide submasters to supervisors and officials on a need basis, with facilities divided into different zones or areas?
24. If master keys are used, are they devoid of marking identifying them as master keys?
25. Are master keys controlled more closely than change keys?
26. Must all requests for reproduction or duplication of keys be approved by the key control officer?
27. Are key holders ever allowed to duplicate keys? If so, under what circumstances?
28. Where the manufacturer's serial number on combination locks and padlocks might be visible

*Prepared by John E. Hunter, U.S. National Park Service.

to unauthorized persons, has this number been recorded and then obliterated?

29. Are locks on inactive gates and storage facilities under seal? Are seals checked regularly by supervisory or key control personnel?

30. Are measures in effect to prevent the unauthorized removal of locks on open cabinets, gates, or buildings?

31. Are losses or thefts of keys and padlocks promptly reported by personnel and promptly investigated by key control personnel?

32. If the building was recently constructed, did the contractor retain keys during the period when construction was being completed? Were

locks changed since that time? Did the contractor relinquish all keys after the building was completed?

33. If removable-core locks are in use, are unused cores and core change keys given maximum security against theft, loss, or inspection?

34. Are combination lock, key, and key control records safeguarded separately (i.e., in a separate safe or file) from keys, locks, cores, and other such hardware?

35. Are all locks of a type which offer adequate protection for the purpose for which they are used?

Appendix 6b

Terms and Definitions for Door and Window Security*

Access Control. A method of providing security by restricting the movement of persons into or within a protected area.

Accessible Window. (1) Residential—any window located within 3.7 meters (12 feet) of grade or a building projection. (2) Commercial—any window located within 4.6 meters (18 feet) of grade or within 3 meters (10 feet) of any fire escape or other structure accessible from public or semipublic areas.

Accordion Gate. See **Sliding Metal Gate.**

Ace Lock. A type of pin tumbler lock in which the pins are installed in a circle around the axis of the cylinder, and move perpendicularly to the face of the cylinder. The shear line of the driver and bottom tumblers is a plane parallel to the face of the cylinder. This type of lock is operated with a push key.

Active Door (or Leaf). The leaf of a double door that must be opened first and which is used in normal pedestrian traffic. This leaf is usually the one in which a lock is installed.

Anchor. A device used to secure a building part or com-

ponent to adjoining construction or to a supporting member. See also **Floor Anchor, Jamb Anchor** and **Stud Anchor.**

Anti-Friction Latch. A latch bolt that incorporates any device which reduces the closing friction between the latch and the strike.

Applied Trim. A separately applied molding used as the finishing face trim of a frame.

Apron. The flat member of a window trim placed against the wall immediately beneath the windowsill.

Architectural Hardware. See **Finish Builders' Hardware.**

Areaway. An open subsurface space adjacent to a building which is used to admit light or to provide a means of access to the building.

Armored Front. A plate or plates which is secured to the lock front of a mortised lock by machine screws in order to provide protection against tampering with the cylinder set screws. Also called *armored face plate.*

Astragal. A member fixed to, or a projection of, an edge of a door or window to cover the joint between the meeting of stiles; usually fixed to one of a pair of swinging doors to provide a seal against the passage of weather, light, noise or smoke.

Auxiliary Lock. A lock installed on a door or window to

*Reprinted courtesy of United States Department of Commerce, National Bureau of Standards.

supplement a previously installed primary lock. Also called a secondary lock. It can be a mortised, bored, or rim lock.

Back Plate. A metal plate on the inside of a door which is used to clamp a pin or disc tumbler rim lock cylinder to the door by means of retaining screws. The tail piece of the cylinder extends through a hole in the back plate.

Backset, Flush Bolt. The distance from the vertical centerline of the lock edge of a door to the centerline of the bolt.

Backset, Hinge. On a door, the distance from the stop face to the edge of the hinge cutout. On a frame, the distance from the stop to the edge of the hinge cutout.

Backset, Lock. The horizontal distance from the vertical centerline of the face plate to the center of the lock cylinder keyway or knob spindle.

Backset, Strike. The distance from the door stop to the edge of the strike cutout.

Baffle. See **Guard Plate.**

Balanced Door. A door equipped with double-pivoted hardware so designed as to cause a semicounterbalanced swing action when it is opened.

Barrel Key. A key with a bit projecting from a round, hollow key shank which fits on a post in the lock.

Barricade Bolt. A massive metal bar that engages large strikes on both sides of a door. Barricade bolts are available with locking devices, and are completely removed from the door when not in use.

Bead. See **Glazing Bead.**

Bevel (of a door). The angle of the lock edge of the door in relation to its face. The standard bevel is 0.32 cm in 5.1 cm ($\frac{1}{8}''$ in 2$''$).

Bevel (of a latch bolt). A term used to indicate the direction in which a latch bolt is inclined: regular bevel for doors opening in, reverse bevel for doors opening out.

Bevel (of a lock front). The angle of a lock front when not at a right angle to the lock case, allowing the front to be applied flush with the edge of a beveled door.

Bicentric Pin Tumbler Cylinder. A cylinder having two cores and two sets of pins, each having different combinations. This cylinder requires two separate keys, used simultaneously, to operate it. The cam or tail piece is gear operated.

Bit. A blade projecting from a key shank which engages with and actuates the bolt or level tumblers of a lock.

Bit Key. A key with a bit projecting from a round shank. Similar to the barrel key but with a solid rather than hollow shank.

Bitting. See **Cut.**

Blank. An uncut key or an unfinished key as it comes from the manufacturer, before any cuts have been made on it.

Blind Stop. A rectangular molding, located between the outside trim and the outside sashes, used in the assembly of a window frame. Serves as a stop for storm, screen, or combination windows and to resist air infiltration.

Bolt. That part of a lock which, when actuated, is projected (or "thrown") from the lock into a retaining member, such as a strike plate, to prevent a door or window from moving or opening. See also **Dead Bolt, Flush Bolt,** and **Latch.**

Bolt Attack. A category of burglary attack in which force, with or without the aid of tools, is directed against the bolt in an attempt to disengage it from the strike or to break it.

Bolt Projection (Bolt Throw). The distance from the edge of the door, at the bolt centerline, to the furthest point on the bolt in the projected position.

Bored Lock (or **Latch**). A lock or latch whose parts are intended for installation in holes bored in a door. See also **Key-In-Knob Lock.**

Bottom Pin. One of the pin tumblers which determines the combination of a pin tumbler cylinder and is directly contacted by the key. These are varied in length and usually tapered at one end, enabling them to fit into the "V" cuts made in a key. When the proper key is inserted, the bottom pins level off at the cylinder core shearline, allowing the core to turn and actuate the lock.

Bottom Rail. The horizontal rail at the bottom of a door or window connecting the vertical edge members (stiles).

Box Strike. A strike plate that has a metal box or housing to fully enclose the projected bolt and/or latch.

Breakaway Strike. See **Electric Strike.**

Buck. See **Rough Buck.**

Builders' Hardware. All hardware used in building construction, but particularly that used on or in connection with doors, windows, cabinets, and other moving members.

Bumping. A method of opening a pin tumbler lock by means of vibration produced by a wooden or rubber mallet.

Burglar-Resistant Glazing. Any glazing which is more difficult to break through than the common window or plate glass, designed to resist burglary attacks of the hit-and-run type.

Butt Hinge. A type of hinge which has matching rectangular leaves and multiple bearing contacts, and is designed to be mounted in mortises in the door edge and in the frame.

Buttress Lock. A lock which secures a door by wedging a bar between the door and the floor. Some incorporate a movable steel rod which fits into metal receiving slots on the door and in the floor. Also called police bolt/brace.

Cabinet Jamb. A door frame in three or more pieces, usually shipped knocked down for field assembly over a rough buck.

Cam. The part of a lock or cylinder which rotates to actuate the bolt or latch as the key is turned. The cam may also act as the bolt.

Cam, Lazy. A cam which moves less than the rotation of the cylinder core.

Cam Lock. See **Crescent Sash Lock.**

Cane Bolt. A heavy cane-shaped bolt with the top bent at right angles; used on the bottom of doors.

Case. The housing in which a lock mechanism is mounted and enclosed.

Casement Hinge. A hinge for swinging a casement window.

Casement Window. A type of window which is hinged on the vertical edge.

Casing. Molding of various widths and thicknesses used to trim door and window openings at the jambs.

Center-Hung Door. A door hung on center pivots.

Center Rail. The horizontal rail in a door, usually located at lock height to separate the upper and lower panels of a recessed panel type door.

Chain Bolt. A vertical spring-loaded bolt mounted at the top of a door. It is manually actuated by a chain.

Chain Door Interviewer. An auxiliary locking device which allows a door to be opened slightly, but restrains it from being fully opened. It consists of a chain with one end attached to the door jamb and the other attached to a keyed metal piece which slides in a slotted metal plate attached to the door. Some chain door interviewers incorporate a keyed lock operated from the inside.

Change Key. A key that will operate only one lock or a group of keyed-alike locks, as distinguished from a master key. See also **Keyed-Alike Cylinders** and **Master Key System.**

Changes. The number of possible key changes or combination changes to a lock cylinder.

Checkrails. The meeting rails of double-hung windows. They are usually beveled, and thick enough to fill the space between the top and bottom sash due to the parting stop in the window frame.

Clearance. A space intentionally provided between components, either to facilitate operation or installation, to insure proper separation, to accommodate dimensional variations, or for other reasons. See also **Door Clearance**.

Clevis. A metal link used to attach a chain to a padlock.

Code. An arrangement of numbers or letters which is used to specify a combination for the bitting of a key or the pins of a cylinder core.

Combination. (1) The sequence and depth of cuts on a key. (2) The sequence of numbers to which a combination lock is set.

Combination Doors Or Windows. Storm doors or windows permanently installed over the primary doors or windows. They provide insulation and summer ventilation and often have self-storing or removable glass and screen inserts.

Common Entry Door (of a multiple dwelling). Any door in a multiple dwelling which provides access between the semi-public, interior areas of the building and the out-of-doors areas surrounding the building.

Communicating Frame. A double rabbeted frame with both rabbets prepared for single-swing doors that open in opposite directions. Doors may be of the same or opposite hand.

Component. A subassembly which is combined with other components to make an entire system. Door assembly components include the door, lock, hinges, jamb/strike, and jamb/wall.

Composite Door. A door constructed of a solid core material with facing and edges of different materials.

Connecting Bar. A flat metal bar attached to the core of a cylinder lock to operate the bolt mechanism.

Construction Master Keying. A keying system used to allow the use of a single key for all locks during the construction of large housing projects. In one such system, the cylinder cores of all locks contain an insert that permits the use of a special master key. When the dwelling unit is completed, the insert is removed and the lock then accepts its own change key and no longer accepts the construction master key.

Continuous Hinge. A hinge designed to be the same length as the edge of the moving part to which it is applied. Also called a piano hinge.

Coordinator. A mechanism which controls the order of closing of a pair of swing doors, used with overlapping astragals and certain panic hardware which require that one door close ahead of the other.

Core. See **Cylinder Core.**

Crash Bar. The cross bar or level of a panic exit device which serves as a push bar to actuate the lock. See also **Panic Hardware.**

Cremone Bolt. A surface-mounted device that locks a door or sash into the frame at both the top and bottom when a knob or lever is turned.

Crescent Sash Lock. A simple camshaped latch, not requiring a key for its operation, usually used to secure double-hung windows. Also called a cam lock.

Cut. An indention made in a key to make it fit a pin tumbler of a lock. Any notch made in a key is known as a cut, whether it is square, round, or V-shaped. Also called bitting.

Cylinder. The cylindrical subassembly of a lock, including the cylinder housing, the cylinder core, the tumbler mechanism, and the keyway.

Cylinder Collar. See **Cylinder Guard Ring.**

Cylinder Core (or **Plug**). The central part of a cylinder, containing the keyway, which is rotated to operate the lock bolt.

Cylinder Guard Ring. A hardened metal ring, surrounding the exposed portion of a lock cylinder, which protects the cylinder from being wrenched, turned, pried, cut, or pulled with attack tools.

Cylinder Housing. The external case of a lock cylinder. Also called the cylinder shell.

Cylinder Lock. A lock in which the locking mechanism is controlled by a cylinder. A double cylinder lock has a cylinder on both the interior and exterior of the door.

Cylinder, Mortise Type. A lock cylinder that has a threaded housing which screws directly into the lock case, with a cam or other mechanism engaging the locking mechanism.

Cylinder, Removable Core. A cylinder whose core may be removed by the use of a special key.

Cylinder, Rim Type. A lock cylinder that is held in place by tension against its rim, applied by screws from the interior face of the door.

Cylinder Ring. See **Cylinder Guard Ring**.

Cylinder Screw. A set screw that holds a mortise cylinder in place and prevents it from being turned after installation.

Cylindrical Lock (or **Latch**). See **Bo-Red Lock**.

Dead Bolt. A lock bolt which does not have an automatic spring action and a bevelled end as opposed to a latch bolt, which does. The bolt must be actuated to a projected position by a key or thumb turn and when projected is locked against return by end pressure.

Dead Latch. A spring-actuated latch bolt having a bevelled end and incorporating a feature that automatically locks the projected latch bolt against return by end pressure.

Dead Lock. A lock equipped with a dead bolt.

Dead Locking Latch Bolt. See **Dead Latch**.

Disc Tumbler. A spring-loaded, flat plate that slides in a slot which runs through the diameter of the cylinder. Inserting the proper key lines up the disc tumblers with the lock's shear line enables the core to be turned.

Dogging Device. A mechanism which fastens the cross bar of a panic exit device in the fully depressed position, and retains the latch bolt or bolts in the retracted position to permit free operation of the door from either side.

Dogging Key. A key-type wrench used to lock down, in the open position, the cross bar of a panic exit device.

Door Assembly. A unit composed of parts or components which make up a closure for a passageway through a wall. It consists of the door, hinges, locking device or devices, operational contacts (such as handles, knobs, push plates), miscellaneous hardware and closures, the frame including the head and jambs, the anchorage devices to the surrounding wall, and the surrounding wall.

Door Bolt. A rod or bar manually operated without a key, attached to a door to provide a means of securing it.

Door Check/Closer. A device used to control the closing of a door by means of a spring and either hydraulic or air pressure, or by electrical means.

Door Clearance. The space between a door and either its frame or the finished floor or threshold, or between the two doors of a double door. See also **Clearance**.

Door Frame. An assembly of members surrounding and supporting a door or doors, and perhaps also one or more transom lights and/or sidelights. See also **Integral Frame**.

Door Jambs. The two vertical components of a door frame called the hinge jamb and the lock jamb.

Door Light. See **Light**.

Door Opening. The size of a doorway, measured from jamb to jamb and from floor line or sill to head of frame. The opening size is usually the nominal door size, and is equal to the actual door size plus clearances and threshold height.

Door Stop. The projections along the top and sides of a door frame against which a one-way swinging door closes. See also **Rabbeted Jamb**.

Double Cylinder Lock. See **Cylinder Lock**.

Double Door. A pair of doors mounted together in a single opening. See also **Active Door** and **Inactive Door**.

Double-Acting Door. A swinging door equipped with hardware which permits it to open in either direction.

Double-Bitted Key. A key having cuts on two sides.

Double Egress Frame. A door frame prepared to receive two single-acting doors swinging in opposite directions, both doors being of the same hand.

Double Glazing. Two thicknesses of glass, separated by an air space and framed in an opening, designed to reduce heat transfer or sound transmission. In factory-made double glazing units, referred to as insulating glass, the air space between the glass sheets is desiccated and sealed airtight.

Double-Hung Window. A type of window, composed of upper and lower sashes which slide vertically.

Double-Throw Bolt. A bolt that can be projected beyond its first position, into a second, or fully extended one.

Double-Throw Lock. A lock incorporating a double-throw bolt.

Driver Pin. One of the pin tumblers in a pin tumbler cylinder lock, usually flat on both ends, which are in line with and push against the flat ends of the bottom pins. They are projected by individual coil springs into the cylinder core until they are forced from the core by the bottom pins when the proper key is inserted into the keyway.

Drop Ring. A ring handle attached to the spindle which operates a lock or latch. The ring is pivoted to remain in a dropped position when not in use.

Dry Glazing. A method of securing glass in a frame by use of a preformed resilient gasket.

Drywall Frame. A knocked down (KD) door frame for installation in a wall constructed with studs and gypsum board or other drywall facing material after the wall is erected.

Dummy Cylinder. A mock cylinder without an operating mechanism, used for appearance only.

Dummy Trim. Trim only, without lock; usually used on the inactive door in a double door.

Dutch Door. A door consisting of two separate leaves, one above the other, which may be operated either independently or together. The lower leaf usually has a service shelf.

Dutch Door Bolt. A device for locking together the upper and lower leaves of a Dutch door.

Dwelling Unit Entry Door. Any door giving access to a private dwelling unit.

Electric Strike. An electrically operated device that replaces a conventional strike plate and allows a door to be opened by using electric switches at remote locations.

Escutcheon Plate. A surface-mounted cover plate, either protective or ornamental, containing openings for any or all of the controlling members of a lock such as the knob, handle, cylinder or keyhole.

Exit Device. See **Panic Hardware**.

Expanded Metal. An open mesh formed by slitting and drawing metal sheet: It is made in various patterns and metal thicknesses, with either a flat or an irregular surface.

Exterior Private Area. The ground area outside a single family house, or a ground floor apartment in the case of a multiple dwelling, which is fenced off by a real barrier, which is available for the use of one family and is accessible only from the interior of that family's unit.

Exterior Semi-Private Area. The ground area outside a multiple dwelling which is fenced off by a real barrier, and is accessible only from the private or semi-private zones within the building.

Exterior Semi-Public Area. The ground area outside a single family house or multiple dwelling, which is accessible from public zones, but is defined as belonging to the house or building by symbolic barriers only.

Exterior Public Area. The ground area outside a multiple dwelling which is not defined as being associated with the building or building entry in any real or symbolic fashion.

Face (of a lock). See **Face Plate**.

Face Glazing. A method of glazing in which the glass is set in an L-shaped or rabbeted frame, the glazing compound is finished off in the form of a triangular bead, and no loose stops are employed.

Face Plate. The part of a mortise lock through which the bolt protrudes and by which the lock is fastened to the door.

Fast Pin Hinge. A hinge in which the pin is fastened permanently in place.

Fatigue. Structural failure of a material caused by repeated or fluctuating application of stresses, none of which is individually sufficient to cause failure.

Fence. A metal pin that extends from the bolt of a lever lock and prevents retraction of the bolt unless it is aligned with the gates of the lever tumblers.

Fidelity Loss. A property loss resulting from a theft in which the thief leaves no evidence of entry.

Filler Plate. A metal plate used to fill unwanted mortise cutouts in a door or frame.

Finish Builders' Hardware. Hardware that has a finished appearance as well as a functional purpose and which may be considered as part of the decorative treatment of a room or building. Also called finish hardware and builders' finish hardware.

Fire Stair. Any enclosed stairway which is part of a fire-resistant exitway.

Fire Stair Door. A door forming part of the fire-resistant fire stair enclosure, and providing access from common corridors to fire stair landings within an exitway.

Floor Anchor. A metal device attached to the wall side of a jamb at its base to secure the frame to the floor.

Floor Clearance. The width of the space between the bottom of a door and the rough or finished floor or threshold.

Flush Bolt. A door bolt so designed that, when installed, the operating handle is flush with the face or edge of the door. Usually installed at the top and bottom of the inactive door of a double door.

Flush Door. A smooth-surface door having faces which are plane and which conceal its rails and stiles or other structure.

Foot Bolt. A type of bolt applied at the bottom of a door and arranged for foot operation. Generally the bolt head is held up by a spring when the door is unbolted.

Forced Entry. An unauthorized entry accomplished by the use of force upon the physical components of the premises.

Frame. The component that forms the opening of and provides support for a door, window, skylight, or hatchway. See also **Door Frame**.

Frame Gasket. Resilient material in strip form attached to frame stops to provide tight closure of a door or window.

Front (of a lock). See **Face Plate**.

Gate. A notch in the end of a lever tumbler, which when aligned with the fence of the lock bolt allows the bolt to be withdrawn from the strike.

General Circulation Stair. An interior stairway in a non-elevator building which provides access to upper floors.

Glass Door. A door made from thick glass, usually heat tempered, and having no structural metal stiles.

Glass Stop. See **Glazing Bead**.

Glazing. Any transparent or translucent material used in windows or doors to admit light.

Glazing Bead. A strip of trim or a sealant such as caulking or glazing compound, which is placed around the perimeter of a pane of glass or other glazing to secure it to a frame.

Glazing Compound. A soft, dough-like material used for filling and sealing the spaces between a pane of glass and its surrounding frame and/or stops.

Grand Master Key. A key designed to operate all locks under several master key systems.

Grating, Bar Type. An open grip assembly of metal bars in which the bearing bars, running in one direction, are spaced by rigid attachment to cross bars running perpendicular to them or by bent connecting bars extending between them.

Grout. Mortar of such consistency that it will just flow into the joints and cavities of masonry work and fill them solid.

Grouted Frame. A frame in which all voids between it and the surrounding wall are completely filled with the cement or plaster used in the wall construction.

Guard Bar. A series of two or more cross bars, generally fastened to a common back plate, to protect the glass or screen in a door.

Guard Plate. A piece of metal attached to a door frame, door edge, or over the lock cylinder for the purpose of reinforcing the locking system against burglary attacks.

Hand (of a door). The opening direction of the door. A right-handed door (RH) is hinged on the right and swings inward when viewed from the outside. A left-handed door (LH) is hinged on the left and swings inward when viewed from the outside. If either of these doors swings outward, it is referred to as a right-hand reverse (RHR) door or a left-hand reverse (LHR) door, respectively.

Handle. Any grip-type door pull. See also **Lever Handle**.

Hasp. A fastening device which consists of a hinged plate with a slot in it that fits over a fixed D-shaped ring, or eye.

Hatchway. An opening in a ceiling, roof, or floor of a building which is large enough to allow human access.

Head. Top horizontal member of a door or window frame.

Head Stiffener. A heavy-gauge metal angle or channel section placed inside, and attached to, the head of a wide door frame to maintain its alignment; not a load-carrying member.

Heel of a Padlock. That end of the shackle on a padlock which is not removable from the case.

Hinge. A device generally consisting of two metal plates having loops formed along one edge of each to engage and rotate about a commonpivot rod or "pin," used to suspend a swinging door or window in its frame.

Hinge Backset. The distance from the edge of a hinge to the stop at the side of a door or window.

Hinge Edge Or Hinge Stile. The vertical edge or stile of a door or window to which hinges or pivots are attached.

Hinge Reinforcement. A metal plate attached to a door or frame to receive a hinge.

Hold-Back Feature. A mechanism on a latch which serves to hold the latch bolt in the retracted position.

Hollow Core Door. A door constructed so that the space (core) between the two facing sheets is not completely filled. Various spacing and reinforcing material are used to separate the facing sheets; some interior hollow core doors have nothing except perimeter stiles and rails separating the facing sheets.

Hollow Metal. Hollow items such as doors, frames, partitions, and enclosures which are usually fabricated from cold formed metal sheet, usually carbon steel.

Horizontal Sliding Window. A type of window, composed of two sections, one or both of which slide horizontally past the other.

Impression System. A technique to produce keys for certain types of locks without taking the lock apart.

Inactive Door (or **Leaf**). The leaf of a double door that is bolted when closed; the strike plate is attached to this leaf to receive the latch and bolt of the active leaf.

Integral Lock (or **Latch**). See **Preassembled Lock.**

Integral Frame. A metal door frame in which the jambs and head have stops, trim and backbends all formed from one piece of material.

Interior Common-Circulation Area. An area within a multiple dwelling which is outside the private zones of individual units and is used in common by all residents and the maintenances staff of the building.

Interior Private Area. The interior of a single family house; the interior of an apartment in a multiple dwelling; or the interior of a separate unit within a commercial, public, or institutional building.

Interior Public Area. An interior common-circulation area or common resident-use room within a multiple dwelling to which access is unrestricted.

Interior Semi-Public Area. An interior common-circulation area or common resident-use room within a multiple dwelling to which access is possible only with a key or on the approval of a resident via an intercom, buzzer-reply system.

Invisible Hinge. A hinge so constructed that no parts are exposed when the door is closed.

Jalousie Window. See **Louvered Window.**

Jamb. The exposed vertical member of either side of a door or window opening. See also **Door Jambs.**

Jam Anchor. A metal device inserted in or attached to the wall side of a jamb to secure the frame to the wall. A masonry jamb anchor secures a jamb to a masonry wall.

Jamb Depth. The width of the jamb, measured perpendicular to the door or wall face at the edge of the opening.

Jamb Extension. The section of a jamb which extends below the level of the flush floor for attachment to the rough door.

Jamb Peeling. A technique used in forced entry to deform or remove portions of the jamb to disengage the bolt from the strike. See **Jimmying.**

Jamb/Strike. That component of a door assembly which receives and holds the extended lock bolt. The strike and jamb are considered a unit.

Jamb/Wall. That component of a door assembly to which a door is attached and secured by means of the hinges. The wall and jamb are considered a unit.

Jimmying. A technique used in forced entry to pry the jamb away from the lock edge of the door a sufficient distance to disengage the bolt from the strike.

Jimmy-Pin. A sturdy projecting screw, which is installed in the hinge edge of a door near a hinge, fits into a hole in the door jamb and prevents removal of the door if the hinge pins are removed.

Keeper. See **Strike.**

Key. An implement used to actuate a lock bolt or latch into the locked or unlocked position.

Key Changes. The different combinations that are available or that can be used in a specific cylinder.

Keyed-Alike Cylinders. Cylinders which are designed to be operated by the same key. (Not to be confused with master-keyed cylinders).

Keyed-Different Cylinders. Cylinders requiring different keys for their operation.

Keyhole. The opening in a lock designed to receive the key.

Key In-Knob Lock. A lock having the key cylinder and the other lock mechanism, such as a push or turn button, contained in the knobs.

Key Plate. A plate or escutcheon having only a keyhole.

Keyway. The longitudinal cut in the cylinder core, being an opening or space with millings in the sides identical to those on the proper key, thus allowing the key to enter the full distance of the blade. See also **Warded Lock.**

Knifing. See **Loiding.**

Knob. An ornamental or functional round handle on a door; may be designed to actuate a lock or latch.

Knob Latch. A securing device having a spring bolt operated by a knob only.

Knob Shank. The projecting stem of a knob into which the spindle is fastened.

Knocked Down (Abbr. KD). Disassembled; designed for assembly at the point of use.

Knuckle. The enlarged part of a hinge into which the pin is inserted.

Laminate. A product made by bonding together two or

more layers of material.

Laminated Glass. A type of glass fabricated from two layers of glass with a transparent bonding layer between them. Also called safety glass.

Laminated Padlock. A padlock, the body of which consists of a number of flat plates, all or most of which are of the same contour, superimposed and riveted or brazed together. Holes in the plates provide spaces for the lock mechanism and the ends of the shackle.

Latch (or **Latch Bolt**). A bevelled, spring-actuated bolt which may or may not include a dead-locking feature.

Leading Edge. See **Lock Edge**.

Leaf, Door. An individual door, used either singly or in multiples.

Leaf Hinge. The most common type of hinge, characterized by two flat metal plates or leaves, which pivot about a metal hinge pin. A leaf hinge can be surface mounted, or installed in a mortise. See also **Butt Hinge** and **Surface Hinge**.

Lever Handle. A bar-like grip which is rotated in a vertical plane about a horizontal axis at one of its ends, designed to operate a latch.

Lever Lock. A key operated lock that incorporates one or more lever tumblers, which must be raised to a specific level so that the fence of the bolt is aligned with the gate of the tumbler in order to withdraw the bolt. Lever locks are commonly used in storage lockers, and safety deposit boxes.

Lever Tumbler. A flat metal arm, pivoted on one end with a gate in the opposite end. The top edge is spring loaded. The bitting of the key rotates against the bottom edge, raising the lever tumbler to align the gate with the bolt fence. Both the position of the gate and the curvature of the bottom edge of the lever tumbler can be varied to establish the key code.

Light. A space in a window or door for a single pane of glazing. Also, a pane of glass or other glazing material.

Lintel. A horizontal structural member that supports the load over an opening such as a door or window.

Lip (of a strike). The curved projecting part of a strike plate which guides the spring bolt to the latch point.

Lobby. That portion of the interior common area of a building which is reached from an entry door and which provides access to the general circulation areas, elevators, and fire stairs and from these to other areas of the building.

Lock. A fastener which secures a door or window assembly against unauthorized entry. A door lock is usually key-operated and includes the keyed device (cylinder or combination), bolt, strike plate, knobs or levers, trim items, etc. A window lock is usually hand operated rather than key operated.

Lock Clip. A flexible metal part attached to the inside of a door face to position a mortise lock.

Lock Edge. The vertical edge or stile of a door in which a lock may be installed. Also called the leading edge, the lock stile and the strike edge.

Lock Edge Door (or **Lock Seam Door**). A door which has its face sheets secured in place by an exposed mechanical interlock seam on each of its two vertical edges. See also **Lock Seam**.

Lock Faceplate. See **Face Plate**.

Locking Dog (of a padlock). The part of a padlock mechanism which engages the shackle and holds it in the locked position.

Lock In-Knob. See **Key-In-Knob Lock**.

Lock Pick. A tool or instrument, other than the specifically designed key, made for the purpose of manipulating a lock into a locked or unlocked condition.

Lock Rail. The horizontal member of a door intended to receive the lock case.

Lock Reinforcement. A reinforcing plate attached inside of the lock stile of a door to receive a lock.

Lock Seam. A joint in sheet metal work, formed by doubly folding the edges of adjoining sheets in such a manner that they interlock.

Lock Set. See **Lock**.

Lock Stile. See **Lock Edge**.

Loiding. A burglary attack method in which a thin, flat, flexible object such as a stiff piece of plastic is inserted between the strike and the latch bolt to depress the latch bolt and release it from the strike. The loiding of windows is accomplished by inserting a thin stiff object between the meeting rails or stiles to move the latch to the open position, or by inserting a thin stiff wire through openings between the stile or rail and the frame to manipulate the sash operator of pivoting windows. Derived from the word "celluloid." Also called knifing and slip-knifing.

Loose Joint Hinge. A hinge with two knuckles. The pin is fastened permanently to one and the other contains the pinhole. The two parts of the hinge can be disengaged by lifting.

Loose Pin Hinge. A hinge having a removable pin to permit the two leaves of the hinge to be separated.

Louver. An opening with a series of horizontal slats so arranged as to permit ventilation but to exclude rain, sunlight, or vision.

Louvered Window. A type of window in which the glazing consists of parallel, horizontal, movable glass slats. Also called a *jalousie window*.

Main Entry Door. The most important common entry door in a building, which provides access to the building's lobby.

Maison Keying. A specialized keying system, used in apartment houses and other large complexes, that enables all individual unit keys to operate common-use locks such as main entry, laundry room, etc.

Masonry. Stone, brick, concrete, hollow tiles, concrete blocks, or other similar materials, bonded together with mortar to form a wall, pier, buttress, or similar member.

Master Disc Tumbler. A disc tumbler that will operate with a master key in addition to its own change key.

Master Key System. A method of keying locks which allows a single key to operate multiple locks, each of which will also operate with an individual change key. Several levels of master keying are possible: a single master key is one which will operate all locks of a group of locks with individual change keys: a grand master key will operate all locks of two or more master key systems: a great grand master key will operate all locks of two or more grand master key systems. Master key systems are used primarily with pin and disk tumbler locks, and to a limited extent with lever or warded locks.

Master Pin. A segmented pin, used to enable a pin tumbler to be operated by more than one key cut.

Meeting Stile. The vertical edge member of a door or horizontal sliding window, in a pair of doors or windows, which meets with the adjacent edge member when closed. See also **Checkrails**.

Metal-Mesh Grille. A grille of expanded metal or welded metal wires permanently installed across a window or other opening in order to prevent entry through the opening.

Mill Finish. The original surface finish produced on a metal mill product by cold rolling, extruding or drawing.

Millwork. Generally, all building components made of finished wood and manufactured in millwork plants and planing mills. It includes such items as inside and outside doors, window and doorframes, cabinets, porchwork, mantels, panelwork, stairways, moldings, and interior trim. It normally does not include flooring, ceiling, or siding.

Molding. A wood strip used for decorative purposes.

Mono Lock. See **Preassembled Lock**.

Mortise. A rectangular cavity made to receive a lock or other hardware; also, the act of making such a cavity.

Mortise Bolt. A bolt designed to be installed in a mortise rather than on the surface. The bolt is operated by a knob, lever or equivalent.

Mortise Cylinder. See **Cylinder, Mortise Type**.

Mortise Lock. A lock designed for installation in a mortise, as distinguished from a bored lock and a rim lock.

Mullion. (1) A movable or fixed center post used on double door openings, usually for locking purposes. (2) A vertical or horizontal bar or divider in a frame between windows, doors, or other openings.

Multiple Dwelling. A building or portion of a building designed or used for occupancy by three or more tenants or families living independently of each other (includes hotels and motels).

Muntin. A small member which divides the glass or openings of sash or doors.

Mushroom Tumbler. A type of tumbler used in pin tumbler locks to add security against picking. The diameter of the driver pin behind the end in contact with the bottom pin is reduced so that the mushroom head will catch the edge of the cylinder body at the shear line when it is at a slight angle to its cavity. See also **Spool Tumbler**.

Night Latch. An auxiliary lock having a spring latch bolt and functioning independently of the regular lock of the door.

Non-Removable Hinge Pin. A type of hinge pin that has been constructed or modified to make its removal from the hinge difficult or impossible.

Offset Pivot (or **Hinge**). A pin-and-socket hardware device

with a single bearing contact, by means of which a door is suspended in its frame and allowed to swing about an axis which normally is located about 1.9cm (¾ in.) out from the door face.

One-Way Screw. A screw specifically designed to resist being removed, once installed. See also **Tamper-Resistant Hardware**.

Opening Size. See **Door Opening**.

Operator (of a window sash). The mechanism, including a crank handle and gear box, attached to an operating arm or arms for the purpose of opening and closing a window. Usually found on casement and awning type windows.

Overhead Door. A door which is stored overhead when in the open position.

Padlock. A detachable and portable lock with a hinged or sliding shackle or bolt, normally used with a hasp and eye or staple system.

Panel Door. A door fabricated from one or more panels surrounded by and held in position by rails and stiles.

Panic Bar. See **Crash Bar**.

Panic Hardware. An exterior door locking mechanism which is always operable from inside the building by pressure on a crash bar or lever.

Patio-Type Sliding Door. A sliding door that is essentially a single, large transparent panel in a frame (a type commonly used to give access to patios or yards of private dwellings); "single" doors have one fixed and one movable panel: "double" doors have two movable panels.

Peeling. See **Jamb Peeling**.

Picking. See **Lock Picking**.

Pin (of a hinge). The metal rod that serves as the axis of a hinge and thereby allows the hinge (and attached door or window) to rotate between the open and closed positions.

Pin Tumbler. One of the essential, distinguishing components of a pin tumbler lock cylinder, more precisely called a bottom pin, master pin or driver pin. The pin tumblers, used in varying lengths and arrangements, determine the combination of the cylinder. See also **Bottom Pin, Driver Pin**, and **Master Pin**.

Pin Tumbler Lock Cylinder. A lock cylinder employing metal pins (tumblers) to prevent the rotation of the core until the correct key is inserted into the keyway. Small coil compression springs hold the pins in the locked position until the key is inserted.

Pivoted Door. A door hung on pivots rather than hinges.

Pivoted Window. A window which opens by pivoting about a horizontal or vertical axis.

Plug Retainer. The part often fixed to the rear of the core in a lock cylinder to retain or hold the core firmly in the cylinder.

Preassembled Lock. A lock that has all the parts assembled into a unit at the factory and, when installed in a rectangular section cut out of the door at the lock edge, requires little or no assembly. Also called *integral* lock, *mono* lock, and *unit* lock.

Pressed Padlock. A padlock whose outer case is pressed

into shape from sheet metal and then riveted together.

Pressure-Locked Grating. A grating in which the cross bars are mechanically locked to the bearing bars at their intersections by deforming or swaging the metal.

Privacy Lock. A lock, usually for an interior door, secured by a button, thumb-turn, etc., and not designed for key operation.

Projection. See **Bolt Projection**.

Push Key. A key which operates the Ace type of lock.

Quadrant. See **Dutch Door Bolt**.

Rabbet. A cut, slot or groove made on the edge or surface of a board to receive the end or edge of another piece of wood made to fit it.

Rabbeted Jamb. A door jamb in which the projection portion of the jamb which forms the door stop is either part of the same piece as the rest of the jamb or securely set into a deep groove in the jamb.

Rail. A horizontal framing member of a door or window sash which extends the full width between the stiles.

Removable Mullion. A mullion separating two adjacent door openings which is required for the normal operation of the doors but is designed to permit its temporary removal.

Restricted Keyway. A special keyway and key blank for high security locks, with a configuration which is not freely available and which must be specifically requested from the manufacturer.

Reversible Lock. A lock which may be used for either hand of a door.

Rim Cylinder. A pin or disc tumbler cylinder used with a rim lock.

Rim Hardware. Hardware designed to be installed on the surface of a door or window.

Rim Latch. A latch installed on the surface of a door.

Rim Lock. A lock designed to be mounted on the surface of a door.

Rose. The part of a lock which functions as an ornament or bearing surface for a knob, and is normally placed against the surface of the door.

Rotary Interlocking Dead Bolt Lock. A type of rim lock in which the extended dead bolt is rotated to engage with the strike.

Rough Buck. A subframe, usually made of wood or steel, which is set in a wall opening and to which the frame is attached.

Rough Opening. The wall opening into which a frame is to be installed. Usually, the rough opening is measured inside the rough buck.

Sash. A frame containing one or more lights.

Sash Fast. A fastener attached to the meeting rails of a window.

Sash Lock. A sash fast with a locking device controlled by a key.

Screwless Knob. A knob attached to a spindle by means of a special wrench, as distinguished from the more commonly used side-screw knob.

Screwless Rose. A rose with a concealed method of attachment.

Seamless Door. A door having no visible seams on its faces or edges.

Secondary Lock. See **Auxiliary Lock**.

Security Glass Or Glazing. See **Burglar-Resistant Glazing**.

Setback. See **Backset**.

Shackle. The hinged or sliding part of a padlock that does the fastening.

Shear Line. The joint between the shell and the core of a lock cylinder; the line at which the pins or discs of a lock cylinder must be aligned in order to permit rotation of the core.

Sheathing. The structural exterior covering, usually wood boards or plywood, used over the framing studs and rafters of a structure.

Shell. A lock cylinder, exclusive of the core. Also called *housing*.

Shutter. A movable screen or cover used to protect an opening, especially a window.

Side Light. A fixed light located adjacent to a door within the same frame assembly.

Signal Sash Fastener. A sash-fastening device designed to lock windows which are beyond reach from the floor. It has a ring for a sash pole hook. When locked, the ring lever is down; when the ring lever is up, it signals by its upright position that the window is unlocked.

Sill. The lower horizontal member of a door or window opening.

Single-Acting Door. A door mounted to swing to only one side of the plane of its frame.

Skylight. A glazed opening located in the roof of a building.

Slide Bolt. A simple lock which is operated directly by hand without using a key, a turnpiece, or other actuating mechanism, Slide bolts can normally only be operated from the inside.

Sliding Door. Any door that slides open sideways.

Sliding Metal Gate. An assembly of metal bars, jointed so that it can be moved to and locked in position across a window or other opening, in order to prevent unauthorized entry through the opening.

Slip-Knifing. See **Loiding**.

Solid Core Door. A door constructed so that the space (core) between the two facing sheets is completely filled with wood blocks or other rigid material.

Spindle. The shaft that fits into the shank of a door knob or handle, and that serves as its axis of rotation.

Split Astragal. A two-piece astragal, one piece of which is surface mounted on each door of a double door and is provided with a means of adjustment to mate with the other piece and provide a seal. See also **Astragal**.

Spool Tumbler. A type of tumbler used in pin tumbler locks to add security against picking. Operates on the same principal as the mushroom tumbler.

Spring Bolt. See **Latch**.

Spring Bolt With Anti-Loiding Device. See **Dead Latch**.

Stile. One of the vertical edge members of a paneled door or window sash.

Stool. A flat molding fitted over the window sill between the jambs and contacting the bottom rail of the lower sash.

Stop (of a door or window frame). The projecting part of a door or window frame against which a swinging door or window closes, or in which a sliding door or window moves.

Stop (of a lock). A button or other device that serves to lock and unlock a latch bolt against actuation by the outside knob or thumb piece. Another type holds the bolt retracted.

Stop Side. That face of a door which contacts the door stop.

Store Front Sash. An assembly of light metal members forming a continuous frame for a fixed glass store front.

Storm Sash, Window, Or Door. An extra window or door, usually placed on the outside of an existing one as additional protection against cold or hot weather.

Strap Hinge. A surface hinge of which one or both leaves are of considerable length.

Strike. A metal plate attached to or mortised into a door jamb to receive and hold a projected latch bolt and/or dead bolt in order to secure the door to the jamb.

Strike, Box. See **Box Strike**.

Strike, Dustproof. A strike which is placed in the threshold or sill of an opening, or in the floor, to receive a flush bolt, and is equipped with a spring-loaded follower to cover the recess and keep out dirt.

Strike, Interlocking. A strike which receives and holds a vertical, rotary, or hook dead bolt.

Strike Plate. See **Strike**.

Strike Reinforcement. A metal plate attached to a door or frame to receive a strike.

Strike, Roller. A strike for latch bolts, having a roller mounted on the lip to reduce friction.

Stud. A slender wood or metal post used as a supporting element in a wall or partition.

Stud Anchor. A device used to secure a stud to the floor.

Sub-Buck Or Sub-Frame. See **Rough Buck**.

Surface Hinge. A hinge having both leaves attached to the surface and thus fully visible.

Swing. See **Hand**.

Swinging Bolt. A bolt that is hinged to a lock front and is projected and retracted with a swinging rather than a sliding action. Also called hinged or pivot bolt.

Tail Piece. The unit on the core of a cylinder lock which actuates the bolt or latch.

Tamper-Resistant Hardware. Builders' hardware with screws or nut-and-bolt connections that are hidden or cannot be removed with conventional tools.

Template. A precise detailed pattern used as a guide in the mortising, drilling, etc., of a door or frame to receive hardware.

Template Hardware. Hardware manufactured within template tolerances.

Tension Wrench. An instrument used in picking a lock. It is used to apply torsion to the cylinder core.

Three-Point Lock. A locking device required on "A-label" fire double doors to lock the active door at three points

—the normal position plus top and bottom.

Threshold. A wood or metal plate forming the bottom of a doorway.

Throw. See **Bolt Projection**.

Thumb Piece (of a door handle). The small pivoted part above the grip of a door handle, which is pressed by the thumb to operate a latch bolt.

Thumb Turn. A unit which is gripped between the thumb and forefinger, and turned to project or retract a bolt.

Tolerance. The permissible deviation from a nominal or specified dimension or value.

Transom. An opening window immediately above a door.

Transom Bar. The horizontal frame member which separates the door opening from the transom.

Transom Catch. A latch bolt fastener on a transom, having a ring by which the latch bolt is retracted.

Transom Chain. A short chain used to limit the opening of a transom; usually provided with a plate at each end for attachment.

Transom Lift. A device attached to a door frame and tramsom by means of which the transom may be opened or closed.

Trim Hardware. See **Finish Builders' Hardware**.

Tryout Keys. A set of keys which includes many commonly used bittings. They are used one at a time in an attempt to unlock a door.

Tumbler. A movable obstruction in a lock which must be adjusted to a particular position, as by a key, before the bolt can be thrown.

Turn Piece. See **Thumb Turn**.

Unit Lock. See **Preassembled Lock**.

Vertical Bolt Lock. A lock having two deadbolts which move vertically into two circular receivers in the strike portion of the lock attached to the door jamb.

Wire Glass. Glass manufactured with a layer of wire mesh approximately in the center of the sheet.

Vision Panel. A fixed transparent panel of glazing material set into an otherwise opaque wall, partition, or door; a nonopening window. See also **Light**.

Ward. An obstruction which prevents the wrong key from entering or turning in a lock.

Warded Lock. A lock containing internal obstacles which block the entrance or rotation of all but the correct key.

Weatherstripping. Narrow or jamb-width sections of flexible material which prevent the passage of air and moisture around windows and doors. Compression weather-stripping also acts as a frictional counterbalance in double-hung windows.

Wet Glazing. The sealing of glass or other transparent material in a frame by the use of a glazing compound or sealant.

Window Frame. See **Frame**.

Window Guard. A strong metal grid-like assembly which can be installed on a window or other opening; types of window guards include metal bars, metal-mesh grilles, and sliding metal gates.

Chapter 7

Safes, Vaults, and Accessories

Choose the Right Container

A safe or vault ideally should occupy the innermost ring of concentric *protective rings* around a secured premises. Other security equipment (fences, gates, vehicle barriers, doors, and access controls) selected for the outer protective rings is usually specifically designed for its function, but the security vault at center often is not.

The value and physical nature of a vault container's contents should dictate the type of container and degree of protection sought; but people tend to categorize all combination-locked security containers as "safes" because of one common denominator—combination locks. This is a mistake.

There are fire-resistant safes, burglary-resistant chests, safes for EDP media, and insulated filing cabinets. Each can be combination-locked, but to regard any combination-locked container as a safe is to disregard the fact that different types and levels of protection exist. Such disregard invites losses.

High-value items stored in a fire-resistant safe or insulated filing cabinet are vulnerable to burglary —the average insulated container can quickly be forced open with a few simple, accessible hand tools. Similarly, important documents stored in a burglary chest are much more secure from burglars than in an insulated container, but are also more likely to be incinerated in a fire.

Underwriters' Laboratories (UL) performs systematic testing of fire and burglary-resistant qualities of representative security containers submitted for testing by their manufacturers (see Chapter Appendix). Makers of those containers which meet specific test requirements may affix a UL rating label to their products. The presence of a UL label signifies that a comparable unit of the same design successfully passed systematic tests performed by Underwriters' Laboratories for resistance to burglary or fire. The label denotes the type and severity of test conditions.

Possibly the best protection are those safes which bear UL labeling for both fire and burglary protection. Such containers are simply burglary chests housed inside insulated containers. Similar protection can be obtained by buying a burglary chest and a fire safe separately, then placing the burglary-resistant chest inside the fire safe, thus establishing separate storage areas for documents and high-value items.

Because UL ratings are recognized by the American insurance industry as reliable rating standards for security containers, comprehensive insurance policies often specify or otherwise require minimum UL security container ratings. Reduced merchantile insurance rates may be applicable if a selected security container exceeds the recommended minimum rating.

Whether or not a security container provides fire or burglary protection, its inherent security can increase with special-function locks. Very often, the purchaser of a fire safe or money chest isn't told of all the optional equipment available with the security container being considered. Salespeople often prefer not to risk confusing their clients with too many options. Optional equipment boosts the sale price, thus can jeopardize a sale. People who buy security containers should nevertheless be aware of what is available and decide for themselves. If unwisely chosen, the security container itself can cause new operational and logistical problems which could be solved by the use of special-function equipment.

For instance, the presence of a quality burglary-resistant chest on the premises of a cash-handling business means that a bank deposit doesn't necessarily have to be made daily, even if daily deposits are supposed to be the usual procedure. An attitude of "nothing to worry about—just put it in the safe overnight" can easily develop. But an after hours visit by a dishonest employee with the combination can double the loss potential. So, too, can a properly timed holdup. The situations that can be prevented or alleviated by wisely chosen security equipment are numerous, and safe buyers should be aware of them. The following pages describe a few such possibilities and the security equipment that is presently available for prevention.

UL-Rated Combination Locks

A good quality combination lock is a basic need. On well made containers, the most commonly encountered combination locks are those certified in accordance with Underwriters' Laboratories standards (UL 768). Combination locks can earn a Group 1, IR, or 2 classification. A lock bearing a UL label has met or exceeded detailed criteria for quality, security, and durability.

The UL testing procedure for combination locks involves ascertaining that the lock can be set to various combinations and operated within specified tolerances. According to Section 11.10 of UL 768, "A three-tumbler wheel lock shall not open with the dial turned more than 1-1/4 dial graduations on either side of the proper gradation for each tumbler. A four-tumbler lock shall not open with the dial turned more than 1-1/2 dial gradation on either side of the proper gradation for each number."

Other sections of UL 768 describe tests for mechanical strength, impact resistance, manufacturing tolerance, product endurance, and operability after prolonged exposure to adverse conditions. The testing for UL Group 1 (manipulation resistant) and Group 1R (manipulation and radiographic resistant) labels includes all tests performed on Group 2 rated locks plus the requirement that the lock tested must by virtue of its design and construction resist skilled surreptitious attempts to learn the combination numbers by manipulation, the use of instruments, or radioactive isotopes (Group 1R test only) for 20 man-hours of net working time.

In most instances, a Group 2 combination lock will provide adequate security. Although many legitimate safe and vault technicians are trained in combination lock manipulation techniques, criminals with the skill and knowledge necessary to surreptitiously open a Group 2 lock by manipulation are few in number. Most safe burglars use forceful methods. High-security installations, however, such as jewelry safes or containers protecting extremely sensitive or classified information, should be outfitted with manipulation-resistant Group 1 locks to block every possible avenue of criminal approach.

Defense contractors who deal with classified information are required to protect such information in security containers which meet certain government specifications. One such specification, MIL-L-15596, defines the type of combination lock that is acceptable. This specification covers much the same territory as the UL standard regarding Group 1 and 1R manipulation- and radiation-resistant locks.

Relocking Devices

A relocking device, or relocker, is an auxiliary bolt or bolt-blocking mechanism for which there is no control from outside the container. Relockers protect security containers against torch, drill, and punching attacks. The relocker is an especially important feature on burglary resistant units, because these containers are designed to protect items of high dollar value, and are therefore more attractive to skilled burglars. Relockers are important enough in preserving a container's security to warrant a separate standard for rating them, UL 140.

Known in bygone days as dynamite triggers, relockers can be simple in design; often they are no more than spring-driven bolts held in a cocked (loaded) position until activated by a burglar's attack. With normal usage of a relock-equipped container, the relocker's presence is undetectable to the user. When activated, though, the relocker blocks the retraction of the door bolts, combination bolt, or both, even if the correct combination for the lock is known.

Relocking devices are often held cocked by a piece of metal attached by screws to the combination lock's back cover. When thus situated, relockers protect against spindle or dial punching, the most common (and in earlier times one of the most effective) forms of forceful burglary attack.

In a typical punching attack the burglar first

knocks the dial off the safe to expose the end of the spindle, a threaded shaft which connects the numbered safe dial to the combination lock's wheels. The spindle end is then punched inward with a hand sledge and drift punch. When the spindle is driven inward in this manner, one or more of the lock's wheels are slammed against or even through the back cover of the lock. A punching attack may completely dislodge all the wheels (or tumblers) in the lock.

Most currently manufactured combination lock back covers are purposely designed to be dislodged by a punching attack. Because the relock checking device is either fastened to the lock cover or located very near it, dislodging the cover also dislodges the relock check. A spring (or in some cases gravity) then takes over, moving the relock to its triggered position.

After spindle punching the burglar can insert tools through the spindle hole and fish the combination bolt to a retracted position. If not for relockers the safe door could be opened. A triggered relocker, however, is neither easily located nor easily released from outside the container. Containers incorporating some form of relocking device now outnumber older, nonrelock-equipped containers; an unsuccessful punching attempt on a recently built container signifies a lack of knowledge and skill.

Although makers of fire-resistant containers are not required to include a relocking device in the container design, many do so to thwart the type of punching attack just described. Safemakers realize that because the cost per cubic inch of space in a fire-resistant container is appreciably less than that of a burglary-resistant container of the same size, many clients will store high-value items in fire-resistant containers instead of burglary chests, even after being advised not to.

Thermal relocking devices hinder skilled burglars who use cutting torches or other burning tools. A thermal relock activates when that part of the mechanism which holds the relock cocked (usually a fusible link made from a metal with an extremely low melting-point) heats to its melting point, at which time a spring can activate a bolt-blocking mechanism. A thermal relock isn't necessarily part of the combination lock but is usually nearby, because torching burglars tend to burn in an area fairly close to the combination lock.

Current Group 1, 1R, and 2 combination locks have simple but effective built-in relocking devices, designed to be activated by spindle-punching attacks. Some also incorporate thermal protection. Many safemakers, however, do not rely totally on

the protection provided by these built-in relockers, referring to include relockers of their own design, situated outside the combination lock.

Some safemakers use a sophisticated type of relocking device that simultaneously guards against punching, drilling, and burning attacks. A *nerve plate* of tempered glass is mounted between the combination lock and the inner surface of the container door. Taut wires or cords are strung from one or more spring-driven relocking devices and fastened to the glass. The placement of such nerve plates ensures that most unskilled and semiskilled burglary attacks will severely shock and thus shatter the the glass nerve plate. Similarly, a skilled operator who attempts to drill into the lock case and manipulate the combination wheels will encounter the nerve plate before penetrating the lock. Any attempt to penetrate further will shatter the glass and release the tension on the wires that hold the relocks cocked.

Glass nerve plates have been popular with foreign safemakers for some time. They are an extremely efficient way to hinder even highly skilled burglars. Some makers of high-security units string the relock wires around a series of posts before attaching them to the nerve plate in front of the combination lock. Relockers and the wires can thus be placed randomly within a production run of like models, defeating those burglars armed with blueprints made by taking exact measurements from a comparable model.

Underwriters' Laboratories performs testing and certification of relocking devices under the standard UL 140. Safemakers whose relocking devices are successfully tested under the conditions described in UL 140 are entitled to affix labels to that effect on their containers.

Locking Dials

Locking combination dials are used to ensure that no one person has control of a security container's contents. Companies whose employees handle large amounts of cash or other valuables use locking dials to satisfy dual custody requirements. Typically, one person is assigned the key that unlocks the dial and another is assigned the combination. A locked dial will not turn to allow the combination to be dialed until the keyholder unlocks it. The keyholder can lock or unlock the dial but cannot open the container without the combination.

A typical application of dual custody is for a

supermarket safe. Usually notice is posted to the effect that two people are required to open the safe; the store manager has the only combination, and the armored car guard has the dial key. When this procedure is used such arrangements deter or complicate holdups.

When used according to strictly observed procedures, locking dials also help reduce the opportunity for a lone dishonest person to abuse a position of trust, and can help to protect innocent persons from unwarranted suspicion when mysterious losses are noted.

Lockable Handles

Lockable bolt control handles perform much the same function as lockable dials. A locking handle allows the combination to be dialed, but the bolt control handle will not retract the door bolts until it is unlocked. Again, this arrangement allows dual custody of the container's contents.

Users of walk-in vaults often leave the combination dialed and the door bolts retracted during business hours. Hold-up gangs have used this fact to advantage, herding their victims into the vault and then simply turning the bolt handle and spinning the combination dial to lock them in, thus helping to ensure a clean getaway. When installed on the door of a walk-in vault, locking bolt control handles helps to prevent this tactic, because the door bolts can be immobilized during the business day.

Time Locks

Time locks are considered standard equipment on bank vault doors but may also be used on any security container whose door has enough usable surface area to permit installation. A time lock ensures that once closed and locked, the safe or vault door will remain so for a predetermined amount of time. Time locks were hailed by nineteenth century bankers as devices which would discourage the kidnapping of bank officials and their family members in order to force disclosure of vault combinations. Before time locks, this was a commonly used tactic of holdup and burglary gangs, who did not balk at committing brutal crimes in order to learn vault combinations.

The most common time locks are mechanical windup mechanisms; their internal design and operation is quite similar to that of ordinary time-pieces, but their mainsprings perform additional duties besides powering the clockworks.

When a mechanical time lock is wound, a shutter in its case closes. There is usually a rod or projection extending from the door bolts; when the bolts move, the rod moves. During bolt retraction (i.e., opening the safe door), this rod would normally enter the time lock case via the shutter hole, but the closed shutter blocks the rod's passage, which translates itself to a door bolt blockage. As the time lock's movements wind down, the mainspring's energy is harnessed to open the shutter. The shutter reopens fully when the first movement has wound down.

A typical time lock relies on at least two, but as many as three or four separate windup movements in a single case. It can be used on safes as well as vaults. The presence of at least two movements gives reasonable assurance that a single movement's failure won't cause a lockout; the more movements used, the more the chance for lockout is reduced. Only one movement must wind down for the container to open.

Time-Delay Combination Locks

No lock can prevent an armed robber from forcing another person to disclose a combination. This type of robbery is often committed against restaurant or store employees in the hours before or after closing. Such crimes often net rich hauls for criminals and can easily involve injuries to the victims.

The robber(s) gain entry to the premises by various methods; by capturing an employee while entering or exiting, by using a seemingly legitimate pretext, or sometimes by breaking into the premises and lying in wait for the holder of the safe combination. Once identified, that person is forced to open the safe.

Time delay combination locks, also known as Delayed Action Timers (D.A.T.s) are one solution to the problem, because such locks can foil or deter robberies. A time delay lock is a combination lock with one or more timer movements attached. The action of dialing the safe combination winds a timer. The operator must wait for a predetermined period after dialing before the delay mechanism will permit the combination lock bolt to retract. Delay times range from as few as three minutes to as many as forty-five minutes, and in some cases are changeable.

The most sophisticated time-delay combination locks boast alarm compatibility. A store manager who is ordered by a robber to open the safe can discreetly dial a special combination and activate a holdup alarm. Alarm-compatible time-delay combination locks give police a better chance of arriving in time to make an arrest.

Time-delay locks reduce both robbery losses and the incidence of robbery. Businesses using time-delay locks usually post conspicuous notices to this effect, causing prospective robbers to take their business elsewhere. Robbers rely on speed of execution—even the hint of a delay reduces a target's appeal.

Alarmed Combination Locks

Alarmed combination locks incorporate micro-switches capable of shunting alarms and signaling unauthorized opening attempts or openings made under duress.

Perhaps the most generally useful are the switches designed to send *duress* alarm signals. They are designed to discreetly send an alarm signal when a special duress combination is dialed. Like the regularly used combination, the duress combination also opens the safe, so that a robber won't realize an alarm is being sent.

The typical robber orders the victim not to set off an alarm, and things can get ugly if the robber suspects otherwise. Because the alarm is set off by a seemingly innocent dialing procedure performed in accord with robbers' demands, combination locks with duress or ambush features could be categorized as compliance alarms.

Tamper switches help protect combination-locked containers during those hours when no persons, not even authorized combination holders, are allowed access to the contents. The dial is set at a predetermined number and sometimes locked in place, then alarm protection is turned on. Any attempt to dial the combination while the protection is on will cause an alarm.

Another switch arrangement can be used to monitor the status of the container or as an alarm shunt. This switch is placed in such a way that when the combination lock bolt is retracted to the open position, the switch is actuated. This lets remote monitors track the container's openings and closings. A shunt switch allows the burglary alarm circuit to remain active 24 hours a day while still allowing combination holders access to the contents.

Vision-Restricting and Shielded Dials

Standard combination dials are known as *front-reading*, meaning their numbers are visible from a horizontal line of sight. It is possible for prying eyes to see the numbers that are dialed when a front-reading dial is used, which of course makes the safe's protection ineffective. If a combination must be dialed while persons not authorized to know the numbers are nearby, a front-reading dial is best replaced with a vision-restricting, or *spyproof* dial.

There are various types of vision-restricting dials available—each safe lock manufacturer has its own version. One of the most common is the top reading dial, whose numbers are are etched into an outer rim that is perpendicular to the safe door. To effectively see the combination numbers, the dialer must stand squarely in front of the dial and look down at the numbers while dialing. A raised flange guards the sides of the dial from view; only a small portion of the dial's numbered area can be seen at any given time.

Other vision-restricting designs incorporate covered dials with louvered windows or tinted and polarized lenses at the index area. Covering the entire dial except the turning knob shields the dial face from finger marks. People who dial safe combinations tend to place one finger on the dial face as a brake. This leaves smudges on the safe dial at fairly regular distances from the actual combination numbers, thus making it possible to learn a safe's combination by composing test combinations as suggested by the smudges' locations.

Combination Changing

A positive aspect of combination locks is user changeability. Although many companies leave this task to service vendors as a matter of policy, some have policies which dictate that company personnel do the changing to absolutely ensure exclusive knowledge of combination numbers. New safes, chests, and insulated files, if combination-locked, usually come with detailed instructions for changing and special change keys.

Safe dealers often remove the changing instructions and changing keys before delivery, and with good reason. The customer's first suspicion might be that the safe dealer would much rather profit from future service calls to change combinations than let the clients do it themselves. This is partly true, but there is a valid reason for withholding changing tools and instructions.

Safe buyers who have changing instructions and try to change keys often fall victim to a common syndrome. They attempt combination changes before having fully read or understood the instructions, and thus cause a lockout.

The client calls the dealer for help and, because the lockout is attributable to error rather than a defective product, is charged for the work. Not wishing to pay a service fee, the client won't admit the error, claiming instead that the unit is defective and that the work should be covered by warranty. The dealer's representative knows better: combination-changing errors are glaringly obvious to a technically experienced person. The dealer's subsequent refusal to write the work off as a warranty job incurs the client's wrath and creates bad will.

Combination changing is a relatively simple task, but mistakes can be costly in terms of both lost time and dollars. Safes are unforgiving—a lockout resulting from a combination-changing error may dictate that the container be forced open. Lockouts can be avoided by exercising a high degree of care when working with the combination lock components and always trying new combinations several times with the safe door open. This is probably the most important yet most-ignored part of combination changing.

Safe Burglaries

There was a time in the not-so-distant past when gangs of skilled safe burglars operated in America; pickings were easy and plentiful. In today's world, where the need for instant gratification often supersedes reason, fewer criminals will spend the time necessary first to learn safe burglary skills and then to properly plan and execute safe burglaries. Contemporary criminals tend to prefer crimes that don't require much time or technical skill; a fast exchange of drugs and money in a motel parking lot can easily net more than a weekend of work with a cutting torch.

Highly skilled and knowledgeable safecrackers are by no means extinct in America, but there are a lot fewer of them today. Those remaining safecrackers with sufficient skill to breach a well-built jeweler's chest or bank vault don't need to work as often as other thieves; consequently, their exploits don't get the continual press coverage that more prolific criminals receive.

The burglar most likely to visit a business or residential premises is fairly average in terms of technical skills. Such individuals work fast and often. While very good at defeating or circumventing door and window locks, this type of burglar is usually stumped when confronted by even a thin-walled insulated safe—quite often one's best effort will be

an unsuccessful attempt at prying or dial punching, after which the container may be locked more securely than before. In addition to technical ignorance, the erstwhile safecracker usually suffers from a faint heart, and would rather leave than invest much time in the effort.

Some burglars, however, inhabit a middle ground with respect to skill. They have learned to recognize and prepare for those situations in which they have a fair chance of getting into some of the safes they may encounter. These individuals find enough opportunities and enjoy enough successes within the parameters of their limited skills that they usually don't make the effort to become more technically proficient. They pose a real threat, though, because part of their expertise is in the exploitation of human error and complacency, failings that even users of high-security containers are subject to.

The only defense against the semiskilled opportunistic safe burglar is knowledge, awareness, and strict adherence to proper security procedures. Following are some of the ways these individuals gain access to safe contents, and suggestions for defeating them.

Hidden Combinations

Many people, fearful of forgetting the safe combination, write down the numbers and dialing sequences and secrete them somewhere near the safe or in a wallet or address book. Smart burglars know more places to look for combination numbers than the average person can dream of, and will systematically search for and discover them, no matter how well hidden the safe user may think they are. Combination numbers can be memorized, a fact that makes combination locks more secure than the majority of key-operated mechanisms. Writing out the combination is a real help for burglars, and can complicate police investigations. Safe users who write down combinations often do so in violation of company security policies. Therefore, they are reluctant to admit it, thus forcing investigators to guess at the facts. Prevention is simple: memorize the numbers.

Using Birthdays, Phone Numbers, Addresses, etc.

Such numbers are appealing because they are already committed to the user's memory, but smart burglars have been known to take the time to do some research on their victims, learning the same numbers and composing test combinations with them. Similarly, many safe users tend to select combination numbers ending in 5 or 0, like 10-20-30 or 25-35-45, because such numbers are more clearly marked on the safe dial. Doing so greatly limits the combination possibilities. A safe combination should ideally be a random set of numbers with no special significance to the user.

Failing to Fully Scramble the Combination When Locking

This is especially common in cases where the safe is outfitted with a locking dial. For daytime convenience the combination numbers are left dialed and then the bolt is left extended and the dial locked with the key. The safe door can then be opened by merely turning the dial key and moving the dial just a few numbers' worth of travel, rather than having to redial completely. Safe users mistakenly think the dial lock and combination lock afford equal protection, but they do not. The combination lock is protected inside the safe door while the dial lock is exposed on the outside. Safes without locking dials can also be locked but not fully scrambled, and thus afford opportunities for patient thieves to walk the dial a number at a time in hopes of finding the last number of the combination. Whenever a safe is closed it is a good practice to turn the dial at least four full revolutions before considering it locked.

Smart burglars confronted with a locking dial can sometimes make a big score by merely clamping a heavy pair of pliers on the dial and twisting, because people who hate to dial safe combinations can easily slip into the habit of using the dial lock for nighttime locking as well as daytime convenience. Daytime robbers have also been known to give the same treatment to safes secured only by locking dials during business hours. Simply stated, the dial lock protects the dial, and the combination lock protects the safe.

Punching

The majority of burglary-resistant safes are protected in some way against punching; relocking devices and punch-resistant spindles are the most popular methods. Many insulated safes built in the last twenty to thirty years also feature relocking devices. Punching is generally a sign of technical ignorance. The safe dial is pried or knocked off and a punch or lineup tool is used in conjunction with a

hand sledge to drive the spindle inward. The intent is to knock the lock components completely out of position so they no longer block the retraction of the door bolts. Except in safes not equipped with relocking devices or other protective measures, punching is usually ineffective. The best defense against punching attacks is to buy a safe that is equipped with a UL-listed relocking device.

While protection against burglary is not an absolute necessity in a fire-resistant container, many makers of such containers realize that safe users will often treat their products as if they were burglary-resistant chests and store high-value items in them. With this in mind, the safemakers will usually include relocking protection of some sort, if only by being certain to use a combination lock with built-in relock protection.

Peeling

Insulated containers can often be *peeled* open in much the same way as a sardine can. Often the burglar will pound with a sledge near one of the door's corners in an effort to buckle it inward, thus permitting the insertion of wedging and prying tools. The door is then peeled back by virtue of sheer force until the contents can be removed. In another type of peeling attack, a chisel separates the outer metal skin from the door. This outer skin of older fire safes was in many cases merely spot-welded in several locations along the door's edge. When the initial separation has been achieved, a larger chisel (fire axes and heavy prying tools have been used) continues the process of breaking the remaining spot welds all the way down the door's edge, until the outer skin can be bent or peeled out of the way. The intent in such attacks is to dig or chop through the door insulation and inner skin, eventually expose the combination lock or door bolts, and overcome them with heavy tools and brute force. More recently-made insulated containers have seam-welded door skins to make this type of attack extremely difficult if not unfeasible. Although fire safes can be peeled by both semi-skilled and skilled criminals, the neatness and efficiency of the work will give an indication of the criminal's skill and experience. A sturdily built money or jewelry chest cannot be peeled.

Ripping or Chopping

These forms of attack are most often successful when carried out against insulated containers. The burglar may be unskilled, semiskilled, or professional. Heavy metal-cutting tools literally cut a hole in the container's door, side, or bottom. When the hole is made the burglar simply reaches in and removes the contents. Defeating the peelers and rippers of the world requires only that the safe purchased be a burglary chest rather than an insulated container. If both fire and burglary protection are necessary, a burglary-resistant container can be installed inside an insulated container.

Cartoffs

Also known by burglary investigators as a *kidnap* or *pack-off*, this is the simplest but perhaps the nerviest safe defeat. If the container can be moved and transported easily enough, the burglar or burglars simply steal the entire container and open it at their leisure in a secure location. The majority of existing insulated containers are wheeled, making this task even easier than it should be. Often a bolt-down kit is available which will enable the safe owner to attach the safe to the floor of the premises and hinder burglars who might try stealing it. At the very least, the wheels of a fire safe should be removed after delivery. To protect a smaller burglary-resistant chest, install it inside a box or metal jacket which is bolted or anchored to the floor and then filled with concrete. The concrete jacket will add appreciably to the weight of the unit and severely complicate its unauthorized removal as well as side attacks by skilled and semiskilled safecrackers.

Skilled Attacks

The skilled safecracker is relatively rare in America, but there are a few in business. Their skills and specialties vary, and they have a wide variety of easily available equipment to choose from: high-speed drills, low-R.P.M./high torque drills, core-drills, carborundum cutters, saber-saws, cutting torches, oxy-arc lances, burning bars, and explosives. The only way to defeat safe burglars who work with such effective gear is to ensure that the actual attack will be time-consuming and fraught with the danger of discovery or capture. The less appealing the target, the more likely the professional will be to seek easier pickings.

If there is genuine concern about the possibility of skilled attack, the first and most obvious thing to do is to buy a burglary-resistant container with a rating equal to or exceeding the recommendation of a knowledgeable insurance agent. Today there are safes designed to put up a staunch fight against even the well-equipped and highly skilled professional safecrackers of the world. A reliable intrusion detection system is necessary; it should protect both the premises perimeter and the safe itself. If the safe is to be used commercially, a security policy should be established and rigorously adhered to. A security policy should define and expressly prohibit breaches of security such as those described earlier; i.e., writing down combination numbers or leaving the combination partially dialed—all such actions should be expressly forbidden.

Overcoming Safe-Opening Problems

Safe users often experience difficulty when trying to open a safe. The combination just doesn't seem to catch when it is dialed. This problem is on the surface an operational inconvenience, but there are security implications as well.

Safe users often learn to live with balky safes and combination locks—either the money for repairs and adjustment just isn't in the budget, or they may wonder if the fault is entirely the safe's. Many people hesitate to make an issue of a dialing problem for fear of exhibiting ignorance or inability to perform what is on the surface a simple rote task. Consequently, they accept the fact that they must dial and redial to open the safe each day, breathe a sigh of relief when the combination finally takes, and then do something which may constitute a breach of their employers' security policies. Rather than opening the safe, removing what is needed, closing the door and throwing the door bolts and rescrambling the combination, the safe user who has been irritated thus will leave the combination dialed for the day in order to avoid the added irritation of the dial-redial routine several more times during the business day.

This usually works nicely until that one day when everybody goes out for lunch and forgets that a turn of the door handle is all that is necessary to open the safe door. A lunchtime office prowler will find it hard to resist trying the safe handle, and will be rewarded for this small expenditure of energy. The scenario changes, but is generally the same—people who use safes and combination locks often will adapt to the inconveniences caused by malfunctioning locks, improper dialing procedures, or maintenance-starved mechanisms by shortchanging their own security procedures.

Another all-too-possible situation, the robbery, presents more grave considerations. If the same person who must routinely make several tries at opening the safe is ordered by armed robbers to open the safe immediately, the criminals could interpret fumbling as a delay tactic and react violently.

Those are only a few reasons why it is in the best interests of all concerned to have a properly-maintained security container and well-trained users of that container. The following information will help safe users open those balky safes with fewer tries. These guidelines should not be interpreted as another set of adaptive measures that will forestall necessary maintenance.

- When dialing a safe combination, stand squarely in front of the safe and look directly at the numbers. Viewing them from an angle will cause improper dial settings.
- Align the dial numbers exactly with the index mark at the top of the dial.
- Follow the safemaker's dialing instructions exactly. If the safe used does not have factory-supplied dialing instructions, contact the factory or a local safe dealer for some. Usually they will be supplied at no charge.
- Don't spin the dial—this accelerates wear and can cause breakage.

When the safe doesn't open after the combination has been correctly dialed, there are a few dialing techniques that usually get results. The first is to add one number to each of the combination numbers and dial as if this were the actual combination. For example, the combination numbers are 20-60-40.

Try 21-61-41, using the same dialing procedure as usual.

If adding 1 to each of the combination numbers doesn't help, next subtract 1 from each of the actual combination numbers. For example, with an actual combination of 20-60-40, the next combination to try would be 19-59-39. One these two procedures will work surprisingly often.

If neither of the first two procedures are successful, the next procedure is to progressively add 1 to each setting and dial the other numbers as usual, again using the normal dialing procedure. For example, if the correct combination is 20-60-40, the progression would be to dial 21-60-40, 20-61-40, then 20-60-41. If this procedure is unsuccessful, the next procedure is to progressively subtract 1 from each combination setting. For example, if the original combination is 20-60-40, dial 19-60-40, 20-59-40, 20-60-39.

These procedures will overcome lock wear and dialing errors—users may habitually and unconsciously misalign combination numbers at the dialing index mark. Interpret the success of any of these procedures as a signal that the mechanism needs inspection and service. It is a mistake to simply continue using the safe without correcting the condition that required using a set of numbers other than those actually set. If the condition that necessitated these dialing procedures was caused by a need for service or adjustment, a future lockout is a strong possibility if service is not obtained.

Appendix 7a

Rating Files, Safes, and Vaults*

GION GREEN

The final line of defense at any facility is at the high security storage areas where papers, records, plans

*From *Introduction to Security*, 3rd ed, by Gion Green (Stoneham, MA: Butterworths, 1981).

or cashable instruments, precious metals, or other especially valuable assets are protected. These security containers will be of a size and quantity which the nature of the business dictates.

The choice of the proper security container for

specific applications is influenced largely by the value and the vulnerability of the items to be stored in them. Irreplaceable papers or original documents may not have any intrinsic or marketable value, so they may not be a likely target for a thief; but since they do have great value to the owners, they must be protected against fire. On the other hand, uncut precious stones, or even recorded negotiable papers which can be replaced, may not be in danger from fire, but they would surely be attractive to a thief; they must therefore be protected.

In protecting property, it is essential to recognize that, generally speaking, protective containers are designed to secure against burglary *or* fire. Each type of equipment has a specialized function, and each type provides only minimal protection against the other risk. There are containers designed with a burglary-resistant chest within a fire-resistant container which are useful in many instances; but these, too, must be evaluated in terms of the mission.

Whatever the equipment, the staff must be educated and reminded of the different roles played by the two types of container. It is all too common for company personnel to assume that the fire-resistant safe is also burglary-resistant, and vice versa.

Files

Burglary-resistant files are secure against most surreptitious attack. On the other hand, they can be pried open in less than half an hour if the burglar is permitted to work undisturbed and is not concerned with the noise created in the operation. Such files are suitable for nonnegotiable papers or even proprietary information, since these items are normally only targeted by surreptitious assault.

Filing cabinets, with fire-rating of one hour, and further fitted with a combination lock, would probably be suitable for all uses but the storage of government classified documents.

Safes

Safes are expensive, but if they are selected wisely, they can be one of the most important investments in security. Safes are not simply safes. They are each designed to perform a particular job to a particular level of protection. To use fire-resistant safes for the storage of valuables—an all too common practice—is to invite disaster. At the same time, it

would be equally careless to use a burglary-resistant safe for the storage of valuable papers or records, since, if a fire were to occur, the contents of such a safe would be reduced to ashes.

Ratings

Safes are rated to describe the degree of protection they afford. Naturally, the more protection provided, the more expensive the safe will be. In selecting the best one for the requirements of the facility, an estimate of the *maximum* exposure of valuables or irreplaceable records will have to be examined along with a realistic appraisal of their vulnerability. Only then can a reasonable permissible capital outlay of their protection be achieved.

Fire-resistant containers are classified according to the maximum internal temperature permitted after exposure to heat for varying periods (Table 7a–1). A record safe rated 350-4 (formerly designated "A") can withstand exterior temperatures building to 2000 degrees Fahrenheit for four hours without permitting the interior temperature to rise above 350 degrees Fahrenheit.

The Underwriters' Laboratories (UL) tests which result in the various classifications are conducted in such a way as to simulate a major fire with its gradual build-up of heat to 2,000 degrees Fahrenheit and where the safe might fall several stories through the fire damaged building. Additionally, an explosion test simulates a cold safe dropping into a fire which has already reached 2,000 degrees Fahrenheit.

The actual procedure for the 350-4 rating involves the safe staying four hours in a furnace temperature that reaches 2,000 degrees Fahrenheit. The furnace is turned off after four hours but the safe remains inside until it is cool. The interior temperature must remain below 350 degrees Fahrenheit during the heating and cooling-out period. This interior temperature is determined by sensors sealed inside the safe in six specified locations to provide a continuous record of the temperatures during the test. Papers are also placed in the safe to simulate records. The explosion impact test is conducted with another safe of the same model which is placed for one-half hour in a furnace preheated to 2,000 degrees Fahrenheit. If no explosion occurs, the furnace is set at 1,550 degrees Fahrenheit and raised to 1,700 degrees Fahrenheit over a half-hour period. After this hour in the explosion test, the safe is removed and dropped thirty feet onto rubble. The safe is then returned to the furnace and reheated for one hour at 1,700 degrees Fahrenheit. The furnace and

Table 7a–1.   Fire Resistant Containers

UL Record Safe Classifications				
Classification	*Temperature*	*Time*	*Impact*	*Old Label*
350-4	2,000°F	4 hrs.	yes	A
350-2	1,850°F	2 hrs.	yes	B
350-1	1,700°F	1 hr.	yes	C
350-1	1,700°F	1 hr.	yes	A
(Insulated Record Container)				
350-1	1700°F	1 hr.	no	D
(Insulated Filing Device)				
UL Computer Media Storage Classification				
150-4	2,000°F	4 hrs.	yes	
150-2	1,850°F	2 hrs.	yes	
150-1	1,700°F	1 hr.	yes	
UL Insulated Vault Door Classification				
350-6	2,150°F	6 hrs.	no	
350-4	2,000°F	4 hrs.	no	
350-2	1,850°F	2 hrs.	no	
350-1	1,700°F	1 hr.	no	

Classification	*Description*	*Construction*	
TL-15	Tool resistant	Weight:	At least 750 pounds or anchored.
		Body:	At least 1 inch thick steel or equal.
		Attack:	Door and front face must resist attack with common hand and electric tools for 15 minutes.
TL-30	Tool resistant	Weight:	At least 750 pounds or anchored.
		Body:	At least 1 inch thick steel or equal.
		Attack:	Door and front face must resist attack with common hand and electric tools plus abrasive cutting wheels and power saws for 30 minutes.
TRTL-30*	Tool & torch resistant	Weight:	At least 750 pounds.
		Attack:	Door and front face must resist attack with tools listed above and oxy-fuel gas cutting or welding torches for 30 minutes.
TRTL-30X6	Tool & torch resistant	Weight:	At least 750 pounds.
		Attack:	Door and *entire body* must resist attack with tools and torches listed above plus electric impact hammers and oxy-fuel gas cutting or welding torches for 30 minutes.
TXTL-60	Tool, torch & explosive resistant	Weight:	At least 1,000 pounds.
		Attack:	Door and entire safe body must resist attack with tools and torches listed above plus 8 ounces of nitroglycerine or equal for 60 minutes.

*As of January 31, 1980, UL stopped issuing the TRTL-30 label, replacing it with the TRTL-30X6 label which requires equal protection on all six sides of the safe. Some manufacturers, however, continue to produce safes meeting TRTL-30 standards in order to supply lower priced containers which provide moderate protection against tool and torch attack.

safe are allowed to cool; the papers inside must be legible and uncharred.

350-2 record safes protect against exposure up to 1,850 degrees Fahrenheit for two hours. The explosion/impact tests are conducted at slightly less time and heat.

350-1 gives one hour of protection up to 1,700 degrees Fahrenheit and a slightly less vigorous explosion/impact test.

Computer media storage classifications are for containers which do not allow the internal temperature to go above 150 degrees Fahrenheit.

Insulated vault door classifications are much the same as for safes except that they are not subject to the explosion/impact test.

UL testing for burglary-resistance in safes does not include the use of diamond core drills, thermic lance, or other devices yet to be developed by the safecracker.

In some businesses, a combination consisting of a fire-resistant safe with a burglary-resistant safe welded inside may serve as a double protection for different assets, but in no event must the purposes of these two kinds of safes be confused if there is one of each on the premises. Most record safes have combination locks, relocking devices, and hardened steel lockplates to provide a measure of burglar resistance, but it must be reemphasized that record safes are designed to protect documents and other similar flammables against destruction by fire. They provide only slight deterrence to the attack of even unskilled burglars. Similarly, burglar-resistance is powerless to protect their contents in a fire of any significance.

Chapter 8
Security Lighting*

CHARLES M. GIRARD, Ph.D

The Miracle of Light

The idea that lighting can provide improved protection for people and facilities is as old as civilization. Equally old, however, is the problem of providing good lighting. Babylon dealt with the situation by "burning thick wicks in bowls of fat during crowded festival times."[1] Other approaches included those used in fourth-century Jerusalem, where crossroads were illuminated with wood fires; and in the tenth century, when the Arabs paved and lighted miles of streets in Cordova. These efforts improved throughout the years when, by the seventeenth century, both London and Paris made attempts to provide effective street lighting. In England, for example, street lights were provided at public expense where individual citizen action could not be expected; while in France, a program was initiated involving a system of guides with lanterns for which the night traveler would pay a small fee for the privilege of being protected by the light.[2]

Over the years, protective lighting evolved from candle and wood power to more sophisticated gas lights, with the first systems installed by the early 1800s. Finally, with the perfection and expanded use of electricity, the first electric filament street lights began appearing during the 1870s, increasing visibility and providing communities with a feeling of security.[3]

Police officers are, of course, aware of the effect that lighting has in reducing criminal opportunity. Nonetheless, it is interesting to note that a variety of studies and experiments have recently been conducted that have documented this fact. In December 1973, in response to national appeals for energy conservation, a small town in Indiana turned off its street lights. An immediate outbreak of vandalism and petty thefts occurred. The outbreak peaked with four firms in a commercial district being burglarized in a single evening. As a result, the conservationists' ideas were replaced by the realities of the community with public demand forcing a return to the properly lighted street.[4]

Clearly, this example is extreme. However, experience has shown the close relationship between illumination and crime. In fact, installation of improved, brighter street lighting in a number of cities has resulted in the following reported effects:[5]

St. Louis, Missouri	40 percent reduction in stranger-to-stranger crime; a 29 percent drop in auto theft; and a 13 percent reduction in commercial burglaries.
New York City, New York (public parks)	50 to 80 percent decrease in vandalism.
Detroit, Michigan	55 percent decrease in street crimes.
Washington, D.C.	25 percent decrease in robbery, compared with an 8 percent decrease city-wide.
Chicago, Illinois	85 percent decrease in robbery; a 10 percent decline in auto theft; and a 30 percent reduction in purse snatching.

---

*Adapted in part from "An Introduction to the Principles and Practices of Crime Prevention" by Koepsell-Girard and Associates, Inc. Also adapted in part from the revised edition, "An Introduction to the Principles and Practices of Crime Prevention," 1975, and "Principles and Practices of Crime Prevention for Police Officers," Texas Crime Prevention Institute, San Marcos, Texas. Permission to reproduce obtained from Charles M. Girard.

It is because of this clear relationship that street lighting intensity has been increased in many communities well above standards required for traffic safety. Street lights, however, are not the only type of lighting important to crime prevention and security. Other types of illuminating devices such as flood lights, search lights, and fresnel units can also be used to increase security around homes, businesses, and industrial complexes.

Transitional Lighting

Good lighting is the single most cost-effective deterrent to crime, but what is *good* lighting? Ideally, a good lighting system would be reproduced daylight. Realistically, however, the system must furnish a high level of visibility and at the same time a low level of glare. One of the most critical problems that needs to be considered is that the evenness of outdoor light is more important than an absolute level. Too much lighting can actually be a hazard in itself. Outdoor evening activity areas, such as a tennis court or playgrounds, can be hazardous because of the difficulty of seeing clearly into the surrounding area. When an individual leaves a brightly lighted area such as this and walks into a dark area, vision is momentarily reduced and vulnerability is increased. The opportunity for criminal attack is more of a likelihood when a situation like this exists.

Transitional lighting can be effectively used to minimize this hazard. Transitional lighting merely provides a gradual light level change from a brightly lighted area to a dark area. A lower light level can be employed adjacent to the bright area and this would help to provide a safe transition.

Understanding Lighting Technology: A Definition of Terms

Lighting technology involves a whole new language. Generally, the terms, definitions, and discussions that appear in most texts are designed for the lighting engineer who has a strong foundation in the jargon and specifics of this subject. The terms presented below give you a better understanding of the subject. Some of the basic lighting terms that a crime prevention officer should be familiar with include:

- *Watt*. A term used to measure the amount of electrical energy consumed.
- *Lumen*. The lamps (light bulbs) used in various lighting equipment are rated in lumens. The lumen is frequently used as a term to express the output of a light source.
- *Foot Candle*. This is another unit of illumination. It is defined as the illumination on a surface one square foot in area on which is uniformly distributed one lumen of light.
- *Coverage Factor*. The coverage factor is the minimum number of directions from which a point or area should be lighted, depending upon the use of the area. For example, a coverage factor of two is required for parking areas and for protective lighting to reduce the effect of shadows between automobiles, piles of materials, and similar bulky objects.
- *Quality of Lighting*. This term refers to the distribution of brightness and color rendition in a particular area. The term is generally used to describe how light can favorably contribute to visual performance, visual comfort, ease of scene, safety and aesthetics for specific tasks.
- *Reflector*. A device used to redirect the light by the process of reflection.
- *Refractor*. A glass band, globe or bowl designed to control the direction of the light by the use of prisms.
- *Luminaire*. A complete lighting device consisting of a light source, together with its globe, reflector, refractor, and housing. The pole, post, or bracket is not considered a part of the luminaire.
- *Visibility*. This term refers to the ability to be seen or to facilitate seeing or the distinctness with which objects may be observed. There are four visual factors that must be considered in planning effective security lighting—size, brightness, contrast, and time. Size is an important consideration in that larger objects reflect a greater amount of light. The comparative brightness of objects is important in that brightly polished silver reflects a greater intensity of light to an area than tarnished silver with the same lighting source. Contrast is important in that an object placed against a strongly contrasting background will seem to reflect more light to the eye than when the object and the background are alike. Time is critical because it requires less time to see accurately under good illumination than it does with poor lighting.[6]

General Types of Outside Security Lighting

There are four general types of outside security lighting. These are continuous lighting, standby lighting, movable lighting, and emergency lighting. Each is described briefly here.[7]

Continuous Lighting

Continuous lighting, the most familiar type of outdoor security lighting, can be designed to provide two specific results: glare projection or controlled lighting. The glare method of continuous lighting originated in prisons and correctional institutions where it is still used to illuminate walls and outside barriers. It has been described by some security experts as a *barrier of light* and is particularly effective for lighting boundaries around a facility and approaches to the site. This technique is normally used when the glare of lights directed across an area will not annoy or interfere with neighboring or adjacent properties. The utility behind this method is that a potential intruder has difficulty seeing inside an area protected by such a barrier; thus, the lighting method creates a strong visual and psychological deterrent. The guard, on the other hand, is able to observe the intruder, even at a considerable distance. Generally, flood lights are used in this way because the beam, although easy to direct, produces a great deal of glare that a possible intruder must face.

The controlled lighting approach, that is, the second type of continuous lighting, is generally employed in situations where due to surrounding property owners, nearby highways, or other limitations, it is necessary for the light to be more precisely focused. For example, the controlled lighting method would be used when the width of the lighted strip outside of an area must be controlled and adjusted to fit a particular need, such as illuminating a wide strip inside a fence and a narrow strip outside, or the lighting of a wall or roof. One of the most popular methods of controlled lighting for industrial and commercial use is the *surface method*. This method provides for the complete illumination of a particular area or structure within a defined site; not only are the perimeters of the property lighted, but so are the various parking areas, storage lots, and other locations that require improved security. Another advantage of the surface method is that the lighting units are directed at a building rather than away from it so that its appearance is enhanced at night. This same principle is used in some locations to illuminate the front and surroundings of residential sites.

Standby Lighting

A second type of outside security lighting is standby lighting. Standby lighting systems generally consist of continuous systems, but are designed for reserve or standby use, or to supplement continuous systems. These systems are engaged, either automatically or manually, when the continuous system is inoperative or the need for additional lighting arises. A standby system can be most useful to selectively light a particular portion of a site should prowlers or intruders be suspected, or to light an area merely for occasional use.

Movable or Portable Lighting

A third type of system uses movable lighting hardware. This system is manually operated and usually is made up of movable search or flood lights that can be located in selected or special locations which will require lighting only for a temporary period. The movable system can also be used to supplement continuous or standby lighting. This type of system would be particularly useful at a construction site.

Emergency Lighting

The fourth system is emergency lighting. Emergency lights may duplicate any or all of the other three types of lighting. Generally, the emergency lighting system is used in times of power failure or other emergencies when other systems are inoperative. The unique feature of the emergency system is that it is based on an alternative power source such as a gas power generator or batteries.

General Types of Lighting Sources

Listed below are the general lighting sources that are mostly used in providing indoor or outdoor lighting. Their characteristics are described and their lumen output is summarized in Table 8–1. The lighting sources discussed are: Incandescent, Mercury Vapor, Fluorescent, Metal Halide, and Sodium Vapor.

Incandescent

Incandescent lighting systems have low initial cost and provide good color rendition. However, incandescent lamps are relatively short in rated life (500–4,000 hours) and low in lamp efficiency (17–22 LPW) when compared to other lighting sources.

Table 8–1. Lamp Information

Lamp Type	Watts	Initial Lumens	Life (10 hours/start)
High Pressure Sodium	100	9,500	24,000
	150	16,000	24,000
	250	25,000–30,000	24,000
	400	50,000	24,000
	1,000	140,000	24,000
Mercury	100	3,850– 4,200	24,000
	100	6,500– 8,150	24,000
	175	9,500–12,100	24,000
	250	20,000–22,500	24,000
	400		
	1,000	57,000–63,000	24,000
Low Pressure Sodium	35	4,800	18,000
	55	8,000	18,000
	180	33,000	18,000
Incandescent	150	2,300– 2,700	600–1,500
	500	10,950	2,000
	1,000	21,600	1,000
	1,250	28,000	2,000
	1,500	34,400–35,800	1,000–2,000
Fluorescent*	70	4,700	12,000
	60	4,300	12,000
	110	7,000– 9,200	12,000
	215	14,500–17,000	12,000
Metal Halide	400	32,000	20,000
	1,000	95,000–98,000	12,000
	1,500	145,000	3,000

*Fluorescent ratings based on 3 hours per start.

Mercury Vapor

Mercury Vapor lamps emit a purplish-white color, caused by an electric current passing through a tube of conducting and luminous gas. This type of light is generally considered more efficient than the incandescent lamp and is widespread in exterior lighting. Approximately 75 percent of all street lighting is mercury vapor. Because mercury lamps have a long life (24,000+ hours) and good lumen maintenance characteristics, they are widely used in applications where long burning hours are customary. Good color rendition is provided and the lumen per watt is 31-63.

Metal Halide

Metal halide is similar in physical appearance to mercury vapor, but provides a light source of higher luminous efficiency and better color rendition. The rated life of 6,000 hours is short when compared to the 24,000+ of mercury lamps. It is used in applica-tions where color rendition is of primary importance and generally where the burning hours per year are low. Rated at 80–115 LPW.

Fluorescent

Fluorescent lights provide good color rendition, high lamp efficiency (67–100 LPW) as well as long life (9,000–17,000 hours). However, their long length, relative to their small diameter, causes luminaires to have very wide horizontal beam spreads. Fluorescent lamps are temperature sensitive and low ambient temperatures can decrease the efficiency. Fluorescent lights cannot project light over long distances and thus are not desirable as flood type lights.

High Pressure Sodium Vapor

This light source was introduced in 1965 and has gained acceptance for exterior lighting of parking

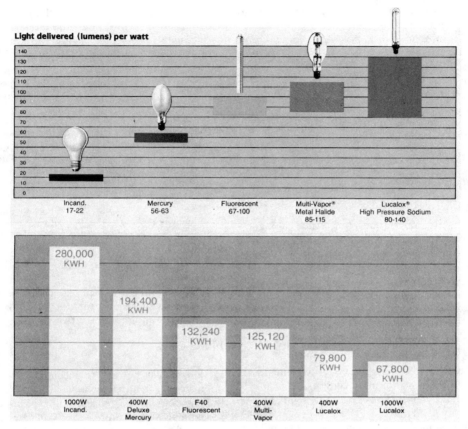

Figure 8–1. Some light sources convert electricity into light much more efficiently than others. The difference in light per watt (LPW) can have a dramatic effect on the energy required to operate a lighting system. (Courtesy of Geneal Electric).

areas, roadways, buildings, and industrial and commercial interior installations. Constructed on the same principle as mercury vapor lamps, they emit a golden-white to light pink color. High pressure sodium vapor lamps provide high lumen efficiency (80–140) and relatively good color rendition. Expected lamp life is up to 24,000 hours. Maintenance of light output is good and averages about 90 percent throughout its rated life (see Figure 8–1).

Low Pressure Sodium Vapor

This light source has similar principles of operation to other types of vapor lights but provides a much higher ratio (135–180). Color produced is yellow and is within a very narrow band of yellow wavelength. For this reason very poor color rendition is provided. LPSV lights have about 95 percent lumen maintenance throughout their rated life. The higher

wattage LPSV lamps increase to about 40″ in length and thus reduce optical control. LPSV will normally restrike within a few seconds should there be a momentary power loss.

Color Rendition Comparison

Color rendition affects your ability to discriminate, grade or select colors, and determine whether colors will appear natural. Good color rendition can improve worker confidence and productivity or enhance salability of merchandise.

- *Metal Halide Lamps.* Slightly emphasizes blues, yellows, greens. Has good overall color balance, comparable to daylight.

  Clear lamps give better color rendition than deluxe white mercury. Phosphor-coated lamps offer even better color rendition, comparable to cool white fluorescent.

- *High Pressure Sodium Vapor.* All colors present, but relatively weak in blues, greens, deep reds. Generally acceptable for all but the most color-critical tasks.
- *Mercury Lamps.* Clear lamp emphasizes green and blue, very weak in reds and warmer colors. Phosphor-coated lamps reveal all colors reasonably well but emphasize blues and greens.

Application Notes

Industrial Lighting:
- Metal halide lamps (phosphor-coated) for good color discrimination or judgments and especially where copper or brass are involved.
- Multi-vapor lamp (clear) provides crisp, cool highlights for improved visibility of cutting tools and abrasive processes.
- Lucalox lamp generally provides lowest cost of light, where precise color discrimination is not needed.

Commercial Lighting:
- Metal halide lamps for good color discrimination, natural appearance of merchandise.
- Clear multi-vapor lamps for cool highlights on diamonds, silverware.
- For best appearance, room colors should be selected under the light source used (especially with Lucalox lamps).

Area Lighting:
- Metal Halide lamps enhance appearance of green foliage, flowers, weathered bronze. Clear mercury also good for green foliage.
- Lucalox lamps enhance color of red/brown brick, other earth-tone colors.
- Multi-vapor lamps good for building and area floodlighting and color TV pick-up.

Further Comparison: Due to the improvements in lighting technology, Mercury vapor, although it provides good color rendition, is not as efficient as it should be to meet today's energy needs.

Guidelines for Recommending a Lighting System

The location of lights, the direction of beams, and the types of general and back up systems that you may recommend will be dependent upon a number of variables. These include such things as the size of the area to be secured, the amount of light needed to adequately protect the facility, the nature of other protective systems that the facility may already be using, and the type and nature of the facility to be protected, i.e., warehouse, retail outlet, commercial facility, or residential site. As a rule of thumb, the following formula should be considered:

> When traffic safety is considered, approximately one to two foot candles is a typical light level for high traffic streets and interchanges, while a level of .4 foot candles is typical for residential streets. Crime deterrent lighting, by comparison, usually approaches a lighting level of 10 foot candles. For reference, indoor office lighting usually approaches the 100 foot candle level, while moonlit streets are at the .02 foot candle level.[8]

Types of Lighting Equipment

Three types of lighting equipment generally used or associated with security lighting are: flood lights, street lights, and search lights.

Floodlights

Floodlights can be used to accommodate most outdoor security lighting needs, including the illumination of boundaries, fences, and buildings and for the emphasis of vital areas or particular buildings.

Floodlights are designated by the type and wattage of the lamp they use and the light distribution or the beam spread. The beam spread can be described in degrees or by the NEMA Type (see Table 8–2).

The standard incandescent PAR (parabolic aluminized reflector) lamps could be classified as floodlights. The beam widths available in PAR lamps are classified as spot, medium flood, or wide flood and can be obtained in a variety of sizes and wattages.

Incandescent floodlights are commonly used

Table 8–2. Outdoor Floodlight Designations

Beam Spread (Degrees)	NEMA Type
10 up to 18	1
18 up to 29	2
29 up to 46	3
46 up to 70	4
70 up to 100	5
100 up to 130	6
130 up	7

in commercial, industrial, and residential security situations where instant light is needed. The other type lamps—the gaseous discharge lamps—will take two to five minutes to warm up to full light output. In addition, if a voltage interruption occurs while they are operating, the gaseous types require a slightly longer period to relight.

Street Lights

Street lights have received the most widespread notoriety for their value in reducing crime. Generally, street lights are rated by the size of the lamp and the characteristics of the light distributed. More specifically, there are four types of lighting units that are utilized in street lighting. The oldest is the incandescent lamp. Although it is the least expensive in terms of purchase, it is the most expensive to operate in terms of energy consumed and the number needed. As such, incandescent lighting is generally recognized as the least efficient and economical type of street lighting for use today.[9]

The second type of lighting unit that has been acclaimed by some police officials as the best source available is the high pressure sodium vapor-lamp. This lamp produces more lumens per watt than most other types, is brighter, cheaper to maintain, and has acceptable color rendering—a point that should be considered strongly in traffic control lighting and also in crime situations.[10]

The third and fourth types of devices commonly used for street lighting are the mercury vapor and metal halide lamps. Both are bright and emit a good color rendition. However, some officials maintain that they are not as efficient as the newer high intensity sodium vapor lights. In addition, they are more expensive to operate and do not produce as many lumens of light per watt. Moreover, high intensity sodium vapor lighting has been claimed to produce almost double the illumination of any other lighting source. In addition, it is claimed as the best source of available street lighting for not only the protection of highway travelers, but also as a crime deterrent.[11]

Moreover, there are a number of street lighting systems and varieties that must be considered when recommending the adoption of street lighting as a crime prevention technique within a community. Placement and quality of lighting equipment depends in a large part on characteristics and needs of the areas to be served. For example, lighting that might be sufficient for a low-crime suburban area might not be adequate in a high-crime, inner city area. In addition, the value and effectiveness of an approved lighting program should not be judged only on the basis of measurable crime reduction. If streets and parks are more secure and inviting, they can help bring people together, enhance the community, and foster a sense of mutual independence and participation. Based on these arguments, the National Advisory Commission on Criminal Justice Standards and Goals developed the following recommendation on street lighting programs for high crime areas.

> Units of local government [should] consider the establishment of approved street lighting programs in high crime areas. The needs and wishes of the community should be a determining factor from the outset and public officials should carefully evaluate the experience of other jurisdictions before initiating their own programs.[12]

When discussing the type of street lighting system that a community should adopt, a crime prevention officer must keep a number of factors in mind. That is, the kind of light source and wattage needed to light a particular street depends on such variables as the height and placement of existing light poles, the amount of reflection offered by surrounding surfaces, and potential glare, among others. In addition, cost factors for installation and maintenance are also important. Finally, the nature of the community should be assessed—residential versus commercial versus industrial. Remember, realistically, few cities will have the resources to become involved in a total relighting program.

For the most part, critical areas of the city should be lighted, or old light sources should be replaced. It will be your responsibility to identify these areas after analysis of sites, crime statistics and other factors that you feel are pertinent to the question of security and the reduction of criminal opportunity.

Search Lights

Although offering more limited opportunities for application, search lights also provide a type of crime related lighting system. Search lights are generally of an incandescent light bulb type and are designed for simplicity and dependability. These lights commonly range from 12 to 24 inches in diameter, with a direct, but restricted beam. Power generally ranges from 250 watts to 3,000 watts.

In correctional institutions, search lights are usually permanently mounted. When used in industrial areas, trucking installations and similar areas, they are often on portable mounts. Portable battery-powered search lights are often used to supplement continuing light systems, or to serve construction sites prior to the installation of lighting of a more permanent nature.[13]

Automatic Lighting Control

Two basic means of automatic light control used to regulate the hours of operation are the *timer* and *photoelectric cell*. A timer is essentially an electric clock which operates a set of contacts through a preset turn on/turn off cycle. Some timers can be multiprogrammed to turn a light off and on numerous times within a 24-hour period. Timers are versatile in that they can also be used to operate other appliances such as a radio or television. Portable timers will cost between 5 and 15 dollars. The built-in type with more sophisticated programming and more capabilities costs considerably more.

The photoelectric cell is widely used to control outside lighting and also building exterior lighting. With the photocell, the amount of light falling on the cell determines whether the light is off or on. The photocell works on current and resistance principles. If there is a low light level hitting the photocell, the resistance of the cell is lowered and current will flow to energize the light. As the light level increases, the resistance also increases, cuts off the current and turns off the light. The advantage of the photocell over the timer is that the photocell automatically compensates for the change in times of sunset and sunrise. Photocells are built in as a component of many outdoor light fixtures or can be easily added to the fixture. One photocell can be used to control a number of lights or each light may be equipped with a photocell. For residential lighting, photocell units can also be supplied with the fixture or it can be added to an existing fixture.

Lighting and the Energy Crisis

Other than street lighting, no statistical accounts have been made as to the effect various types of lighting have on reducing crime. While the nation is facing an energy crisis and conservation recommendations have been common, there is a critical question to homeowners, industrialists, and businessmen as to whether or not it is cost-effective to reduce security lighting.

Before the question of reducing security lighting is considered, however, an analysis of the present system should be conducted to determine whether the most cost-effective lighting sources are being

utilized. As Figure 8–1 demonstrates, the amount of light delivered per watt differs considerably among the various lighting sources. To figure out your security lighting costs, use the following formula:

$$\frac{\text{Watts} \times \text{Hours}}{1{,}000} = \underline{\quad}\text{KWH} \times \underline{\quad}\text{¢ per/KWH}$$

A decision as to what light source is most efficient cannot be made without assessing the facility's lighting needs as well as the characteristics of the various types of lights.

Publicly supported systems, however, may be questioned in light of the current crisis. Generally street lights utilize about 0.7 percent of the electrical energy generated in this nation. The public's return for this consumption of now scarce energy is a general feeling that street lights have a deterrent effect on street crimes. This effect is somewhat sustained by research conducted by the Law Enforcement Assistance Administration and the fact that various communities which have installed improved street lighting in certain areas have reported reductions in the rate of street crime. Thus, it is the judgment of LEAA that any American community is justified in not taking any action toward reducing street lighting if it so chooses.[14]

Moreover, the use of security lighting as a crime deterrent has been supported, although in a limited fashion, through research and is accepted by the federal government as a viable tool in assisting a community in its fight against crime. As a crime prevention officer, it will be your duty to inform your city officials and various groups of residents and businessmen of the value of improved lighting. In fact, more and more police officials are beginning to see the need to assign high priority to improved lighting as a valuable and necessary technique to reduce criminal opportunity.[15]

References

1. Joyce Siemon and Larry Vardell, "A Bright Answer to the Crime and Energy Question," *The Police Chief*, Vol. SLI, No. 6, June, 1974, p. 53.
2. *Ibid.*
3. *Ibid.*
4. LEAA Emergency Energy Committee, *Energy Report No. 2: Street Lighting, Energy Conservation and Crime*, a report prepared by the U.S. Department of Justice, Law Enforcement Assistance Administration, Wash., D.C.: U.S. Government Printing, 1974, p. 3.
5. National Advisory Commission on Criminal Justice Standards and Goals, *Report on Community Crime Prevention* (Washington, D.C.: U.S. Government

Printing Office, 1973), pp. 198–199.

6. These definitions were adopted from the following sources by Koepsell-Girard Associates: Richard J. Healy, *Design for Security* (New York: John Wiley & Sons, Inc. 1968), p. 140 and General Electric, *Glossary of Terms Used in Street and Highway Lighting*, Hendersonville, S.C.: General Electric, 1973), pp. 1–5.

7. Richard J. Healy, *Design for Security* (New York: Wiley, 1968) pp. 142–145. The discussion on types of lighting was drawn from this publication. It should be noted that all reference to residential lighting was added to the discussion by Koepsell-Girard and Associates.

8. LEAA Emergency Energy Committee, Energy Report No. 2, p. 16.
9. Siemon and Vardell, p. 54.
10. *Ibid.*
11. *Ibid.*, pp. 54–55.
12. National Advisory Commission on Criminal Justice Standards and Goals, *Report on Community Crime Prevention*, pp. 199–200.
13. Healy, *Design for Security*, p. 151.
14. *Ibid.*, p. 151.
15. LEAA Emergency Energy Committee, *Energy Report No. 2*, p. 1.

Appendix 8a

Protective Lighting Requirement and Applications*

Protective lighting provides a means of continuing, during hours of darkness, a degree of protection approaching that maintained during daylight hours. Figure 8a–1 illustrates a floodlight often used for security purposes. This safeguard has considerable value as a deterrent to thieves and vandals and may make the job of the saboteur more difficult. It is an essential element of an integrated physical security program.

Requirements

A. Protective or security lighting needs at installations and facilities depend on each situation and the areas to be protected. Each situation requires careful study to provide the best visibility practicable for such security duties as identification of badges and people at gates, inspection of vehicles, prevention of illegal entry, detection of intruders outside and inside buildings and other structures, and inspection of unusual or suspicious circumstances.

B. When such lighting provisions are impractical, additional security posts, patrols, sentry dog patrols, or other security means will be necessary.

C. Protective lighting should not be used as a psychological deterrent only. It should be used on a perimeter fence line only where the fence is under continuous or periodic observation. Protective lighting may be unnecessary where the perimeter fence is protected by a central alarm system.

D. Protective lighting may be desirable for those sensitive areas or structures within the perimeter, which are under specific observation. Such areas or structures include pier and dock areas, vital buildings, storage areas, and vulnerable control points in communications, power, and water distribution systems. In interior areas where night operations are conducted, adequate lighting of the area facilitates detection of unauthorized persons approaching or attempting malicious acts within the area.

Characteristics

Lighting is inexpensive to maintain and, when properly employed, may reduce the need for security

*From Field Manual, No. 19–30, March 1, 1979, Department of the Army, Washington, D.C.

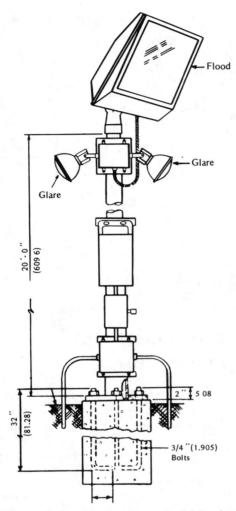

Figure 8a–1. Typical perimeter security lighting details. (From Physical Security Field Manual, No. 19–30, Dept. of the Army, Washington, D.C., 1979.)

forces. It may also provide personal protection for forces by reducing the advantages of concealment and surprise for a determined intruder. Security forces thus relieved may be used to better advantage elsewhere.

Protective lighting usually requires less intensity than working light, except for identification and inspection at authorized portals and in emergencies. Each area of an installation or facility presents its particular problem based on physical layout, terrain, atmospheric and climatic conditions, and the protective requirements. Data are available from the manufacturers of lighting equipment and from the Army Corps of Engineers, which will assist in designing a lighting system. Included in these data are:

- Descriptions, characteristics, and specifications of various incandescent, arc, and gaseous discharge lamps.
- Lighting patterns of the various luminaries.
- Typical layouts showing the most efficient height and spacing of equipment.
- Minimum protective lighting intensities required for various applications.

Security Director's Responsibility

A. Each security director must determine perimeter lighting needs dependent upon the threat, perimeter extremities, surveillance capabilities, and available guard forces.

B. Security director must insure that protective lighting is designed and employed to discourage unauthorized entry and to facilitate detection of intruders approaching or attempting to gain entry into protected areas.

C. The director must insure that protective lighting operates continuously during periods of reduced visibility, and that standby lighting is maintained and periodically tested for use during times of emergency and mobilization alerts.

Planning Considerations

In planning a protective lighting system, the physical security manager must give specific consideration to the following areas:

A. Cleaning and replacement of lamps and luminaries, particularly with respect to costs and means (such as ladders, mechanical buckets) required and available.

B. Advisability of including timers or photoelectric controls.

C. The effects of local weather conditions may be a problem in cases where flourescent units are used.

D. Fluctuating or erratic voltages in the primary power source.

E. Requirement for grounding of fixtures and the use of a common ground on an entire line to provide a stable ground potential.

F. Establishment of a ledger to maintain a burning-time (80 percent) record based on the life expectancy of the lamp. The ledger should contain, as a minimum, the following:

- Type and wattage of lamp
- Area, facility, or utility pole used
- Date of insertion
- Programmed date (based on life expectancy) for extraction and where used

G. Limited and exclusion areas:

(1) All limited and exclusion areas must have protective lighting on a permanent basis at perimeter and access control points. The lighting must be positioned to:

(a) Prevent glare that may temporarily blind the guards.

(b) Avoid silhouetting or highlighting the guards.

(2) Lighting in these areas must be under the control of the security force.

(3) The perimeter band of lighting must provide a minimum intensity of 0.2 foot candles, measured horizontally six inches (15.2 cm) above ground level, at least 30 feet (9.1 m) outside the exclusion area barrier. Lighting inside exclusion areas must be of sufficient intensity to enable detection of persons in the area or at structure entrance(s). Lighting at entrance control points must be of sufficient intensity to enable guards to compare and identify bearers and badges.

(4) Protective lighting systems will be operated continuously during hours of darkness.

(5) Protective lights should be employed so that the failure of one or more lights will not affect the operation of remaining lights.

H. Other suitable employment locations:

(1) Warehouses

(2) Motorpools/parks

(3) Commissaries

(4) Post exchanges/annexes

(5) Clubs

(6) Bank/finance and accounting office

(7) Medical/dental facilities

(8) Salvage yards

(9) Helipads and hangars

(10) Museums

(11) Gasoline dispensing areas

(12) Recreational areas (isolated/administrative areas)

(13) Housing areas

(14) Perimeter entrance exits (isolated/used)

Principles of Protective Lighting

Protective lighting should enable guard force personnel to observe activities around or inside an installation without disclosing their presence. Adequate lighting for all approaches to an installation not only discourages attempted unauthorized entry, but also reveals persons within the area (Table 8a–1).   However, lighting should not be used alone. It should be used with other measures such as fixed security posts or patrols, fences, and alarms. Other principles of protective lighting are listed:

A. Good protective lighting is achieved by adequate, even light upon bordering areas, glaring lights in the eyes of the intruder, and relatively little light on security patrol routes. In addition to seeing long distances, security forces must be able to see low contrasts, such as indistinct outlines of silhouettes, and must be able to spot an intruder who may be exposed to view for only a few seconds. All of these abilities are improved by higher levels of brightness.

B. In planning protective lighting, high brightness contrast between intruder and background should be the first consideration. With predominantly dark, dirty surfaces or camouflage-type painted surfaces, more light is needed to produce the same brightness around installations and buildings than when clean concrete, light brick, and grass predominate. When the same amount of light falls on an object and its background, the observer must depend on contrasts in the amount of light reflected. The ability of the observer to distinguish poor contrasts is significantly improved by increasing the level of illumination.

C. When the intruder is darker than the background, the observer sees primarily the outline or silhouette. Intruders who depend on dark clothing and even darkened face and hands may be foiled by using light finishes on the lower parts of buildings and structures. Stripes on walls have also been used effectively, as they provide recognizable breaks in outlines or silhouettes. Good observation conditions can also be created by providing broad lighted areas around and within the installation, against which intruders can be seen.

D. Two basic systems, or a combination of both, may be used to provide practical and effective protective lighting. The first method is to light the boundaries and approaches. The second is to light the area and structures within the general boundaries of the property.

E. To be effective, protective lighting should:

(1) Discourage or deter attempts at entry by

Table 8a–1. Lighting Specifications

Location	Foot-Candles on Horizontal Plane at Ground Level
Perimeter of outer area	0.15
Perimeter of restricted area	0.4
Vehicular entrances	1.0
Pedestrian entrances	2.0
Sensitive inner area	0.15
Sensitive inner structure	1.0
Entrances	0.1
Open yards	0.2
Decks on open piers	1.0

Type of area	Type of Lighting	Width of Lighted Strip (ft)	
		Inside Fence	Outside Fence
Isolated perimeter	Glare	25	200
Isolated perimeter	Controlled	10	70
Semi-isolated perimeter	Controlled	10	70
Nonisolated perimeter	Controlled	20–30	30–40
Building face perimeter	Controlled	50 (total width from building face)	
Vehicle entrance	Controlled	50	50
Pedestrian entrance	Controlled	25	25
Railroad entrances	Controlled	50	50
Vital structures	Controlled	50 (total width from structure)	

intruders. Proper illumination may lead a potential intruder to believe detection is inevitable.

(2) Make detection likely if entry is attempted.

Types of Lighting

The type of lighting system to be used depends on the overall security requirements of the installation concerned. Lighting units of four general types are used for protective lighting systems—continuous, standby, movable, and emergency.

A. Continuous lighting (stationary luminary). This is the most common protective lighting system. It consists of a series of fixed luminaries arranged to flood a given area continuously during the hours of darkness with overlapping cones of light. Two primary methods of employing continuous lighting are glare projection and controlled lighting:

(1) The glare projection lighting method is useful where the glare of lights directed across surrounding territory will not be annoying nor interfere with adjacent operations. It is a strong deterrent to a potential intruder because it makes it difficult to see the inside of the area. It also protects the guard by keeping her or him in comparative darkness and enabling the guard to observe intruders at considerable distance beyond the perimeter (see Figure 8a–1).

(2) Controlled lighting is best when it's necessary to limit the width of the lighted strip outside the perimeter because of adjoining property or nearby highways, railroads, navigable waters, or airports. In controlled lighting, the width of the lighted strip can be controlled and adjusted to fit the particular need, such as illumination of a wide strip inside a fence and a narrow strip outside; or floodlighting a wall or roof. This method of lighting often illuminates or silhouettes security personnel as they patrol their routes. (Figure 8a–2 shows controlled lighting.)

B. Standby lighting (stationary luminary). The layout of this system is similar to continuous lighting. However, the luminaries are not continuously lighted, but are either automatically or manually turned on only when suspicious activity is detected or suspected by the security force or alarm systems.

C. Movable lighting (stationary or portable). This

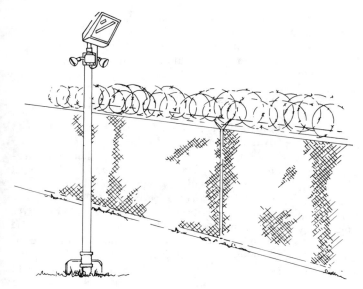

Figure 8a–2. Example of boundary lighting near adjoining property (controlled lighting). (From Physical Security Field Manual.)

type of system consists of manually operated movable searchlights which may be lighted either during hours of darkness or only as needed. The system normally is used to supplement continuous or standby lighting.

D. Emergency lighting. This system may duplicate any or all of the above systems. Its use is limited to times of power failure or other emergencies which render the normal system inoperative. It depends on an alternative power source, such as installed or portable generators, or batteries.

Lighting Applications

A. Fenced perimeters.
   (1) Isolated fenced perimeters are fence lines around areas where the fence is 100 feet or more from buildings or operating areas, plus the approach area is clear of obstruction for 100 or more feet outside the fence and is not used by other personnel. Both glare projection and controlled illumination are acceptable for these perimeters. Patrol roads and paths should be kept unlighted.
   (2) Semi-isolated fenced perimeters are fence lines where approach areas are clear of obstruction for 60 to 100 feet outside the fence and the general public or installation personnel seldom have reason to be in the area. Patrol roads and paths should be kept in relative darkness.
   (3) Nonisolated fence perimeters are fence lines

immediately adjacent to operating areas within the installation, other installations or to public thoroughfares, where outsiders or installation personnel may move about freely in the approach area. The width of the lighted strip in this case depends on the relative clear zone inside and outside the fence. It may not be practicable to keep the patrol area dark.

B. Building face perimeters consist of faces of buildings on or within 20 feet of the property line or area line to be protected, and where the public may approach the buildings. Guards may be stationed inside or outside of the buildings. Doorways or other insets in the building's face should receive special attention for lighting to eliminate shadows.

C. Active entrances for pedestrians and vehicles should have two or more lighting units with adequate illumination for recognition of persons and examination of credentials. All vehicle entrances should have two lighting units located to facilitate complete inspection of passenger cars, trucks, and freight cars as well as their contents and passengers. Semiactive and inactive entrances should have the same degree of continuous lighting as the remainder of the perimeter, with standby lighting of sufficient illumination to be used when the entrance becomes active. Gate houses at entrances should have a low level of interior illumination to enable guards to see better, increase their night vision adaptability, and avoid making them targets.

D. Areas and structures within the installation property line consist of yards, storage spaces, large open working areas, piers, docks, and other sensitive areas and structures.
  (1) Open yards (defined as unoccupied land only) and outdoor storage spaces (defined as material storage areas, railroad sidings, motor pools, and parking areas) should be illuminated as follows:
    (a) An open yard adjacent to a perimeter (between guards and fences) should be illuminated in accordance with the illumination requirements of the perimeter. Where lighting is deemed necessary in other open yards, illumination should not be less than 0.2 foot candle at any point.
    (b) Lighting units should be placed in outdoor storage spaces to provide an adequate distribution of light in aisles, passageways, and recesses to eliminate shadowed areas where unauthorized persons may conceal themselves.
  (2) Piers and docks should be safeguarded by illuminating both water approaches and the pier area. Decks on open piers should be illuminated to at least 1.0 foot candle and the water approaches (extending to a distance of 100 feet from the pier) to at least 0.5 foot candle. The area beneath the pier floor should be lighted with small wattage floodlights arranged to the best advantage with respect to piling. Movable lighting capable of being directed as required by the guards is recommended as a part of the protective lighting system for piers and docks. The lighting must not in any way violate marine rules and regulations; it must not be glaring to pilots. The U.S. Coast Guard should be consulted for approval of proposed protected lighting adjacent to navigable waters.
  (3) Critical structures and areas should be the first consideration in designing protective fencing and lighting. Power, heat, water, communications, explosive materials, critical materials, delicate machinery, areas where highly classified material is stored or produced, and valuable finished products need special attention. Critical structures or areas classified as vulnerable from a distance should be kept dark (standby lighting available), and those that can be damaged close at hand should be well lighted. The surroundings should be well lighted to force an intruder to cross a lighted area, and any walls should be lighted to a height of eight feet to facilitate silhouette vision.

Wiring Systems

Both multiple and series circuits may be used to advantage in protective lighting systems, depending on the type of luminary used and other design features of the system. The circuit should be arranged so that failure of any one lamp will not leave a large portion of the perimeter line or a major segment of a critical or vulnerable position in darkness. Connections should be such that normal interruptions caused by overloads, industrial accidents, and building or brush fires will not interrupt the protective system. In addition, feeder lines should be located underground (or sufficiently inside the perimeter in the case of overhead wiring) to minimize the possibility of sabotage or vandalism from outside the perimeter. The design should provide for simplicity and economy in system maintenance and should require a minimum of shutdowns for routine repairs, cleaning, and lamp replacement. It is necessary in some instances to install a duplicate wiring system.

Maintenance

A. Periodic inspections should be made of all electrical circuits to replace or repair worn parts, tighten connections, and check insulation. Luminaries should be kept clean and properly aimed.
B. Replacement lamps can be used in less sensitive locations. The actuating relays on emergency lines, which remain open when the system is operating from the primary source, need to be cleaned frequently since dust and lint collect on their contact points and can prevent their operation when closed.
C. The intensity of illumination and specification for protective lighting for fences or other antipersonnel barriers should meet the minimum requirements.

Power Sources

Power sources should meet the following criteria:

A. Primary—usually a local public utility.

B. Alternate—the following should be provided:
  (1) Standby batteries or gasoline-driven generators may be used.
     (a) If cost-effective, a system should start automatically upon failure of outside power.
     (b) Must insure continuous lighting.
     (c) May be inadequate for sustained operations; therefore, additional security precautions must be considered.
     (d) Tested to insure efficiency and effectiveness. The frequency and duration of tests depend on:

       • Mission and operational factors
       • Location, type and condition of equipment

       • Weather (temperature affects batteries very strongly)

  (2) Located within a controlled area for additional security.
  (3) Generator or battery-powered portable and/or stationary lights:
     (a) For use in a complete power failure
     (b) Includes alternate power supply
     (c) Available at designated control points for security personnel.

C. Security—a must.
  (1) Starts at the points where power feeder lines enter the installation or activity.
  (2) Continual physical security inspections of power sources is required to determine security measures and replacement of equipment (transformers, lines, etc.).

Chapter 9

Alarms: Intrusion Detection Systems

MIKE ROLF

Burglary is a big business. The latest crime figures available from the FBI show that four burglaries occur every minute of every day. Moreover, the crime figures show a staggering rate of increase for burglaries involving private homes.

It is no wonder then that many homeowners and businesspeople are giving serious consideration to electronic alarm protection. Unfortunately, some people in the burglar alarm industry are out to take advantage of the anxious buyer. These operators are in the market to make a fast dollar and the unwary customer who buys what seems to be a bargain too often ends up being cheated.

The selection of a proper alarm system is not a simple matter, because the needs of each individual homeowner or businessperson is different, like a set of fingerprints. Some factors which determine the requirements of an individual alarm system and the questions which must be answered when selecting a system include:

- The threat or risk—what is the system to protect against?
- The type of sensors needed—what will be protected?
- What methods are available to provide the level of protection needed?
- The method of alarm signal transmission—how is the signal to be sent and who will respond?

Most of the confusion regarding intrusion detection systems is a result of the variety of methods available to accomplish the proper protection needed. The combination of detection ranges into the thousands. An intrusion detection system may serve to deter a would-be intruder. However, the primary function of the alarm system is to signal the presence of an intruder. An intrusion detection

system can be just a portion of the overall protection needed. Many large businesses supplement them with security guards and other security personnel. The successful operation of any type of an alarm system depends upon its proper installation and maintenance by the alarm installing company and the proper use of the system by the customer.

Components of Alarm Systems

Sensing devices are used in the actual detection of an intruder   (see Figures 9–1 and 9–2).   They each have a specific purpose and can be divided into three categories: perimeter protection, area/space protection, and object/spot protection.

Perimeter Protection

Perimeter protection is the line in the defense to detect an intruder. The most common points equipped with sensing devices for perimeter protection are doors, windows, vents, skylights, or any opening to a business or home. Since over 80 percent of all break-ins occur through these openings, most alarm systems provide this type of protection. The major advantage of perimeter protection is its simple design. The major disadvantage is that they protect only the openings. If the burglar bursts through a wall, comes through the ventilation system, or stays behind after closing, perimeter protection is useless.

1. *Door switches (contacts).* These devices are usually magnet-operated switches. They are installed on a door or window in such a way that opening

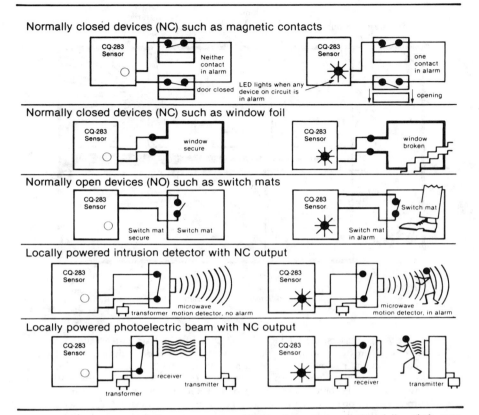

Figure 9–1.   Typical application of the use of magnetic contacts, window foil, switch mats, motion detection, and photoelectric beam. (Courtesy of Aritech Corporation.)

the door or window causes the magnet to move away from the contact switch which activates the alarm. They can be surface-mounted, recessed into the door and frame. A variety of types of switches are manufactured for all types of doors or windows.

2. *Metallic foil (window tape)*. This method is widely used to detect glass breakage in show windows, doors, and transoms. When the glass cracks and breaks the foil, it interrupts the low voltage electrical circuit and activates the alarm.

3. *Glass break detectors (window bugs)*. These detectors are shocksensing devices which are attached to the glass and sense the breakage of the glass by shock or sound.

4. *Wooden screens*. These devices are made of wooden dowel sticks assembled in a cage-like fashion no more than four inches from each other. A very fine, brittle wire runs in the wooden dowels and frame. The burglar must break the doweling to gain entry and thus break the low voltage electrical circuit, causing the alarm.

These devices are primarily used in commercial applications.

5. *Window screens*. These devices are similar to regular wire window screens in a home, except that a fine, coated wire is a part of the screen and when the burglar cuts the screen to gain entry, the flow of low voltage electricity is interrupted and causes the alarm. These devices are used primarily in residential applications.

6. *Lace and paneling*. The surfaces of door panels and safes are protected against entry by installing a close lace-like pattern of metallic foil or a fine brittle wire on the surface. Entry cannot be made without first breaking the foil or wire, thus activating the alarm. A panel of wood is placed over the lacing to protect it.

Area/Space Protection

These devices protect interior spaces in a business or home. They protect against intrusion whether or

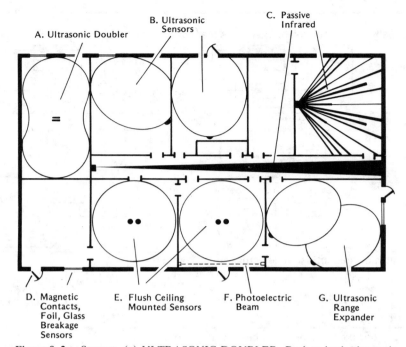

A. Ultrasonic Doubler

B. Ultrasonic Sensors

C. Passive Infrared

D. Magnetic Contacts, Foil, Glass Breakage Sensors

E. Flush Ceiling Mounted Sensors

F. Photoelectric Beam

G. Ultrasonic Range Expander

Figure 9–2. Sensors. (a) ULTRASONIC DOUBLER. Back-to-back ultrasonic transceivers provide virtually double the coverage of single detectors at almost the same wiring and equipment cost. With more than 50 by 25 feet of coverage, the doubler is your best value in space protection. (b) ULTRASONIC SENSORS. Easy to install, no brackets needed. Mount it horizontally or vertically or in a corner, surface or flush, or with mounting feet on a shelf. Each UL listed sensor protects a threedimensional volume up to 30 feet wide and high. (c) PASSIVE INFRARED. For those zones where the lower cost ultrasonic sensor is inappropriate, there is no need to buy a complete passive infrared system. Both ultrasonic and passive infrared can be used in the same system. (d) MAGNETIC CONTACTS, FOIL, GLASS BREAKAGE. SENSORS. The building's perimeter protection detectors can be wired into the system via universal interface sensor. There is no need for running a separate perimeter loop. (e) FLUSH CEILING MOUNTED SENSORS. Only the two small two-inch diameter transducer caps are visible below the ceiling tiles. Designed for where minimum visibility is needed for aesthetic or security purposes. (f) PHOTOELECTRIC BEAM. The universal interface sensor allows the connection of any NO or NC alarm device into the system for zoned annunciation. It can be used with photoelectric beams, switch matting, microwave motion detectors, and many other intrusion detectors. (g) ULTRASONIC RANGE EXPANDER. Adding an ultrasonic range expander can increase the coverage of an ultrasonic sensor by 50 to 90 percent, depending on where it is positioned and the surrounding environment. (Courtesy of Aritech Corporation.)

not the perimeter protection was violated. It is particularly effective for a stay-behind intruder or the burglar who cuts through the roof or bursts a block wall. Space protection devices are only a part of the complete alarm system. They should always be supplemented with perimeter protection. The major advantage of space protection devices is that they provide a highly sensitive, invisible means of detec-

tion. The major disadvantage is that improper application and installation by the alarm company can result in frequent false alarms (see Table 9–1).

The types of area/space protection are:

1. *Photoelectric eyes (beams).* These devices transmit a beam across a protected area. When an intruder interrupts the beam, the beam circuit is

Table 9–1.   Motion Sensor Survey Checklist

Environmental and Other Factors Affecting Sensor Usage	(Circle one)	Effect on Sensor			Recommendations and Notes
		Ultrasonics	Microwave	Passive I/R	
1. If the area to be protected is enclosed by thin walls, or contains windows, will there be movement close by the outside of this area?	Yes No	None	Major	None	Avoid using a microwave sensor unless it can be aimed way from thin walls, glass, etc., which can pass an amount of microwave energy.
2. Will protection pattern see sun, moving headlamps, or other sources of infrared energy passing through windows?	Yes No	None	None	Major	Avoid using a passive I/R sensor unless pattern can be positioned to avoid rapidly changing levels of infrared energy.
3. Does area to be protected contain HVAC ducts?	Yes No	None	Moderate	None	Ducts can channel microwave energy to other areas. If using a microwave sensor, aim it away from duct openings.
4. Will two or more sensors of the same type be used to protect a common area?	Yes No	None	None (see note)	None	Note: Adjacent units must operate on different frequencies.
5. Does area to be protected contain fluorescent or neon lights that will be on during Protection-On period?	Yes No	None	Major	None	Microwave sensor, if used, must be aimed away from any fluorescent or neon light within 20'.
6. Are incandescent lamps that are cycled on-and-off during protection-on period included in the protection pattern?	Yes No	None	None	Major	If considering use of passive I/R sensor, make a trial installation and, if necessary, redirect protection pattern away from incandescent lamps.
7. Must protection pattern be projected from a ceiling?	Yes No	None, but only for ceiling heights up to 15'	Major	Major	Only *ultrasonic* sensors can be used on a ceiling, but height is limited to 15'. At greater ceiling heights, either (1) use rigid ceiling brackets to suspend sensor so as to maintain 15' limitation, or (2) in large open areas try using a microwave sensor mounted high on a wall and aimed downward.

Table 9–1.   *Continued*

Environmental and other Factors Affecting Sensor Usage	(Circle one)	Effect on Sensor			Recommendations and Notes
		Ultrasonics	**Microwave**	**Passive I/R**	
8. Is the overall structure of flimsy construction (corrugated metal, thin plywood, etc.)?	Yes No	Minor	Major	Minor	*Do not* use a *microwave* sensor! Where considerable structural movement can be expected, use a rigid mounting surface for ultrasonic or passive infrared sensor.
9. Will protection pattern include large metal objects or wall surfaces?	Yes No	Minor	Major	Minor (major if metal is highly polished)	1. Use ultrasonic sensor. 2. Use passive I/R sensor.
10. Are there any nearby radar installations?	Yes No	Minor	Major when radar is close and sensor is aimed at it.	Minor	Avoid using a microwave sensor.
11. Will protection pattern include heaters, radiators, air conditioners, etc.?	Yes No	Moderate	None	Major, when rapid changes in air temperature are involved.	1. Use ultrasonic sensor, but aim it away from sources of air turbulence (desirable to have heaters, etc., turned off during Protection-On period.) 2. Use microwave sensor.
12. Will area to be protected be subjected to ultrasonic noise (bells, hissing sounds, etc.)?	Yes No	Moderate, can cause problems in severe cases	None	None	1. Try muffling noise source and use an ultrasonic sensor. 2. Use a microwave sensor. 3. Use passive infrared sensor.
13. Will protection pattern include drapes, carpets, racks of clothing, etc.?	Yes No	Moderate, reduction in range	None	Minor	1. Use ultrasonic sensor if some reduction in range can be tolerated. 2. Use a microwave sensor.
14. Is the area to be protected subject to changes in temperature and humidity?	Yes No	Moderate	None	Major	1. Use an ultrasonic sensor unless changes in temperature and humidity are severe. 2. Use a microwave sensor.
15. Is there water noise from faulty valves in the area to be protected?	Yes No	Moderate, can be a problem	None	None	1. If noise is substantial, try correcting faulty valves and use an ultrasonic sensor.

Table 9–1. *Continued*

Environmental and other Factors Affecting Sensor Usage	(Circle one)	Effect on Sensor			Recommendations and Notes
		Ultrasonics	Microwave	Passive I/R	
					2. Use a microwave sensor. 3. Use a passive I/R sensor.
16. Will protection pattern see moving machinery, fan blades, etc.?	Yes No	Major	Major	Minor	1. Have machinery, fans, etc. turned off during Protection-On period. 2. Use careful placement of ultrasonic sensor. 3. Use passive infrared sensor.
17. Will drafts or other types of air movement pass through protection pattern?	Yes No	Major	None	None, unless rapid temperature changes are involved	1. If protection pattern can be aimed away from air movement, or if air movement can be stopped during Protection-On period, use an ultrasonic sensor. 2. Use a microwave sensor. 3. Use a passive I/R sensor.
18. Will protection pattern see overhead doors that can be rattled by wind?	Yes No	Major	Major	Minor	1. If protection pattern can be aimed away from such doors, use an ultrasonic sensor. 2. Use a passive I/R sensor.
19. Are there hanging signs, calendar pages, etc. which can be moved by air currents during Protection-On period?	Yes No	Major	Major	Moderate, can be a problem	1. Use ultrasonic sensor, but aim pattern away from objects that can move or remove such objects. 2. Use passive infrared sensor.
20. Are there adjacent railroad tracks that will be used during Protection-On period?	Yes No	Major	Minor	Minor	A trial installation is required if using an ultrasonic sensor.
21. Can small animals (or birds) enter protection pattern?	Yes No	Major	Major	Major (particularly rodents)	Install a physical barrier to prevent intrusion by animals or birds.
22. Does area to be protected contain a corrosive atmosphere?	Yes No	Major	Major	Major	None of these sensors can be used.
Approximate ADT cost per square foot of coverage:	——	(3¢)	(4¢)	(6¢)	

disrupted and the alarm is initiated. Photoelectric devices use a pulsed infrared beam that is invisible to the naked eye. Some units have a range over 1,000 feet and can be used outdoors.

2. *Ultrasonic detectors.* Movement of an intruder in a protected area disrupts a high-pitched sound (ultrasonic) wave pattern which, in turn, activates the alarm signal. Ultrasonic motion sensors generate signals in the range between 19 and 40 kilohertz, which is above the frequencies that the average human can hear. Ultrasonic energy is contained completely in the area it is operating. It will not penetrate walls or windows but is absorbed by carpet, draperies, and acoustical tile. Obstructions within a room will reflect the ultrasonic energy and distort its shape pattern. Typical detection range of ultrasonic units is 20 feet wide by 30 feet long in a room with a ceiling up to 12 feet high. More complex ultrasonic systems can detect movement anywhere within the protected area. Ultrasonic devices can be mounted on either the ceiling or the wall. Ultrasonic detectors can be prone to false alarms due to excessive air currents and other extraneous ultrasonic noises. Proper application and installation of this equipment is very important.

3. *Microwave detectors.* These detectors use high frequency radio waves (microwaves) to detect movement. The most commonly used frequencies range between 915 and 10.525 megahertz. The microwave energy will penetrate and pass through all building construction materials (wood, sheet rock, cinder block, plastic, glass and brick) and is reflected by metal. Because microwave energy will penetrate, application and installation are very critical. Microwave has a much greater range than ultrasonic and can be used outdoors.

4. *Infrared detectors.* These detectors are passive sensors, because they do not transmit a signal for an intruder to disturb. Rather, a source of moving infrared radiation (the intruder) is detected against the normal radiation/temperature environment of the room. They sense the radiation from a human body moving through the optical field of view of the detector.

5. *Pressure mats.* These mats are basically mechanical switches. Pressure mats are most frequently used as a back-up system to perimeter protection. When used as traps they can be hidden under the carpet in front of a likely target or in hallways where an intruder would travel.

6. *Sound sensors.* Sound sensors detect intrusion by picking up on the noise created by the burglar during an attempt to break into a protected area. These sensors consist of a microphone and an electronic amplifier/processor. When the sound level increases beyond the limit normally encountered, the unit signals an alarm. Some units have a pulse-counting and time-interval feature. Other types have the capacity for actually listening to the protected premises from a central monitoring station.

Object/Spot Detection

Object/spot detection is used to detect the action or presence of an intruder at a single location. It provides direct security for things. Such a detection method is the final stage of an in-depth system for protection. The objects which are most frequently protected include: safes, filing cabinets, desks, art objects, models, statues and expensive equipment.

The types of object/spot protection are:

1. *Capacitance/proximity detectors.* The object being protected becomes an antenna, electronically linked to the alarm control. When an intruder approaches or touches the object-antenna, an electrostatic field is unbalanced and the alarm is initiated. Only metal objects can be protected in this manner.

2. *Vibration detectors.* These devices utilize a highly sensitive and specialized microphone called an electronic vibration detector (EVD). The EVD is attached directly to the object to be protected. They can be adjusted to detect a sledge hammer attack on a concrete wall or a delicate penetration of a glass surface. They will alarm only when the object is moved, whereas capacitance devices will detect when the intruder is close to the protected object. Other types of vibration detectors are similar to tilt switches used in pinball machines.

Alarm Controls

All sensing devices are wired into the alarm control panel that receives their signals and processes them. Some of the most severe burglary losses are caused not by a failure in equipment but simply by someone turning off the alarm system. The type of control panel needed is dependent upon the sophistication of the overall intrusion alarm system. Some control panels provide zoning capabilities for separate annunciation of the sensing devices. It may also provide the low voltage electrical power for the sensing devices.

Included in the control panel is the backup or standby power in the event of an electrical power failure. Batteries are used for standby power. Some equipment uses rechargeable batteries, whereby the control has a low-power charging unit—a trickle charger—and maintains the batteries in a fully-charged condition.

The alarm control unit will normally incorporate a key-operated switch to turn the system on or off. Some control panels will accept a remote on-off switch so that the system can be turned on and off at more than one location.

If the alarm control panel is connected to a central monitor station, the times that the system is turned on and off are recorded and logged. When the owner enters the building in the morning, the alarm is activated. If this happens at a time that has been prearranged with the central station, it is considered a normal opening. If it happens at any other time, the police are dispatched.

It is possible for the owner or other authorized persons to enter the building during the closed times. The person entering must first call the central station and identify himself by a special coding procedure. Records are kept at the central station company for these irregular openings and closings.

Tamper protection is a feature that provides an alarm signal to be generated when the system is compromised in any way. Tamper protection can be designed into any or all portions of the alarm system (control panel, sensing devices, loop wiring, alarm transmission facilities).

Alarm Transmission/Signalling

The type of alarm transmission/signalling system used in a particular application depends upon the location of the business or residence, the frequency of police patrols, and the ability of the customer to afford the cost. Remember that, after deterrence, the purpose of an alarm is to summon the proper authorities to stop a crime during the act of commission or lead to the apprehension of the intruder. It is very important that the response by proper authorities to the alarm comes in the shortest possible time. There are four types of alarm signalling systems in general use:

1. *Local alarm.* A bell or light indicates that an attempted or successful intrusion has taken place. The success of the system relies on some-

one hearing or seeing the signal and calling the responsible authorities. The local alarm also serves to notify burglars that they have been detected. This may be advantageous in frightening off the less experienced intruder.

2. *Central station system.* The alarm signal is transmitted over telephone lines to a specially constructed building called the central station. Here, trained operators are on duty 24 hours a day to supervise, record, and maintain alarms. Upon receipt of an alarm, the police are dispatched, and, in some cases, the alarm company guard or runner. This recordkeeping function and guard-response assure thorough documentation of any alarm signal. Alarm transmissions to the central station are of six types. Each type of transmission has certain advantages and disadvantages which must be considered in determining the risk. The transmission of an alarm signal to the UL-listed central station is generally regarded as the most reliable method for reducing burglary losses.

a. *Direct wire systems.* High risk locations (banks, jewelers, furriers) are generally protected with a direct wire system. A single dedicated telephone line is run from the protected premises to the central station or police station where a separate receiver supervises only that alarm. A fixed DC current is sent from the central station to the protected premises and is read on a meter at the central station. The advantage of a direct wire system is that problems can be very quickly traced to a specific alarm system. This makes compromising the alarm signal by a professional burglar more difficult.

The disadvantage of such a system is the higher cost of leased telephone lines. This becomes a more serious economic factor as the distance from the central station to the protected premises increases. Proper transmission of the alarm signal to the central station is essential. Problems can result on these telephone lines from shorts and broken wires. Most central stations expect these problems and are well equipped to rapidly make repairs. However, some of today's burglars are more sophisticated. They know they can prevent the transmission of the alarm signal to the central station by shunting or jumpering out the leased telephone line. Special methods are used by the alarm company to protect against jumpering of the alarm signal. Alarm systems having this special line security are classified as *AA Grade Central Station* alarms by Underwriters Laboratories.

b. *Circuit (party line) systems.* Alarm signals transmitted over circuit transmission systems can be compared to a party line where several alarm customers defray the cost of the telephone line by sharing it. With a circuit transmission system, as many as 15 alarm transmitters may send alarm signals to a single receiving panel at the central station over the same line, or loop. The alarm signals at the central station are received on strips of paper. Each alarm has a distinct code to identify it from the others. The advantage of a circuit-loop alarm transmission system is the lower telephone line cost. Thus, a central station can make its services available to more customers by subdividing the cost of the telephone line among different users. The disadvantage of circuit-loop alarm transmission systems is that problems on a leased telephone line are more difficult to locate than with a direct wire system.

c. *Multiplex systems.* This system is the newest method used by central station companies to receive alarm signals. The multiplex system is designed to reduce leased telephone line charges while at the same time providing a higher degree of line security than circuit-loop alarms. Multiplex systems have introduced data processing—computer based techniques—to the alarm industry.

d. *Digital communicators.* This computer-based type of alarm transmission equipment sends its signal through the regular switch line telephone network. The alarm signal transmitted is a series of coded electronic pulses that can only be received on a computer-type terminal at the central station.

The signals are then displayed visually and also provide a hard copy print-out of the activity received. The receiving terminal can also provide additional data for the alarm operator.

e. *Telephone dialer.* The dialer delivers a prerecorded, verbal message to a central station, answering service, or police department when an alarm is activated. Many of the earlier tape dialers were a source of constant problem to police departments, because of their unsophistication. Basically, they were relabeled tape recorders. It was not uncommon for the tape dialer to play most of the

message before the police could answer the phone. The police knew that an alarm signal had been sent, but did not know its location. The newer, modern tape dialers have solved these problems and are reasonably reliable.

f. *Radio signal transmission.* This method takes the alarm signal from the protected premises and sends it via radio signals to either a central station or police dispatch center. Additionally, the alarm signal can be received in a police patrol car.

Alarms Deter Crime

Those who find fault with the alarm industry for too many false calls have some obvious justification. Indeed, the alarm field suffers from a few high pressure salesmen, poor installers, untrained servicers, and other causes of false alarms. False calls waste police resources. They also waste alarm company resources. The police and alarm industry are acutely aware of this, and both have initiated efforts across the country to relieve the dilemma.

Yet, there are other problems that dwarf false alarms. Foremost, there is crime; burglary alone cost the public $1.4 billion in 1987. The average victim lost $750.

Of course, the police community is more aware of this than anyone. Their awareness decreases, though, when it comes to the value of alarm systems. This may be fallout from their rage over false alarms.

The police should set aside that anger for a time and attempt to see the value of alarm systems in the war on crime. It is a fact that alarm systems prevent crime. These electronic and electrical systems deter burglars, arsonists, vandals, and other criminals. They are both the most effective and most economical crime prevention tool available.

Consider a few statistics:

- Premises protected by alarm systems are burglarized from one-half to one-sixth as often as those without alarms.
- Burglar alarm systems currently protect about 1.4 million residences and about 2.2 million business establishments across the nation.
- Police budgets have been reduced in most locales and frozen in others, while private investment in alarm security is growing yearly by about 10 percent.
- Alarm systems in 1987 helped police capture from 25,000 to 30,000 criminals in the act of committing a crime, according to best estimates available to

the National Burglary and Fire Alarm Association (NBFAA).

- Criminals caught in the act of committing a crime are nearly always convicted, and at costs substantially lower than the funds spent investigating and prosecuting those arrested away from the scene of the crime.

Alarm systems are a prime deterrent to burglars. For this reason, the Scarsdale (New York) police have been encouraging residents to install alarm systems ever since the late 1960s. The attitude of Scarsdale police rests on a decade of favorable experience with alarm systems. The experience began when they allowed about half of the city's 900 home alarm systems to be connected directly to the station.

Burglary statistics over the five-year period of 1967–71 indicate that the policy change paid off. During that period, the number of burglaries in Scarsdale ranged from 58 percent below the national average in 1969 to 23 percent below in 1971, according to the Uniform Crime Reports.

These statistics are especially significant, because Scarsdale—a quiet, tree-lined suburb of 5,440 private homes, where the average family earns about $40,000 yearly—is a high target community, a burglar's paradise.

Most certainly, the low crime rates were not due entirely to burglar alarms. Yet, the role they did play is evident from the stark fact that homes equipped with alarms were burglarized only 15 times during that five-year period, in which a total of 423 burglaries took place, according to alarm companies who serve the area. Yearly, unprotected homes suffered five times as many attacks as those monitored by alarm systems, 16 per 1,000 contrasted with 3.3 per 1,000.

Such striking rate differences persist to this day. During the three-year period of 1975–77 when 392 burglaries occurred, alarmed homes were burglarized only 24 times, for a yearly rate of 8.4 in 1,000, according to the Scarsdale police. This is contrasted with a yearly attack rate of 27.4 per 1,000 on unprotected homes.

Another case study produced similar results. This study covered Multnomah County, Oregon, an urban area encompassing Portland, an environment far different from the serene, affluent suburb of Scarsdale.

In Multnomah County, the police station monitored about 5,200 alarm systems for one year: March, 1976 through February, 1977. In that time, commercial premises without alarms were burglarized at a rate of 80 per 1,000 while alarmed premises experienced exactly half that rate.

Even more striking were the findings on residential attacks: Burglars hit unprotected homes six times as often as those protected by alarm systems. The rates were 6 attacks per 1,000 alarmless homes versus 1 per 1,000 for alarmed homes.

The view expressed by skeptics that alarms fail to deter crime and provide, at best, a false sense of security, does not consider common sense and experience. The fact that alarms proved a highly effective deterrent in two locales as different as Scarsdale and Multnomah County makes a strong case for their value in preventing crime across the nation.

The National Crime Prevention Institute has long endorsed alarm systems as the best available crime deterrent. This educational institution realizes that most criminals fear alarm systems. They much prefer to break into an unprotected building rather than risk capture by a hidden sensor.

Problem deterrence is the alarm business, a field which, in fact, extends far beyond protecting premises from burglary. Crisis prevention duties of alarm firms range from monitoring sprinkler systems and fire sensors, and watching temperature levels in buildings, to supervising industrial processes such as nuclear fission and the manufacturing of dangerous chemicals.

To alarm companies, deterrence becomes a sophisticated and specialized art. In the area of crime prevention, companies take pride in spotting potential weaknesses in a building and designing an alarm system that will confound the most intelligent criminals.

Crime prevention, in fact, is the area where police need the most help. The rise in burglary and other crimes has often put police officers in a response posture.

By protecting such places as hospitals, office buildings and schools, alarm systems free up police resources and enable patrol officers to spend more time in areas with high crime rates and with fewer premises protected by alarm systems. Police may also dedicate more officers to apprehending criminals. In this manner, police and alarm companies can work together, complementing one another, and waging a mutual war on crime.

Critics have suggested that adding more police officers would answer the need for more effective crime prevention. To fill this need, the Aerospace Corporation, in a 1976 report, "Survey and System Concepts for a Low Cost Burglary Alarm System for Residences and Small Businesses," estimated that police manpower would have to nearly double, at an extra taxpayers' cost of about $5 billion annually. Such dollar figures are prohibitive.

One fact is certain: those thousands of alarm arrests saved the courts and detectives considerable time and the tax-paying public many millions of dollars.

False Alarms

The full crime prevention potential in alarm systems has yet to be realized. Relatively speaking, the number of premises not protected by alarms is great, although those businesses and residences holding the most valuable goods are thoroughly guarded by the most sophisticated sensor systems.

Yet the main drag on the potential of alarms, as industry leaders and police are well aware, remains the false alarm problem. A modern instance of *the boy who cried wolf* phenomenon, false alarms erode alarm system effectiveness. They are costly to alarm companies and police agencies—both in dollars and, more importantly, in the loss of mutual respect and cooperation.

Many law enforcement leaders believe alarm companies are oblivious to the problem. No doubt some are. Yet there is no question that the overwhelming majority of NBFAA member companies are highly aware.

The NBFAA has asked its members—who monitor about 70 percent of the nation's alarm systems—to rate their priorities on association activities. The outstanding response asked for a comprehensive program to help member companies reduce false alarms. Moreover, while researching possible programs, the NBFAA learned that many members had already embarked on significant reduction efforts.

The nation's largest alarm company, American District Telegraph (ADT) has always concerned itself with reducing false alarms. However, this effort has been increased extensively in recent years. ADT has a multifaceted program that includes product design and testing, extensive training programs for installation, maintenance, and sales personnel, coupled with subscriber education and audits of installations, all aimed at reducing false alarms and their associated costs.

These and other efforts have reduced ADT's false alarm rate to 2.07 false calls per system per year, well below the Underwriters' Laboratory's ceiling rate of four per system per year.

Morse Signal Devices' San Diego office implemented a beeper device and designed a decal to remind subscribers to deactivate their alarm systems when entering the premises at unscheduled times. Morse has experienced dramatic declines in its false alarm rate. For instance, from 1975, when Morse's Los Angeles office began its effort, to 1977, the number of false calls dropped by 37 percent.

It should be noted that part of Morse's success lies in the enactment of alarm ordinances by local jurisdictions. For instance, the Los Angeles County Ordinance demands that users take out permits in order to install an alarm system on their premises. More than three false alarms by a subscriber over a calendar year would result in a fine or suspension of the permit. Also, newly enacted state legislation provides for the licensing of all alarm firms in California. There are many other cities across the U.S. that have implemented ordinances. Some have been very successful; others have failed miserably.

Morse, with other firms in the area all represented by the Western Burglar and Fire Alarm Association (WBFAA), aided the county and state in developing and enforcing the regulations. In fact, WBFAA now endorses legal efforts, properly and responsibly developed, aimed at reducing false alarms.

Yet, such legal actions alone did not account for the Los Angeles area success. The reduction in false calls occurred after police started meeting with the subscribers and alarm personnel who were primarily responsible for the problem. It was the friendly arm-twisting by police that caused the offenders to take the problem seriously.

The Greater Cincinnati Regional Chapter #1 (GCRC) of the NBFAA has developed many successful programs to assist crime prevention officers. The general theme has been "Teamwork Prevents False Alarms." Cooperation between the police, the alarm company, and the customer will voluntarily reduce false alarms. The most successful of their programs has been the false alarm brochure that they supply on a no-charge basis to all police departments in the area.

The officer responding to an alarm run fills in an Alarm Reduction Survey (see Figure 9–3) in the brochure and leaves it at the premises. It is part of the educational process to make the alarm customer more aware of the false alarm problem.

Some of the police departments have initiated a written letter program from the police chief to those who have an excessive number of alarm runs. Others have the crime prevention officer do a follow-up visit to the business or residence, after the other steps have failed. On many situations, a representative of GCRC #1 accompanies the crime prevention

Figure 9–3. Alarm reduction survey form.

ALARM REDUCTION SURVEY

Date: _____

Business Name: _____

Business Address: _____ Zip: _____

Name of Alarm: _____

Type of Alarm: _____

Reasons alarm went off (check all boxes applicable)

1. Improper Installation: _____
   A. Sending unit _____
   B. Receiver _____
   C. Sensor unit _____
   D. Placement _____
   E. Other _____

2. Mechanical Failure: _____
   A. Sending unit _____
   B. Sensor unit _____
   C. Receiver _____
   D. Other _____

3. Human Error: _____
   A. Training _____
   B. Carelessness _____
   C. Placement _____
   D. Other _____

4. Robbery in Progress: _____
   A. Yes _____
   B. No. _____

5. Unknown Causes: _____
   A. Describe in detail _____

officer on the visit. Members of GCRC #1 also provide instructors on alarm-intrusion detection systems at the regional police academy where three-day crime prevention courses are given to other line police officers.

The NBFAA also endorses efforts towards eliminating equipment failure, the second leading cause of false alarms; and there is evidence that the industry is embarking upon a major equipment overhaul.

Alarm Equipment Overhaul

A California alarm station recently undertook a major overhaul. The effort began with a false alarm inventory, in which subscribers whose systems produced four or more false alarms per week were weeded out. Service workers then replaced, virtually reinstalled, the alarm systems for those subscribers. New sensors, new batteries, new wiring, and new soldering jobs were required in many instances. The process was costly, but it paid off in the long run.

The office then had fewer service calls and a relationship with the local police that has improved and increased business.

Many NBFAA member companies have instituted training programs for their sales, installation, and service personnel. Also, subscribers are being educated on the operation of their systems three times: by salespeople, installers, and by supervisors when they inspect newly installed systems.

One member company weeded out and entirely rebuilt its problem systems. This approach is the most feasible way for smaller firms to attack the problem. Lacking sufficient capital to initiate a comprehensive program, such companies can nevertheless cut down the number of false alarms by renovating the relatively few systems that cause the majority of problems.

Police chiefs and crime prevention officers working in areas troubled by false alarms should meet with the heads of the firms in their areas and discuss reduction programs like the ones above.

Additional Resources

Now NBFAA members have a guide in the form of a comprehensive quality control manual outlining measures they can undertake and alleviate false alarms.

To provide an idea of how this *False Alarm Handbook* looks, an outline of it follows:

1. Determine false alarm rate and causes.
2. Form an alarm equipment evaluation committee.
3. Institute equipment testing procedures.
4. Develop equipment training facilities.
5. Know how to plan and make alarm installations.
6. Be familiar with sensor zoning procedures.
7. Inspect installations.
8. Educate the subscriber.
9. Cooperate with local law enforcement officers.

The theory behind the handbook is evident in the section titles. Companies are encouraged to begin with a series of statistical studies—from the general rate per total alarms and systems, to causes distinguishing among equipment, user, telephone line, and environmental problems. A separate study helps companies determine how much money false alarms are costing them.

The results of these studies should then be reviewed by the company's alarm equipment evaluation committee. That committee, made up of the chief engineer and plant, sales, and general managers, next decides which systems to keep, which to drop, and which to research further.

Sections 3 and 4 are self-explanatory, both aimed at eliminating equipment-related problems through further testing and by educating all personnel on equipment operations. It should be noted that salespeople will be particularly urged to go through the training process.

The next two parts cover installation procedures. Service workers are warned about environmental hazards that can affect different sensors. Such hazards include heat, static electricity, vibration, and electromagnetic interference from radio waves. The zoning section tells companies how they may set up their installations to isolate faults in different sensors and pieces of equipment.

Under subscriber education, firms are urged to inundate their customers with training films, brochures, seminars, and whatever else it takes to teach them how to operate their alarm systems properly.

The NBFAA has also developed a separate booklet to help educate alarm subscribers. It incorporates a discussion of alarm system fundamentals along with procedures customers may take to reduce mistakes by their employees who operate the systems.

Lastly, the *False Alarm Handbook* asks alarm companies to work closely with the local police on this problem. Here, the NBFAA endorses community-wide research efforts, and the forming of a local private security advisory council to oversee the efforts.

An attitude of aloof disdain by either the police or alarm company officials can only perpetuate the problem. Suspicious of one another, police and alarm personnel will lack sincerity: the former may persist in responding slowly to alarm calls, while the latter may only make a half-hearted effort to reduce false calls.

Each must recognize they need the other. Like surgeons and other medical specialists who need sophisticated drugs and instruments to prevent diseases from occurring, the law enforcement community needs the alarm industry. Prevention, the reason for alarm protection, must lead the war on crime.

At the same time, the alarm industry must remove from its ranks the flimflam-man selling placebos and faulty systems. Users must be taught to care for their security.

Police should take action against such companies and customers when they aggravate the false alarm problem. If some friendly arm-twisting fails to stop such practices, then police should meet with responsible alarm firms, and together they should develop programs and, if necessary, ordinances to penalize negligent subscribers and deceitful companies.

Appendix 9a

Application Guidelines For Exterior Intrusion Detectors*

ROBERT BARNARD

Many false alarms can be prevented by selecting the proper sensor for the application and by using good installation practices. Guides listed below should be considered in the intrusion detection system design along with the guides recommended in the manufacturer's installation manual for the specific equipment being installed.

Before listing guides for specific exterior detectors, some general guidelines apply to all detectors. The guides are not listed in any order of priority.

General

a. Check all equipment for shipping damage prior to installation.
b. Check the equipment after installation for damage.
c. Check that all electrical connections are secure.
d. Mount detector transducers, especially active motion detector transducers, rigidly on vibration-free surfaces.
e. Adjust detector sensitivity level for adequate detection in the worst case operating environment.
f. Areas containing sources of electromagnetic energy (radio transmitters, radar, electrical switches, large motors, generators, etc.) could cause severe operational problems.
g. Avoid adjusting any detector sensitivity so high that it will be susceptible to false alarms.
h. Detector enclosures should be tamper-protected and the tamper alarms monitored continuously.
i. Detector processor units installed out-of-doors should be in weatherproof enclosures and the

*From *Intrusion Detection Systems*, by Robert Barnard (Stoneham, MA: Butterworths, 1981).

circuit boards should be conformal coated.
j. All interconnecting cables should be installed in sealed conduit and, where applicable, buried in the ground.
k. Exterior detection zone lengths should be limited to about 1,000 linear feet.

Fence Disturbance Sensors

a. The fence fabric should be reasonably tight and the fence posts well anchored.
b. All fence signs should be removed or secured so they will not rattle.
c. Gates should be well secured so that they will not rattle.
d. Bottom of fence fabric should be in close proximity to the ground or, better yet, anchored down.
e. All brush and tree branches should be cut or removed so they will not rub against the fence.

Microwave Detectors

a. Ground should be level with no dips or obstructions between the transmitter and receiver.
b. Zones of detection should be overlapped (approximately twice the distance from the transmitter to where the beam touches the ground).
c. Grass should be removed or maintained at a length of no greater than 4 inches between the transmitter and receiver.
d. Snow should not accumulate more than about 4 inches.
e. Dectectors should be located far enough from the fence that the fence will not interfere with the microwave beam.

Infrared Detectors

a. Ground should be level with no dips or obstructions between the detector columns.
b. Bottom beam should be no greater than 6 inches above the ground.
c. Top infrared beam should be at least 4 feet above the ground.
d. Zones of detection should be overlapped or top of detector columns protected with pressure switch.

Electric-Field Detectors

a. When detector is installed on chain-link fences, the fence fabric should be reasonably tight.
b. All vegetation must be removed from under the electric-field fence.

Geophone Sensors

a. Locate sensor to avoid objects anchored in ground that could move in the wind.

b. Backfill dirt for geophone trench should be well tamped.

Strain/Magnetic Line Sensors

a. Locate sensor cable to avoid objects anchored in the ground.
b. When crossing over or under power lines with the sensor line cannot be avoided, then cross perpendicular to them.
c. Avoid routing signal and power cables in the same trench with the transducer cable.
d. Backfill dirt should be well compacted.

Ported Coaxial Sensor Systems

a. Avoid locating sensor near moving body of water.
b. Between dual fences, maintain factory recommended distances.
c. Adhere to the special instructions used near asphalt and concrete.

Appendix 9b

Application Guidelines For Interior Intrusion Detectors*

ROBERT BARNARD

This summary presents a list of basic guidelines that should be considered in the selection, design, installation, and operation of interior intrusion detectors.

Ultrasonic Motion Detectors

a. Avoid using ultrasonic detectors in areas with large volumes of moving air caused by open

*From *Intrusion Detection Systems*, by Robert Barnard (Stoneham, MA: Butterworths, 1981).

windows, doors, vents, etc.
b. Avoid directing the transceivers at large glass windows, nonrigid partitions, warehouse doors, etc., that might vibrate and cause false alarms.
c. Avoid directing transceivers at each other unless they are separated by an adequate distance to prevent interference (usually about 60 feet).
d. Avoid locating individual receivers or transceivers close to air conditioning and heating registers.
e. Position the transceivers and separate receivers

at least 10 feet from telephone bells or any type of bell (unless otherwise indicated by the manufacturer).

Microwave Motion Detectors

a. Avoid locating detectors closer than 10 feet to bare fluorescent lamps, especially if the detector will be pointed toward the lamp, without first determining that the fluorescent lamps will not affect the detectors.
b. Avoid directing the transmitted energy toward nonrigid metal partitions, thin metal walls, or large metal doors that might be vibrated by wind, passing trucks, airplanes, etc.
c. Avoid directing the transmitted energy toward windows, wooden walls, or any wall that the energy can penetrate and perhaps detect outside movement.
d. Avoid directing the transceivers toward rotating or moving machinery.
e. After an installation is complete, check movement outside the protected area that might cause alarms. (Remember, cars and trucks are larger targets and can cause alarms when at greater distances than human movement.)

Sonic Motion Detectors

a. Consider the fact that sonic detectors generate an audible high frequency tone that might be heard several hundred feet from the area being protected, depending on the building construction.

Infrared Motion Detectors

a. Avoid directing the detectors toward heat sources that cycle on and off.
b. Avoid directing the detectors toward burning incandescent lamps.
c. Avoid mounting the detectors over heat sources such as radiators or hot pipe lines.
d. Avoid a heat source directed to the sensor case itself.

Audible Detectors

a. Avoid locating the receivers close to inside noise

sources or near outside walls or doors where exterior noises could be a problem.

Vibration Detectors

a. Both structural and glass breakage detectors should be well secured to the surface where they are detecting penetrations.
b. Structural vibration detectors should be connected to a pulse-accumulating supervisory circuit that can be adjusted for the specific application and not alarm on a single impact.

Operable Opening Switches

a. Doors and windows should be well secured to prevent excessive motion that might cause false alarms.

Photoelectric Detectors

a. Mount transmitters and receivers along with any mirrors securely on vibration-free surfaces.
b. Avoid using mirrors with detectors covering long ranges or ranges over 100 feet.
c. Conceal transmitters and receivers to reduce compromise.

Capacitance Proximity Detectors

a. Avoid using wooden blocks to isolate the protected metal object from the ground plane.
b. Reference ground plane should be well grounded to provide adequate electrical potential differential between the metal object and ground.

Pressure Mats

a. Conceal pressure mats to reduce compromise.

Infra Sonic Sensors

a. Do not employ where large vehicles pass close to building windows.
b. Will cover 15,000 square feet if properly installed.

Appendix 9c

Terms and Definitions for Intrusion Alarm Systems*

Access Control. The control of pedestrian and vehicular traffic through entrances and exits of a **Protected Area** or premises.

Access Mode. The operation of an **Alarm System** such that no **Alarm Signal** is given when the **Protected Area** is entered; however, a signal may be given if the **Sensor, Annunciator**, or **Control Unit** is tampered with or opened.

Access/Secure Control Unit. See **Control Unit**.

Access Switch. See **Authorized Access Switch**.

Accumulator. A circuit which accumulates a sum. For example, in an audio alarm control unit, the accumulator sums the amplitudes of a series of pulses, which are larger than some threshold level, subtracts from the sum at a predetermined rate to account for random background pulses, and initiates an alarm signal when the sum exceeds some predetermined level. This circuit is also called an integrator; in digital circuits it may be called a counter.

Active Intrusion Sensor. An active sensor which detects the presence of an intruder within the range of the sensor. Examples are an **Ultrasonic Motion Detector, a Radio Frequency Motion Detector**, and a **Photoelectric Alarm System**. See also **Passive Intrusion Sensor**.

Active Sensor. A sensor which detects the disturbance of a radiation field which is generated by the sensor. See also **Passive Sensor**.

Actuating Device. See **Actuator**.

Actuator. A manual or automatic switch or sensor such as **Holdup Button, Magnetic Switch**, or thermostat which causes a system to transmit an **Alarm Signal** when manually activated or when the device automatically senses an intruder or other unwanted condition.

Air Gap. The distance between two magnetic elements in a magnetic or electromagnetic circuit, such as between the core and the armature of a relay.

Alarm Circuit. An electrical circuit of an alarm system which produces or transmits an **Alarm Signal**.

Alarm Condition. A threatening condition, such as an intrusion, fire, or holdup, sensed by a **Detector**.

Alarm Device. A device which signals a warning in response to a **Alarm Condition**, such as a bell, siren, or **Annunciator**.

Alarm Discrimination. The ability of an alarm system to distinguish between those stimuli caused by an **Intrusion** and those which are a part of the environment.

Alarm Line. A wired electrical circuit used for the transmission of **Alarm Signals** from the protected premises to a **Monitoring Station**.

Alarm Receiver. See **Annunciator**.

Alarm Sensor. See **Sensor**.

Alarm Signal. A signal produced by a **Control Unit** indicating the existence of an **Alarm Condition**.

Alarm State. The condition of a **Detector** which causes a **Control Unit** in the **Secure Mode** to transmit an **Alarm Signal**.

Alarm Station. (1) A manually actuated device installed at a fixed location to transmit an **Alarm Signal** in response to an **Alarm Condition**, such as a concealed **Holdup Button** in a bank teller's cage. (2) A well-marked emergency control unit, installed in fixed locations usually accessible to the public, used to summon help in response to an **Alarm Condition**. The **Control Unit** contains either a manually actuated switch or telephone connected to fire or police headquarters, or a telephone answering service. See also **Remote Station Alarm System**.

Alarm System. An assembly of equipment and devices designated and arranged to signal the presence of an **Alarm Condition** requiring urgent attention such as unauthorized entry, fire, temperature rise, etc. The system may be **Local, Police Connection, Central Station** or **Proprietary**. (For individual alarm systems see alphabetical listing by type, e.g., **Intrusion Alarm System**.)

Annunciator. An alarm monitoring device which consists of a number of visible signals such as flags or lamps indicating the status of the **Detectors** in an alarm system or systems. Each circuit in the device is usually labelled to identify the location and condition being monitored. In addition to the visible signal, an audible signal is usually associated with the device. When an alarm condition is reported, a signal is indicated visibly, audibly, or both. The visible signal is generally maintained until reset either manually or automatically.

Answering Service. A business which contracts with sub-

*Courtesy U.S. Department of Justice, Law Enforcement Assistance Administration, National Institute of Law Enforcement and Criminal Justice.

scribers to answer incoming telephone calls after a specified delay or when scheduled to do so. It may also provide other services such as relaying fire or intrusion alarm signals to proper authorities.

Area Protection. Protection of the inner space or volume of a secured area by means of a **Volumetric Sensor**.

Area Sensor. A sensor with a detection zone which approximates an area, such as a wall surface or the exterior of a safe.

Audible Alarm Device. (1) A noisemaking device such as a siren, bell, or horn used as part of a local alarm system to indicate an **Alarm Condition**. (2) A bell, buzzer, horn or other noisemaking device used as a part of an **Annunciator** to indicate a change in the status or operating mode of an alarm system.

Audio Detection System. See **Sound Sensing Detection System**.

Audio Frequency (Sonic). Sound frequencies within the range of human hearing, approximately 15 to 20,000 Hz.

Audio Monitor. An arrangement of amplifiers and speakers designed to monitor the sounds transmitted by microphones located in the **Protected Area**. Similar to an **Annunciator**, except that supervisory personnel can monitor the protected area to interpret the sounds.

Authorized Access Switch. A device used to make an alarm system or some portion or zone of a system inoperative in order to permit authorized access through a **Protected Port**. A **Shunt** is an example of such a device.

B.A. Burglar alarm.

Beam Divergence. In a **Photo-Electric Alarm System**, the angular spread of the light beam.

Break Alarm. (1) An **Alarm Condition** signaled by the opening or breaking of an electrical circuit. (2) The signal produced by a break alarm condition (sometimes referred to as an open circuit alarm or trouble signal, designed to indicate possible system failure).

Bug. (1) To plant a microphone or other **Sound Sensor** or to tap a communication line for the purpose of **Surreptitious** listening or **Audio Monitoring**; loosely, to install a sensor in a specified location. (2) The microphone or other sensor used for the purpose of surreptitious listening.

Building Security Alarm System. The system of **Protective Signaling** devices installed at a premise.

Burglar Alarm (B.A.) Pad. A supporting frame laced with fine wire or a fragile panel located with **Foil** or fine wire and installed so as to cover an exterior opening in a building, such as a door, or skylight. Entrance through the opening breaks the wire or foil and initiates an **Alarm Signal**. See also **Grid**.

Burglar Alarm System. See **Intrusion Alarm System**.

Burglary. The unlawful entering of a structure with the intent to commit a felony or theft therein.

Cabinet-for-Safe. A wooden enclosure having closely spaced electrical **Grids** on all inner surfaces and **Contacts** on the doors. It surrounds a safe and initiates an alarm signal if an attempt is made to open or penetrate the cabinet.

Capacitance. The property of two or more objects which enables them to store electrical energy in an electric field between them. The basic measurement unit is the farad. Capacitance varies inversely with the distance between the objects, hence the change of capacitance with relative motion is greater the nearer one object is to the other.

Capacitance Alarm System. An alarm system in which a protected object is electrically connected as a **Capacitance Sensor**. The approach of an intruder causes sufficient change in **Capacitance** to upset the balance of the system and initiate an **Alarm Signal**. Also called proximity alarm system.

Capacitance Detector. See **Capacitance Sensor**.

Capacitance Sensor. A sensor which responds to a change in **Capacitance** in a field containing a protected object or in a field within a protected area.

Carrier Current Transmitter. A device which transmits **Alarm Signals** from a sensor to a **Control Unit** via the standard AC power lines.

Central Station. A control center to which alarm systems in a subscriber's premises are connected, where circuits are supervised, and where personnel are maintained continuously to record and investigate alarm or trouble signals. Facilities are provided for the reporting of alarms to police and fire departments or to other outside agencies.

Central Station Alarm System. An alarm system, or group of systems, the activities of which are transmitted to, recorded in, maintained by, and supervised from a **Central Station**. This differs from **Proprietary Alarm Systems** in that the central station is owned and operated independently of the subscriber.

Circumvention. The defeat of an alarm system by the avoidance of its detection devices, such as by jumping over a pressure sensitive mat, by entering through a hole cut in an unprotected wall rather than through a protected door, or by keeping outside the range of an **Ultrasonic Motion Detector**. Circumvention contrasts with **Spoofing**.

Closed Circuit Alarm. See **Cross Alarm**.

Closed Circuit System. A system in which the sensors of each zone are connected in series so that the same current exists in each sensor. When an activated sensor breaks the circuit or the connecting wire is cut, an alarm is transmitted for that zone.

Clutch Head Screw. A mounting screw with a uniquely designed head for which the installation and removal tool is not commonly available. They are used to install alarm system components so that removal is inhibited.

Coded-Alarm System. An alarm system in which the source of each signal is identifiable. This is usually accomplished by means of a series of current pulses which operate audible or visible **Annunciators** or recorders or both, to yield a recognizable signal. This is usually used to allow the transmission of multiple signals on a common circuit.

Coded Cable. A multiconductor cable in which the insulation on each conductor is distinguishable from all others by color or design. This assists in identification of the point of origin or final destination of a wire.

Coded Transmitter. A device for transmitting a coded signal when manually or automatically operated by an **Actuator**. The actuator may be housed with the transmitter or a number of actuators may operate a common transmitter.

Coding Siren. A siren which has an auxiliary mechanism to interrupt the flow of air through its principal mechanism, enabling it to produce a controllable series of sharp blasts.

Combination Sensor Alarm System. An alarm system which requires the simultaneous activation of two or more sensors to initiate an **Alarm Signal**.

Compromise. See **Defeat**.

Constant Ringing Drop (CRD). A relay which when activated even momentarily will remain in an **Alarm Condition** until **Reset**. A key is often required to reset the relay and turn off the alarm.

Constant Ringing Relay (CRR). See **Constant Ringing Drop**.

Contact. (2) Each of the pair of metallic parts of a switch or relay which by touching or separating make or break the electrical current path. (2) switch-type sensor.

Contact Device. A device which when actuated opens or closes a set of electrical contacts; a switch or relay.

Contact Microphone. A microphone designed for attachment directly to a surface of a **Protected Area** or object; usually used to detect surface vibrations.

Contact Vibration Sensor. See **Vibration Sensor**.

Contactless Vibrating Bell. A **Vibrating Bell** whose continuous operation depends upon application of an alternating current, without circuit-interrupting contacts such as those used in vibrating bells operated by direct current.

Control Cabinet. See **Control Unit**.

Control Unit. A device, usually **Electronic**, which provides the interface between the alarm system and the human operator and produces an **Alarm Signal** when its programmed response indicates an **Alarm Condition**. Some or all of the following may be provided for: power for sensors, sensitivity adjustments, means to select and indicate **Access Mode** or **Secure Mode**, monitoring for **Line Supervision** and **Tamper Devices**, timing circuits, for **Entrance** and **Exit Delays**, transmission of an alarm signal, etc.

Covert. Hidden and protected.

CRD. See **Constant Ringing Drop**.

Cross Alarm. (1) An **Alarm Condition** signaled by crossing or shorting an electrical circuit. (2) The signal produced due to a cross alarm condition.

Crossover. An insulated electrical path used to connect foil across window dividers, such as those found on multiple pane windows, to prevent grounding and to make a more durable connection.

CRR. Constant ringing relay. See **Constant Ringing Drop**.

Dark Current. The current output of a **Photoelectric Sensor** when no light is entering the sensor.

Day Setting. See **Access Mode**.

Defeat. The frustration, counteraction, or thwarting of an **Alarm Device** so that it fails to signal an alarm when a protected area is entered. Defeat includes both **Circumvention** and **Spoofing**.

Detection Range. The greatest distance at which a sensor will consistently detect an intruder under a standard set of conditions.

Detector. (1) A sensor such as those used to detect **Intrusion**, equipment malfunctions or failure, rate of temperature rise, smoke or fire. (2) A demodulator, a device for recovering the modulating function or signal from a modulated wave, such as that used in a modulated photoelectric alarm system. See also **Photoelectric Alarm System, Modulated**.

Dialer. See **Telephone Dialer, Automatic**.

Differential Pressure Sensor. A sensor used for **Perimeter Protection** which responds to the difference between the hydraulic pressures in two liquid-filled tubes buried just below the surface of the earth around the exterior perimeter of the **Protected Area**. The pressure difference can indicate an intruder walking or driving over the buried tubes.

Digital Telephone Dialer. See **Telephone Dialer, Digital**.

Direct Connect. See **Police Connection**.

Direct Wire Burglar Alarm Circuit (DWBA). See **Alarm Line**.

Direct Wire Circuit. See **Alarm Line**.

Door Cord. A short, insulated cable with an attaching block and terminals at each end used to conduct current to a device, such as **Foil**, mounted on the movable portion of a door or window.

Door Trip Switch. A **Mechanical Switch** mounted so that movement of the door will operate the switch.

Doppler Effect (Shift). The apparent change in frequency of sound or radio waves when reflected from or originating from a moving object. Utilized in some types of **Motion Sensors**.

Double-Circuit System. An **Alarm Circuit** in which two wires enter and two wires leave each sensor.

Double Drop. An alarm signaling method often used in **Central Station Alarm Systems** in which the line is first opened to produce a **Break Alarm** and then shorted to produce a **Cross Alarm**.

Drop. (1) See **Annunciator**. (2) A light indicator on an annunciator.

Duress Alarm Device. A device which produces either a **Silent Alarm** or **Local Alarm** under a condition of personnel stress such as holdup, fire, illness, or other panic or emergency. The device is normally manually operated and may be fixed or portable.

Duress Alarm System. An alarm system which employs a **Duress Alarm Device**.

DWBA. Direct wire burglar alarm. See **Alarm Line**.

E-Field Sensor. A **Passive Sensor** which detects changes in the earth's ambient electric field caused by the movement of an intruder. See also **H-Field Sensor**.

Electromagnetic. Pertaining to the relationship between current flow and magnetic field.

Electromagnetic Interference (EMI). Impairment of the reception of a wanted electromagnetic signal by an electromagnetic disturbance. This can be caused by lightning, radio transmitters, power line noise and other electrical devices.

Electromechanical Bell. A bell with a prewound spring-driven striking mechanism, the operation of which is initiated by the activation of an electric tripping mechanism.

Electronic. Related to, or pertaining to, devices which utilize electrons moving through a vacuum, gas, or semiconductor, and to circuits or systems containing such devices.

EMI. See **Electromagnetic Interference**.

End Of Line Resistor. See **Terminal Resistor**.

Entrance Delay. The time between actuating a sensor on an entrance door or gate and the sounding of a **Local Alarm** or transmission of an **Alarm Signal** by the **Control Unit**. This delay is used if the **Authorized Access Switch** is located within the **Protected Area** and permits a person with the control key to enter without causing an alarm. The delay is provided by a timer within the **Control Unit**.

E.O.L. End of line.

Exit Delay. The time between turning on a control unit and the sounding of a **Local Alarm** or transmission of an **Alarm Signal** upon actuation of a sensor on an exit door. This delay is used if the **Authorized Access Switch** is located within the **Protected Area** and permits a person with the control key to turn on the alarm system and to leave through a protected door or gate without causing an alarm. The delay is provided by a timer within the **Control Unit**.

Fail Safe. A feature of a system or device which initiates an alarm or trouble signal when the system or device either malfunctions or loses power.

False Alarm. An alarm signal transmitted in the absence of an **Alarm Condition**. These may be classified according to causes: environmental, e.g., rain, fog, wind, hail, lightning, temperature, etc.; animals, e.g., rats, dogs, cats, insects, etc.; human-made disturbances, e.g., sonic booms, EMI, vehicles, etc.; equipment malfunction, e.g., transmission errors, component failure, etc.; operator error; and unknown.

False Alarm Rate, Monthly. The number of false alarms per installation per month.

False Alarm Ratio. The ratio of **False Alarms** to total alarms; may be expressed as a percentage or as a simple ratio.

Fence Alarm. Any of several types of sensors used to detect the presence of an intruder near a fence or any attempt to climb over, go under, or cut through the fence.

Field. The space or area in which there exists a force such as that produced by an electrically charged object, a current, or a magnet.

Fire Detector (Sensor). See **Heat Sensor** and **Smoke Detector**.

Floor Mat. See **Mat Switch**.

Floor Trap. A **Trap** installed so as to detect the movement of a person across a floor space, such as a **Trip Wire Switch** or **Mat Switch**.

Foil. Thin metallic strips which are cemented to a protected surface (usually glass in a window or door), and connected to a closed electrical circuit. If the protected material is broken so as to break the foil, the circuit opens, initiating an alarm signal. Also called tape. A window, door, or other surface to which foil has been applied is said to be taped or foiled.

Foil Connector. An electrical terminal block used on the edge of a window to join interconnecting wire to window **Foil**.

Foot Rail. A **Holdup Alarm Device**, often used at cashiers' windows, in which a foot is placed under the rail, lifting it, to initiate an **Alarm Signal**.

Frequency Division Multiplexing (FDM). See **Multiplexing, Frequency Division**.

Glassbreak Vibration Detector. A **Vibration Detection System** which employs a **Contact Microphone** attached to a glass window to detect cutting or breakage of the glass.

Grid. (1) An arrangement of electrically conducting wire, screen, or tubing placed in front of doors or windows or both which is used a part of a **Capacitance Sensor**. (2) A lattice of wooden dowels or slats concealing fine wires in a closed circuit which initiates an **Alarm Signal** when forcing or cutting the lattice breaks the wires. Used over accessible openings. Sometimes called a protective screen. See also **Burglar Alarm Pad**. (3) A screen or metal plate, connected to earth ground, sometimes used to provide a stable ground reference for objects protected by a **Capacitance Sensor**. If placed against the walls near the protected object, it prevents the sensor sensitivity from extending through the walls into areas of activity.

Heat Detector. See **Heat Sensor**.

Heat Sensor. (1) A sensor which responds to either a local temperature above a selected value, a local temperature increase which is at a rate of increase greater than a preselected rate (rate of rise), or both. (2) A sensor which responds to infrared radiation from a remote source, such as a person.

Hi-Field Sensor. A **Passive Sensor** which detects changes in the earth's ambient magnetic field caused by the movement of an intruder. See also **E-Field Sensor**.

Holdup. A **Robbery** involving the threat to use a weapon.

Holdup Alarm Device. A device which signals a holdup. The device is usually **Surreptitious** and may be manually or automatically actuated, fixed or portable. See **Duress Alarm Device**.

Holdup Alarm System, Automatic. An alarm system which employs a holdup alarm device, in which the signal transmission is initiated solely by the action of the intruder, such as a money clip in a cash drawer.

Holdup Alarm System, Manual. A holdup alarm system in which the signal transmission is initiated by the direct action of the person attacked or of an observer of the attack.

Holdup Button. A manually actuated **Mechanical Switch** used to initiate a duress alarm signal; usually constructed to minimize accidental activation.

Hood Contact. A switch which is used for the supervision of a closed safe or vault door. Usually installed on the outside surface of the protected door.

Impedance. The opposition to the flow of alternating current in a circuit. May be determined by the ratio of an input voltage to the resultant current.

Impedance Matching. Making the **Impedance** of a **Terminating Device** equal to the impedance of the circuit to which it is connected in order to achieve optimum signal transfer.

Infrared (IR) Motion Detector. A sensor which detects changes in the infrared light radiation from parts of the **Protected Area**. Presence of an intruder in the area changes the infrared light intensity from that direction.

Infrared (IR) Motion Sensor. See **Infrared Motion Detector**.

Infrared Sensor. See **Heat Sensor, Infrared Motion Detector**, and **Photoelectric Sensor**.

Inking Register. See **Register, Inking**.

Interior Perimeter Protection. A line of protection along the interior boundary of a **Protected Area** including all points through which entry can be effected.

Intrusion. Unauthorized entry into the property of another.

Intrusion Alarm System. An alarm system for signaling the entry or attempted entry of a person or an object into the area or volume protected by the system.

Ionization Smoke Detector. A **Smoke Detector** in which a small amount of radioactive material ionizes their air in the sensing chamber, thus rendering it conductive and permitting a current to flow through the air between two charged electrodes. This effectively gives the sensing chamber an electrical conductance. When smoke particles enter the ionization area, they decrease the conductance of the air by attaching themselves to the ions causing a reduction in mobility. When the conductance is less than a predetermined level, the detector circuit responds.

IR. Infrared.

Jack. An electrical connector which is used for frequent connect and disconnect operations; for example, to connect an alarm circuit at an overhang door.

Lacing. A network of fine wire surrounding or covering an area to be protected, such as a safe, vault, or glass panel, and connected into a **Closed Circuit System**. The network of wire is concealed by a shield such as concrete or paneling in such a manner that an attempt to break through the shield breaks the wire and initiates an alarm.

Light Intensity Cutoff. In a **Photoelectric Alarm System**, the percent reduction of light which initiates an **Alarm Signal** at the photoelectric receiver unit.

Line Amplifier. An audio amplifier which is used to provide preamplification of an audio **Alarm Signal** before transmission of the signal over an **Alarm Line**. Use of an amplifier extends the range of signal transmission.

Line Sensor (Detector). A sensor with a detection zone which approximates a line or series of lines, such as a **Photoelectric Sensor** which senses a direct or reflected light beam.

Line Supervision. Electronic protection of an **Alarm Line** accomplished by sending a continuous or coded signal through the circuit. A change in the circuit characteristics, such as a change in **Impedance** due to the circuit's having been tampered with, will be detected by a monitor. The monitor initiates an alarm if the change exceeds a predetermined amount.

Local Alarm. An alarm which when activated makes a loud noise (see **Audible Alarm Device**) at or near the **Protected Area** or floods the site with light or both.

Local Alarm System. An alarm system which when activated produces an audible or visible signal in the immediate vicinity of the protected premises or object. This term usually applies to systems designed to provide only a local warning of **Intrusion** and not to transmit to a remote **Monitoring Station**. However, local alarm systems are sometimes used in conjunction with a **Remote Alarm**.

Loop. An electric circuit consisting of several elements, usually switches, connected in series.

Magnetic Alarm System. An alarm system which will initiate an alarm when it detects changes in the local magnetic field. The changes could be caused by motion of ferrous objects such as guns or tools near the **Magnetic Sensor**.

Magnetic Contact. See **Magnetic Switch**.

Magnetic Sensor. A sensor which responds to changes in magnetic field. See also **Magnetic Alarm System**.

Magnetic Switch. A switch which consists of two separate units: a magnetically-actuated switch, and a magnet. The switch is usually mounted in a fixed position (door jamb or window frame) opposing the magnet, which is fastened to a hinged or sliding door, window, etc. When the movable section is opened, the magnet moves with it, actuating the switch.

Magnetic Switch, Balanced. A **Magnetic Switch** which operates using a balanced magnetic field in such a manner as to resist **Defeat** with an external magnet. It signals an alarm when it detects either an increase or decrease in magnetic field strength.

Matching Network. A circuit used to achieve **Impedance Matching**. It may also allow audio signals to be transmitted to an **Alarm Line** while blocking direct current used locally for **Line Supervision**.

Mat Switch. A flat area switch used on open floors or under carpeting. It may be sensitive over an area of a few square feet or several square yards.

McCulloh Circuit (Loop). A supervised single wire **Loop** Connecting a number of **Coded Transmitters** located in different **Protected Areas** to a **Central Station** receiver.

Mechanical Switch. A switch in which the **Contacts** are opened and closed by means of a depressible plunger or button.

Mercury Fence Alarm. A type of **Mercury Switch** which is sensitive to the vibration caused by an intruder climbing on a fence.

Mercury Switch. A switch operated by tilting or vibrating which causes an enclosed pool of mercury to move, making or breaking physical and electrical contact with conductors. These are used on tilting doors and windows, and on fences.

Microwave Alarm System. An alarm system which employs **Radio Frequency Motion Detectors** operating in the **Microwave Frequency** region of the electromagnetic spectrum.

Microwave Frequency. Radio frequencies in the range of approximately 1.0 to 300 GHz.

Microwave Motion Detector. See **Radio Frequency Motion Detector**.

Modulated Photoelectric Alarm System. See **Photoelectric Alarm System, Modulated**.

Monitor Cabinet. An enclosure which houses the **Annunciator** and associated equipment.

Monitor Panel. See **Annunciator**.

Monitoring Station. The **Central Station** or other area at which guards, police, or commercial service personnel observe **Annunciators** and **Registers** reporting on the condition of alarm systems.

Motion Detection System—See **Motion Sensor**.

Motion Detector. See **Motion Sensor**.

Motion Sensor. A sensor which responds to the motion of an intruder. See also **Radio Frequency Motion Detector, Sonic Motion Detector, Ultrasonic Motion Detector**, and **Infrared Motion Detector**.

Multiplexing. A technique for the concurrent transmission of two or more signals in either or both directions, over the same wire, carrier, or other communication channel. The two basic multiplexing techniques are time division multiplexing and frequency division multiplexing.

Multiplexing, Frequency Division (FDM). The multiplexing technique which assigns to each signal a specific set of frequencies (called a chennel) within the larger block of frequencies available on the main transmission path in much the same ay that many radio stations broadcast at the same time but can be separately received.

Multiplexing, Time Division (TDM). The multiplexing technique which provides for the independent transmission of several pieces of information on a time-sharing basis by sampling, at frequent intervals, the data to be transmitted.

Neutralization. See **Defeat**.

NICAD. Nickel cadmium. A high performance, long-lasting rechargeable battery, with electrodes made of nickel and cadmium, which may be used as an emergency power supply for an alarm system.

Night Setting. See **Secure Mode**.

Nonretractable (One-Way) Screw. A screw with a head designed to permit installation with an ordinary flat bit screwdriver but which resists removal. They are used to install alarm system components so that removal is inhibited.

Normally Closed (NC) Switch. A switch in which the **Contacts** are closed when no external forces act upon the switch.

Normally Open (NO) Switch. A switch in which the **Con-**

tacts are open (separated) when no external forces act upon the switch.

Nuisance Alarm. See **False Alarm**.

Object Protection. See **Spot Protection**.

Open-Circuit Alarm. See **Break Alarm**.

Open-Circuit System. A system in which the sensors are connected in parallel. When a sensor is activated, the circuit is closed, permitting a current which activates an **Alarm Signal**.

Panic Alarm. See **Duress Alarm Device**.

Panic Button. See **Duress Alarm Device**.

Passive Intrusion Sensor. A passive sensor in an **Intrusion Alarm System** which detects an intruder within the range of the sensor. Examples are a **Sound Sensing Detection System**, a **Vibration Detection System**, an **Infrared Motion Detector**, and an **E-Field Sensor**.

Passive Sensor. A sensor which detects natural radiation or radiation disturbances, but does not itself emit the radiation on which its operation depends.

Passive Ultrasonic Alarm System. An alarm system which detects the sounds in the **Ultrasonic Frequency** range caused by an attempted forcible entry into a protected structure. The system consists of microphones, a **Control Unit** containing an amplifier, filters, an **Accumulator**, and a power supply. The unit's sensitivity is adjustable so that ambient noises or normal sounds will not initiate an **Alarm Signal**; however, noise above the preset level or a sufficient accumulation of impulses will initiate an alarm.

Percentage Supervision. A method of **Line Supervision** in which the current in or resistance of a supervised line is monitored for changes. When the change exceeds a selected percentage of the normal operating current or resistance in the line, an **Alarm Signal** is produced.

Perimeter Alarm System. An alarm system which provides perimeter protection.

Perimeter Protection. Protection of access to the outer limits of a **Protected Area**, by means of physical barriers, sensors on physical barriers, or exterior sensors not associated with a physical barrier.

Permanent Circuit. An **Alarm Circuit** which is capable of transmitting an **Alarm Signal** whether the alarm control is in **Access Mode** or **Secure Mode**. Used, for example, on foiled fixed windows, **Tamper Switches**, and supervisory lines. See also **Supervisory Alarm System, Supervisory Circuit**, and **Permanent Protection**.

Permanent Protection. A system of alarm devices such as **Foil, Burglar Alarm Pads**, or **Lacings** connected in a permanent circuit to provide protection whether the **Control Unit** is in the **Access Mode** or **Secure Mode**.

Photoelectric Alarm System. An alarm system which employs a light beam and **Photoelectric Sensor** to provide a line of protection. Any interruption of the beam by an intruder is sensed by the sensor. Mirrors may be used to change the direction of the beam. The maximum beam length is limited by many factors, some of which are the light source intensity, number of mirror reflections, detector sensitivity, **Beam Divergence**, fog, and haze.

Photoelectric Alarm System, Modulated. A photoelectric

alarm system in which the transmitted light beam is modulated in a predetermined manner and in which the receiving equipment will signal an alarm unless it receives the properly modulated light.

Photoelectric Beam Type Smoke Detector. A **Smoke Detector** which projects a light beam across the area to be projected onto a photoelectric cell. Smoke between the light source and the receiving cell reduces the light reaching the cell, causing actuation.

Photoelectric Detector. See **Photoelectric Sensor**.

Photoelectric Sensor. A device which detects a visible or invisible beam of light and responds to its complete or nearly complete interruption. See also **Photoelectric Alarm System** and **Photoelectric Alarm System, Modulated**.

Photoelectric Spot Type Smoke Detector. A **Smoke Detector** which contains a chamber with covers which prevent the entrance of light but allow the entrance of smoke. The chamber contains a light source and a photosensitive cell so placed that light is blocked from it. When smoke enters, the smoke particles scatter and reflect the light into the photosensitive cell, causing an alarm.

Point Protection. See **Spot Protection**.

Police Connection. The direct link by which an alarm system is connected to an **Annunciator** installed in a police station. Examples of a police connection are an **Alarm Line**, or a radio communications channel.

Police Panel. See **Police Station Unit**.

Police Station Unit. An **Annunciator** which can be placed in operation in a police station.

Portable Duress Sensor. A device carried on a person which may be activated in an emergency to send an **Alarm Signal** to a **Monitoring Station**.

Portable Intrusion Sensory. A sensor which can be installed quickly and which does not require the installation of dedicated wiring for the transmission of its **Alarm Signal**.

Positive Noninterfering (PNI) and Successive Alarm System. An alarm system which employs multiple alarm transmitters on each **Alarm Line** (like **McCulloh Loop**) such that in the event of simultaneous operation of several transmitters, one of them takes control of the alarm line, transmits its full signal, then release the alarm line for successive transmission by other transmitters which are held inoperative until they gain control.

Pressure Alarm System. An alarm system which protects a vault or other enclosed space by maintaining and monitoring a predetermined air pressure differential between the inside and outside of the space. Equalization of pressure resulting from opening the vault or cutting through the enclosure will be sensed and will initiate an **Alarm Signal**.

Proprietary Alarm System. An alarm system which is similar to a **Central Station Alarm System** except that the **Annunciator** is located in a constantly guarded room maintained by the owner for internal security operations. The guards monitor the system and respond to all **Alarm Signals** or alert local law enforcement agencies or both.

Printing Recorder. An electromechanical device used at a **Monitoring Station** which accepts coded signals from alarm lines and converts them to an alphanumeric printed record of the signal received.

Protected Area. An area monitored by an alarm system or guards, or enclosed by a suitable barrier.

Protected Port. A point of entry such as a door, window, or corridor which is monitored by sensors connected to an alarm system.

Protection Device. (1) A sensor such as a **Grid, Foil, Contact,** or **Photoelectric Sensor** connected into an **Intrusion Alarm System**. (2) A barrier which inhibits **Intrusion**, such as a grille, lock, fence or wall.

Protection, Exterior Perimeter. A line of protection surrounding but somewhat removed from a facility. Examples are fences, barrier walls, or patrolled points of a perimeter.

Protection Off. See **Access Mode**.

Protection On. See **Secure Mode**.

Protective Screen. See **Grid**.

Protective Signaling. The initiation, transmission, and reception of signals involved in the detection and prevention of property loss due to fire, burglary, or other destructive conditions. Also, the electronic supervision of persons and equipment concerned with this detection and prevention. See also **Line Supervision** and **Supervisory Alarm System**.

Proximity Alarm System. See **Capacitance Alarm System**.

Punching Register. See **Register, Punch**.

Radar Alarm System. An alarm system which employs **Radio Frequency Motion Detectors**.

Radar (Radio Detecting And Ranging). See **Radio Frequency Motion Detector**.

Radio Frequency Interference (RFI). Electromagnetic Interference in the radio frequency range.

Radio Frequency Motion Detector. A sensor which detects the motion of an intruder through the use of a radiated radio frequency electromagnetic field. The device operates by sensing a disturbance in the generated RF field caused by intruder motion, typically a modulation of the field referred to as a **Doppler Effect**, which is used to initiate an **Alarm Signal**. Most radio frequency motion detectors are certified by the FCC for operation as field disturbance sensors at one of the following frequencies: 0.915 GHz (L-Band), 2.45 GHz (S-Band), 5.8 GHz (X-Band), 10.525 GHz (X-Band), and 22.125 GHz (K-Band). Units operating in the **Microwave Frequency** range are usually called **Microwave Motion Detectors**.

Reed Switch. A type of **Magnetic Switch** consisting of contacts formed by two thin movable magnetically actuated metal vanes or reeds, held in a normally open position within a sealed glass envelope.

Register. An electromechanical device which makes a paper tape in response to signal impulses received from transmitting circuits. A register may be driven by a prewound spring mechanism, an electric motor, or a combination of these.

Register, Inking. A register which marks the tape with ink.

Register, Punch. A register which marks the tape by cutting holes in it.

Register, Slashing. A register which marks the tape by cutting V-shaped slashes in it.

Remote Alarm. An **Alarm Signal** which is transmitted to a remote **Monitoring Station**. See also **Local Alarm**.

Remote Station Alarm System. An alarm system which employs remote **Alarm Stations** usually located in building hallways or on city streets.

Reporting Line. See **Alarm Line**.

Resistance Bridge Smoke Detector. A **Smoke Detector** which responds to the particles and moisture present in smoke. These substances reduce the resistance of an electrical bridge grid and cause the detector to respond.

Retard Transmitter. A **Coded Transmitter** in which a delay period is introduced between the time of actuation and the time of signal transmission.

RFI. See **Radio Frequency Interference**.

Rf Motion Detector. See **Radio Frequency Motion Detector**.

Robbery. The felonious or forcible taking of property by violence, threat, or other overt felonious act in the presence of the victim.

Secure Mode. The condition of an alarm system in which all sensors and **Control Units** are ready to respond to an intrusion.

Security Monitor—See **Annunciator**.

Seismic Sensor. A sensor, generally buried under the surface of the ground for **Perimeter Protection**, which responds to minute vibrations of the earth generated as an intruder walks or drives within its **Detection Range**.

Sensor. A device which is designed to produce a signal or offer indication in response to an event or stimulus within its detection zone.

Sensor, Combustion. See **Ionization Smoke Detector**, **Photoelectric Beam Type Smoke Detector**, **Photoelectric Spot Type Smoke Detector** and **Resistance Bridge Smoke Detector**.

Sensor, Smoke. See **Ionization Smoke Detector**, **Photoelectric Beam Type Smoke Detector**, **Photoelectric Spot Type Smoke Detector** and **Resistance Bridge Smoke Detector**.

Shunt. (1) A deliberate shorting-out of a portion of an electric circuit. (2) A key-operated switch which removes some portion of an alarm system for operation, allowing entry into a **Protected Area** without initiating an **Alarm Signal**. A type of **Authorized Access Switch**.

Shunt Switch. See **Shunt**.

Signal Recorder. See **Register**.

Silent Alarm. A **Remote Alarm** without an obvious local indication that an alarm has been transmitted.

Silent Alarm System. An alarm system which signals a remote station by means of a silent alarm.

Single Circuit System. An **Alarm Circuit** which routes only one side of the circuit through each sensor. The return may be through either ground or a separate wire.

Single-Stroke Bell. A bell which its struck once each time its mechanism is activated.

Slashing Register. See **Register, Slashing**.

Smoke Detector. A device which detects visible or invisible products of combustion. See also **Ionization Smoke Detector, Photoelectric Beam Type Smoke Detector, Photoelectric Spot Type Smoke Detector**, and **Resistance Bridge Smoke Detector**.

Solid State. (1) An adjective used to describe a device such as a semiconductor transistor or diode. (2) A circuit or system which does not rely on vacuum or gas-filled tubes to control or modify voltages and currents.

Sonic Motion Detector. A sensor which detects the motion of an intruder by her or his disturbance of an audible sound pattern generated within the protected area.

Sound Sensing Detection System. An alarm system which detects the audible sound caused by an attempted forcible entry into a protected structure. The system consists of microphones and a **Control Unit** containing an amplifier, **Accumulator** and a power supply. The unit's sensitivity is adjustable so that ambient noises or normal sounds will not initiate an **Alarm Signal**. However, noises above this preset level or a sufficient accumulation of impulses will initiate an alarm.

Sound Sensor. A sensor which responds to sound; a microphone.

Space Protection. See **Area Protection**.

Spoofing. The defeat or compromise of an alarm system by tricking or fooling its detection devices such as by short circuiting part or all of a series circuit, cutting wires in a parallel circuit, reducing the sensitivity of a sensor, or entering false signals into the system. Spoofing contrasts with **Circumvention**.

Spot Protection. Protection of objects such as safes, art objects, or anything of value which could be damaged or removed from the premises.

Spring Contact. A device employing a current-carrying cantilever spring which monitors the position of a door or window.

Standby Power Supply. Equipment which supplies power to a system in the event the primary power is lost. It may consist of batteries, charging circuits, auxiliary motor generators or a combination of these devices.

Strain Gauge Alarm System. An alarm system which detects the stress caused by the weight of an intruder as he or she moves about a building. Typical uses include placement of the strain gauge sensor under a floor joist or under a stairway tread.

Strain Gauge Sensor. A sensor which, when attached to an object, will provide an electrical response to an applied stress upon the object, such as a bending, stretching or compressive force.

Strain Sensitive Cable. An electrical cable which is designed to produce a signal whenever the cable is strained by a change in applied force. Typical uses including mounting it in a wall to detect an attempted forced entry through the wall, or fastening it to a fence to detect climbing on the fence, or burying it around a perimeter to detect walking or driving across the perimeter.

Subscriber's Equipment. That portion of a **Central Station Alarm System** installed in the protected premises.

Subscriber's Unit. A **Control Unit** of a **Central Station Alarm System**.

Supervised Lines. Interconnecting lines in an alarm system which are electrically supervised against tampering. See also **Line Supervision**.

Supervisory Alarm System. An alarm system which monitors conditions or persons or both and signals any deviation from an established norm or schedule. Examples are the monitoring of signals from guard patrol stations for irregularities in the progression along a prescribed patrol route, and the monitoring of production or safety conditions such as sprinkler water pressure, temperature, or liquid level.

Supervisory Circuit. An electrical circuit or radio path which sends information on the status of a sensor or guard patrol to an **Annunciator**. For **Intrusion Alarm Systems**, this circuit provides **Line Supervision** and monitors **Tamper Devices**. See also **Supervisory Alarm System**.

Surreptitious. Covert, hidden, concealed or disguised.

Surveillance. (1) Control of premises for security purposes through alarm systems, closed circuit television (CCTV), or other monitoring methods. (2) Supervision or inspection of industrial processes by monitoring those conditions which could cause damage if not corrected. See also **Supervisory Alarm System**.

Tamper Device. (1) Any device, usually a switch, which is used to detect an attempt to gain access to intrusion alarm circuitry, such as by removing a switch cover. (2) A monitor circuit to detect any attempt to modify the alarm circuitry, such as by cutting a wire.

Tamper Switch. A switch which is installed in such a way as to detect attempts to remove the enclosure of some alarm system components such as control box doors, switch covers, junction box covers, or bell housings. The alarm component is then often described as being tampered.

Tape. See **Foil**.

Tapper Bell. A **Single-Stroke Bell** designed to produce a sound of low intensity and relatively high pitch.

Telephone Dialer, Automatic. A device which, when activated, automatically dials one more preprogrammed telephone numbers (e.g., police, fire department) and relays a recorded voice or coded message giving the location and nature of the alarm.

Telephone Dialer, Digital. An automatic telephone dialer which sends its message as a digital code.

Terminal Resistor. A resistor used as a **Terminating Device**.

Terminating Capacitor. A capacitor sometimes used as a terminating device for a **Capacitance Sensor** antenna. The capacitor allows the supervision of the sensor antenna, especially if a long wire is used as the sensor.

Terminating Device. A device which is used to terminate an electrically supervised circuit. It makes the electrical circuit continuous and provides a fixed **Impedance** reference (end of line resistor) against which changes are measured to detect an **Alarm Condition**. The impedance changes may be caused by a sensor, tampering, or circuit trouble.

Time Delay. See **Entrance Delay** and **Exit Delay**.

Time Division Multiplexing (TDM). See **Multiplexing, Time Division**.

Timing Table. That portion of **Central Station** equipment which provides a means for checking incoming signals from **McCulloh Circuits**.

Touch Sensitivity. The sensitivity of a **Capacitance Sensor** at which the **Alarm Device** will be activated only if an intruder touches or comes in very close proximity (about 1 cm or ½ in.) to the protected object.

Trap. (1) A device, usually a switch, installed within a protected area, which serves as secondary protection in the event a **Perimeter Alarm System** is successfully penetrated. Examples are a **Trip Wise Switch** placed across a likely path for an intruder, a **Mat Switch** hidden under a rug, or a **Magnetic Switch** mounted on an inner door. (2) A **Volumetric Sensor** installed so as to detect an intruder in a likely traveled corridor or pathway within a security area.

Trickle Charge. A continuous direct current, usually very low, which is applied to a battery to maintain it at peak charge or to recharge it after it has been partially or completely discharged. Usually applied to nickel cadmium (NICAD) or wet cell batteries.

Trip Wire Switch. A switch which is actuated by breaking or moving a wire or cord installed across a floor space.

Trouble Signal. See **Break Alarm**.

UL. See **Underwriters Laboratories, Inc.**

UL Certificated. For certain types of products which have met UL requirements, for which it is impractical to apply the UL Listing Mark or Classification Marking to the individual product, a certificate is provided which the manufacturer may use to identify quantities of material for specific job sites or to identify field installed systems.

UL Listed. Signifies that production samples of the product have been found to comply with established Underwriters Laboratories' requirements and that the manufacturer is authorized to use the Laboratories' Listing Marks on the listed products which comply with the requirements, contingent upon the follow-up services as a check of compliance.

Ultrasonic. Pertaining to a sound wave having a frequency above that of audible sound (approximately 20,000 Hz). Ultrasonic sound is used in ultrasonic detection systems.

Ultrasonic Detection System. See **Ultrasonic Motion Detector** and **Passive Ultrasonic Alarm System**.

Ultrasonic Frequency. Sound frequencies which are above the range of human hearing; approximately 20,000 Hz and higher.

Ultrasonic Motion Detector. A sensor which detects the motion of an intruder through the use of **Ultrasonic** generating and receiving equipment. The device operates by filling a space with a pattern of ultrasonic waves; the modulation of these waves by a moving object is detected and initiates an **Alarm Signal**.

Underdome Bell. A bell most of whose mechanism is concealed by its gong.

Underwriters Laboratories, Inc. (UL). A private independent research and testing laboratory which tests and lists various items meeting good practice and safety standards.

Vibrating Bell. A bell whose mechanism is designed to strike repeatedly and for as long as it is activated.

Vibrating Contact. See **Vibration Sensor**.

Vibration Detection System. An alarm system which employs one or more **Contact Microphones** or **Vibration Sensors** which are fastened to the surfaces of the area or object being protected to detect excessive levels of vibration. The contact microphone system consists of microphones, a **Control Unit** containing an amplifier and an **Accumulator**, and a power supply. The unit's sensitivity is adjustable so that ambient noises or normal vibrations will not initiate an **Alarm Signal**. In the vibration sensor system, the sensor responds to excessive vibration by opening a switch in a **Closed Circuit System**.

Vibration Detector. See **Vibration Sensor**.

Vibration Sensor. A sensor which responds to vibrations of the surface on which it is mounted. It has a **Normally Closed Switch** which will momentarily open when it is subjected to a vibration with sufficiently large amplitude. Its sensitivity is adjustable to allow for the different levels of normal vibration, to which the sensor should not respond, at different locations. See also **Vibration Detection System**.

Visual Signal Device. A pilot light, **Annunciator** or other device which provides a visual indication of the condition of the circuit or system being supervised.

Volumetric Detector. See **Volumetric Sensor**.

Volumetric Sensor. A sensor with a detection zone which extends over a volume such as an entire room, part of a room, or a passageway. **Ultrasonic Motion Detectors** and **Sonic Motion Detectors** are examples of volumetric sensors.

Walk Test Light. A light-on-motion detector which comes on when the detector senses motion in the area. It is used while setting the sensitivity of the detector and during routine checking and maintenance.

Watchman's Reporting System. A **Supervisory Alarm System** arranged for the transmission of a patrolling watchman's regularly recurrent report signals from stations along the patrol route to a central supervisory agency.

Zoned Circuit. A circuit which provides continual protection for parts of zones of the **Protected Area** while normally used doors and windows or zones may be released for access.

Zones. Smaller subdivisions into which large areas are divided to permit selective access to some zones while maintaining other zones secure and to permit pinpointing the specific location from which an **Alarm Signal** is transmitted.

Chapter 10

Closed Circuit Television Security

HERMAN KRUEGLE

In today's complex society, security personnel are responsible for the many factors required to produce an effective security and safety system. An important factor in these systems is closed circuit television (CCTV). Today, more than ever before, with spiraling labor costs, CCTV has earned its place as a cost-effective means for expanding security control and safety, while reducing budgets.

Equipment and time loss due to theft is a growing cancer that eats away at every business, be it retail, service, or manufacturing. The size of the organization makes no difference to the thief. The larger the company, the larger the theft, and the greater the opportunity for losses. The more valuable the product is, the easier it is to dispose of, and thus, the greater the temptation to steal it. The implementation of a business CCTV system properly designed and applied can be an extremely profitable investment to the institution. The main objective of the CCTV system should not be in the apprehension of thieves but rather in increasing security so as to prevent thievery. If a company can deter an incident from occurring in the first place, the problem has been solved. A successful thief needs privacy in which to operate. It is the function of the television system to prevent this privacy from occurring.

Use of CCTV systems in public and industrial facilities has been accepted, and resistance by workers to its presence and use is decreasing significantly. With present business economics getting worse, people begin looking for other ways to increase their income and means for paying the bills. CCTV is being applied to counteract this and increase corporation profits. There are many case histories in which CCTV is installed and shoplifting and employee thefts drop sharply. The number of thefts cannot be counted exactly, but the reduction in shrinkage can be measured, and it has been shown that CCTV is an effective psychological deterrent to crime. An expected by-product of CCTV systems use has been improved employee efficiency and a resultant rise in productivity. Theft takes the form of removing valuable property from premises, as well as removing information in the form of: (1) computer software; (2) magnetic tape; (3) microfilm; and (4) data on paper. CCTV surveillance systems provide a means for successfully deterring such thievery and/or detecting or apprehending offenders. Another form of loss which CCTV prevents is the willful destruction of property. Such crimes include: (1) vandalizing buildings; (2) defacing elevator interiors; (3) painting graffiti on priceless art objects and facilities; (4) demolishing furniture or other valuable equipment; and (5) destroying computer rooms.

The greatest potential for CCTV is the integration of it with other sensing systems so that it can be called upon for use to view remote areas with potential safety problems or fire hazards. CCTV, combined with smoke detectors where the cameras are located in inaccessible areas, can be used to give advance warning of a fire.

Closed Circuit Television Theory

Many closed circuit television applications require only one television camera as shown in Figure 10–1. This may be used to monitor employees, visitors, people entering or leaving a front reception area of a building, or other applications which require viewing only a single location. In general, the CCTV monitor is located remotely from the televi-

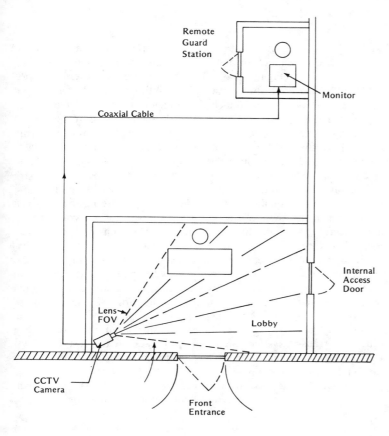

Figure 10–1. Closed circuit television system.

sion camera. For instance, a camera is located in a lobby close to the ceiling and looking at a scene in the reception area viewing the front door and internal access door. The monitor might be located hundreds or thousands of feet away—even in another building, with the security personnel viewing that same lobby, front door, and reception area. The television camera monitor system effectively acts as an extension of the eyes, removing the camera from the location of the observer to the observed location. The one camera system shown in Figure 10–1 contains the following subsystems:

1. *Lens.* The function of the lens is to collect the light from the scene and form an image of the scene on the sensitive camera tube.
2. *Camera.* The camera containing the sensitive image tube converts the visible scene formed by the lens onto the tube, into an electrical signal which is then made suitable for transmission via a coaxial cable or other transmission means to the remote monitor.
3. *Coaxial Cable or Wireless Tranmission Means.*

The function of the cable or wireless transmission means is to transmit the electrical camera scene signal to the remote monitor screen.

4. *Monitor.* The monitor displays the camera picture by converting the electrical signal back into a visible picture on the monitor.
5. *Video Cassette, Video Tape Recorder, or Video File.* These machines permanently record the monitor picture from the camera onto a magnetic tape cassette, tape reel, or hard disk.

Several items are not directly parts of the closed circuit television system but play very important parts in determining the scene: (1) the scene lighting; (2) the contrast of objects in the scene; (3) the system resolution; (4) whether the system's function is to detect, identify, or recognize objects or personnel. As will be seen later, how the scene is illuminated, i.e., via sunlight, moonlight, or artificial illumination, and the actual scene contrast will play important roles in the type of lenses and cameras necessary, and the quality in the resultant scene on the monitor.

Lens/Camera System

Figure 10–2 shows the essentials of a CCTV camera including the lens and the field of view (FOV), or scene, the camera sees.

The camera sees the scene in the following manner. A light source (sunlight, lamps, etc.) illuminates the scene. A part of the light reaching the scene from the source is reflected toward the camera, and is intercepted and collected by the camera lens. The camera lens collects the reflected radiation much like the lens of your eye or a film camera lens. The lens focuses the scene onto the television image tube, which acts like a detector similar to the retina of your eye or the film in a camera. The image tube and camera electronics convert the visible image into an equivalent electrical signal suitable for transmission to a remote monitor. Although the scene image is focused onto the image tube continuously, the camera electronics transforms the visible image to an electrical signal point by point. The camera video signal (containing all picture information) contains frequencies from 30 Hz (cycles/second) to 4 MHz, which are transmitted via the coaxial cable. Most camera external controls include mechanical focus (vidicon position) and electronic focus. Some may have beam and target controls.

Vidicon Camera Size

All standard CCTV cameras use either a ⅔-inch diameter or one-inch diameter vidicon image tube (see Figure 10–3). Which one to use is determined primarily by cost and reliability factors. A ⅔-inch tube has a .26 inch × .35 inch (6.6mm × 8.8mm) image format, i.e., the visible scene falling in the central 6.6mm × 8.8mm (11mm diagonal) region of the vidicon is later displayed on the monitor. Likewise, a one-inch diameter vidicon has 9.6mm × 12.8mm active area (16mm diagonal). If cost is a primary factor, the ⅔-inch system is the choice. If image quality and reliability are the criteria, the one-inch system is superior. It is somewhat like comparing a super 8mm to 16mm movie system.

In the case of the 16mm movie system, approximately four times the area of the film is used. In the case of the one-inch versus the ⅔-inch television system, a 16mm diameter versus an 11mm diagonal target area is used, and therefore the signal-to-noise ratio in a television system for the one-inch vidicon is significantly higher than that for the ⅔-inch system. Signal-to-noise ratio in the television system is analogous to the amount of grain in the film system.

As a result of the lower cost of the ⅔-inch system, this is used more commonly in security systems.

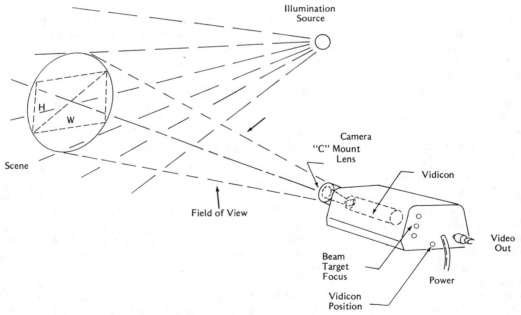

Figure 10–2. CCTV camera, scene, and source illumination.

Camera Field of View (FOV)

The task of choosing the right lens to do the job is probably the most difficult part of designing a CCTV system. Understanding the following step-by-step procedure should make the task considerably easier.

Just as your own eyes have a FOV, i.e., the scene you can see, so does the television camera. The camera FOV is determined by the simple geometry shown in Figure 10–3. The scene has width (W) and height (H) and is a distance (D) away from the camera lens. Once a decision has been made on what scene the camera should view, there are three factors which determine the correct focal length lens to use: (1) size of the scene to be televised (H, W); (2) distance between the scene and camera lens (D); and (3) image tube size, ⅔-inch or one-inch diameter. Table 10–1 lists the scene sizes viewed by one-inch cameras for common lens focal lengths and for a range of subject distances. A simple multiplication factor (.7) converts the numbers to a ⅔-inch tube format. Understanding Figure 10–3 and Table 10–1 makes it easy to choose the right lens for most applications. As an example, choose a lens for viewing all of a 10 foot high by 15 foot long wall from a distance of 30 feet, with a one-inch diameter CCTV camera. From Table 10–1, a 25mm FL lens will just do the job. If a ⅔-inch diameter CCTV camera were used, a lens with a focal length of (.7) × 25mm = 15.5mm (choose 16mm) would be used. Alternately, just multiply the required scene size by 1.43 to get: 1.43 × (10 ft. × 15 ft.) = 14.3 ft. × 21.45 ft. Then proceed as before. A 16mm (.63 inch) FL lens will do the job.

Several comments and observations can be made about CCTV lenses:

- Lenses invert the picture image; the camera electronics reinverts the picture so that it is displayed right side up on the monitor.
- A short FL lens has a wide FOV (Table 10–1; 6.5mm, one-inch tube sees 59.1 ft × 44.4 ft. at 30 ft.).
- A long FL lens has a narrow FOV (Table 10–1; 150mm, one-inch tube, sees 2.5 ft. × 1.9 ft. at 30 ft.).
- The 25mm FL lens is considered the standard or reference lens and has an FL in between the two just mentioned. It is defined to have a magnification (M) of 1. Using the 25mm lens as a reference

Figure 10–3. Camera tube geometry and formats.

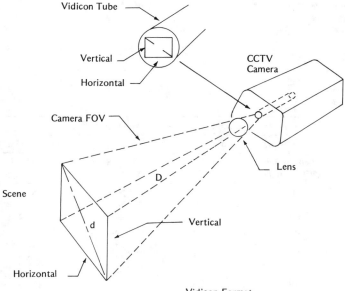

Tube Size	Vidicon Format					
	Diagonal (d)		Horizontal		Vertical	
	mm	inches	mm	inches	mm	inches
2/3 inch	11	.43	8.8	.35	6.6	.26
1 inch	16	.63	12.8	.50	9.6	.38

Table 10–1. Camera scene FOV versus lens focal length

		W x H (5)	W x H (15)	W x H (25)
4.0*	.16	16x12	48x36	80x 60
4.8*	.19	13.3x10	40x30	66.7x50
6.5	.26	9.8x7.4	29.4x22.2	49x37
8.5	.33	8.2x5.9	24.6x17.7	41x29.5
12.5	.5	5x3.8	15x11.3	25x18.8
16	.63	4x3	12x9	20x15
15	1	2.5x1.9	7.5x5.6	12.5x9.4
50	2	1.3x.9	3.8x2.8	6.3x4.7
75	3	.8x.6	2.5x1.9	4.1x3.2
100	4	.6x.5	1.9x1.4	3.1x2.3
150	6	.4x.3	1.3x.9	2.1x1.6
		W x H	W x H	W x H
mm	inch	5	15	25
Lens	F.L.	Distance (D) In Feet (Note 1)		

Camera to Scene Distance (D) in Feet (See Note 1)

Lens mm	F.L. inches	10 W+ x H+	20 W x H	30 W x H	40 W x H	50 W x H	60 W x H	70 W x H	80 W x H	90 W x H	100 W x H
4.0*	.16	32x24	64x48	96x72							
4.8*	.19	26.7x20	53.3x40	80x60							
6.5	.26	19.7x14.8	39.4x29.6	59.1x44.4	78.8x59.2	98.5x74	118.8x88.8				
8.5	.33	16.3x11.7	32.6x23.4	48.9x35.1	65.2x46.8	81.5x58.5	97.8x70.2	114x81.9			
12.5	.5	10x7.5	20x15	30x22.5	40x30	50x37.5	60x45	70x52.5	80x60	90x67.5	100x75
16	.63	8.1x6	16.2x12	24.3x18	32.4x24	41x30	48.6x36	56.7x42	64.8x48	72.9x54	81x60
25	1	5x3.75	10x7.5	15x11.25	20x15	25x18.75	30x22.5	35x26.25	40x30	45x33.75	50x37.5
50	2	2.5x1.9	5x3.8	7.5x5.6	10x7.5	12.5x9.4	15x11.3	17.5x13.1	20x15	22.5x16.9	25x18.7
75	3	1.7x1.3	3.3x2.5	5x3.8	6.7x5	8.3x6.3	10x7.5	11.7x8.8	13.3x10	15x11.3	16.7x12.5
100	4	1.3x0.9	2.5x1.9	3.8x2.8	5x3.8	6.3x4.7	7.5x5.6	8.8x6.6	10x7.5	11.3x8.4	12.5x9.4
150	6	0.8x0.6	1.7x1.3	2.5x1.9	3.3x2.5	4.2x3.1	5x3.8	5.8x4.4	6.7x5	7.5 x5.6	8.3x6.3

*4.0 and 4.8mm lenses are available only for ⅔" Format. Multiply W x H by 0.7
+ W and H is width and height in feet.

Notes: 1) Scene sizes (W x H) are for 1 inch vidicon. 2) To get scene size for ⅔ inch vidicon, multiply W by .7 and H by .7. Example: For a F.L. = 25mm and a ⅔ inch vidicon at 20 ft., W = 10 ft. x .7 = 7 ft.
H = 7.5 ft. x .7 = 5.25 ft.

Table 10–2. Camera Angular View Versus Focal Length

Lens FL (mm)	Maximum Lens Aperture* (inches)		⅔" Vidicon Horizontal View Angle	⅔" Vidicon Vertical View Angle	1" Vidicon Horizontal View Angle	1" Vidicon Vertical View Angle
4.0	.16	f/1.4	96	79	N/A	N/A
4.8	.19	f/1.8	86.3	70.2	N/A	N/A
6.5	.26	f/1.8	69.4	54.8	89.1	72.9
8.5	.33	f/1.5	54.8	42.5	78.3	60.8
12.5	.5	f/1.4	38.7	29.5	54.5	42.1
16	.63	f/1.6	31	23.4	44	33.3
25	1	f/1.4	20	15	28.5	21.5
50	2	f/1.4	10	7.5	14.5	11
75	3	f/1.4	6.7	5	9.6	7.2
100	4	f/2.8	5	3.7	7.1	5.3
150	6	f/2.8	3.4	2.5	4.8	3.6

*These values are for common CCTV lenses.
†For any distance (D).

with M = 1, the 75mm lens has a magnification of 3, and the 8.5mm, a magnification of 1/3. In general, the magnification of a lens is:

$$\text{Magnification} = \frac{\text{Lens Focal Length (mm)}}{25\text{mm}}$$

or

$$M = \frac{FL \text{ (mm)}}{25\text{mm}}$$

Table 10–2 converts the lens focal length of a lens into the actual FOV the camera sees. For example, a 25mm FL lens on a 2/3-inch vidicon camera sees a 20 degree horizontal by 15 degree vertical FOV.

Zoom Lenses

A zoom lens is a variable focal length lens. Several elements in these lenses are physically moved to vary the FL and thereby vary the angular FOV and magnification. Figure 10–4 shows the external characteristics of the zoom lens. By rotating an external member of the lens manually or via a motor with remote control, the angular FOV, and hence the scene observed by the camera, can be changed. Typical ranges of variation are from 20mm focal length to 100mm (or 200mm) giving a

Table 10–3. Zoom Lens Characteristics

Zoom Range (mm)	Magnification Ratio	Optical f/number	Camera Format Vidicon Size (in)
11.5 to 90	8:1	f/2	⅔"
20 to 100	5:1	f/1.8	⅔" or 1
15 to 150	10:1	f/1.8	1
16 to 160	10:1	f/1.8	1
15 to 225	15:1	f/2.8	1
25 to 350	14:1	f/2.8	1

5 to 10 times change in the angular FOV. These lenses have the advantage that a range of focal lengths can be dialed in, thereby accommodating a large number of different fields of view with one lens. Zoom lenses generally cost two to ten times as much as a fixed FL lens. A manual and a motorized zoom lens are shown in Figure 10–4. Table 10–3 lists a variety of common zoom lenses available with ranges in zoom ratio from 20 to 1, to 4 to 1, and focal ranges from 11mm to 400mm.

Camera Vidicon Types

Several different sensor types are available for CCTV security applications. These include the most common antimony trisulphide vidicon type (Sb S),

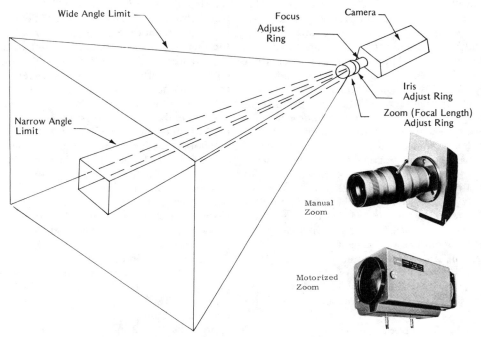

Figure 10–4. Zoom lens characteristics.

low light level silicon (Si) and Newvicon* (Cadmium Selenide, CdSe) types, and the new solid state silicon charge coupled devices (CCD). Extreme low light level applications are solved using silicon intensifier tubes (SIT) and intensified SIT tubes (ISIT).

The low light level cameras (Silicon, Newvicon, SIT, and ISIT) require some form of automatic iris control in order to control the light level reaching the camera. The Silicon and Newvicon cameras can be operated down to dusk conditions but the SIT and ISIT cameras can be used viewing scenes that are illuminated only by natural moonlight or starlight or some other very low light level artificial illumination. The SIT tube camera combines a silicon target vidicon structure with a stage of light amplification ahead of it. For ultra low light level viewing such as under a heavily overcast nighttime condition, the ISIT camera should be considered. This camera uses a SIT tube with an additional light amplification stage and is about the lowest light level camera available today. Some resolution is lost in the ISIT camera compared to the SIT camera, but if ultra low light level performance is required it is probably the best choice.

The CCTV camera image tube responds to the reflected light from the scene. If the scene is illuminated via sunlight or artificial lighting (fluorescent, tungsten, etc.), a standard vidicon using an antimony trisulfide target is generally satisfactory. This vidicon has advantages and disadvantages. Its primary advantages are: (1) excellent image resolution; and (2) the ability to be operated and controlled over wide variations in lighting levels from bright sunlight (10,000 FtCd) to a relatively dim (1 FtCd) indoor scene. This represents a 10,000 to 1 variation in light level. With some sacrifice in picture quality, a 100,000 to 1 variation in light level can be achieved. A third advantage is its low cost and availability. The primary disadvantages of this type vidicon are: (1) a fixed scene being viewed will slowly *burn* into the vidicon over an extended period of time; and (2) if the camera inadvertently receives direct sunlight, a bright reflection, or direct light from an ordinary tungsten lamp, the tube will be damaged, and a burn spot (white spot on the monitor) will be seen.

When an application requires viewing bright lights or occasionally the sun or its reflections, a camera having a silicon, Newvicon, or Ultracon† target (instead of antimony trisulfide) is the better

choice. If size is important, or all solid state design is required, the CCD camera is the choice. These cameras are about 10 to 20 times more sensitive (can see at dusk or low level lighting) depending on the type of illumination, and they will not burn. The tubes, however, are not a panacea since they cannot operate over more than about a 100 to 1 change in light level. An application having a larger light level change requires an additional automatic optical attenuator (automatic iris) for proper operation. Also, these tubes cost considerably more than standard vidicons.

A brief description of the television camera scanning process and video signal will now be given with the aid of Figure 10–5. The television tube and camera converts the optical image into an electrical signal called *composite video*, which contains the picture information and various synchronization pulses. Signals are transmitted in what is called a *frame of picture video*, which is made up of two fields of information. Each field is transmitted in 1/60 of a second, the entire frame in 1/30 of a second.

A picture field is made by scanning approximately 262 horizontal lines. The second field of the frame contains the second 262 lines which are synchronized so that they fall between the gaps of the first field lines, thus producing one completely interlaced picture frame. If the requirement that the scan lines of the second field fall exactly halfway between the lines of the first field, a 2 to 1 interlace system results. As shown in Figure 10–5, the first field starts at the upper left hand corner and progresses down the screen line by line until it ends at the bottom center of the screen. Likewise the second field starts at the top center of the scan and ends at the lower right hand corner. Each time one line in the field traverses from the left hand side of the scan to the right hand side, it corresponds to one horizontal line as shown in the video wave form at the bottom of Figure 10–5. The video wave form consists of negative synchronization pulses, and positive picture information. Horizontal and vertical synchronization pulses are used by the television monitor to synchronize the video picture and lay an exact replica in time and intensity of the camera scanning function. Black picture information is indicated on the wave form at the bottom of the picture information and white picture information at the top. The peak to peak amplitude of a standard NTSC signal should be 1.4 volts peak to peak. The frame of picture information consists of approximately 512 lines with the 525 line system, providing the additional lines necessary for vertical

---

*Trademark Matsushita Electric Co., Inc.
†Trademark of Radio Corporation of America.

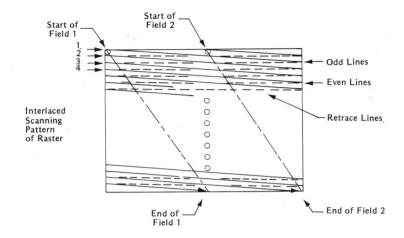

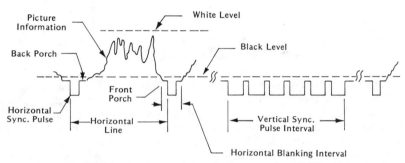

Figure 10–5. CCTV scanning and standard composite NTSC video signal.

blanking (the time during which retrace occurs as the camera tube beam moves from the bottom to the top to start a new field). Random interlace cameras do not provide complete synchronization between the first and second fields. Horizontal and vertical scan frequencies are not locked together; therefore, fields do not interlace exactly. This condition, however, results in an acceptable picture quality and is difficult to detect. The 2 to 1 interlace system has an advantage when multiple cameras are used with multiple monitors and/or video tape or cassette recorders in that they prevent jump or jitter when switching from one camera to the next.

Scene Illumination

The illumination present in the scene affects the amount of light ultimately reaching the television camera—an important factor contributing to successful CCTV operation. The illumination can be either from natural sources such as the sun, moon, or starlight, or from artificial sources such as tungsten, fluorescent, sodium, or Xenon lamps. It almost goes without saying that the more light available on the scene, the better the ultimate television picture. Some factors which must be considered in the source illuminating the scene include: 1) the source spectral characteristics; 2) the beam angle over which the source radiates; 3) the intensity of the source; and 4) the variations in the source intensity. Factors to be considered in the scene include: 1) the reflectance of objects in the scene; and 2) the complexity of the scene. The CCTV camera image tube responds to the reflected light from the scene. Figure 10–2 shows the illumination source, the scene to be televised, and the camera with the lens. The radiation from the illuminating source reaches the television camera by first reflecting off the objects in the scene.

To obtain a better understanding of scene and camera illumination, consider Figure 10–6. For practical purposes in planning a television system, it is necessary to know the amount of illumination

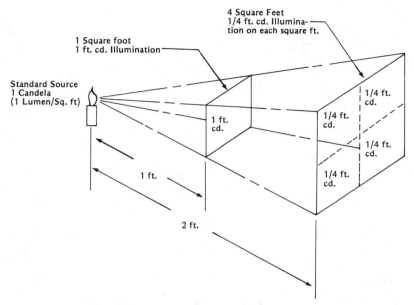

Figure 10–6. Geometry for defining illumination.

and intensity of light falling on a surface and how the illumination varies as a function of distance from the light source.

The amount of light (luminous intensity) produced by any light source is the candela. One foot candle of illumination is defined by the amount of light received from a one candela source at a distance of one foot. A light meter calibrated in foot candles will measure one foot candle at a distance of one foot. As shown in Figure 10–6, the light falling on a one square foot area at a distance of two feet is one-quarter foot candle. This indicates that the light level varies inversely and is the square

of the distance. That is, doubling the distance from the source reduces the light level to one-quarter of its original level. It should also be noted that exactly four times the area is now being illuminated by the same amount of light and this exactly corresponds to why each one-quarter of the area receives only one-quarter of the light. In Figure 10–2, if the scene is illuminated by sunlight, or moonlight, it will get a relatively uniform illumination. If, on the other hand, it is illuminated by several sources (i.e., lamps), the illumination may vary considerably over the field of view of the camera. Table 10–4 summarizes the overall light level ranges produced

Table 10–4. Source Light Level Variations and Applicable Cameras

Illumination Condition*	Illumination (ft cd)	Camera Tube Sensitivity Range[†]				
		Standard Vidicon	Silicon/ Newvicon	CCD	SIT	ISIT
Direct sunlight	10,000					
Full daylight	1,000					
Overcast day	100					
Very dark day	10					
Twilight	1					
Deep twilight	.1					
Full moon	.01					
Quarter moon	.001					
Starlight	.0001					
Overcast night	.00001					

*Natural light illumination (sun, star, or moonlight) using an f/1.4 lens and viewing a scene with 50% reflectance.
[†]Shaded region indicates useful operating range of TV camera.

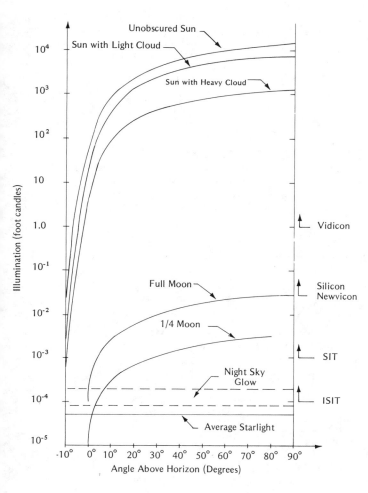

Figure 10–7. Natural illumination levels and camera sensitivities.

by direct sunlight down to the condition of overcast night. The measure of illumination is the foot candle (FtCd). For outdoor conditions, the camera system must operate over the full range of direct sunlight to nighttime conditions. It must have an automatic light control means to compensate for this light level change. Figure 10–7 summarizes the radiation characteristics of natural sources, i.e., the sun, the moon, and starlight, and how different types of cameras available operate with these light sources.

Standard daylight type vidicon cameras have automatic light level controls which permit operating from direct sunlight levels down to twilight conditions. Low light level cameras systems have automatic iris and electronic light control systems which can automatically adjust from direct sunlight conditions down to overcast night conditions.

Artificial light or illuminating sources consist of several types of lamps. These lamps may be used either in outdoor conditions, i.e., parking lots, out-door storage facilities, fence lines, or in indoor environments for general room lighting, hallway, work area, or elevator locations. The lamps are of two general types: tungsten or tungsten iodine lamps having solid filaments, and gaseous lamps having a low or high pressure gas in an envelope. Examples of the gaseous type include mercury, low and high pressure sodium, fluorescent, multi alkali, and Xenon. For special applications, some of these lamps are covered with a dark filter so that only invisible or infrared radiation illuminates the scene. Since the different camera types respond to different colors, it is important to know what type of illumination exists in a typical surveillance area, as well as what type might have to be added in order to get a suitable television picture. Figure 10–8 shows the light output characteristics of the various artificial sources available, as well as the natural sunlight and moonlight radiation characteristics. Superimposed on this figure are the spectral sensitivities

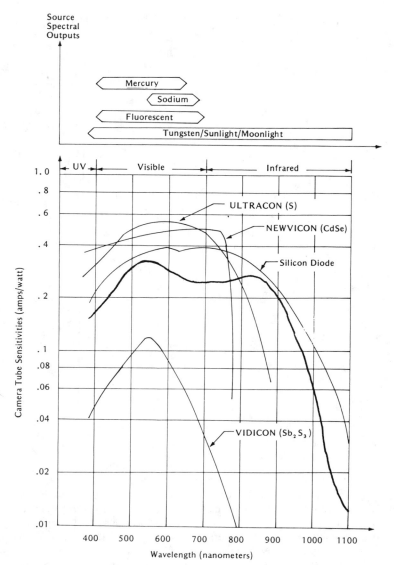

Figure 10–8. Natural and artificial light sources versus camera tube sensitivities.

of the different types of cameras that are available. Each of the different sources produce light in different wavelengths or colors. In order to obtain the maximum utility from any television camera, the camera must be sensitive to the light produced by the artificial or natural source. Sunlight, moonlight, and tungsten lamps produce energy in a range that most TV cameras are sensitive in. It is for this reason that low light level cameras are sensitive in both daylight and nighttime environments. Vidicon and Newvicon tubes are more sensitive to the visible wavelength (tungsten, mercury, sodium) than the silicon television tube. For covert applications,

the silicon, SIT or ISIT tubes are best, although the Newvicon tube has some sensitivity in the near-infrared region.

Another characteristic important in determining the amount of light needed for a scene is the beam angle over which the source radiates. It is obvious that the sun and moon radiate over the entire scene. Artificial light sources and lamps can be adjusted to produce narrow or wide angle beams. If a large area is to be viewed, it is necessary to either have a single wide beam source or multiple sources located within the scene to fully illuminate the scene. If, on the other hand, a small scene at a long range is to be viewed, it is only necessary to illuminate that part of the scene to be viewed with the beam, thereby reducing the total power needed from the source.

Scene Characteristics

The quality of the television picture depends on various scene characteristics. These characteristics include the contrast of the object(s) to be observed relative to the scene background, and whether the object(s) to be viewed are in a simple uncluttered background or a complicated scene. Actually, how well a television system operates depends on whether the information required to do the job consists of: (1) detecting an object or movement in the scene; (2) recognizing the type of object in the scene, i.e., adult or child, car or truck; and (3) identifying the object (If it is a person, who is the person? Exactly what kind of truck?). Whether or not or how well these distinctions can be made depends on the resolution of the system and the contrast obtained at that resolution.

The probability that you can see an object in a field is influenced not only by the illumination level and the contrast of the object with respect to the scene background and the complexity of the scene,

but also by how large that object is with respect to the scene, i.e., the angle of that object, as seen by the camera. In a typical scene it has been determined that the average observer can see a target about one-tenth of a degree in angle. Relating this information to the television picture having 525 horizontal lines and having about 350 line vertical and 500 line horizontal resolution, Table 10–5 summarizes the number of lines required to detect, orient, recognize, or identify an object in the television picture.

Coaxial Cable and Wireless Transmission

There are several techniques for transmitting the video signal from the CCTV camera to the monitor. The most common, reliable, and lowest-cost form is via coaxial cable. There are basically four types of cable for use in video transmission systems: 1) 75 ohm unbalanced coaxial cable for installations in buildings; 2) 75 ohm coaxial cable for outdoor use; 3) 124 ohm balanced indoor coaxial cable; 4) 124 ohm balanced outdoor cable. The type of cable used for any particular installation depends on the environment in which the cable will be used and the electrical characteristics required for the system. By far, the most common forms of coaxial cable

Table 10–5. Number of TV lines to detect, orient, reorganize, and identify

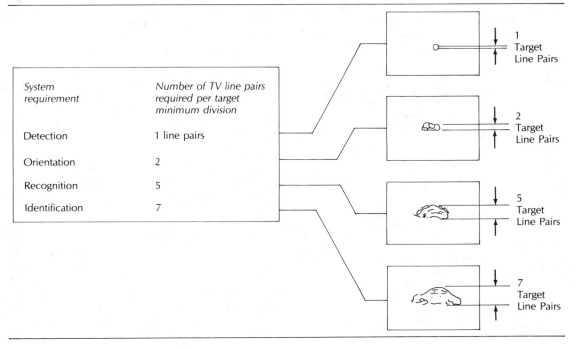

System requirement	Number of TV line pairs required per target minimum division
Detection	1 line pairs
Orientation	2
Recognition	5
Identification	7

1 Target Line Pairs

2 Target Line Pairs

5 Target Line Pairs

7 Target Line Pairs

used are the RG-59/U and the RG-11/U, 75 ohm impedance type. Common forms of this coaxial cable are RG 59/U and RG 11/U. For a short camera-to-monitor distances (a few hundred feet), preassembled sections of RG 59/U coaxial cable with connectors at each end are used. These cables come in lengths of 25, 50, and 100 feet, with either UHF or BNC type connectors attached. Long cable runs (several hundred feet and up) should have a single length of coaxial cable with a connector at each end. For most interior CCTV installations, use 75 ohm unbalanced coaxial cables. When very long cable runs (several 1,000 feet or more) are used, particularly between several buildings, the balanced 124 ohm cable system should be considered. The equipment at the ends of the cable run, i.e., in two different buildings, may be at a slightly different ground potential, but may be impressed on the video signal and show up as an interference (wide bars on the video screen) and make the picture unacceptable. A two-wire balanced cable can eliminate this problem.

Television camera manufacturers generally specify the maximum distance between camera and monitor over which their equipment will operate. Table 10–6 is a guide for choosing the right type of cable for the application.

In situations of several thousand feet of cable runs, video amplifiers are required. These amplifiers are located at the camera output and/or somewhere along the coaxial cable run. These amplifiers permit the camera to monitor distances up to 3,400 feet for Rg 59 cable to 6,500 feet for Rg 11 cable.

Closed circuit television refers to transmitting the video signal (Figure 10–5), at what is referred

Table 10–6. CCTV Coaxial Cable Characteristics

| | Maximum Recommended Camera to Monitor Range for Each Type Cable* | | |
Cable Type	Cable Only[1] (ft.)	With Video Amplifier[2] (ft.)	Powered[3] Coaxial (ft.)
Rg 59/U	500	3,400	2,000
Rg 6/U	750	4,800	
Rg 11/U	1,000	6,500	3,000
Rg 15/U	1,500	8,600	

*If a coaxial cable can't be installed, the video signal can be transmitted over a twisted pair of telephone wires. A special transmitter and receiver permit transmission over a range of 4,000 ft. using #22 or #24 wire.
[1] All cables have a 75 ohm impedance necessary for CCTV.
[2] The video amplifier is connected at the camera output to extend the coaxial cable effective range.
[3] Single coax cable powers the camera and transmits the video signal.

to baseband frequencies, over coaxial cable. Figure 10–9 shows the single channel television bandwidth requirements for black and white and color systems. Each channel requires approximately 6 MHz; however, black and white pictures can be transmitted for security and safety applications with a 4.5 MHz bandwidth. If more than one channel of television information is to be transmitted over a single cable, the video signal is modulated at RF frequencies, transmitted over the cable, then demodulated at the remote end, and the multiple camera signals presented on multiple monitors (Figure 10–9). This type of system is often used when the video information from a large number of cameras must be transmitted to a large number of receivers over long distances. These systems require careful analysis and choice of the modulator, coaxial cable run, and demodulator. Table 10–7 summarizes some of the television transmission frequencies used in video. The VHF and UHF frequency ranges are commonly used in the RF transmission systems.

Most cameras operate from 117 VAC or 24 VAC. If a 117 VAC outlet is available at the camera location, use it. If power is to be run from a remote location to the camera, a 117 VAC to 24 VAC step-down transformer powering a 24 VAC camera has an advantage; any technician can install it. No electrician is required. A 50 volt-amp (VA) power rating on the transformer is readily available and adequate to power the camera. When a CCD solid state camera is used, either a 12 volt DC power source or a wall plug mounted 117 VAC to 12 volt AC power converter can be used.

There are cameras available which require only a coaxial cable for operation. The coaxial cable (RG 59 or RG 11) transmits both the camera power and the video signal. This is referred to as vidiplexing. This single cable camera model reduces installation costs, eliminates costly utility wiring and conduit, and is ideal for installing into hard-to-reach places.

If a coaxial cable is not available or difficult to install (perhaps because two buildings are separated by a street), a technique exists for transmitting the television picture over a dedicated pair of wires. These wires can be run parallel or as a twisted pair but they cannot run through a telephone switching station. The system uses a small transmitter and receiver at each end of the pair of wires and will transmit the picture over a maximum distance of about 3,000 feet. Surprisingly good television transmission quality is obtained. In addition, a variation of this system includes transmitting simultaneously in both directions CCTV pictures with one-half the

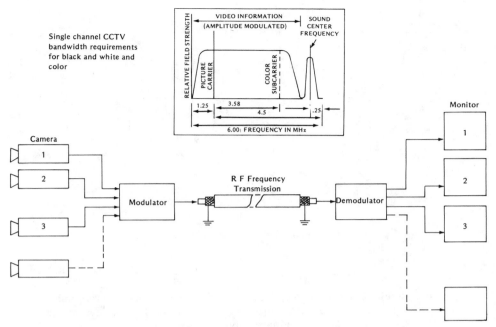

Figure 10–9. CCTV bandwidth requirements for transmission.

Table 10–7. Television Transmission Frequencies

Band Designation	Frequencies Allocated
CCTV-Closed Circuit Television	0–30 MHz
VHF-Very High Frequency	
1. Channels 2,3,4	54–72 MHz
2. Channels 5,6	76–88 MHz
3. Channels 7 thru 13	174–216 MHz
UHF-Ultra High Frequency	
Channels 14 thru 83	470–890 MHz
X Band Microwave (Security)	10.525 GHz*

* 1 GHz = 1,000 MHz

resolution of a normal picture. This is real-time duplex television. Two-way voice communication and control signals for switching cameras, adjusting the camera lenses, and other functions can be added. This system is shown in Figure 10–10.

Other means for transmitting television pictures without cables (wireless) include the use of microwave transmission and gallium arsenide (GaAs) infrared laser transmission. The microwave system has a range of approximately 3,500 feet with excellent picture quality but may require an FCC license for operation. On the other hand, the infrared laser transmission requires no FCC approval, but does have a shorter range; generally 2,000 feet or less in good visibility conditions and down to a few hundred feet in poor visibility conditions. A microwave system exists which has a built-in intrusion detection function, so that if the beam is disturbed by a person walking between the transmitter and receiver, an alarm output is registered. Both these systems permit independent placement of the CCTV camera in locations which might be inaccessible for a coaxial cable transmission.

The above wireless transmission systems all result in real-time television transmission. A scheme for transmitting the television picture over large distances, i.e., anywhere in the world, makes use of what is called slow scan television transmission. This nonrealtime technique involves storing one television picture (snapshot) and sending it slowly over the telephone network anywhere within a country or from one country to another. The received picture is reconstructed to produce a continuously displayed television snapshot. Each snap-shot is transmitted in 32 seconds with a resulting picture having a resolution of approximately one-half that of a conventional closed circuit TV system. Every subsequent scene is transmitted in 32 seconds so that a time lapse effect is achieved. Shorter transmission times are possible at corresponding decreases in picture resolution. Figure 10–11 shows the system.

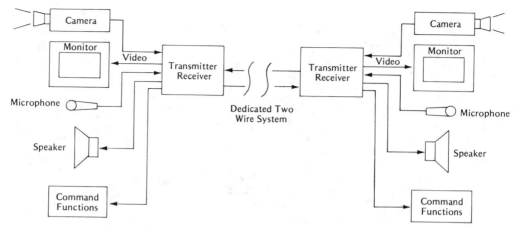

Figure 10–10. Realtime CCTV transmission via telephone lines.

CCTV Monitors

Standard television monitors are available with screen sizes from 5-inch to 23-inch diameter diagonal with the 9-inch diagonal monitor in most common use. These monitors are available for 117 volt AC operation. Several are available for 12 volt DC operation. Connections are made via UHF or BNC connectors on the rear, and terminated in either 75 ohm or high impedance inputs. If only one monitor is used, the switch on the rear of the monitor is set to the 75 ohm or Low Impedance position for best results. If multiple monitors are used, all but the last monitor in the series is set to the High Impedance position. The last monitor is set to the Low Impedance position. All cameras and monitors have a 4 × 3 format, i.e., horizontal size is in a 4 to 3 ratio to the vertical size.

Small viewfinders and portable type monitors are available having 1½ inch to 4½ inch diameter tube sizes and are powered by 9 or 12 volts DC or 117 VAC. These monitors are used in portable applications and for servicing equipment out in the field. One such monitor utilizes a new rear surface, flat tube which results in a monitor with an inherently brighter (more contrast) picture, and a very thin profile package. One of these Sony flat screen monitors is shown in Figure 10–12.

Once the single camera-lens system is understood, most of the design toward multiple camera systems has been accomplished. A question remaining is whether an individual monitor is sufficient to

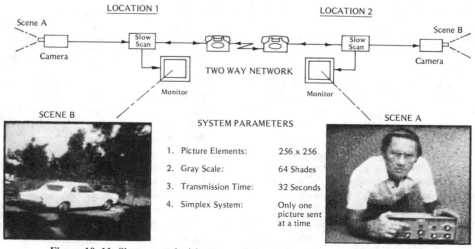

Figure 10–11. Slow scan television transmission and resulting snapshot pictures.

Figure 10–12. Portable flat screen monitor. (Courtesy of the Sony Corporation.)

display each camera or whether the picture from each individual camera should be switched into a single display monitor via an electronic switcher. Depending on the preference of individual viewers, the number of people entering and leaving each of the camera areas, the activity in the scenes, one or the other will be chosen. If the scene activity, i.e., the number of people passing into or out of an area is relatively high, all cameras should be displayed on separate monitors. For installations with infrequent activity or casual surveillance, an electronic switcher should be used. There are switchers available having manual and automatic switching sequences.

Video Switchers

There are many different types of video switchers available for connecting multiple cameras to a single monitor or multiple monitors. The simplest type switcher is the manual switcher (Figure 10–13) which provides the function of choosing one camera from a number of cameras and presenting that one camera on a single video monitor. The switches are activated manually to connect the individual cameras to the monitor. Shown in Figure 10–13 are the two basic types available: manual passive switcher and manual active switcher. The basic difference between the two is that the passive switcher uses a simple contact switch whereas the active switcher uses an electronic switch. Switchers are generally built to accommodate from 4 to 16 different cameras.

Figure 10–14 shows a second type of switcher

called a homing sequential switcher. This switcher can operate in an automatic sequencing mode, whereby each of the individual cameras is presented on the television monitor, one after the other automatically. The length of time each camera picture is presented on the monitor is variable by the operator. The three position front panel switches provide three separate functions for operation: automatic sequencing, bypass, and select (homing). When a switch is set to *bypass*, that particular camera is not displayed. When the switch is set to *Select*, that camera picture is presented continuously on the monitor and in essence overrides the automatic sequencing function. This permits continuous observation of any particular camera at the operator's command.

Figure 10–15 shows the block diagram for a bridging sequential switcher. This switcher system operates in a similar way to the homing sequential switcher but has the additional feature that two monitors can view the television cameras. The first monitor (the sequential monitor) has all the functions of the homing sequential switcher. The bridging monitor sees whatever camera is selected on the switcher when in the *Select* mode of operation. When the particular camera is selected for the bridging monitor, the automatic sequence continues for the sequential monitor.

Figure 10–16 shows the block diagrams for looping homing and looping bridging sequential systems. The looping homing system is similar to the homing sequential switchers with the additional capability that all camera inputs can be brought out to a second switcher which in turn operates as a homing sequential switcher. The looping bridging sequential switchers operate in the same manner as the bridging sequential switchers except that looping input capability is added.

Another type of switcher is called an alarming switcher. This switcher displays a picture on a monitor or starts a video tape recorder each time a camera activated by a motion detector system or another alarm is activated. When it is used with a video cassette or tape recorder, a switch closure on the back of the switcher turns on the recorder which can be set up for either a realtime or time lapse mode of operation.

CCTV Equipment

Lenses: Fixed Focal Length

The majority of lenses used in CCTV applications are referred to as fixed focal length lenses. These

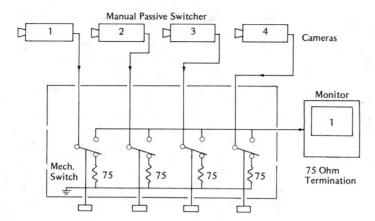

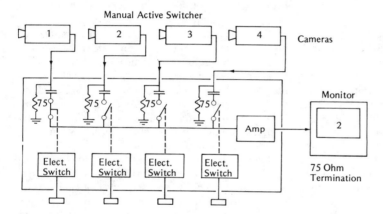

Figure 10–13. Manual CCTV switching systems.

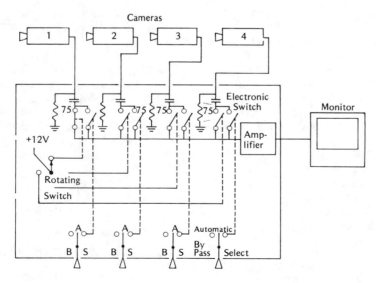

Figure 10–14. Homing sequential switcher system.

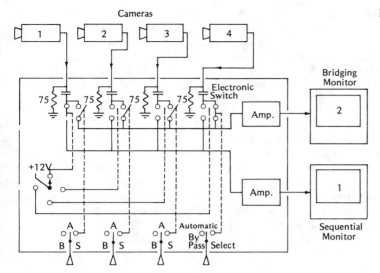

Figure 10–15. Bridging sequential switcher system.

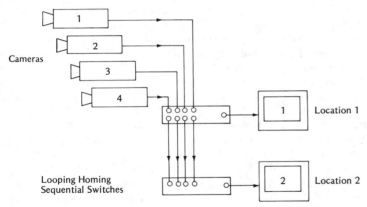

Figure 10–16. Looping-homing sequential switcher system.

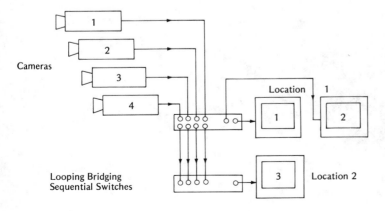

all have a *C* mount (1 inch × 32 threads per inch) mounting. They are used on a ⅔-inch or 1-inch vidicon camera and have a fixed field of view (FOV). Commonly used focal lengths vary from 4.0mm (wide angle) to 150mm (telephoto). Most of the available focal lengths between these values and their corresponding areas of coverage are shown in Tables 10–1 and 10–2.   Most of these lenses are available with a manually adjustable iris, and those lenses down to approximately 8.5mm focal length are available with an adjustable focus ring. The 4.0mm to 4.8mm focal length lenses are available only for ⅔-inch vidicon cameras and show some image distortion in the picture. The 4.0mm lens has a 96 degree horizontal by 79 degree vertical FOV and considerable distortion. It can, however, effectively view an extremely wide area in close quarters. Long focal length lenses—150mm to 1,000mm—are generally used outdoors, viewing parking lots or other remote areas, and usually are quite large and require very stable mounts (or pan/tilt drives) to obtain good quality pictures. From 4.0mm focal length up to several hundred millimeters, the lenses are of the refractive or glass type. Beyond a few hundred millimeters focal length, in order to achieve reasonably fast lenses, reflective type mirror optics or mirror/lens optics are used. Table 10–2 shows the angular FOV obtainable with lenses from 4mm focal length up to 600mm focal length. Above approximately 150mm focal length, lenses become large and expensive. Although long focal length lenses can be designed with small lens or mirror elements the amount of light passed through these lenses to the television camera is too small to be of practical use. Therefore, as the focal length becomes longer, the diameter of the lens increases, and costs increase substantially. Most fixed focal length lenses are

available in a motorized or auto iris form for use in remote control applications. When they are used with low light level television cameras such as the Newvicon, Silicon, SIT, and ISIT types, the iris or light level control must be varied depending on the scene illumination. This is usually accomplished via automatic iris and neutral density filters.

Zoom Lens

The zoom lens is a second class of lens used particularly in remote control applications (pan/tilt) where the FOV seen by the lens and camera must be varied from wide angle to narrow angle and vice versa (Figure 10–4). The zoom lens has a variable focal length (variable magnification) and the ability to change its FOV. This lens permits viewing narrow, medium, and wide angle scenes depending on its setting (which may be motorized), thereby permitting initial wide field viewing of an area and then close-in telephoto viewing of one portion of the area. Focal length ranges for various classes of zoom lenses vary from 20 to 200mm and anywhere from 3 to 1 focal length change to 20 to 1 focal length change. These lenses are available for either manual or motorized operation.

Split Image Lenses

A lens for imaging two independent scenes onto a single television camera is called an *image splitting optical* or *bifocal* system. The lens system views the two scenes with two separate lenses with the same or different magnifications and combines them on the camera tube (Figure 10–17);   depending on

Figure 10–17. Split image lens.

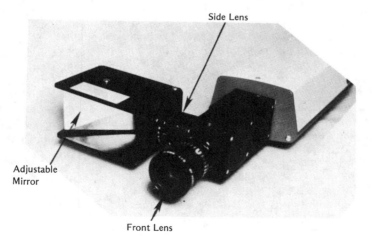

Side Lens

Adjustable Mirror

Front Lens

Front section moves up and down
to point lenses far out or close in

Figure 10–18. Tri-split lens.

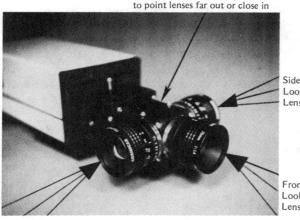

Side
Looking
Lens

Front
Looking
Lens

Side
Looking
Lens

the orientation of the lens system on the camera, either a vertical or horizontal split is obtained. The C mount lenses can have the same or different focal lengths, and any lens which mechanically fits can be used. The adjustable mirror on the side lens permits looking in many directions. The adjustable mirror can be oriented so that it is pointing at the same scene as the front lens. In this case, if the front lens is a wide angle lens (say, 6.5mm focal length) and the side lens is a narrow angle lens (say, 75mm focal length) a bifocal length system results; i.e., *simultaneous* wide field and narrow field coverage *with one camera* results. The split FOV covered by each of the lenses is one-half of the total lens FOV. For example, with the 6.5mm and 75mm focal length lenses, on a ⅔-inch camera and a vertical split, the 6.5mm lens will display a 49.3 ft. × 74 ft. scene, and the 75mm will display a 4.1 ft. × 6.3 ft. scene at a distance of 50 ft. The horizontal FOV of each lens has been reduced by one-half. The bifocal lens inverts the picture on the monitor, a condition which is rectified by either inverting the camera or its vertical deflection coil.

Another image splitting lens which can produce a 3-way optical image is shown in Figure 10–18. The lens is designed primarily for viewing three hallways at one time. This lens provides the ability to view three (3) different scenes with the same or different magnifications on one monitor with one camera with no electronic splitters required, thereby replacing two cameras and two monitors. Each scene occupies one-third of the monitor face. Adjustable optics in the lens permits changing the pointing elevation angle of the three front lenses so that they can look close in for short hallway appli-

cations, and all the way out for long hallways. This lens inverts the monitor image as does the bisplit lens.

In complex video systems containing many television cameras, it is sometimes desirable to combine several television pictures onto one monitor. Combining four full camera pictures on one monitor is accomplished using a Quad Combiner. This Quad system takes four standard CCTV camera signals, compresses the pictures they represent, and displays the four compressed pictures on a single monitor. Figure 10–19 shows a typical Quad picture. Each individual picture on the monitor is from the full camera picture.

Figure 10–19. One monitor using a Quad Combiner.

Covert Lenses

A technique for accomplishing television surveillance obtaining particular attention is the use of covert cameras and lenses. Using this technique, the camera and lens are out of view of anyone in the area under surveillance, and the result is still a high quality television picture of the area. By this method, unsuspecting violators are viewed on closed circuit television, their actions recorded, and, if necessary, apprehended. Figure 10–20 shows how these lenses and cameras are mounted behind a wall with the lens viewing through a small hole in the wall. The illuminating source for indoor applications is generally fluorescent or tungsten light. Figure 10–21 shows two alternate configurations for the television systems in which a straight or right angle system is used. The right angle version permits locating the camera and lens inside a narrow wall or above a ceiling. In both cases, i.e., straight pinhole or right angle, it is imperative to locate the front element of the lens as close to the front surface of the wall as possible. This prevents tunneling of the light reaching the lens through the hole. When the front element of the lens is close to the front barrier, a full FOV of the scene is obtained. If the lens is back from the front surface of the barrier opening, vignetting occurs and less than the designed FOV is obtained. A porthole effect is obtained. The optical speed of the pinhole lens is important for the successful implementation of a covert camera system. The lower the f/number (f/#) the more light is reaching the television camera and hence the better the television picture. The best theoretical f/# is equal to the focal length (FL) divided by the entrance lens diameter (d):

$$f/\# = \frac{FL}{d}$$

xx

In practice, the f/# obtained is worse than this as determined by various lens losses such as lens transmission, reflection, absorption, and other lens imaging properties. For a pinhole lens, the light getting through the lens to the television tube is limited primarily by the diameter of the lens or the mechanical opening through which it views. For this reason, the larger the entrance diameter of the lens, the more light getting through to the television tube. More light means a better picture quality, all other conditions remaining the same.

The amount of light getting through the lens system varies as the square of the lens f/#. Small f/# differences make large differences in the television picture quality obtained. The f/# relationship is analogous to water flowing through a pipe; i.e., if the pipe diameter is doubled, four times as much water flows through it. Table 10–8 shows the large light level differences between pinhole lenses having different f/– numbers. These parameters are representative of commercially available lenses. Types of pinhole lenses available today are analyzed below. One pinhole lens type has a focal length of 9mm and a very small entrance diameter of 2.5mm (.10 inches). This lens has a theoretical f/# of:

$$f/\# = \frac{9mm}{2.5mm} = 3.6$$

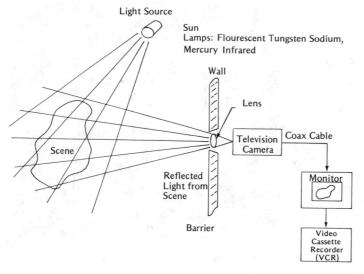

Figure 10–20. Covert CCTV Surveillance system.

Light Source
Sun
Lamps: Flourescent Tungsten Sodium, Mercury Infrared
Wall
Lens
Scene
Television Camera
Coax Cable
Reflected Light from Scene
Barrier
Monitor
Video Cassette Recorder (VCR)

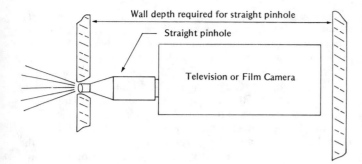

Figure 10–21. Straight and right-angle pinhole lens installations.

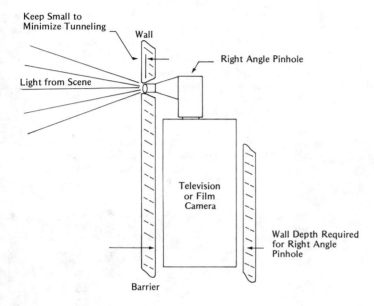

Table 10–8. Pinhole Camera Lens Characteristics

System Type	Lens Focal Length	Lens Diameter	Lens f/#	Light Power*	Camera FOV Horizontal × Vertical	Configuration
Pinhole camera	11.5mm	.25 inch (6mm)	1.8	5	47 × 38	Straight
	11.5mm	.25 inch (6mm)	1.8	5	47 × 38	Right angle
Manual iris	9mm	.10 inch (2.3)	4.0	1	58 × 48	Straight
8mm lenses	9mm	.125 inch (3.2)	4.0	1	67 × 53	Straight
Pinhole lenses	9mm	.100 inch (2.5)	4.0+	0.9	67 × 53	Right angle
	11.5mm	.25 inch (6mm)	2.5	2.6	47 × 38	Straight
	11.5mm	.25 inch (6mm)	2.8	2.1	47 × 38	Right angle
Auto iris	11.5mm	.25 inch (6mm)	2.5	2.6	47 × 38	Straight
Pinhole lenses	11.5mm	.25 inch (6mm)	4.0	1	47 × 38	Right angle

*Light power is a figure of merit for the lens system based on the f/4 pinhole lens having a lens efficiency of 1 (one). The *higher* the number the better the system. Example:

$$\text{Light Power for Pinhole Camera} = \frac{(4.0)^2}{(1.8)^2} = 5$$

This lens is optically low by design. Real optical losses mentioned above result in this lens having an f/# of approximately f/4.0. A second type pinhole lens available has a focal length of 11.5mm and an entrance lens diameter of 6mm. This lens has a theoretical f/# of:

$$f/\# = \frac{11.5mm}{6mm} = 1.9$$

Lens losses result in this lens having an f/number of f/2.5. To emphasize, the most important characteristics of pinhole lenses are: fast optical speed: what is the f/number (the lower the better), and how easy they are to use. Figure 10–22 shows a straight pinhole lens and a right angle pinhole lens for mounting a camera parallel to a wall or ceiling. Both are designed for ⅔-inch format television cameras and have a manual iris control to adjust the initial light level reaching the camera.

When low light level covert applications exist, a sensitive camera such as a Newvicon or Silicon camera is required, and a pinhole lens with an automatic iris controlling the light reaching the camera is necessary Figure 10–23 shows straight and right angle pinhole lenses with automatic irises able to control the light level reaching the camera over a 300,000 to 1 light level range. If a requirement exists for viewing through a 6 to 12-inch thick wall, where the pinhole lens cannot approach the area on the viewing side of the wall, a rigid fiber optic pinhole lens is used (Figure 10–24). This lens has a 50 degree field of view and is less than ½ inch in diameter. The ½-inch diameter rigid fiber optic tube is available in lengths from 6 to 12 inches long. The fiber optic lens speed is f/4, which is slower than the standard, all lens type system. It should also be pointed out that the picture obtained with the fiber optic system is not as clean as that obtained with an all lens pinhole lens. There are some cosmetic imperfections which look like dust spots, as well as a geometric pattern caused by packing of the fibers. The picture is adequate for identification of people and actions, and has a resoluion similar to a standard ⅔-inch camera system. The fiber optic pinhole is available with

Iris

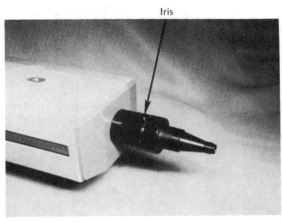

Straight

Iris

Right Angle

Figure 10–22. Straight and right-angle pinhole lenses.

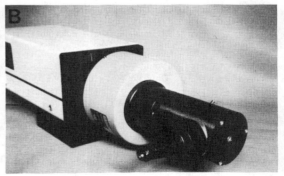

Figure 10–23. Automatic iris pinhole lenses. (a) Straight. (b) Right-angle.

Iris

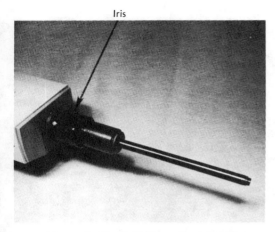

Figure 10–24. Rigid fiberoptic pinhole lens.

tions to date, this system integrates the fastest pinhole lens directly into the camera. The lens has a 11.5mm FL and a front barrel diameter of 3/8 inch (9.5mm) and a taper which makes it easy to mount behind a barrier (See Figure 10–20 or 10–21). A means for focusing the lens while it is installed is located at the rear of the camera. Table 10–8 summarizes the characteristics of the pinhole camera and commercially available pinhole lenses. In order to compare different lenses with a respect to their ability to transmit light to the camera tube, a light power factor is defined with an f/4.0 lens as a base or reference (see Table 10–8). Note the difference in light passing through the pinhole camera as compared to the pinhole lenses. The f/1.8 pinhole camera transmits five (5) times as much light as an f/4 pinhole lens.

automatic iris and for a ⅔-inch television format.

When the utmost flexibility between the front objective lens and the television camera is required, (pinhole lens or otherwise) a flexible fiber optic bundle is used. This system is shown in Figure 10–25. The 36 inch long fiber optic bundle encased in a braided stainless steel sheathing can be twisted through 360 degrees with no image degradation. It, too, has spots like the rigid fiber optic. All pinhole lenses and rigid and flexible fiber optic systems invert the picture on the camera.

A unique *pinhole camera* (Figure 10–26) is now in use, which combines a very fast pinhole lens—f/1.8—with a new television camera design. Unlike all other covert pinhole lens and camera combina-

Right Angle Lens

Another very useful lens for mounting cameras parallel to a wall or ceiling is shown in Figure 10–27. This right angle optical system permits use of wide angle lenses (4.0mm, 100 degree) looking at right angles to the camera axis. This cannot be accomplished by using a mirror and a wide angle lens directly on the camera, since the entire scene will not be reflected by the mirror to the lens on the camera. The edges of the scene will not appear on the monitor because of picture vignetting. The right angle adapter permits the use of any focal length lens that will mechanically fit into its C mount. It is designed for ⅔-inch or one-inch camera formats.

Figure 10–25. Flexible fiberoptic pinhole lens.

Camera   Iris

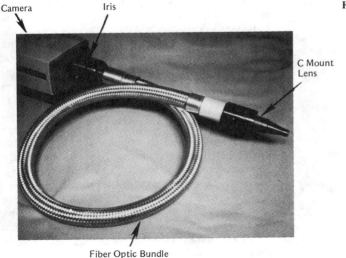

C Mount Lens

Fiber Optic Bundle

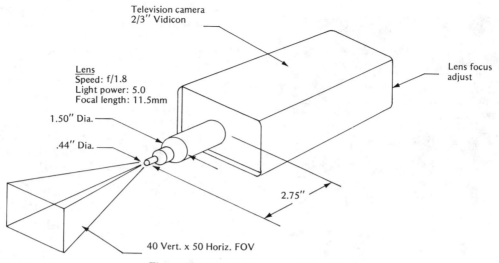

Television camera
2/3″ Vidicon

Lens focus
adjust

Lens
Speed: f/1.8
Light power: 5.0
Focal length: 11.5mm

1.50″ Dia.

.44″ Dia.

2.75″

40 Vert. x 50 Horiz. FOV

Figure 10–26. Pinhole camera geometry.

Figure 10–27. (a) Right angle and (b) auto iris right angle lenses.

CCTV Cameras

Most cameras used for security have a ⅔-inch vidicon format, and use a standard antimony trisulfide (Sb_2S_3) tube. One-inch vidicon cameras are used when the highest level of reliability and the best resolution are required. All vidicon cameras utilize automatic light control (ALC)—this changes the camera amplification to adapt to large variations in light level conditions. ALC compensation over a 10,000:1 range is standard, although cameras having a 100,000:1 ALC capability are available. When the ALC capability of the camera, in addition to the auto iris mechanism in the lens, are utilized, light level compensation of 660,000:1 or more are accomplished for low light level cameras. Other features available as options in many cameras include: (1) camera identification number, (2) electronic screen splitter, (3) RF modulator, and (4) external synchronization. The RF modulator option permits taking the composite video output from the camera and connecting directly into the antenna input of a home-type television receiver.

When standard vidicon cameras will not produce an adequate picture, lower light level cameras using the Newvicon, Silicon, or Ultracon tube, or the solid state CCD sensors cameras are used. These cameras have a sensitivity between 10 to 100 times better than the standard vidicon. In general, all three are relatively immune to image burn which can occur in standard vidicon cameras when they are pointed at bright lights or the sun, or continually at the same scene. When the available scene illumination is in the visible spectrum, the Newvicon is the better choice since it has slightly better resolution than the silicon types. When these lower light level cameras cannot produce an adequate picture, very low light level cameras such as the SIT (silicon intensified target) and ISIT (intensified SIT) cameras are required. These cameras are extremely sensitive and must use lenses having special automatic iris characteristics. Likewise, these cameras are expensive and are only justified when the light level cannot be raised by providing additional lighting.

Video Tape and Cassette Recorders

For many years, the reel-to-reel video tape recorders (VTR) have dominated the security field. This type recorder provided real time recording of the television picture, as well as time lapse recording for long periods of time. The ease of use of video cassettes and video cassette recorders (VCR) has resulted in widespread use of this type system. Present realtime recording systems record 2, 4, or 6 hours continuous black and white or color with more than 300 line resolution. Time lapse recorders have total recording time up to 200 hours and an alarming mode in which the recorder reverts to realtime when an alarm condition exists. Every television scene that can be displayed on a monitor is capable of being recorded on a VCR for a permanent record for later use. The tapes can be erased and reused many times so that tape cost remains relatively low.

Hard Disk Video File

Two new hard disk magnetic storage media have become available. These video files make use of microcomputer hard disks and can store from a few hundred to several thousand monochrome video frames on one 20 megabyte drive. While similar to the time lapse video recorder in that single frames (or fields) of video are stored, the hard disk can provide rapid random access to the stored pictures. Two generic systems

- Microcomputer based, digitized hard disk file
- Analog hard disk video file

An example of the microcomputer based hard disk video file is an IBM PCXT or AT with a video analog to digital conversion board and software to store the video frames. A PCXT with a 20 megabyte hard disk drive would typically store about 2,000 pictures, with any picture being able to be retrieved in a few seconds.

An example of an analog hard disk video file using a 20 megabyte hard disk drive would typically store about 2,450 pictures, and have a retrieval time of 0.2 seconds.

Pan and Tilt Systems

There are many accessories available for CCTV cameras and systems. Some of these accessories include pan/tilt mechanisms to rotate and tilt the camera to the direction of interest. These mechanisms are available for light-weight duty, indoor, small camera applications as well as large, heavy-weight outdoor systems for larger lens and camera installations. These mechanisms can operate in an automatic mode or via control from a remote control joystick mounted on a control console. Figure 10–28 shows a typical indoor and outdoor pan/tilt system.

Housings

There are many housings available for overt and covert camera installation for indoor and outdoor applications. One requirement for these housings is that they be vandalproof. The housing must protect the camera and lens and be rigidly attached to its mount. Another requirement for some housings is that they be unobtrusive, attractive, and fit into the surrounding decor. Some housings have these characteristics are shown in Figure 10–29. Indoor and outdoor housings are fabricated from metal as well as high impact plastic.

Time/Date Generators

Time/date generators are available to annotate the television picture with the time and date. Likewise, camera identification numbers can be annotated on the picture via generators either built into the camera or from external units in order to identify the camera being viewed or recorded.

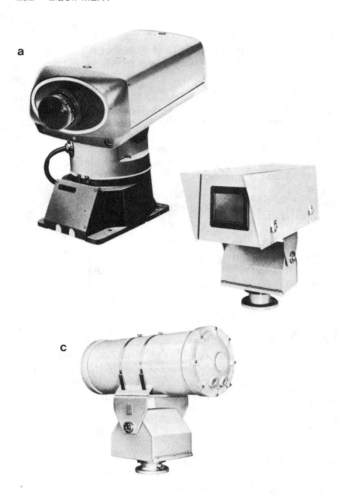

Motion Detectors

The output of a television camera when provided with appropriate processing electronics can make the camera operate as an alarm sensor. The processing electronics (motion detector) memorizes the instantaneous television picture and then, if the television picture changes by a prescribed amount somewhere in the scene, an alarm signal can be generated to alert a guard or record the video scene on the VCR. Although two general types of processing electronics have been used—analog processing and digital processing—the digital form provides more capability and reliability. The digital processor analyzes the picture and presents to the security operator such information as: location in the picture where a motion or intrusion has occurred: a record of the intrusion through the use of the VCR, and various audible and visible alarm signals. Figure 10–30 shows the block diagram for the motion detection system and illustrates in principle the type of information which can be obtained.

Microprocessor Control Console

Just as microprocessors and microcomputers are revolutionizing other fields, so are they providing giant steps in the security field. There are now microcomputer-based control systems for preprogramming and automating; pan/tilt, preset pointing location for the camera, camera identification number, automatic switching functions, all provided in one small console unit. Figure 10–31 illustrates a current state-of-the-art microcomputer console and the functions it can control.

Prior to microcomputer systems, these functions were provided by manually programmed dedicated

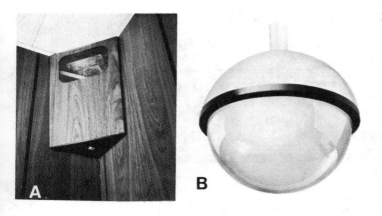

Figure 10–29. Examples of attractive, unobtrusive housings. (a) Corner ceiling housing. (b) Dome housing. (c) Outdoor housing.

Scene

Camera

White band
indicates
movement
in scene

Motion
Detection
Processing
Electronic

Figure 10–30. CCTV motion detection system.

function systems, which provided only limited flexibility in use. The new microcomputer-based systems, functioning via programming of small microcomputers, provide substantially expanded capabilities, ease of operation, and far greater flexibility in one single system.

Pinhole Camera

The availability of ultra fast pinhole cameras provide new and expanding capabilities in covert surveillance. This camera is shown in Figure 10–32. As indicated, this camera lens system has an optical

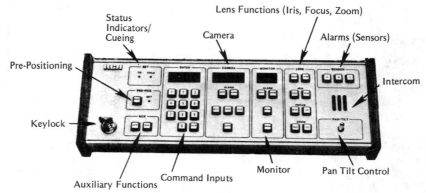

Figure 10-31. Microcomputer security console.

Figure 10–32. Pinhole camera with f/1.8 optics.

speed of f/1.8 (See Figure 10–26 for dimension and optical field of view.) Auto iris pinhole lenses for use with low light level cameras will significantly expand covert surveillance applications.

CCTV Applications

There is a wide variety of CCTV applications for meeting security and safety requirements. The power of the CCTV system with respect to its low investment cost attests to its widespread use. Since the CCTV applications are as varied as the environments in which they are used, only some guidelines and a few examples are presented here. The specific applications covered here are: single and multiple camera systems, wide angle indoor and outdoor CCTV systems, elevator security, parking lot and perimeter surveillance, multiple hallway surveillance, and photo ID access control systems.

Figure 10–1 shows a simple but often encountered CCTV problem—monitoring people entering and leaving the front lobby of a building with one camera CCTV system. The monitor is located at a remote guard station. The camera is located in the lobby

close to the ceiling and looks at the scene with a lens having a FOV large enough to see most of the lobby, the front door, and the internal access door. Aside from choosing the equipment, camera location is most important. The camera lens should not be pointed in the direction of the sun or toward an outside door. Large light level changes degrade the picture quality. The camera in Figure 10–1 is pointed toward the inside of the building, thereby receiving relatively constant illumination. If the camera uses a standard vidicon tube, direct sunlight or a bright target (common tungsten bulbs) would burn a permanent spot on the camera tube. This is seen as a white image on the monitor screen. With the camera location shown, it views people coming in and out, most of the lobby, and the internal access door.

There are many ways to install CCTV cameras. Three general methods are: simple camera bracket, recessed in the wall or ceiling, and attractive housings. Camera installations generally require protection from vandalism. Outdoor installations also require protection from the environment (temperature, precipitation, dirt).

Camera brackets are expedient but generally unattractive. Wall or ceiling installations are often custom-made and expensive. Attractive housings have several advantages: They keep dirt and flying debris away from the camera and lens, they protect the camera and lens from vandalism, and they can be heated or cooled to expand the camera temperature operating range.

Elevator Security

One application encountered quite often is the viewing of an entire room or elevator with one television

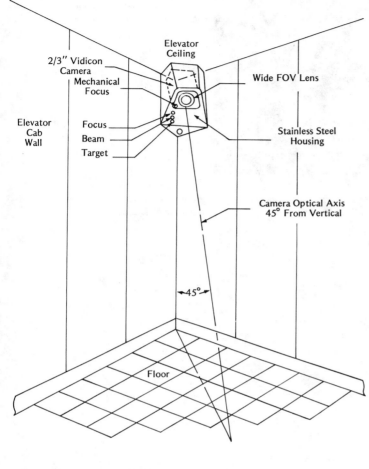

Figure 10–33. Optimum elevator CCTV system viewing.

Elevator Ceiling

2/3″ Vidicon Camera

Mechanical Focus

Wide FOV Lens

Elevator Cab Wall

Focus

Beam

Target

Stainless Steel Housing

Camera Optical Axis 45° From Vertical

◄45°►

Floor

camera. In this application, the picture should contain a maximum facial view of the occupants of the room or elevator and have sufficient resolution to permit identification of persons as well as their actions. A camera located in the ceiling corner of the room or elevator will best satisfy these requirements (see Figure 10–33). A small, unobtrusive, vandalproof CCTV surveillance system for elevators is shown in Figure 10–34 The lens used in the system has a 95 degree horizontal field of view and about 75 degrees vertical field of view and fast f/1.8 optical speed. The lens camera optical axis is directed 45 degrees from each wall and 45 degrees down from the horizontal (ceiling). This viewing geometry results in a 100 percent coverage of the room or elevator volume and provides excellent probability of occupant and activity identification. The rugged welded stainless steel system is vandalproof, can withstand abuse, and provides adequate protection for the lens and camera inside. The camera views

through a mar-resistant ¼-inch Lexan* window. The camera is a standard ⅔-inch vidicon, Newvicon or Silicon design. The housing is lockable and extremely difficult to open, break, or remove from the room or elevator. The small housing size—only 10½ inches high—makes it completely suitable for elevator installations. If an elevator installation requires a covert or near covert installation, or essentially no protrusion into the elevator cab, the television configuration shown in Figure 10–35 is used. This system, with a wide FOV lens (95 degrees horizontal), is used with the television camera via right angle optics. The key component in this system is the right angle optical adapter. This module bends the wide field image from the lens without vignetting. This right angle configuration permits the camera to be installed in the cab above the ceiling and out of view of the passengers.

*Trademark, General Electric Company.

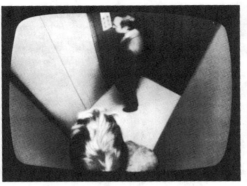

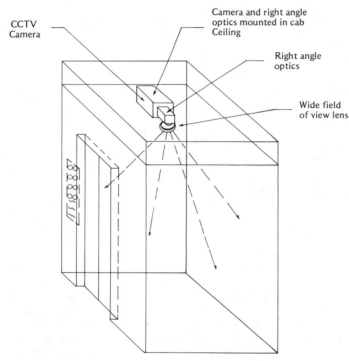

CCTV
Camera

Camera and right angle
optics mounted in cab
Ceiling

Right angle
optics

Wide field
of view lens

Figure 10–35. Covert elevator CCTV system using rightangle lens.

Two new variations of the elevator camera system shown in Figure 10–34 is a small housing for CCD solid state cameras—only six inches high—and an infrared illumination (IR) system shown in Figure 10–36. The CCD housing is very small because of the small camera size. The IR illuminator housing accommodates all CCD and small ⅔-inch Silicon tube cameras and provides an excellent picture in a totally darkened room.

Figure 10–37 illustrates the elevator system block diagram for a four-cab installation. In this particular application, four monitors are located in the building lobby and single monitor in the security room. An optional video tape recorder is shown.

Figure 10–38 illustrates a suitable location for the lobby monitors at ground floor of the building. As with other television systems, the cable is run up the elevator shaft along with the traveling cable and out to the monitors.

Wide FOV CCTV: Parking Lots

There are generally four techniques for solving the wide FOV CCTV application. These are: (1) a camera on a pan/tilt platform with a fixed focus or zoom lens, (2) multiple cameras to split the wide FOV into narrower FOV's, (3) a camera with a

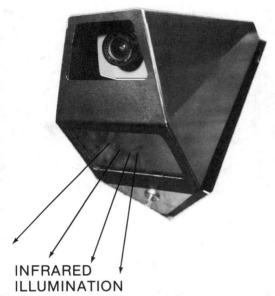

INFRARED
ILLUMINATION

Figure 10–36. Infrared Illumination (IR) system.

fixed, wide FOV lens, and (4) a camera on a pan/tilt with two lenses having a wide FOV and a narrow FOV lens. This last technique provides maximum surveillance of the area.

The pan/tilt system permits the television camera to rotate in a horizontal and vertical plane, thereby permitting the camera to look at scenes substantially outside the FOV of the lens used. The fixed lens and

camera systems (single or multiple cameras), on the other hand, only look at the FOV as determined by the lens FL and the camera tube diameter (see Tables 10–1 and 10–2).

Each of the four techniques have distinct advantages and disadvantages. The pan/tilt system has a primary advantage that it can look at any part of the scene by changing the lens-camera pointing direction. If a zoom lens (variable focal length and therefore a variable FOV) is used, it can provide excellent resolution when in the high magnification mode and good area coverage in the low magnification mode. The main disadvantages of the pan/ tilt installations are: high initial and maintenance costs, inherent optical dead zone, and operator time and dexterity required to manipulate pan/tilt and zoom functions. Maintenance costs come from periodically replacing electric motors, gearing, limit switches, etc. An additional maintenance item is the coaxial cable which bends and flexes each time the camera is moved and therefore must be replaced periodically.

The inherent optical dead zone of the pan/tilt system originates because the system cannot be looking at all places at the same time. When it is pointing in a particular direction, all areas outside the FOV of the lens are not under surveillance, and, hence, there is effectively no surveillance in those areas part of the time. Figure 10–39 illustrates this condition. The cross-hatched area is the instantaneous FOV of the camera (fixed focus lens FOV shown). The outer lines show the total pan/tilt

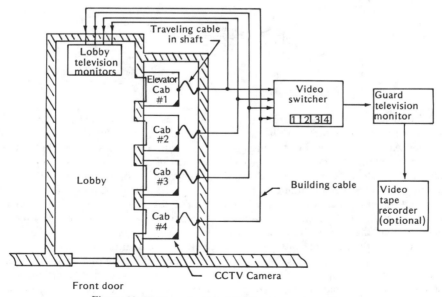

Figure 10–37. Four elevator CCTV system schematic.

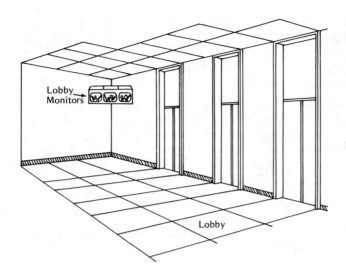

Figure 10–38. Lobby with CCTV monitors displaying elevator cab interiors.

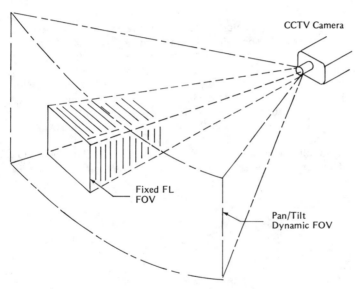

Figures 10–39. Static FOV versus pan tilt dynamic FOV.

dynamic FOV and lens FOV, and represents the total angular coverage which the pan/tilt camera system can view. At any time, most of the area for which surveillance is desired is not being displayed on the television monitor. To partially overcome this shortcoming, when the person hiding from the camera is out of the instantaneous FOV of the CCTV, the camera and pan/tilt mechanism is sometimes hidden, so that the person does not know where the camera is pointing at any particular instant.

The primary advantage of the fixed CCTV camera installation over the pan/tilt type are: low initial installation costs, low maintenance costs, and no optical dead zone. The primary disadvantage is that only a small FOV can be viewed with good resolution, i.e., the wider the FOV, the smaller the amount of detail that can be seen.

The bifocal optical image splitting lens (Figures 10–17, 10–40) offers a unique solution to the problem of displaying a wide FOV and narrow FOV (telephoto) scene simultaneously on one monitor. It is particularly advantageous when expensive low light level cameras (Newvicon, Silicon, SIT, ISIT) are used, since only one camera is used.

If, for instance, an 8.5mm lens and 75mm lens are used with the optical image splitter shown, FOV's of 27.4 by 42.5 degrees and 3.4 by 5 degrees,

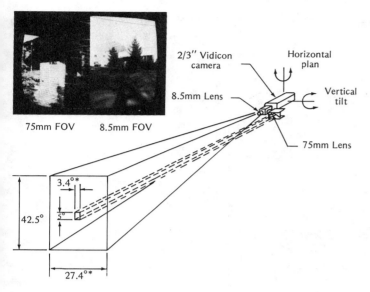

Figure 10–40. Bifocal split image lens FOV. One half the FOV is shown in Table 18-1 since image is split in half.

respectively, would be viewed (see Figure 10–40). At a distance of 50 feet, this represents views of 40.8 feet by 58.5 feet and 4.2 feet by 6.3 feet, respectively. If now the FOV of the telephoto lens is centered on that of the wide FOV lens a very effective CCTV surveillance system results. When the system operates with pan and tilt, wide area coverage is always displayed simultaneously with a close-up of the area of interest. A pan and tilt system, with or without a zoom lens, cannot accomplish this. To obtain maximum flexibility and wide angle area coverage, a bifocal lens, with a zoom lens and a narrow angle (75mm to 200mm FL) lens, is an excellent solution. The zoom lens permits a variable FOV coverage from wide angle (40 degrees) to medium coverage (4 degrees).

This combination is particularly good for outdoor parking lot and fence line (perimeter) applications. In the fence line application, if the pan/tilt, in its normal condition, is left pointing so that the telephoto FOV is looking at a perimeter gate or along the fence line, a video motion sensor programmed to respond only to the narrow FOV scene could be used to activate an alarm, guard cue, or VCR. Simultaneously the wide FOV zoom lens scene assures no dead zone in the scene.

Another common CCTV application is hallway surveillance in public facilities. Locations requiring such surveillance include: hotels and motels, office buildings, government buildings, and manufacturing plants. The CCTV requirement is to view down as many hallways as possible showing who is in the hallway, where they are going, and what they

are doing. Figure 10–41 illustrates the problem of monitoring the activity in a multistory hotel, showing the elevator lobby and room hallway, including the fire escape exits at the ends of the hallway. This application could be solved using three cameras and three monitors. This would not be acceptable since, in a multistory hotel, the guard would have to view too many monitors. Even if they were switched, the guard would be overburdened and ineffective. An improvement would be to connect the three cameras to two electric splitters and display the three cameras on one monitor.

The most cost-effective solution is to use one camera and the trisplit lens (Figure 10–18) and to display the three scenes on one monitor. The lower cost of the trifocal lens solution is emphasized when the cost of one low light level camera is compared to the three which are required in the other solutions. The total trisplit system can be housed in either a dome-shaped or rectangular type enclosure with a clear or tinted one-way mirrored surface. The inset in Figure 10–41 shows the lens, camera, and housing with cover removed.

CCTV Access Control System

The photo ID card has received widespread use providing a means for security personnel to admit or deny access to public, private, and government premises. CCTV provides two important features: positive visual identification and a view (and/or a VCR recording) of the person desiring access and the

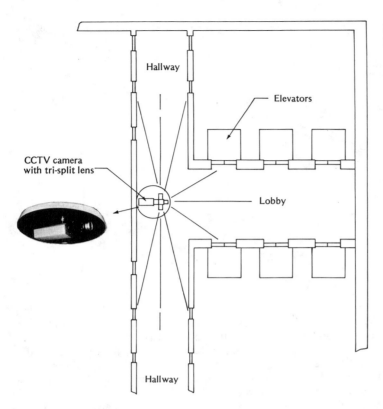

Figure 10–41. Hallway surveillance in hotels, motels, and office buildings.

photo ID card simultaneously in realtime. Since one guard can physically control only one access location at a time, a system permitting monitoring of more than one location by one guard is cost-effective. The photo ID-CCTV access control system lets the security guard view more than one access location and therefore control many entrances. If an installation has only one access location, a CCTV system is still cost-effective since it allows the security officer to perform other functions at the control console during slow periods of activity.

Several CCTV access control applications are listed below:

- Gates, turnstiles, or doors at outdoor perimeter access points
- Vehicle driver identification at perimeter access points
- Limited
- Limited access
- Realtime retrieval of stored personnel pictures and data

This application requires the use of a CCTV to control personnel access from the main lobby into the plant of an industrial building with assurance that only one person enters at a time (no tailgating)

and is not carrying unauthorized materials (equipment, etc.). Figure 10–42 shows all of the parts of the television access control system required in the lobby and the remote guard location to accomplish this. The television ID camera system is mounted in the lobby on the wall next to the access door to view the face of the person desiring access, and the photograph of the person's face on a photo ID card. These two scenes (photo ID and person) are displayed on one television monitor simultaneously, side by side at the remote guard location.

A wide FOV camera system (see Figure 10–34) is mounted in a ceiling corner and views the entire lobby area to determine: how many people are in the area, that only one person after identification gains access, and whether or not the person is carrying unauthorized packages.

In operation, the person desiring access enters the lobby. The guard views the person via the wide FOV camera picture. Alternatively, if the guard has other duties, the person presses an intercom or annunciator call button. The guard then switches to the access control video picture and compares the person's face to the photo ID card face. If the guard confirms a match, she or he presses the door release switch on the console, releasing the access

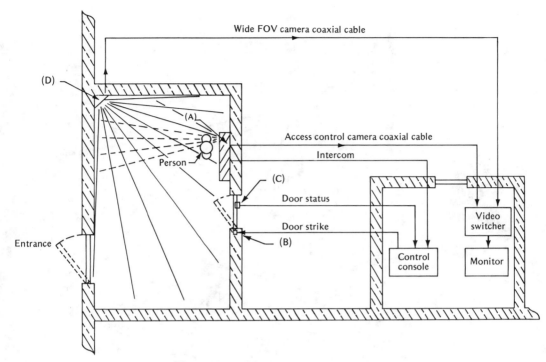

Figure 10–42. CCTV access control system.

door strike. An open door status indicator light indicates an open door to the guard. After the person enters the secured area, a closed door indicator light indicates a secured mode again. The guard switches the video back to the wide FOV camera, thus completing the cycle. It is obvious that this system can be expanded to several access points, each with its own camera, so that one guard can monitor and control several access points. Since 100 percent television monitoring of the lobby is required to prevent tailgating, the wide FOV camera is needed.

The wall-mounted television access control system contains a prealigned television camera, image splitting optics (see Figure 10–43), and lenses which simultaneously view the person desiring access and the photo ID card presented. It also contains a two-way intercom and annunciator switch.

Figure 10–43 shows the CCTV access control guard console containing the television monitor and control functions just described. The video signal from the wide FOV system and the access control system in the lobby is alternately displayed via built-in two position switcher.

Higher security can be achieved by combining the photo ID-CCTV access control system with an electronic ID card code reader. The electronic card

reader (magnetic, capacitance, optical) is installed into the CCTV access control system so that the card is read while the photo on the card and the person's face are simultaneously displayed for the guard at the CCTV monitor. This dual system insures that a lost or stolen coded card is not used by the wrong person.

Two other CCTV access control systems used by banks, armored car services, prisons, government facilities, and other institutions requiring high security make use of turnstiles or locked portals. Figure 10–44 shows the physical arrangement. Using these techniques, a person desiring entry from an unsecured area (A), into a secured area (B), must first pass through a locked area (C). The area (C) contains a wide FOV camera and split image CCTV access control system described previously. To enter, the person in the unsecured area (A) announces a name to the guard. The guard unlocks the entrance port (1), and the person enters the area (C). The door (1) closes and locks.* The guard views the person on the wide FOV camera to ascertain that the person is alone and not carrying an unauthorized

*Depending on the application, entrance port (1) may be left unlocked.

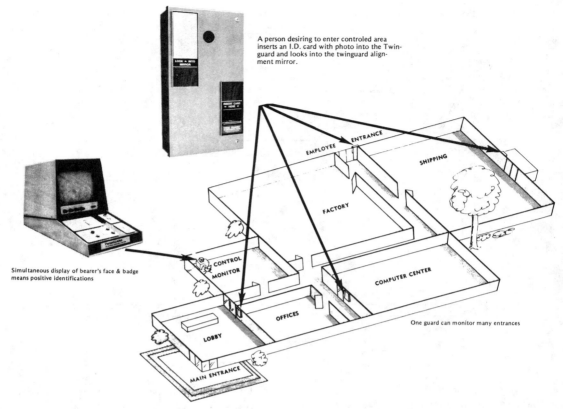

A person desiring to enter controled area inserts an I.D. card with photo into the Twinguard and looks into the twinguard alignment mirror.

Simultaneous display of bearer's face & badge means positive identifications

One guard can monitor many entrances

Figure 10–43. Video access control camera and console equipment.

package. The guard switches to the access control camera and compares the person's face to the photo on the ID card, and permits or denies entry through the door (2). After the person enters the secured area (B), the door (2) relocks, completing the entry procedure. This procedure is a higher level of security since the person must undergo verification while in a locked area, and only one person can enter at a time under full visual surveillance. Obviously, combining the turnstile or portal arrangement while simultaneously reading into an electronic ID card reader adds a still higher level of security.

Figure 10–45 shows an enclosed turnstile system with a photo ID television access control system and card reader installed.

Many industrial and government installations utilize the color photo ID badge system for access control into buildings as well as controlling passage of personnel within the building. A new, cost-effective color photo ID card system utilizing the split image optics described in Figure 10–17 and a one-inch color camera system is shown in Figure 10–46. Utilizing the split image optics, only one television camera is required to simultaneously display on the color monitor the photo ID and photograph and the person's face. Hence, with other CCTV systems, this color picture can be recorded on a VCR for later retrieval.

Another unique photo ID card access control system available uses a photo ID card having a photograph of an authorized card holder which is visible under ordinary illumination but also contains a second identical photograph of the user hidden from visibility (buried) inside the card. When the card is illuminated and viewed by a special lighting system and CCTV, both the visible and the hidden photograph are clearly displayed on the television monitor.

The availability of the visible and hidden photograph permit the guard to determine whether the visible photograph is authentic or counterfeit. Other information on the ID card includes signature, personal printed data, memorized ID code number, and binary code. The system combines high probability of identification with low probability of ID card counterfeiting.

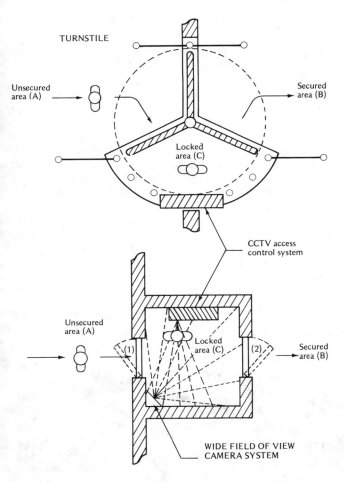

TURNSTILE

Unsecured area (A) →

Secured area (B)

Locked area (C)

Secured area (B)

Figure 10–44. Turnstile and trap CCTV access control layout.

CCTV access control system

Unsecured area (A)

Locked area (C)

Secured area (B)

WIDE FIELD OF VIEW CAMERA SYSTEM

Figure 10–45. Turnstile CCTV access control system.

Figure 10–46. Color CCTV access control system.

Vehicle Access Control

Another part of the personnel access control problem is to control the entry of cars, vans, trucks, and other vehicles and to identify the vehicle driver. Such a vehicle control facility uses an audio-video system located at a vehicle entry location to permit a security person at a remote console to communicate with and identify the driver of the vehicle requesting entry (or exit). Figure 10–47 shows an outdoor system in which the vehicle occupant or remotely located guard can raise or lower the CCTV and lighting system contained inside so that drivers in any height vehicle—from a compact car to a full tractor-trailer rig—can be seen and identified by the guard. Separate lighting is used to assure optimum video pictures under daytime and nighttime conditions. The television pictures on the guard's monitor show: (1) the face of the vehicle occupant, and (2) the photo identification card (or other document) held up against the control facility window by the vehicle driver. Two way audio at the car, van, and truck levels provide full communication between the vehicle driver and the guard.

Realtime Video Retrieval

There always has been a need for realtime or near realtime retrieval of stored CCTV pictures. This is particularly true for access control applications. Up to the recent past the only equipment available was either too expensive, too cumbersome, not near realtime, or too small a storage capacity.

A practical system is now available (Figure 10–12) which stores 2,460 monochrome CCTV frames on one small magnetic hard disk. Any of the individual pictures (frames) can be retrieved in less than 0.2 seconds by entering an ID number from an electronic card reader or keypad. The unit has application for any CCTV requirement in which a half-tone picture, signature, line drawing, alphanumeric information must be stored and retrieved quickly and automatically.

Low Cost Visitor Badge

There is a need to make temporary visitors' badges at many facilities. To be most effective and provide

Vehicle
Access
Control
Unit

Figure 10–47. Vehicle access control system.

Figure 10–48. Temporary badge system.

the highest security, the badge should contain a picture of the visitor, signature, access restrictions (escort required, hours allowed, area restrictions). Figure 10–48 shows a temporary visitor's badge-making system which provides a low cost badge which can be produced in less than 10 seconds and can make a second copy of the badge if a file copy is required. Figure 10–49 shows a typical badge from the thermal printer used in the system.

Checklist and Summary

The full potential of CCTV is only beginning to be utilized by the security industry. CCTV equipment has been reliable and highly developed technically for several years. There are many areas in which CCTV systems can effect tremendous cost savings via reduction in the number of personnel required, and/or in significantly improved deployment of existing personnel.

CCTV should be a part of an integrated security system which includes surveillance, intrusion detection, and access control. The following listing summarizes some of the questions which should be asked when designing a CCTV security system:

ACTUAL PRINT SIZE 3″ x 4″

Figure 10–49. Typical badge from thermal printer.

- Where should the camera be located so that the entire scene to be viewed is covered by the television camera?
- In what direction should the camera be pointed so that the sun, bright lights, or other variable lighting have a minimum effect on picture quality?
- Should the camera have a ⅔-inch or one-inch diameter vidicon tube?
- What field of view should the camera cover?
- Should a fixed focus (constant FOV) or zoom lens (variable FOV) be used? What focal length is best?
- Is there sufficient lighting available?
- Is daytime and/or nighttime operation required?
- Should the camera be mounted with brackets, recessed in the walls or ceiling, or installed in a housing?
- Is a covert (hidden) camera and lens required?
- Should the camera voltage be 117 VAC, 24 VAC, or 12 VDC?
- Should it be powered via the coaxial cable (vidiplexed)?
- What is the distance between the camera and the monitor?
- What coaxial cable type should be used: RG 59 or RG 11?
- Should wireless microwave or other wireless transmission be considered?
- What monitor screen size should be used?
- How should the monitor be connected and terminated?
- Is the monitor to be desk top or rack mounted?
- Should the video recorder use reel-to-reel or tape cassette?
- What is the maximum recording time on the reel or cassette?
- Is time-lapse mode necessary for extending record time?
- Should frames of video be stored on hard disk for later, rapid retrieval?

Glossary

Alarming Sequential Switcher. An automatic switcher which is activated by a variety of sensing devices including magnetic door or window locks and switches, pressure sensitive floor mats, window stripping, motion sensors. Once activated, the switcher connects the camera in the included area onto the monitor or to the recorder.

AM (Amplitude Modulation). The system of transmission based on varying the amplitude of the power output while the frequency remains the same.

AGC (Automatic Gain Control). A circuit for automatically controlling amplifier gain in order to maintain a constant output voltage with a varying input voltage.

ALC (Automatic Light Control). An electro-optical system which maintains near constant output levels when input light levels change over wide ranges. It is usually comprised of an optical attenuator (iris or filter) and an electrical servo system.

Aperture Stop. An optical opening or hole which defines or limits the amount of light passing through a lens system. It takes the form of the front lens diameter in a pinhole lens, an iris diaphraghm, neutral density filter, spot filter.

Automatic Iris. This device optically (by filters and mechanical iris) adjusts automatically to light level changes via the video signal from the television camera. Typical compensation ranges are 300,000 to 1. They are used on Newvicon, Silicon, SIT and ISIT cameras.

Balanced Cable. Balanced cables consist of a pair of inner conductors, often twisted as in audio cable, with each insulated from the other having identical diameters. These are surrounded by additional insulation, a coaxial-type shield, and an outer insulative-protective coating. They offer many advantages for long cable runs, primarily in eliminating grounding or hum problems in long runs. The cables have an impedance of 124 ohms.

Bandpass. A specific range of frequencies that will be passed through a device. Examples: An audio system will pass 20 Hz to 20 KHz. A video system will pass 30 Hz to 6 MHz.

Beta Format. A ½-inch video cassette format found on all Sony VCR equipment. It is not compatible with VHS or other formats.

Bi-focal Lens. A lens system having two different focal length lenses which image the same or two different scenes onto a single television camera. The two scenes appear as a split image on the monitor.

Bridging Sequential Switcher. A sequential switcher with separate outputs for two monitors, one for programmed sequence and the second for extended display of a single area.

Camera Tube. An electron tube that converts an optical image into an electrical current by a scanning process. Also called a pickup tube and a television camera tube.

Camera Format. Standard C mount television cameras are made with nominal ⅔-inch and one-inch vidicon formats. The actual target area used (scanned) on the tubes are 8.8mm horizontal × 6.6mm vertical × 11mm diagonal for the ⅔-inch, and 12.8mm horizontal × 9.6mm vertical by 16mm diagonal for the one-inch.

Cathode Ray Tube (CRT). The video display tube used in video monitors and receivers, radar displays, and video computer terminals.

Charged Coupled Device (CCD). A solid state silicon imaging sensor in which the television scanning function is accomplished by moving the electrical video picture signal (charge) along paths on the silicon chip. It has no electron beam scanning like the vidicon tube and is therefore very small. It has lower resolution than a vidicon, and lower sensitivity than a standard silicon vidicon.

Charge Injection Device (CID). A solid state silicon imaging sensor similar to the CCD sensor, manufactured by General Electric Company. Readout of the signal is different from the CCD.

Charge Transfer Device (CTD). The generic name for CCD, CID, and similar devices.

CCTV (Closed Circuit Television). A distribution system which limits reception of an image to those receivers or monitors which are directly connected to the origination point by coaxial cable or microwave link.

Close-up Lens. A low power accessory lens which permits focusing on objects closer to the lens that it has been designed for.

C Mount. An industry standard for lens mounting. Has a one-inch diameter threaded barrel with 32 threads per inch. The focused image is located .69 inches behind the C mount mounting surface.

Coaxial Cable. See **Balanced, Unbalanced Cables.** A type of cable capable of passing a wide range of frequencies with very low signal loss. It usually consists of a stranded metallic shield with a single wire accurately placed along the center of the shield and isolated from the shield with an insulator. Almost all CCTV coax cables have a 75 ohm impedance.

Composite Video. The combined video picture signal, including vertical and horizontal blanking and synchronizing signals, with a one-volt amplitude.

CPS. Cycles per Second. See **Hertz.**

Depth of Field. Depth of field of a lens is the area along the line of sight in which objects are in reasonable focus. Depth of field increases with smaller lens apertures (higher f/stop numbers), shorter focal lengths, and greater distances from the lens.

Diopter. A term describing the power of a lens. It is the reciprocal of the focal length in meters. For example, a lens with a focal length of 25cm has a power of 4 diopters.

Electronic Focus. An electrical adjustment available on most television cameras, monitors, and receivers for sharpening the picture image.

Electronic Splitter (Combiner). An electronic module which takes the video signals from two (or more) cameras and combines them so that a part of each appears on the final monitor picture. The part of each camera picture used is usually chosen via front panel controls.

Fiber Optic Bundle. This optical device is an assembly of many thousands of hair-like fibers, coherently assembled so that an image is transferred from one end of the bundle to the other.

Field of View (FOV). The field of view is the width and height of a scene to be monitored and is determined by the lens focal length, the lens-to-subject distance, and the camera format size.

F number (f/#). The speed of a lens is determined by the amount of light it transmits. This is the relationship between lens opening (controlled by the iris) and the focal length, and is expressed as a fraction referred to as f/number. Example: an f/4.0 lens is one having an aperture ¼ of the focal length. The markings (f/stops) on lenses are arbitrarily chosen ratios of aperture to focal length, such as f/1.0, 1.4, 2.0, 2.8, 4.0, 5.6, 8, 11, 16, 22. The smaller the f/stop number the faster the lens speed. The light passing through a lens varies as $(1/f\#)^2$. Therefore, an f/2 lens is four times as fast as an f/4 lens.

FM (Frequency Modulation). A system of signal transmission based on varying the frequency to transmit information rather than amplitude. FM has better signal to noise and noise immunity characteristics than AM.

Focal Length (FL). The distance from the lens center to the focal plane (vidicon target) is the lens focal length and is expressed in inches or in millimeters.

Foot Candle (FtCd). A unit of illuminance on a surface one square foot in area on which there is an incident light of one lumen. The illuminance of a surface placed one foot from a light source that has a luminous intensity of one candle.

Frame. The total picture area which is scanned while the picture signal is not blanked. One-thirtieth of a second (525 lines) in standard NTSC CCTV systems.

Front Surface Mirror. A mirror in which the reflective surface is on the front. All common glass mirrors have the reflective surface on the rear of the glass. A front surface mirror does not produce a ghost or secondary image as does a rear surface mirror. Since the reflecting coating on front surface mirrors is on the front, these mirrors should be handled carefully and not touched on the front surface.

Hz (Hertz). Number of variations in a signal. Named after scientist Hertz. Formerly designated as cycles per second (CPS).

Homing Sequential Switcher. A switcher in which: 1) the outputs of multiple cameras can be switched sequentially onto a monitor: 2) one or more cameras can be bypassed (not displayed): or 3) any one of the cameras can be selected for continuous display on the monitor (homing). The lengths of time each camera output is displayed is independently selectable by the operator.

Horizontal Resolution. The maximum number of individual picture elements that can be distinguished in a single horizontal scanning line. Also called horizontal definition. Five hundred lines typical with 4 MHz bandwidth.

Impedance. The input or output electrical characteristic of a system component (camera, etc.) that determines the type of transmission cable to be used. The cable used must have the same characteristic impedance as the component. Expressed in ohms. Video distribution has standardized on 75-ohm coaxial and 124-ohm balanced cable.

Interlace. The relationship between the two scanned fields in a television system. In a 2:1 interlaced system, the two fields are synchronized exactly. See **Random Interlace** for unsynchronized fields.

Iris Diaphragm. The iris is a device for mechanically closing the lens aperture, thus controlling the amount of light transmitted through a lens. In this way the iris adjusts the f/stop of a lens.

ISIT (Intensified Silicon Intensified Target). The ISIT tube is essentially the same as a SIT, the only difference being the use of double intensifier. This means that two intensifiers are stacked in series to yield a gain of about 2,000 over a standard vidicon. Typical sensitivity of an ISIT tube is about 1×10^{-6} foot candles of faceplate illumination.

Lens. A transparent optical component consisting of one or more pieces of glass with surfaces so curved (usually spherical) that they serve to converge or diverge the transmitted rays of an object, thus forming an image of that object onto a focal plane or target.

Lens Speed. See **F/Number**.

Line Amplifier. A video amplifier used to amplify the camera video signal and compensate for the loss of signal level caused by the cable attenuation. It is put in series with the camera and monitor, at the camera or along the cable run.

Magnification. Magnification is usually expressed with a one-inch focal length lens as a reference. For example, a lens with a two-inch (50mm) focal length is said to have a magnification of 2.

Manual Switcher. An electronic module which has multiple front panel switches to permit connecting one of a number of camera outputs into a single CCTV monitor or video tape recorder. The simplest is a passive switcher which contains no active (transistor or integrated circuits). The active switcher contains transistors and/or IC parts.

Monitor. A video display which shows the images detected and transmitted by a television camera or the face of a CRT.

Newvicon Tube. Trade name of Matsushita. The Newvicon tube has a cadmium and zinc telluride target and provides sensitivity about 20 times that of a sulfide target. Spectral response is somewhat narrower than a silicon diode tube, 470 to 850 nm. The Newvicon operates very similar to the silicon tube, in that it uses a fixed target voltage and must use an auto iris lens system.

NTSC Standard Format. National Television Systems Committee. A committee that worked with the FCC in formulating standards for the present-day United States color television system. Uses 525 horizontal scan lines, 30 frames per second. Commonly used in the United States and Japan.

Optical Splitter. An optical lens prism and/or mirror system which combines two or more scenes and images them onto one television or film camera. No electronics are used to combine the scenes.

PAL Format. Phase Alternating Line. Uses 625 horizontal scan lines, 25 frames per second. Used in Western Europe, Australia, parts of Africa and the Middle East.

Pan-Tilt Mechanism. An electro-mechanical platform which has provisions to change the pointing direction of a camera and housing along a horizontal and vertical plane, from a remotely located controller.

Pinhole Camera. An integral television or film camera having a small front lens to permit easy concealment. The lens and camera are a single unit.

Pinhole Lens. A special lens designed to have a small (.1 inch to .25 inch) front lens diameter to permit its use in covert (hidden) camera applications.

Plumbicon. Trade name of N.V. Philips special tube. More sensitive than a Vidicon. Used in some color video cameras and television X-ray inspection systems. Has very low picture lag particularly at low light levels.

Random Interlace. The two scanned fields are not synchronized. See **Interlace**.

Raster. The geometrical pattern scanned on the camera or monitor tube by the electron beam. In standard CCTV, the first field is scanned from the top left corner of the tube to the lower right corner. The second field starts in the top left corner inbetween the first two lines of the first field.

Resolution. See **Horizontal** and **Vertical Resolution**.

SECAM. Sequential Color and Memory. 625 horizontal scan lines, 25 frames per second. Similar to PAL but differs greatly in method of producing color signals. SECAM is used in Saudi Arabia, USSR, and France.

Signal to Noise Ratio. The ratio between the useful television picture signal and the scene, equipment, and interferring noise (snow). Mathematically: signal voltage/total noise voltage.

Silicon Tube. The silicon target is made up of a mosaic of light sensitive silicon material, and depending on light source is between 10 and 50 times as sensitive as a sulfide vidicon. Other advantages are very broad spectral response 380–1,100 nm, and high resistance to vidicon burn. The silicon tube does not permit automatic sensitivity control by means of signal electrode voltage regulation; therefore, an automatic iris must be used.

Slow Scan Television. An electronic video system which transmits single frames of television scenes from a standard CCTV camera via ordinary telephone or twisted pair lines. Each picture is stored in the form of picture elements—an array from 64×64 elements to 256×256 elements (or more). Every 8, 16, or 32 seconds, all the picture elements are transmitted and received, put into memory and displayed on a standard monitor. Since the signal bandwidth is from 300 Hz to 3,000 Hz, the television pictures can be stored on an ordinary audio recorder. The picture is not in realtime.

Switcher. See **Manual, Homing Sequential, Alarming, Looping**.

Target. The light sensitive material in the television camera pickup tube or silicon chip sensor. The standard vidicon tube target material is antimony trisulphide ($Sb_2 S_3$).

UHF (Ultra High Frequency). In television transmission, a term used to designate channels 14 through 83 (470 MHz to 890 MHz).

U-matic. A video cassette format offered by several manufacturers in which ¾-inch tape is used. Not compatible with VHS or Beta.

Unbalanced Cable. The term *unbalanced* refers to the single-conductor shielded coaxial cable commonly used in television installations (RG-11/U and RG-59/U are of this type). It is manufactured in several impedances; however, for purposes of unbalanced video transmission, only the 75-ohm impedance is used. The shielding may be standard braid or double braid or solid aluminum. The dielectric used may be foam, solid plastic or even air.

VHF (Very High Frequency). In television transmission, a term used to designate channels 2 through 13 (54 MHz to 216 MHz).

VHS (Victor Home System). A ½-inch tape video cassette format in widespread use. Not compatible with Sony and U-Matic.

Vehicle Control Facility (VCF). A television system containing cameras, lighting system for daytime and nighttime operation, and two-way audio commumications. The system should move vertically to permit identification of the person and ID document for drivers of cars, vans, and trucks.

Vertical Resolution. The number of horizontal lines that can be seen in the reproduced image of a television pattern. 350 lines maximum with the 525 NTSC system.

Video Cassette Recorder (VCR). A magnetic recorder which records live television pictures in black and white or color, with sound, onto a small cassette containing magnetic tape. Available systems can record continuously from ½ hour to 6 hours on one cassette. Time lapse recorders record up to 200 hours on one cassette.

Standard formats are VHS, Beta, U-Matic, all incompatible.

Video Tape Recorder (VTR). A device which accepts signals from a video camera and a microphone and records images and sound on video magnetic tape in the form of a reel. It can then play back the recorded program for viewing on a television monitor or reciever.

Video Hard Disk File. A magnetic hard disk recording system which records many (thousands) of individual CCTV pictures which can be retrieved rapidly (0.2 seconds) and displayed on a monitor.

Vidicon. Electron tube used to convert light to an electrical signal. The standard vidicon tube utilizes an antimony trisulfide ($Sb_2 S_3$) target and is the most widely used image tube for close circuit surveillance. The spectral response covers most of the visible light range and most closely approximates the human eye. A useful feature of the vidicon is the ability of the target voltage to be controlled to permit variation of sensitivity. The tube has a spectral sensitivity from 300 to 800 nm.

Vignetting. Vignetting refers to the loss of light through a lens system occurring at the edges due to lens design or obstruction. Lenses are usually designed to eliminate vignetting internal to the lens.

Zoom Lens. A zoom lens is a variable focal length lens. The lens components in these assemblies are moved to change their relative physical positions, thereby varying the focal length and angle of view through a specified range of magnifications.

Chapter 11

Access Control and Personal Identification Systems

DAN M. BOWERS

The Security System

Access control devices and systems comprise an important part of almost every security system. This chapter provides an education in access control and personal identification systems, to enable readers to select the proper kind and size of equipment for needs. However, in order for the system design to succeed, other portions of the security system must also be well thought out. Even the simplest access control system, a single-portal push-button device, will require at least an electric door strike to unlock the door, a timer to make sure that the door doesn't stay open all day, and perhaps a bell or light to indicate remotely that the door is opened.

This chapter is solely devoted to the access control devices and systems themselves; it is appropriate, however, to briefly describe the other elements which help to make up the total security system.

Portal Hardware. There is usually an electrically operated door strike to unlock the door, although some access control devices of the simpler kind unlock mechanically. There needs to be a sensor —usually a contact switch or magnetic switch—to determine whether the door is open or closed. And there is usually a remote indicator which lights or sounds (annunciates) when the door is opened.

Physical Barriers. It sounds simplistic to state that in order to make certain that all prospective entrants pass through the access control equipment, they must be prevented from entering elsewhere. Design of physical barriers—walls, fences, barred windows, etc.—is an important part of a security system.

Traps and Turnstiles. Once the door is opened, there may be a need to insure that only one person (or vehicle) comes through it; there are available a variety of traps, turnstiles, parking gates, etc.

Guards. The fact that an automated security system or some electronic security device is installed does not mean that the traditional guard force is to be eliminated. Many of the most effective security system combine the best features of guards and automated systems rather than opting for wholly one means or the other.

Other Sensors and Annunciators. In addition to the *door-open* sensor and annunciator described above, it may be useful to provide intrusion detectors, smoke detectors, etc.; many access control systems provide the facility for wiring-in these sensors and annunciating them along with the door-open signal.

Multiple Systems. Infrequently, access control is provided alone (not in conjunction with other security and life safety systems). The other sensors represent another, if minimal, security system. There are frequently closed-circuit television cameras and monitors. There may be article-surveillance systems. And access control is frequently combined with a time-and-attendance or job-cost-monitoring system, since the required data for these systems can be collected at the access control point. Energy management and other forms of facility automation are increasingly being provided along with the security system.

Clearly, the more functions are provided, the more complex the system design task becomes, and also the more vital it becomes that all of the systems mesh efficiently together.

Processors and Controllers. With a simple one-portal access control device, the controller consists of a single circuit board which can detect that the correct code was entered, then energize a door strike. At the other end of the spectrum, a system encompassing access control, fire detection and alarm, time and attendance, and energy management, will require a sizeable general-purpose computer and a sophisticated communications controller, along with years' experience in computer programming. An interesting design decision arises: Will the savings in processor-controller hardware which is achieved by all subsystems sharing a large computer be cancelled out by the complexity and cost of the software task? What is the exposure to failure of the single large processor and the consequent loss of all of the subsystems? If the exposure to such failure is eliminated by providing redundant processors-controllers or degraded operation through providing intelligent remote units, how much of the originally contemplated savings will be lost? In short, does it better serve the purposes for which the system or systems is being installed to have one large, integrated system, or several smaller, dedicated, systems?

People. Several sets of people play an integral part of an access control system. Some people must be admitted to the facility without delay or aggravation, and different sets of people must be admitted to different areas within the same facility. Some people must not be admitted to the facility. And there are people who are part of the security force who must monitor the activities, respond to alarms, and deal with unusual situations.

In order to narrow down the field in choosing an access control system, there are a number of questions to ask, and the answers to these should already be embodied in the total security system design.

What level of security is required? A storage room containing iron bars requires a different level of security from one containing gold bars.

How many authorized entrants are there? There are card-access systems which can handle 500 different employees and identify each, and there are those which can handle and identify 100,000.

Will there be a separate alarm system? Or must the access control system handle some number of alarms?

Should there be logging of activity for subsequent use in investigating incidents?

What other automated systems will be provided, and will they be centrally-controlled or independent? See the discussion above.

Another fundamental decision which the user must make is who will assume the role of systems integrator. There are a large number of systems houses who will provide a turnkey-packaged security system incorporating all of the subsystems required by the user: access control, CCTV, alarm systems, fire alarm, fence protection, etc. On the other hand, the user may perform as general contractor, buying each of the sub-systems from the vendor thereof, hiring the electrical contractor to run the wiring, and being ultimately responsible that it all works together. Few users have all of the required skills to manage this variety of technical and trade workers and systems.

Errors in Access Control and Personal Identification Systems

An access control system can fail to perform its desired function in either of two ways: It can admit a person who should not have been admitted (a false-accept error), or it can deny admittance to a person who should have been admitted (a false-reject error). The cognoscenti have always referred to these as Class I and Class II errors, but since most of us have always had trouble remembering which was Class I and which Class II, the false-accept and false-reject definitions facilitate much more intelligent communication. The principal purpose of any access control system is to prevent false-accept errors, but it will not be acceptable to accomplish this while having a high number of false-reject errors. A solid brick wall will allow no unauthorized entries, but it will not allow the workers to get in to the plant either.

The performance of automatic access control systems, as measured by false-accept and false-reject errors, varies with the technology used. Barring equipment failure, a keypad system will have neither kind of error—either the correct number is entered or it is not. From there on it goes downhill. A card can become dirty, bent, scratched, demagnetized. It becomes difficult to read, and can therefore give false-reject errors if the card reader cannot detect all of the correct bits on the card. It is extremely unlikely that a non-valid card could become altered in such a way as to create the proper bits in a well-conceived card-access system, so card-access systems should not have false-accept errors.

The personal-attribute, or biometric, systems represent a different class of problem. In these systems, identification is based upon the probability that certain measured physical characteristics are unique to a particular person. The problem is that these physical characteristics may vary from time to time, and that there are limitations to the accuracy and repeatability of the physical measurements. For example, a fingerprint can be both physically different and more difficult to measure on a Monday morning after the person has spent the weekend working on an automobile engine (grease in the grooves), laying brick (the ridges are worn down), or clearing the back yard (cuts and scratches).

Personal attribute systems, therefore, inherently have the potential for both false-accept and false-reject errors. Further, there is always a dependence between the two. If the system is adjusted so that it must absolutely be certain of the identification, and therefore have the fewest possible false-accept errors, this usually results in an unacceptably high level of false-reject errors.

Reducing the acceptable threshold so as to not delay the authorized work force in getting to their tasks, could cause a 10 percent false-accept rate. If, however, the means are in place to apprehend attempted penetrators, even a 10 percent false-accept rate will result in nine out of every ten attempts being foiled and punished.

Again, the risk analysis and system design is the key element, not a blind reliance upon automatic devices. The most effective solution combine several security devices, systems, and procedures and people, carefully designed to function together as a total security system.

Principles of Access Control and Personal Identification Systems

All access control systems utilize one or more of three basic techniques in order to identify a prospective admittee: (1) something a person knows, (2) something a person has, and (3) something a person is or does. We define them as (1) the combination locks, (2) the portable key, and (3) the physical attribute.

The Combination Lock. These systems have also been called stored-code systems, where the code is a series of numbers such as is used to open the ordinary mechanical combination lock. The code is stored both in the human brain and in the lock mechanism, and entry of the code by the human into a set of pushbuttons allows access. Another form of stored-code system is embodied in the key-questions technique frequently used by banks: personal information which is unlikely to be forgotten (e.g., your mother's maiden name) is stored in your bank account and asked of you by the teller as additional verification of your identity.

The Portable Key. An object such as an ordinary metal key (the everyday lock-and-key being the simplest example of a portable-key system), an ID card or badge, or computer-coded plastic card, is in the possession of the person to be allowed entry; the key is inserted into a reading mechanism which senses the code contained, by any of a variety of means, in the key. If it appears specious on the surface to compare the everyday lock and key with a sophisticated card-access system, be advised that there are key-and-lock systems which equal some card-access systems in both security and price; consider also that your post office box and your bank safe deposit box are both opened with a metal key (and in both cases the portable-key system is combined with other elements to comprise an effective total security system).

Another form of portable-key access control device is the kind of disposable cardboard ticket one buys from the movie theater cashier and uses for entry; the movie ticket may only be a $5.00 item, but the same means of access control is used for a $40.00 Broadway play.

A new form of portable-key beginning to achieve considerable usage needs not be inserted into a reader or other mechanism, but will be recognized when in the immediate vicinity (some at a few inches, some at several feet) of the reader. Here again, the concept and technology are not new, only the application of the concept to identification of humans. For many years, radio interrogation and coded response have been used to identify aircraft to the air traffic controller. There have been a number of experimental installations to identify automobiles, for example to collect tolls without the need for the autombile to stop at a toll booth.

The Physical Attribute. Some unique characteristic of the person to be allowed admittance is recognized. Traditionally, this characteristic has been the human face, and the access control system consisted of a guard comparing the actual face against a picture-badge or ID card; this is still the most widespread physical attribute system in use today. There are also automatic and semiautomatic systems using faces, fingerprints, hand geometry, voiceprints, signatures, and the patterns of the retina of the eye.

These three fundamental techniques for access control have always been in use, through the combination lock, the lock-and-key, and guard-recognizes-face. Automatic access control systems merely apply the most current technology to these concepts, providing systems which are more difficult to defeat, and require less high-cost human help.

On the other hand, automation cannot change basic weaknesses in all of these techniques. A code can be told to an accomplice or sometimes observed from afar. A key can be stolen, lost, copied, or loaned. This is true regardless of whether the code and key are meant to open ordinary $1.98 locks, or are recognized by $100,000 computer systems. Physical attribute systems have inherent false-accept and false-reject errors, and the requirement that the two kinds of errors be balanced off against each other. Physical attribute systems have been around for more than a decade, and have been widely predicted to become the dominant form of access control for even longer than that; that they have not done so is partially due to the error problem, but more due to the much higher cost per portal which the manufacturers have not yet been able to overcome.

Combinations of the techniques can greatly increase the security of a system. A code-plus-key system requires that prospective admittees insert their key (e.g., a coded card) into a reader, and enter the proper code into a set of push-buttons. This removes many of the weaknesses of the two simpler systems; of course, it also costs more than either of the two simpler systems alone.

The following sections of this chapter present a detailed discussion of each kind of access control system. In addition, there are system-level features to which the user should give serious attention when procuring his access control system. These are the following:

Tamper Alarms. If a sophisticated penetrator can gain access by disassembling or smashing the access control box and tinkering with its insides, the security provided is clearly diminished. A well-designed access control system will not be capable of being taken apart from the outside of the portal; further, it will incorporate a sensor which can detect that the box is being attacked and will create an alarm.

Power Fail Protection. Some units have internal batteries so that the access control device will continue to perform its function even if the A-C power fails. At the very least, the device should have the acceptable-code stored in nonvolatile memory (static semiconductor, jumpers, switches) so that it does not have to be reprogrammed after power is restored.

Fail-Safe or Fail-Soft. The user's security plan and system design must consider that power will fail occasionally, and equipment will also fail. When failure occurs, should the portal be made permanently open or permanently closed? Should there be a conventional-mechanical-key bypass to allow access under failure conditions?

Code Changes. Part of the security plan and system may be the changing of the access codes occasionally, frequently, or periodically. This will require the ability to change both the code which the person has or knows (the set of numbers to be entered into the pushbuttons or the code contained in the card), and the code within the access control equipment which will be compared against the person's code. In most systems, changing the code in the access control equipment is made easy for the user. Changing the person's code is simple in a pushbutton system: s/he is merely told what the new numbers are. In some card systems, e.g., the magnetic stripe, the coded data can be easily rewritten on the card; other card systems, e.g., Wiegand and magnetic-slug, require that new cards be procured from the manufacturer.

Keypad Access Control Systems

A keypad access control device (stored-code, digital lock, pushbutton, combination lock) requires that a correct sequence of numbers be depressed on a set of pushbuttons to open a door or other mechanism. The system may be mechanically operated, in which case the positions of the pushbuttons operate a mechanism similar in concept to the tumblers in a rotary combination lock, allowing the bolt of the lock to be manually operated (see Figure 11–1), or closing a switch which may be used to operate an electric door strike. Most keypad devices are electrically or electronically operated, in which case the sequence of pushbutton depressions is decoded by electronic logic circuits, and a solenoid is enabled, electrically unlocking the door. As in all electronic logic operations, the decoding function is now most

Figure 11–1. Mechanical push-button access control device, with conventional key bypass. (Courtesy of Simplex Security Systems, Inc.)

commonly done by a microprocessor or microcomputer (which is a microprocessor with additional functional chips for input-output and memory control), and in some cases by a personal computer or even a larger computer.

Sometimes the pushbuttons are recessed or hidden behind a privacy panel to prevent observation of the combination by an outsider. A relatively recent innovation is to eliminate the permanently engraved numbers on the pushbuttons and to replace them with electronic display of the numbers. The positions of the numbers can then be varied by the electronics of the device, so that the same number does not always appear in the same position. This prevents an outsider from deducing the code by observing the positions of the pushbuttons depressed. The price paid for this (since there is never any such thing as a free lunch) is a somewhat longer time taken to enter the numbers and a somewhat higher wrong-number rate, since the human brain is accustomed to storing positional patterns corresponding with the numbers, as on the telephone keypad.

Conventional burglar and intrusion alarm systems for both home and commercial use frequently utilize keypads for arming and disarming the system. Since once the system has been disarmed the premises can be entered, we consider these devices to be included in the family of keypad access control devices.

The code or codes which are to be recognized as correct by the keypad access control device must be stored within the unit's controller, and this is accomplished by a variety of means: jumper wires, rotary switches, solid-state memory. The combination usually can be easily changed by the user in a few minutes. When purchasing a unit, the user should determine whether or not the code-storage mechanism will survive a temporary electrical power outage, and thus be ready to perform its function immediately when the power comes back on, or will need to be recoded. Whether or not this is a serious problem again depends upon the particular security situation.

The various options and features which are available with keypad access control systems and devices are described in the following material.

Combination Time. The system controls the amount of time which is allowed to enter the proper combination, under the assumption that authorized persons can readily enter the numbers, and anyone taking excessive time is probably up to no good.

Error Alarm. Entry of an incorrect number activates an alarm, either locally or remotely. In some cases more than one incorrect entry is required before the alarm is signalled. These error alarms prevent unauthorized persons from trying a large number of combinations in order to improve their odds on getting the right one.

Time Penalty. The system is deactivated for a selectable amount of time after entry of an incorrect number, so that unauthorized persons cannot quickly try a large number of combinations.

Door Delay. The length of time the door remains unlocked is variable. This is only one facet of portal design; for example, a turnstile may be used to admit only one person at a time.

Hostage Alarm. In the event that an authorized entrant is being physically coerced into opening a portal, s/he can secretly and silently cause an alarm to be signalled by depressing an extra digit or an alternate digit. Also known as a duress alarm.

Remote Indication. There may be a remote electrical indication, for example at a guard station or central logging facility, that the portal was opened.

Visitor's Call. An additional button may be provided so that persons not possessing the combination may request entry.

Multiple Zones or Times. The system may be capable of relating the acceptable code to the time of day or area of the facility, so that persons on different shifts will have different codes, and persons can be restricted of access to particular physical areas.

Individual ID. Most systems allow entry to any person possessing the correct code, and can record only that the portal was opened by an authorized person. Some systems provide individual codes, and can thus identify the particular person who opened the portal.

Multiple Doors—Central Control and Logging. The two basic types of keypad access control devices are those which are self-contained, stand-alone, and are intended to operate a single portal, and those which obtain their intelligence from a central control unit which can control a multiplicity of portal devices. As always, there are also systems which do not fit neatly into these simple categories.

Weatherproof Units. These are provided by many manufacturers, in addition to their indoor units and fancy-decor units, for use on outside portals.

Antipassback. To prevent a person who has already passed through the portal using an authorized code from passing-back the ability to enter to another person using the same code, a few keypad-access systems now have the ability to remember that a particular person (code) has entered, and to not allow another entry using that code until an exit has been made. This has been a usual feature of card-access systems for many years, but its incorporation into keypad access control is a new development.

The cost of a simple, single-door, mechanical or electronic keypad access control device can be as low as $30, and including all available options it is difficult to spend more than $50 per portal. For pure combination-lock-level access control, without penalties, remote gadgetry, etc., these units are an attractive buy.

If additional features, multiple portals, etc., will eventually be required, the user is better advised to install the more sophisticated versions initially, since the simple units are usually non-upgradable and non-usable with a central-controlled systems. Intelligent stand-alone units will run in the range of $300–$500, and incorporate most of the optional features. A complete centrally-controlled, multiple-portal system can cost anywhere from $100 to $1,000 per portal; a completely satisfactory installation should be possible for most situations for under $400 per portal.

Card and Other Portable-Key Access Control Systems

A portable-key access control system admits the holder of a device, usually a plastic card but embodied in other forms as well, which contains a predetermined code. The device is inserted into a reader, and if it contains the code which the reader or its controller requires, the portal is unlocked (see Figure 11–2). This process is no different in concept from the ordinary metal key and lock which have been in use for centuries; the modern systems, however, utilize keys which are more difficult to duplicate, and can provide complex logic, control, and logging functions which a simple key cannot. The user should recognize that the more exotic versions of the metal-key-and-lock probably provide as much or more security than the simplest versions of electronic card-access at about the same cost.

The plastic, wallet-size card has become the most popular device used for portable-key access control systems; it is offered by 91 percent of the vendors of such systems, although an additional 14 percent offer other forms as well. The second most popular form of device is a key-shaped token, usually of plastic, with some versions being small enough to fit on an ordinary key ring. There are also metal cards of various sizes, and a number of other kinds of metal and plastic tokens in use. The form of the device is not high on the list of factors which the

Figure 11–2. Access control card reader. (Courtesy of Rusco Electronic Systems.)

user should take into consideration when choosing an access control system, although s/he should be aware that with most of the types of encoding now in use, the larger the device (in flat surface area) the more different codes it can store.

Coding and Reading

There are a variety of technologies utilized to store the access code on the device which will be read in order to allow or not allow access. Many of the early systems used the most convenient technology then available, simple visible *optical bar-codes*, a series of stripes similar to the universal-price-code which is now found on most grocery items (read by photo-cells); or *Hollerith-code*, using physically punched holes identical to those in a conventional computer-card (read by a conventional punched card reader). Some of these are still offered.

There are three types of magnetically encoded devices. The bank-card type has a *magnetic stripe* on the card, much as if a strip of ordinary magnetic tape had been affixed. The code is recorded magnetically onto the stripe, and can therefore be read, erased, altered, with equipment utilizing conventional magnetic tape recording technology. Because this technology is well known and readily available, there is appropriate concern that the cards are easily duplicatable, and a number of additional safeguards are provided in situations requiring a high level of security. Many vendors encrypt the data on the card so that even if read, it is not useful to the perpetrator. Many users use a keypad in conjunction with the card reader, so that the correct number must be entered in addition to an acceptable card. One manufacturer's technique imbeds a unique code into the stripe during the manufacturing process which can only be read by a special reader.

A second kind of magnetic encoding has *magnetic slugs* imbedded in the device during its manufacture, and is read by a magnetic-sensing head which determines that there is or is not a slug at each possible position; these devices cannot be altered. The third type of magnetic encoding utilizes a sandwich construction with a sheet of magnetic material in the center (usually comprised of barium ferrite, hence these cards are usually called *barium ferrite* cards); spots can be magnetized at various positions on the sheet, thus creating coding which is read by a magnetic-sensing head; these devices are usually factory-coded, although some can be coded by the user.

Although strictly speaking a magnetic method of coding, the *Wiegand-effect* operates on a different principle and therefore has different characteristics from the other magnetic techniques. Each bit of data is encoded in a wire which is twisted under tension and heat-tempered, and has a magnetic snap-action which creates a large voltage under the influence of a given strength of magnetic field, regardless of the speed with which it is moved past the read head. In conventional magnetic reading, the size of the read signal is proportionate to the reading speed. Wiegand wires are imbedded into positions in the access control device to create the codes, and dummy nonWiegand wires can also be imbedded so that the position of the coded wires cannot easily be detected. The Wiegand-effect wires are also used in automotive ignition, keyboard sensing, and production-line item-sensing applications.

The nonmagnetic coding techniques are in general peculiar to one vendor who has developed each for certain reasons and uses them in a certain product line alone. There have been *capacitance-coding* techniques, in which the codes are embodied in conductive particles, and sensed capacitively; none are known to be currently offered. There have been cards containing an *electrical matrix* coding, which were read by direct electrical connection to terminals on the card-edge; none are known to be currently offered. There was once a card having the coding in embedded *radioactive slugs* and read by sensing the radioactivity; it did not achieve popular acceptance. There are devices having the coding in embedded *nonmagnetic metal slugs*, which are read by techniques similar to airport metal detecting equipment. There are devices having the code embodied in *nonvisible* (ultraviolet or infrared) *optical* form and read by optical readers. There are devices containing *tuned circuits* which can be sensed by readers emitting radio-frequency waves, similar to the techniques used in electronic article surveillance systems. Devices are beginning to be offered which contain microprocessor-type *integrated-circuit chips* and memory and are read through wireless-communication circuits in the reader.

Reading units for access control devices come in several forms. Most require movement of the access control device past a reading mechanism in the reader. For key-shaped devices this is usually accomplished by insertion of the device into a slot and turning. Some card readers require insertion of the card into the reader; in some it is done manually and others provide a motor drive. The swipe card reader is used on magnetic-stripe cards (which can also be read by the insertion type); the card is grasped by its top and the portion containing the stripe is manually moved through a slot which contains the reading mechanism.

The number of possible combinations of cards, personal identifiers, physical areas, time zones, etc., which can be controlled by an access control system, is determined by the number of binary digits which can be encoded upon or within the access control device. Ten to 40 binary digits will inherently provide one thousand to one million combinations, respectively; since 20 binary digits will provide over one million combinations, the digits beyond those needed for pure access control can be used for other purposes. The access control systems and devices now being offered provide a choice of devices with code storage capabilities from 8 digits (256 combinations) to more than 40 digits.

In systems which have more than the number of codes required to merely open a portal, the extra digits can be used to store employee number, shift of work, etc. This allows control of employee access by time of day, and by area of the facility. It also allows the keeping of a log showing who passed through what portal when; some companies expand this capability into a personnel-locator function. Clearly, also, these systems can be used to provide time-clock (time-and-attendance) function for payroll purposes. It also confers the capability to reject particular cards, for example when the employee is terminated or the card is lost or stolen. Some card systems have *no-passback* protection, in which the card code is remembered (or, in some cases, the code on the card is altered) when the cardholder passes in through a portal, and the card cannot be again used to pass in the portal until it has exited; this eliminates passing-back a card from one person to another, and allows only one person-entry per card.

The reading and control logic of a multi-portal centrally-controlled access control system is usually, but not always, divided between the portal unit and the central computer. Many vendors provide a *degraded* mode of operation so that if the central computer, or the communications between it and the portal unit, fails, the portal unit can still provide basic control of access. This usually consists of admitting all devices containing the correct code for that portal, without having the additional facilities of logging, individual card lockout, etc.

The defeatability of a pure portable-key access control system is largely determined by the encoding mechanism. Optical bar-codes and Hollerith punches are clearly visible, recognizable, decodable, and duplicatable by any person or organization with a little technical know-how. Magnetic stripes require more know-how and equipment, but should not pose a particular problem to the professional with some equipment and resources; the specifications therefore are, after all, published in an ANSI Standard. Embedded materials, both magnetic and non-magnetic, provide another step in security, but analytical equipment is capable of detecting and cracking the code. Organized criminals, competitive corporations, foreign governments, all have sufficient financial resources to buy the technical capability to solve such problems as these. For every security device that is devised, a penetrating method can be devised, even as for every military weapon a counterweapon is made. Total security can be had not through devices alone but by incorporating the appropriate devices into a total system which fits the organization's needs. Observe, for example, the magnetic-stripe card, the specifications for which can be bought through the mail; with the addition of other techniques and devices in the system (key-pads, encryption, computer pattern analysis), it has become the single most accepted device for controlling access not only to physical facilities, but to all of our money as well.

Key-Plus-Keypad Systems

Pushbutton access control systems are simple, reliable, and inexpensive, and the key to them cannot be lost nor stolen. However, the key can be given away without penalty, and there is no personal identification capability: all persons possessing the code look alike to the code recognition unit. Card and other portable-key access control systems can have personal identification, and can be virtually pick-proof; however, cards can be used by nonauthorized persons who came by then through loss, collusion, or theft.

Key-plus-keypad systems combine the positive attributes of both these simpler systems. The person desiring admittance must possess the portable key, and s/he must know the numbers to press on the keypad. The numbers may be the same for every entrant, or each may have a different code to remember; in the latter case, the key numbers are derived from the information on the portable-key.

Two separate recognition devices are required in the system: the portable-key reader and the keypad (see Figure 11–3). Since this includes the equipment needed for a keypad-only and a portable-key-only system, it stands to reason that vendors of key-plus keypad systems could easily offer the two simpler systems, and several do. Options as to stand-alone

Figure 11–3. Card-plus-keypad access control unit. (Courtesy of Continental Instruments Corporation.)

versus centrally controlled, communications techniques, sophisticated logging and control features, etc., are the same for key-plus-keypad systems as for the simpler systems. In many centrally-controlled systems the user may elect to mix and match portals, having keypad-only for ordinary portals, card or token for more protected areas, and key-plus-keypad control of access to the most important portals.

Features and Options

The various features and options which are available with portable-key access control systems, which the user must evaluate when choosing the most suitable system for his or her application, are described in the following material.

Keying Device. Card or token, and the material from which it is made. Anything smaller than the standard wallet-size card, including key-shaped devices, is called a token. Materials are generally plastic, metal, or cardboard.

Coding Means. As described earlier in this section— magnetic stripe, Wiegand, etc.

Maximum Number of Identification Numbers or Devices. The number of different persons or access cards or tokens which the system can uniquely identify.

Device Code Change By. Can the user recode own cards or tokens, or must s/he purchase a new set of coded devices from the manufacturer?

Number of Portals. How many different portals can the manufacturer's system handle, if it is a centrally controlled system?

Central Control. Does the manufacturer offer a centrally-controlled system? Note that many manufacturers offer both single-portal and centrally controlled systems.

Multiple Zones or Times. Can the system restrict access of particular persons to specific areas or during specific times, or both?

Time and Attendance. Does the system provide timekeeping functions for payroll purposes?

Antipassback. Is this feature provided?

Individual Lockout. Can the system remove a single individual's name (i.e., card number) from the authorized list and prevent entry?

Computer Interface. Is a communications facility provided for communication with computing equipment? This could enable a single-portal system to be connected to a centrally-controlled system, a system having few portals to be linked into a larger system, or access control equipment to be made a part of the user's general computer system.

Keypad Available. Can a key-plus-keypad system be got from this manufacturer?

Handles Alarm Points. Many access control portal equipments provide, in addition to the normal function of recognizing the code stored within a card or token, the ability to recognize and report or act upon some number of electrical contact closures, i.e., alarm points. These points could be door-open contacts associated with the access control function, or they could be unrelated points such as smoke detectors or intrusion alarms.

Weatherproof Model. Outside portals will require card or token readers which will withstand extremes of temperature, rain and snow, etc. Many manufacturers have a variety of housings for different decors, types of doors, indoor-outdoor, etc.

Degraded Mode. In a centrally controlled system, if the central controller or the communications link thereto fails, can the portal unit alone provide simple access control without the extra goodies?

Duress Alarm (hostage alarm). In a keypad system this is easily provided through the use of an extra or alternate digit; in a portable-key system the code is embedded in the device, therefore changing of the code or adding a digit is not possible. Several schemes have been devised, such as an over-travel switch on an insertion-type card reader; under normal conditions the user inserts the card to the first, or reading, position, and under duress conditions s/he inserts it further to activate a duress switch.

The cost of a single-portal card or token access control system with only the basic capabilities begins in the $65 range and can go as high as $300. An intelligent single-portal system may provide some time-period control, individual lockout, and capability to be upgraded by connection to a central computer, and will cost from $500–$1,000; another $2,000 will add a logging capability.

Centrally controlled systems begin in the $2,000–$5,000 range for mainstream access control, go up to the $15,000 range for relatively sophisticated features and a large number of terminals, and can get into the hundreds of thousands of dollars when facility management capabilities are added. To this, of course, must be added the cost of the equipment at each portal. In most cases a completely satisfactory installation should be possible for $500–$1,000 per portal for a portable-key system, and $150–$200 more for key-plus-keypad. These estimates are, of course, for the bought equipment alone, not including the wiring and installation costs which will vary depending upon the physical facility.

The cost of the access control card or token must be considered when selecting a system. There are cardboard cards in the disposable range of a few cents each, but these are not suitable for permanent employee passes. Most conventional plastic cards can be obtained for $1.00–$2.00 each in reasonable quantities; addition of logos, employee pictures, pocket clips, etc., can easily drive to $4.00–$6.00.

Proximity Access Control Systems

Proximity access control systems perform the usual function of opening a portal, powering-up a computer terminal, etc., based on a coded device which is in the possession of the person desiring admittance, but without any physical contact between the coded device and the reading and controlling mechanism or system. Some proximity systems operate like coded-card systems without the necessity of inserting the card into a reader (see Figure 11–4); others are actually keypad systems without wiring between the keypad and the access control system. Obviously, in every access control system a code must be communicated from the user or a device in his/her possession to a code comparator in the system; in the usual keypad or card systems this communication takes place electrically over physical

Figure 11–4. Proximity card access control system being used to control vehicle access. (Courtesy of Schlage Electronics.)

wiring. In a proximity system the communication is accomplished through electromagnetic (which includes radio), optical (including infrared) or sound (ultrasonic) transmissions.

Proximity access control was virtually unknown and unused until the late 1970s, but by 1983 most access control market surveys attributed nearly 10 percent of the card-access market to proximity systems. An even more widespread penetration of proximity systems is in the home market. For example, the electronic garage door opener operates by a token coded by the owner's choosing, and on command the code is transmitted by radio to a controller containing the same code; upon recognizing the correct code, the controller activates a relay which turns on a motor which opens or closes the garage door. Home-oriented versions of the garage door opener for ordinary doors are now offered.

Another emerging class of proximity systems is the wireless (RF) alarm system. In conjunction with these systems, several manufacturers offer wireless keypads for arm/disarm, and these comprise access control just as do their equivalents in wired alarm systems.

Principles of Operation

There are two basic classes of proximity access control systems: those in which the user initiates transmission of the code to the system, such as the garage door opener, and those in which the system senses the presence of a coded device without the user having to perform any action at all. We shall call these *user-activated* and *system-sensing* proximity access control systems.

The *user-activated* systems must by their nature incorporate a power source in the token which is carried by the user. This is a battery in the current units, but devices having other power sources are known to be in development. There are several types of user-activated systems, as follow:

Wireless Keypads. The user depresses a sequence of keys on an ordinary keypad, and the coded representation of the keys is transmitted on a radio frequency. The system detects the transmission and decodes it.

Preset Code. The code is already set into the device, and the user depresses a single key which causes the code to be transmitted for the system to detect and decode. In currently-marketed devices, the transmission is variously accomplished by radio-frequency, infrared light, and ultrasound.

The system-sensing systems utilize a variety of concepts, some of which require that the user-possessed device contain its own power, and some of which require no power or obtain power from the system itself. The several types are as follows.

Passive Devices. The device contains one or more passive electronic circuits; when the device is brought into the RF field which is maintained by the system, subharmonic reradiations occur. These are sensed by the system's electronics. This is similar to the principle upon which most EAS (electronic article surveillance) systems operate.

Active but Unpowered Devices. The device contains an active electronic circuit, such as an RF transmitter, and a power supply circuit capable of extracting sufficient power from a strong RF field to accomplish a brief, weak, RF transmission of the code. The RF field which supplies this power is maintained by the system, and therefore the transmission occurs when the device is brought within the field of the system.

Transponders. The device contains a radio receiver, a radio transmitter, and is battery-powered. The system transmits an interrogation signal which is received by the device, which then transmits a return signal containing the code; this is similar to the ordinary poll-response process through which a computer communicates with its network of terminals.

Continuous Transmission. The device is battery-powered and contains a radio transmitter which continuously transmits the entry code. When the device is sufficiently proximate to the system, the transmission is detected and the code is received.

Features and Functions

The user's security system design should take into consideration the attributes of the various systems, and determine which, if any, of the proximity systems suits one's particular needs. Following are some of the parameters which need be studied.

Activation Distance. The distance at which a proximity system can be activated varies from two inches to nearly fifty feet, with the self-powered tokens naturally providing the greatest distance.

Hands-Off versus Triggered. Some devices require the user to push buttons or keys, others require no user action and thus need not be removed from pocket, wallet, or purse.

Concealment. Since there is no need for accessable and visible wall-mounted keypads, card readers, etc., most proximity systems can be installed so that the presence of an access control system is not obvious; this in itself can add to the security of the installation.

Reading through Barriers. Since RF and optical waves pass rather readily through sturdy materials (cement, wood, and brick for RF, bulletproof glass for optical), the access control system can be physically protected from assault, unlike non-proximity systems which must have a reader or keypad accessable in an unprotected area.

The costs of the more sophisticated proximity access control systems are comparable per portal with intelligent card-access systems, and at the low end costs are similar to those of the simple single-portal keypads. Costs of the portable tokens vary widely depending upon whether they are passive cards (cost on the high end of ordinary plastic cards, i.e., $4.00–$7.00) or active transmitters ($15.00–$75.00).

Access Control Systems Based upon Physical Attributes

The ultimate in a reliable access control system would uniquely identify a person and admit that person and only that person, independent of whether the person possessed a particular coded token, and/or knew a particular set of code numbers. This ultimate system would be based upon recognition of one or more physical or personal characteristics of the person. Automated systems for performing such a function have been offered for more than a dozen years; they have variously been called physical attribute systems, personal characteristics systems, and biometric systems.

Physical attribute systems of the nonautomated variety have been in use for centuries, using recognition of the human face by guards who knew all of the persons to be admitted. When the number of persons, and also the number of different guards, became too large, picture-badge systems were introduced, allowing the guard to compare the face on the badge with the face of the person. Such systems use the person's face as the unique physical attribute; two other physical attributes are well-accepted measures of personal identification: the signature (as on your personal checks) and the fingerprint (as in FBI).

Automated and semiautomated systems using these three basic physical attributes have been developed by the score, and many are still offered and in common use; others have been relegated to the Boot Hill of new inventions. Three other physical attributes have formed the basis of access control systems: the voiceprint, hand geometry, and the retinal pattern of the eye. Systems based upon the latter two are currently being aggressively marketed.

Industry experts predict that physical attribute systems are the future of access control, but that future may be much farther away in years than industry experts hope. The problem is cost: the per-portal cost is four to ten times that of a sophisticated card-access system. The second problem is the unavoidability of false-accept and false-reject errors; even though the physical attribute may be unique, the measurement of it may be imprecise. The designer of a security system must consider and resolve a number of questions when considering a physical attribute system as a possible solution to the access control problem. Is it really more secure than the alternatives, e.g., a card-plus-keypad system? If it is really more secure, is it worth the added cost? Is there penetration potential for faking physical attributes, just as a card can be stolen and a number obtained? As before, there is no standard and universal answer. Each security situation must be analyzed and the choices made which are appropriate for that system.

The effective error rate of a personal attribute system depends hugely on how it is used in a system. If the prospective entrant presents his/her finger (or face, voice, hand, etc.) to the system and the system is required to determine whether or not this fingerprint exists in the file of acceptable persons, a rela-tively high rate of both kinds of errors can be expected. If, however, an identifying pin or card is also presented, then the system is required only to determine that the fingerprint does or does not match the fingerprint which is in the file for that person. Very palatable error rates, in the tenths to thousandths of a percent, can be achieved using this method. Of course, the latter system combines two means of access control, which always results in increased security.

Face Recognition

Access control using recognition of the human face, as discussed above, is the most venerable form of physical attribute system. To our knowledge there has never been, nor is there now, a fully-automatic access control system based on this attribute. There are semiautomatic face recognition systems which are really improvements upon the concept of the picture-badge; instead of the picture being carried on a card which is outside of the system's control, and therefore subject to counterfeiting, the reference picture is stored internally (microfilm, video tape, or disk) and presented to the guard for comparison with the actual face; an employee number is used to retrieve the reference picture from the system file, thus making this a sort of face-plus-keypad system.

Signature Comparison

Signature comparison is the basis for personal identification in millions of financial transactions every day; the comparison is done manually, usually by a bank teller with no training in the subject, but frequently aided by combining it with a PIN and key questions. A number of machine-assisted methods facilitate signature verification by automating the presentation of the signature to the teller; a review of the techniques used is instructive and may prove useful in some specialized security system designs.

File Card. The standard method of retrieving a file signature is from a worn file card; in a multibranch operation, copies of the signature cards may be distributed, or one teller may describe the signature over the telephone to the teller who has the customer at hand. There are clearly a number of cumbersome, costly, and risky aspects to this kind of operation.

Microfilm. The signature is stored on microfilm instead of the card, which makes it more convenient to keep updated copies at the branches.

Facsimile and CCTV. One central file of signature cards is maintained, and images are transmitted to the branches on request.

Ultraviolet and Scrambled. The reference signature is in the possession of the customer, on an ID card, or in a passbook, but is in a form which can only be created and read utilizing specialized equipment at the bank.

Computer-Based Video. The signature is read by a video camera or other scanner and digitized, then stored in a central computer; it can be retrieved and displayed on demand at a teller's monitor.

There does not exist an automated system offered for signature comparison, that is, pattern recognition of a person's signature against a file signature. Systems have been introduced using a different approach, that of utilizing as the physical attribute the manner in which the person writes the signature, not the appearance of the finished signature; they use as the physical attributes the speed, accelerations, pressure, etc., during writing of the signature.

Fingerprint Comparison

Fully automatic fingerprint-recognition systems have been marketed for a dozen years by a continually changing series of vendors, driven in part by the large government expenditures of the 1970s. Massive research and development efforts by very substantive companies—including what seems like a list of the top aerospace and DOD contractors—has not produced any profusion of successful products.

Two fundamental approaches have been taken to the fingerprint-recognition problem. One is pattern recognition of the form of the print—the whorls and loops and tilts. The second is the recognition of singular points such as the endings and splittings of ridges and valleys, called the *minutae* approach. There are also semiautomated systems which present a reference print and the actual print of the person, and require a human to make the comparison and the decision.

The Hand Geometry System

The utilization of hand geometry as the physical attribute upon which to base an access control system stemmed from a 1971 study to statistically analyze glove measurements for Air Force pilots, with aim to reduce manufacturing variability and increase inventory efficiency. The study concluded

Figure 11–5. Hand geometry personal identification reader, with card reader feature. (Courtesy of Stellar Systems.)

that (1) hand geometry is a distinct human, measurable characteristic that can be related to individuals, and (2) tolerances can be established so that the probability of a particular individual cross-identifying can be reduced to one out of thousands.

Based upon this premise, and adding additional parameters such as the light transmissivity of the individual's skin, an access control system was introduced in 1972, during a time when interest in physical attribute identification systems was substantial. Most of the efforts were concentrated in the more accepted attributes of face, fingerprint, and voiceprint, and the professional pattern recognition community looked upon handprint recognition in much the same manner as the American Medical Association views a faith healer. Yet the hand geometry system alone survives from the many systems which were promoted during that period (see Figure 11–5).

Retinal Pattern of the Eye

In 1983, a personal attribute access control system was introduced based upon the premise that the pat-

Figure 11–6. Eye retina personal identification system. (Courtesy of Eyedentify, Inc.)

tern on the retina of the human eye is a unique identifier; those who scoff might do well to remember hand geometry. One uses the system by peering into a binocular eyepiece, whilst the patterns of the blood vessels on one's retina are scanned by a low-intensity infrared light beam, detected by a photosensor, and digitized. Comparison is made with a previously-read reference pattern to verify identity (see Figure 11–6).

Voiceprints

There has never been a successful voiceprint access control system, nor is there one today, despite considerable research and development work over the past fifteen years. There are still companies working on such a system, and voiceprint recognition could well be one of the contenders in the 1990s.

Selection of an Access Control System

Every management decision requires the balancing of risk and expenditure, and in choosing an access control system for the facility, the manager must decide what expenditure is warranted for the solution to the particular security problem. A total security system will encompass fire detection, perimeter control, internal surveillance, access control, and nonphysical security such as employee screening and audit trails. In all cases there will be existing measures in place for most or all of these aspects of security, and the manager must weigh the costs of new or additional security measures against those s/he is already incurring.

The keypad-only system is simply a sophisticated combination lock which is quicker to operate, more difficult to defeat, and has more features and options than the version sold at the corner hardware store. Features such as hostage alarm, error alarm, and remote indication can be deciding factors in some situations. Pushbutton systems cannot be employed where there is a large risk of collusion, since the combination can be told without penalty if there is no individual identification feature. Keypad systems will cost ten to twenty times the cost of a common lock, and the increased security and extra features will justify the cost in many cases.

The card-only system is equivalent to a conventional lock-and-key, more difficult to duplicate or master-key, and which can have many additional features. When equipped with personal identification, cancel-that-person ability, and logging of accesses and attempts, these systems provide control, history, and identification, and are virtually undefeatable by an amateur outsider; they can in many cases be completely cost-justified through side benefits such as time-clock information. The risk of lost or stolen cards is still present to a degree, since entry may be effected before the card's loss is known and the card's access privileges cancelled. Card-only systems can cost ten to a hundred times that of the conventional lock-and-key, and with the logging and cancel features they can provide sufficient additional security to justify that cost when the security need requires it.

A few words should be said about the method of encoding a card. Since no amount of ultra-high-technology can create an unloseable or unstealable card, it does not make sense from the user's point of view to pay greatly more money for exotic coding techniques. Granted that sophisticated coding requires the would-be penetrator to expend more effort and resources to crack and duplicate the code. If the stakes are worth it s/he will proceed to do so; further, in most cities s/he can hire a burglar, pickpocket, or mugger to obtain a real card cheaply. The security of card systems does not depend a great deal on the code or its embodiment.

Card-plus-keypad systems plug the loss and theft loopholes in the card-only systems, and the collusion loophole in the keypad-only systems. Card-plus-keypad systems cost very little more than card-only systems, and provide considerably increased security. On a cost/performance basis they are considered a best-buy. The increased security provided by adding a keypad to a card system may well be sufficient that a simple, stand-alone system will suffice for the user's security needs, and the expensive central processor and its options—along with the expensive wiring thereto—can be dispensed with; if this is deemed so, card-plus-keypad could be a cheaper system than a sophisticated card-only system.

Physical attribute systems are—or will be—the ultimate in access control systems, but they have yet to stand the test of time in the mainstream of access control applications. Standing alone, they still suffer from the false-accept and false-reject error problems, but in combination with a keypad or card we consider them even today to be a reliable top-of-the-line means of access control. At present costs, however, there is a rather limited portion of the spectrum of security situations in which they can be justified.

The Future of Access Control

It is appropriate to comment briefly upon what we believe will be the trends in access control technology, equipments, and practices in the coming years. Following are some areas which should be considered by vendors as they plan their new product offerings, and users as they design their new security systems in such a fashion that they are not likely to become oversoon obsolete.

The Active Card or the smart card or token. Complete microcomputers can now be put on a card or into a token, along with a power source. The major credit card companies are test-applying such devices, which will result in manufacturing at the millions-level, which produce such devices at prices approaching that of today's simple coded-cards. The result in the access control field will be that the card-holder carries a computer which is part of the access control system, providing greatly improved ability to provide secure codes. Multiple-purpose cards—access control, credit card credit, bank debit—will be possible, as will a proximity access control system at a much more attractive price than at present.

Wireless Systems. Installation and wiring of an access control system is a major part of the cost of such systems. Wireless alarm, security, and fire systems will continue to become more popular, and the advent of cellular telephone communications will raise some interesting new possibilities in the design of security systems.

Physical Attribute Systems. The viability of these systems will begin to be accepted by users. There will also be recognition that, as we said above concerning the coding of card systems, the security of a personal attribute system does not depend a great deal on which attribute the system is based upon, so long as the total system (e.g., attribute-plus-card) is properly designed. Despite a continuing trend towards reduced prices, these systems will continue to be top-of-the-line and justifiable only in particular situations.

The Security System

Machines alone are not the answer. Guards alone are not the answer. Barriers alone are not the answer. The security system is the answer, a security system designed pursuant to a professional analysis of the risks, threats, and exposures which are characteristic of the operation to be protected.

PART THREE
OPERATIONS

Chapter 12

Operations of a Guard Force

JOSEPH G. WYLLIE

In the five years from 1982 to 1987, the Uniformed Security Guard industry in the United States flourished. Various industries throughout the United States have engaged the services of private security firms. Others replaced their in-house security guard forces with full-time contract security guards.

A close look at the existing situation in the United States today readily indicates the vital need for security guards. The most recent statistics on record with most large metro police departments and the FBI show a definite increase in crime of all types throughout this country. Due to inadequate police protection in large as well as small cities, private concerns are turning to security guards as a deterrent to major crime.

It is a known fact that private security guards, both contract and in-house, outnumber police as much as two to one. In 1973, security guards and investigative services in the United States amounted to $2.5 billion in sales. The New York Times estimated that in the year 1986 this amount had risen to over $20 billion in sales.

In 1973, *in-house guard forces* amounted to approximately 65 percent of the total force of security guards. In 1986, however, the growth of contract security guards had increased to 65 percent, while in-house forces decreased to approximately 35 percent.

Companies presently using in-house security guards are taking a close look at existing costs with the future possibility of converting to contract guards. The salary increases and the fringe benefit packages negotiated at union contract renewals benefit in-house security guards by increasing their hourly rate costs. In many firms, it has become prohibitive to continue with an in-house force that has become so expensive.

Due to the confidentiality of security programs in various large corporations employing in-house guards, there is little information available. Several large in-house guard forces are in actuality police departments. One well regarded in-house guard force with a 150- to 200-person unit is Grumman Aerospace, Bethpage, L.I., New York.

A wealth of information is available regarding private security contract guards. All available records show that the big three in the United States are Pinkerton's Inc., founded in 1850, the oldest and largest with 40,000 employees. Next in size is Burn's International Security Services, Inc., founded in 1914, with 38,000 employees and then the Wackenhut Corporation, founded in 1954, with 25,000 employees. The balance of the contract guard firms is made up of several substantial firms such as Guardsmark, Globe Security Systems, and Wells Fargo. Then there are some medium sized firms as well as thousands of local guard companies. It has been estimated that there are between 5,000 and 6,000 local guard companies throughout the United States.

The basic mission of a guard force is to protect all property within the limits of the client's facility boundaries and protect employees and other persons on the client's property. This type of service offered by a guard agency must start with the basic requirements. The firm's concept of service must be one of integrity and professionalism, implemented by people with years of experience and expertise in their particular field of security. A guard agency may have an assignment that could be protection of a nuclear power plant to the actual guarding of the Alaska Pipeline. The agency may supply a single guard for a small business or provide total security for NASA's Kennedy Space Center. No matter what the size, the commitment to the concept of service remains the same. Total dedication to the job at hand is the paramount issue.

Today's demands for facility security are complex and diverse. Meeting such demands can require an expertise in the guard agency that defies description. The varied requirements of highly sophisticated clients, with far-flung operating facilities, has called for a highly professional approach to begin to meet some of the client's security problems. Guard clients today could be anywhere from the government of an emerging nation concerned with the development of its internal security capability to a giant petro-chemical complex or a nuclear power generating facility.

The watchman service of thirty years ago has evolved into the modern *system approach* to total security. The system approach requires, first, an in-depth analysis of the client's situation and requirements. This assessment of the client's needs is vital to the development of a plan of action for a total security concept.

In the case of a small guard job, such analysis and planning will be brief yet thorough. As larger clients present more detailed requirements, the procedure grows accordingly. And, as occurs frequently in the large agencies, due to worldwide activities, the resolution of extremely complicated and diverse security situations for giant business, industrial, or government facilities at home or abroad results in major analytical and planning procedures for the guard agency management.

Security Guards of the Future

The security guard of the 1980s is a far cry from the night watchman of the 1950s, 1960s, and in most cases even the 1970s. To be considered as an effective guard force in today's competitive market requires a training program that can guarantee a guard of the caliber to make a judgement that could save a multibillion dollar facility from total destruction.

In the past the security guard was principally concerned with protection of the site or facility. The post orders mainly were concerned with calling the fire department in case of fire or explosion. If there was a break-in or intrusion by an individual or group of individuals, then the local police were to be called. For any other problem during the tour of duty, an up-to-date alert list was available for phone calls to the client for decisions not to be handled by the guard force.

With the advent of the terrorism problems throughout the world, the security guard now has an awareness of security that never was considered until the early 1970s. It is a known fact that a successful act of sabotage against a nuclear power plant could result in serious and disasterous consequences to the health and safety of the public.

Security personnel, who are responsible for the protection of special nuclear material on-site and in-transit and for the protection of the facility or shipment vehicles against industrial sabotage, must be required to meet minimum criteria to assure that they will effectively perform their assigned security related job duties.

The new security awareness for guards in our nuclear oriented society has made a radical change in their basic mission. The guard's duties will shift from patrolling to operating of sophisticated equipment. At the time, the guard will remain ready for immediate deployment as part of a coordinated armed response unit.

Capable, confident guards will be no less important in the future, but they will have increasingly greater responsibility and awareness and will need professional training in electronics and other new security requirements. Obviously, it takes more than a snappy uniform and a shiny badge to make a security guard. The guard of the 1990s will be a unique individual, highly trained, specializing in a type of physical security that was unknown as much as ten years ago.

To be competitive in the security guard market of the future, the security firm must be ready to meet the new challenges with new concepts, bold innovations, and unrelenting insistance on high standards.

Guards at a Nuclear Power Plant

The Federal Government has mandated in article 10 CFR 73.55 the basis for security of nuclear power plants. The article is titled *Requirements for Physical Protection of Licensed Activities in Nuclear Power Reactors Against Industrial Sabotage.* In this article, under the physical security organization, four paragraphs stipulate the type of organization that is required:

1. The licensee shall establish a security organization, including guards, to protect the facility against radiological sabotage.
2. At least one full-time member of the security organization who has authority to direct the physical protection activities of the security organization shall be on-site at all times.

3. The licensee shall have a management system to provide for the development, revision, implementation and enforcement of security procedures.
4. The licensee shall not permit an individual to act as a guard, watchman, or armed response person, or other member of security organization unless such individual has been trained, equipped, and qualified to perform each assigned security job duty

Once the security force has been organized, then the licensee shall demonstrate the ability of the physical security personnel to carry out their assigned duties and responsibilities. Each guard, watchman, armed response person, and other members of the security organization shall requalify at least every 12 months. Such requalification must be documented. Each licensee shall submit a training and qualification plan outlining the processes by which guards, watchmen, armed response persons, and other members of the security organization will be selected, trained, equipped, tested, and qualified to assure that these individuals meet the requirements of this paragraph.

The training and qualification plan shall include a schedule to show how all security personnel will be qualified, within two years after the submitted plan is approved.

Executive Protection

Executive protection is a service designed to guard wealthy persons and top executives around the world —especially in Latin America and Europe—from kidnappers and assassins. This offshoot of the security guard service has grown tremendously since the 1960s; in the 1980s it became a very essential service for most large corporations, both in the United States and overseas.

Most security firms offering executive protection start with a survey that will identify vulnerabilities within the corporate and residence environment, plus review of the various executives' social, recreational, and travel activities. The normal transition from the original survey would be the preparation and implementation of a crisis management program. This program will assist senior executives in developing a corporate response during a crisis situation while maintaining continuity of operations. Within this program will be the development of plans, organizations, and procedures to reduce vulnerabilities to potential threats prior to a crisis,

while minimizing loss of assets and reducing corporate liability. Crisis management programs also focus analysis and decisionmaking and demonstrate corporate awareness and preparedness. The security firm's executive protection division provides real-world training, using scenerio formats to exercise the crisis management team's functional areas, which include: legal, personnel, finance, public relations and the negotiator and security. There is also an area where the security firm can provide hostage situation assistance to corporations at the time of an actual hostage situation or extortion demand. The executive protection division also can provide advice and assistance in:

(a) Identifying and obtaining trained hostage negotiators for those corporations desiring such assistance
(b) Developing terms for negotiation, when so asked by the corporation
(c) Establishing methods of ransom payment usually in third country locations
(d) Helping set up operational security matters at the affected location

An additional service offered to the corporation by the security firm is threat analysis. This service includes the following:

(a) evaluation of the threat in specific areas of interest
(b) summary of terrorist/criminal activity and propaganda and assessment of their activity
(c) updated reports of internal situations in specific areas of interest or as requested by the corporation

The executive protection service is responsible for the design and implementation of long-term bodyguard operations, tailored to the corporation's specific situation, usually but not always in response to a stated or perceived threat situation. The international bodyguard operations are coordinated through the security firm's international department utilizing resources from their additional subsidiaries and affiliates worldwide. The domestic bodyguard operations are coordinated through the security firm's network of offices throughout the United States.

The executive protection division of the security firm also can coordinate counterterrorist driver's training through recognized United States and overseas schools specializing in such training. The division negotiates the best price available with the school that, in their professional opinion, presents the best course for the driver. The savings are passed on to the corporate client. On many occasions, the personal chauffeurs of top executives are enrolled in these schools.

Another service that the executive protection division provides is awareness and survival training. This service is offered to corporate executives who travel frequently to high-risk areas. It is also offered to individuals who, by reason of earned or inherited wealth, are targets of criminal or terrorist elements. This training is usually given as an integral part of crisis management but applies to all levels of executives and managers, male or female.

The security firm in the 1980s must now be able to supply executive protection programs which apply experience—validated flexible procedures which bring about tangible improvement in the protected person's security posture. With the terrorism situations in the United States and overseas, the professional security guard firms are now in a position to offer this additional sophisticated service.

Security Services for Air Travel

In 1973, the FAA instituted an antihijack program that is in effect in all major airports throughout the United States. The service is known in the security industry as Predeparture Screening. The security employees at the airports are called PDS screeners. The service supplied has a number of benefits to the air travellers and the airlines which include:

- Prevention of kidnapping and extortion (hijacking and bomb threats)
- Controlled passenger entry
- Acts as a deterrent
- Ensures boarding pass validity
- Detection of weapons and hazardous materials
- Gives a positive public image

The security person(s) must conduct a thorough inspection of ALL passengers and ALL carry-on baggage before anyone or anything is allowed aboard the plane.

Explanation of definitions:

1. Carry-on baggage—Any item the passenger is carrying. This includes all baggage, valet bags, coats, gifts, purses, musical instruments, recording devices, and other items.
2. Dangerous item—Any item that may threaten the safety and security of airline passengers and aircraft. This includes incapacitating gasses, knives, stilettos, fountain pens that might fire a projectile, and cigarette lighters with hidden weapons.

3. Weapons—The word *weapon* is used to denote handguns, rifles, shotguns, and knives.
4. Explosives—Any item that can be triggered to explode. This includes dynamite, black powder, hand grenades, and shells.

The PDS screener's responsibility is to search all passengers and baggage and ensure that none of the above items are carried aboard the aircraft. The PDS screener is to prevent hijacking and criminal acts from occurring.

PDS inspectors use three devices in their screening: (1) X-ray machine, (2) magnetometer, and (3) hand wand.

All carry-on baggage, including pocketbooks, must go through the X-ray machine. All passengers must go through the magnetometer. If the passenger triggers off the magnetometer the second time, then the screener must use the hand wand to find the metal involved.

In 1981, the FAA changed their regulations which required an armed law enforcement officer present at each concourse predeparture screening check point. The FAA changed the requirement to let the airlines use specially trained security personnel from the private security industry to provide the required coverage. The individual involved is now called a check-point security supervisor or CSS and this person is now operating in place of the armed police officer. The CSS is an unarmed, specially trained security officer.

All major airports in the United States are using specially trained security guards for their predeparture screeners (PDS) and their check point security supervisors (CSS). These services have become an integral part of the major airlines security programs.

Liabilities Connected with Guard Force

Various legal aspects of industrial security and plant protection must be fully understood by the security guard.

A guard force is not engaged in law enforcement as such; therefore, the guard is not a law enforcement officer, like a police officer or sheriff. Guards are engaged in the protection of goods and services. The plant management makes the rules regarding the conduct of persons engaged in production. The final end is a smooth flow of production—not law enforcement.

Rules and regulations do not have the same force as law. An employee cannot be deprived of freedom because of breaking a rule or regulation to help production. The most that can be done is to dismiss the employee. Violation of law by someone working in the plant brings the same repercussions as breaking the law elsewhere—the case is under the jurisdiction of law enforcement agencies local, state, or federal. The work performed by a security guard is not related to police work. Execution of the job and training are different. The security guard must leave law enforcement to the responsible agency.

In special situations a security guard may make arrests. A security guard, peace officer, or any other person may arrest an offender without a warrant if the offense is a felony or an offense against public peace. A felony is ordinarily an offense punishable by confinement in a penitentiary for a period of more than one year. Arrests such as these should be made only with the consent of a superior, except in an emergency situation, and only on company property. False arrests and searches can result in civil and criminal suits. A security guard has no authority in a civil case and if required to testify in any civil case, the security guard should report the facts to the supervisor of the force and in turn demand a subpoena in order to testify.

Before making the arrest, the security guard should know that the law has actually been violated, that the violation is a crime, that information proves beyond a reasonable doubt that the person committed the crime. No arrest is legal until after the actual violation of the law. No person may be arrested on a charge of suspicion. The arrest is made by actual restraint of the person or by the guard saying, "You are under arrest." Actual touching of the person is unnecessary—it is enough if the person submits to your custody. The guard has no authority beyond the company property line other than that of a *private citizen*. No person is to be transported as a prisoner off company property by a security guard. The guard must notify the local law enforcement agency and turn the prisoner over to them on the company property. Crimes that may occur on company premises: murder, arson, assault, burglary, larceny, intoxication, violation of sabotage and espionage laws.

When a crime is committed on company property, the guard on duty must take prompt measures to afford protection of the crime scene. In the event of a serious crime, the security guard will not investigate the area. The guard should refrain from touching any evidence in the crime scene area and should prevent unauthorized persons from handling such evidence. The nature of the crime and the type of evidence in the area require that the security guard be extremely careful in moving about so as not to obliterate or otherwise destroy crime evidence.

The security guards will rope off or isolate the area and avenue of entry or escape believed to be used. No one should be allowed to enter or leave the area pending the arrival of representatives of the law enforcement agency having primary investigative jurisdiction. The guard should then obtain the names and addresses of any possible witnesses to be furnished to the law enforcement agency.

Power and Authority of the Security Guards

The accentuation of professionalism in the ranks of law enforcement in the United States has filtered down to the ranks of the contract security guard. Although some of the duties of the security guard are similiar to the duties of the police officer, their overall powers are entirely different.

Recent court decisions have found the security guard is not encumbered by the so-called Miranda warnings of rights. The security guard is *not* a law enforcement officer. Some recent state of Missouri Supreme Court decisions have made the arrest powers of a security guard much easier to understand in this current wave of lawlessness.

As you can see from the following information, the security guard in today's society must of necessity receive a basic training to learn the rules and regulations governing the guard's power and authority.

Private Security Guards Don't Have to Tell Suspects about Their Rights

Between movies and T.V. everybody has heard the expression, "Read them their rights." It refers to the warnings the suspect in custody is supposed to receive before interrogation. Otherwise, a confession can't be introduced at trial. That's why cops chant "You have the right to remain silent. . . ."

Recently, some people have claimed that private security guards must also precede their questioning with a recitation of these rights. *Here's the most recent of a series of decisions that indicate private guards need not give these so-called Miranda warnings**:

> The assistant security manager of the K-mart store in Willowbrook, Illinois, one day saw a shopper take a scarf from a rack, tear off the price tag and put the scarf in her purse. Outside the store, the security officer showed the shopper his badge and asked her to come

*Excerpted from *You & the Law*, February 2, 1981.
Prepared by: The Research Institute of America, Incorporated.

back to the security office. When asked for the receipt for the scarf, the shopper said, "Oh, I must have forgotten to pay for it." The guard made some comment about the shopper driving 50 miles "to steal at K-mart". Reportedly, the shopper said, "Sure, why not?" Another store employee was present in the security office and later corroborated the guard's testimony.

When the shopper was brought to trial for the theft under an Illinois shop-lifting law, the first thing her lawyer did was attempt to suppress the confession, because the guard had not read her rights. But he failed at the beginning and at the end of the trial. His client's conviction sent him to the Appellate Court in Illinois—but he did no better there.

The higher court pointed out that the U.S. Supreme Court in the Miranda case had defined "custodial interrogation" as "questioning initiated by law enforcement officers after a person had been taken into custody or otherwise deprived of his freedom of action in any significant way". This prompted the court to agree with all others that questioning by private security guards is not a "custodial interrogation" because the private guards are not "law enforcement officers." This is so even when they are acting pursuant to a specific shoplifting statute such as the Illinois Retail Theft Act. (*People v. Rattano*, 401 N.E.2d 278)

Don't let the freedom from Miranda restraints give your security people the impression that anything goes. Whether obtained by the police or by private guards, a suspect's confession must be voluntary to stand up in court.

Missouri

Arrest Power of Private Person (Security Guard)

The Missouri Supreme Court in *State v Fritz*, 490 S.W. 2nd 30, 32 (1973), explained: "in Missouri a private citizen may make an arrest on a *showing* of commission of a *felony* and *reasonable grounds* to suspect the arrested party."

In *State v Parker*, 378 S.W. 2nd 274, 282 (1964), the Court held that a private citizen does have the right "to arrest for certain crimes, such as the commission of a *felony* or the commission of *petit larceny* in *his presence*. But he should be sure both of the crime and of the person. . . . a private citizen has the right . . . to arrest in order to prevent a *breach of peace* or an affray."

The more recent Missouri cases which hold that a private person possessed of knowledge that a recent felony has been committed may arrest anyone he has reasonable grounds to believe   committed the

offense, are: *Helming v Adams*, 509 S.W. 2nd 159 (1974); *State v Goodman*, 449 S.W. 2nd 656 (1970); *State v Keeny*, 431 S.W.95 (1968).

Thus, it is clear that in Missouri a security guard may arrest someone who had committed a *felony*, even though not committed in the presence of the guard, as long as the guard knows that a felony has in fact occurred, and she or he has reasonable grounds to believe the person to be arrested is the perpetrator of the crime.

Regarding *misdemeanors*, according to a 1970 opinion by the Missouri Attorney General: "A private citizen may only arrest for those *misdemeanors* which involve *breaches of the peace, petit larceny committed in his presence*, or pursuant to those powers granted him by virtue of (Section 573.125, Missouri Statutes)."

Section 573.125, Missouri Statutes, pertains to *shoplifting*. It provides that a *merchant*, *agent*, or *employee*, who has *reasonable grounds* or *probable cause* to believe that a person has taken money or merchandise, may detain the person in a reasonable manner and for a reasonable length of time in order to make an investigation. The detention does not constitute an unlawful arrest, and it does not render the merchant, agent, or employee either criminally or civilly liable.

The entire shoplifting statute is set forth:

537.125. Shoplifting: Detention of suspect by merchant—liability presumption:

1. As used in this section:
   (a) "Merchant" means any corporation, partnership, association or person who is engaged in the business of selling goods, wares and merchandise in a mercantile establishment;
   (b) "Mercantile establishment" means any mercantile place of business in, at or from which goods, wares and merchandise are sold, offered for sale or delivered from and sold at retail or wholesale;
   (c) "Merchandise", means all goods, wares and merchandise offered for sale or displayed by a merchant;
   (d) "Wrongful taking" includes stealing of merchandise or money and any other wrongful appropriation of merchandise or money.
2. Any merchant, agent, or employee, who has reasonable grounds or probable cause to believe

that a person has committed or is committing a wrongful taking of merchandise or money from a mercantile establishment, may detain such person in a reasonable manner and for a reasonable length of time for the purpose of investigating whether there has been a wrongful taking of such merchandise or money. Any such reasonable detention shall not constitute an unlawful arrest or detention, nor shall it render the merchant, agent, or employee, criminally or civilly liable to the person so detained.

3. Any person willfully concealing unpurchased merchandise of any mercantile establishment, either on the premises or outside the premises of such establishment, shall be presumed to have so concealed such merchandise with the intention of committing a wrongful taking of such merchandise within the meaning of subsection 1, and the finding of such unpurchased merchandise concealed upon the person or among the belongings of such person shall be evidence of reasonable grounds and probable cause for the detention in a reasonable manner and for a reasonable length of time, of such a person by a merchant, agent, or employee, in order that recovery of such merchandise may be effected, and any such reasonable detention shall not be deemed to be unlawful, nor render such merchant, agent, or employee criminally or civilly liable.

Use of Force by Private Person

Missouri has a specific statute covering a private person's use of force in making an arrest. The Statute, as well as the comment interpreting the statute, are reproduced below:

563.051 Private person's use of force in making an arrest

1. A private person who has been directed by a person reasonably believed to be a law enforcement officer to assist such officer to effect an arrest or to prevent escape from custody may, subject to the limitations of subsection 3, use physical force when and to the extent reasonably necessary to carry out such officer's direction unless she or he knows or believes that the arrest or prospective arrest is not or was not authorized.

2. *A private person acting on his own account* may, subject to the limitations of subsection 3, use physical force to effect arrest or prevent escape only when and to the extend such is *immediately necessary* to effect the *arrest*, or to *prevent escape*

from custody, of a person whom he reasonably believes to have committed a crime and who in fact has committed such crime.

3. A private person in effecting an arrest or in preventing escape from custody is justified in using *deadly force only*,
   (a) When such is *authorized under other sections* of this chapter; or
   (b) When he *reasonably believes such to be authorized under the circumstances and he is directed or authorized by law enforcement officer to use deadly force*; or
   (c) When he reasonably *believes such use of deadly force is immediately necessary to effect the arrest of a person who at that time and in his presence*:
      (a) Committed or attempted to commit a *class A felony or murder*; or
      (b) *Is attempting to escape by use of a deadly weapon*.
   (d) The defendant shall have the burden of injecting the issue of justification under this section.
   (L.1977, S.B. No. 60, P. 662, & 1, eff. Jan. 1, 1979.)

Comment to 1973 Proposed Code

Based on Model Penal Code 3.07; Illinois Criminal Code, Ch. 38, 7–5; New York Revised Penal Law 35.30.

In *State v Parker*, 378 S.W. 2d 274, 282 (Mo. 1964), the Missouri Supreme Court stated:

The private citizen is limited in the power of arrest; but he does have the right, without warrant or other process, to arrest for certain crimes, such as the commission of a felony or the commission of petit larceny in the presence. But he should be sure of the crime and the person. ... All authorities seems to agree that a private person has the right (where not abrogated by statute) to arrest in order to prevent a breach of peace or an affray. We know of no statute which abrogates this right of the citizen in this state.

Authorities cited included *Pandjiris v Hartman*, 196 Mo. 539, 94 S.W. 270 (1906) and *Wehmeyer v Melvihill*, 150 Mo. App. 197, 130 S.W. 681 (1910). This *section deals with the private person acting on his own, or with other private persons, in making arrests, subsection 2; and when he is summoned or directed to assist a law enforcement officer, subsection:*
1. *The section distinguishes the occasions when deadly force can be used. Subsection 1 prescribes the amount of non-deadly physical force that a person can use if*

summoned by a law enforcement officer. As with other sections of this Chapter, the section allows a person to act on appearances provided he does so reasonably. To be justified under subsection 1, the private person must, first, be summoned by one he reasonably believes to be a law enforcement officer; second, use only that amount of force which he reasonably believes necessary to carry out the orders of the officer; and lastly, believe the arrest lawful.

Subsection 2 prescribes the amount of nondeadly physical force a private person may use when acting on his own account, which impliedly includes acting in conjunction with other private persons. The applicability of Subsection 2 is contingent on the private person having a *reasonable belief* that the person to be arrested has committed a crime and that such person in fact has committed such crime. Again the defense is dependent on *using physical force only as a final means of effecting an arrest.*

The section makes a slight modification in Missouri law. *The section authorizes the use of physical force even when the crime was committed out of the presence of the private person.* However, the in presence requirement announced in *State v Parker*, supra has not been strictly adhered to by Missouri courts. For example, in *State v Keeney*, 431 S.W. 2d 95 (Mo. 1968), the Missouri Supreme Court held that where a private person had been advised by the victim of a crime as to the description of the robber's automobile and 16 minutes later such person observed the automobile fitting the description in another state, he had the authority to arrest the occupants of the automobile and search the same. The safegards that a private person must reasonably believe the person did in fact commit the crime removes the need for the "in presence" requirement as to the use of non-deadly physical force.

Under *subsection 3* the use of *deadly force* by a private person effecting an arrest is *authorized only if it is allowed under another section of this Chapter, as for example in self-defense under 563.031; or when he is directed by a law enforcement officer to use deadly force and he reasonably believes such to be authorized; or when it is necessary in the arrest of a person who has committed a Class A Felony or murder or who is attempting to escape by using a deadly weapon. Subsection 3 (2) authorized the use of deadly force when the private person is directed to use deadly force by the officer he has been summoned to assist.* The private person must, however, reasonably believe the use of deadly force to be authorized under the circumstances. Mistakes will not vitiate the applicability of the justification unless such mistakes were unreasonable.

Subsection 3(3) is similar to the corresponding paragraph in the preceding section, 563.046, subsection 3(2). However, there are two significant differences. First, *as to the private person, the situations giving rise to the use of deadly force must occur "at that time and in his presence." Thus, the private person must personally detect the crime and immediately thereafter attempt to effect the arrest. Secondly, the situations in which the private person is justified in using deadly force are more limited than those in which a law enforcement officer may use deadly force. For the private person, it must involve a Class A Felony or murder or attempted escape by use of a deadly weapon.*

(A Class A Felony is a crime for which the penalty is death, life imprisonment, or imprisonment for a term of twenty years or more. Examples in addition to murder are: robbery, kidnapping, causing catastrophe, rape, and first degree assault with a deadly weapon.)

Definitions for Misdeameanors and Felonies

The Missouri Statute defining these terms is as follows:
556.016 classes of crimes:

1. An offense defined by this code or by any other statute of this state, for which a sentence of death or imprisonment is authorized, constitutes a "crime". Crimes are classified as felonies and misdemeanors.
2. A crime is a *felony* if it is so designated or if persons convicted thereof may be sentenced to death or imprisonment for a term which is *in excess of one year.*
3. A crime is a *misdemeanor* if it is so designated or if persons convicted thereof may be sentenced to imprisonment for a term of which the *maximum is one year or less.*
   (L.1977, S.B. No.60, p. 662, 1, eff. Jan. 1, 1979).

Crimes are classified for the purpose of sentencing into Class A through Class D felonies, and Class A through Class C misdemeanors.

4. *Larceny* is included in the Missouri Statute entitled *Stealing* Section 570.030, Missouri Statutes. It provides that stealing is a Class C *felony* if the value of the property or services appropriated is *one hundred fifty dollars ($150.00) or more.*
5. *Good Samaritan Act*: The Missouri Good Samaritan Act which is reproduced below applies only to those persons trained to provide first aid. The

Statute would therefore apply to guards who have had legitimate first aid training.

190.195 Personal liability for civil damages removed in certain emergency care situations.

Any person who has been trained to provide first aid in a standard, recognized training program may render emergency care or assistance to the level for which he or she has been trained, at the scene of an emergency or accident, and shall not be liable for civil damages for acts or omissions other than damages occasioned by gross negligence or by willful or wanton acts or omissions by such person in rendering such emergency care.

Laws 1973, p. 306, 20, effective July 1, 1974.

Training

In view of the demands of industry for fully trained security guards, a new phase of the guard industry has come into view. To give the necessary training required for the basic guard who could be working on a one-guard site up to the basic guard working at a nuclear power plant, a new look has been given to guard training.

Training today must be organized so as to provide the initial or basic training as well as the follow-up programs necessary to maintain quality standards for the personnel. Most professional security agencies offer at least a basic security officer's program. These programs can run as long as twenty-four hours and cover subjects ranging from laws of arrest to weapon safety. The present system attempts to package the training in a practical delivery system and to keep quality high in terms of testing.

Many of the basic training courses are tailored to individual client needs. In recent years a number of states have mandated requirements for security officers and most states have mandated requirements for weapon training.

Another offshoot of the training for guards has been the predeparture screening services required at all airports across the United States. In screening carry-on baggage with an X-ray machine, the ability to detect the outline, shape or form of a weapon or an explosive device is critical. The FAA has mandated a training program that must be uniformly given to every screener at every airport in the country. It has been necessary to develop audiovisual training programs prepared in cooperation with the Federal Aviation Agency. Besides instruction in the techniques of discerning the outlines

of X-ray screens, the course offers new pointers in the use of magnetometers, both the walk-through models and the hand-held wands.

As an illustration of the completeness of the Basic Guard Training Program, you will see in the chapter appendixes an outline of an existing program. The importance of training cannot be emphasized enough. The modern day security officer has a great many responsibilities and is often required to make important decisions under sometimes trying conditions. Only thorough training will provide assurance of an effective and competent guard operation. The primary duties of guards and supervisors are treated below.

Report Writing

Very few people like paperwork, yet it seems that the occupation does not exist where paperwork is not required. For the security officer, the paperwork is in the form of reports. There are four basic reasons for completing so many reports.

1. *To inform.* Written communications reduce the chances of misunderstandings or errors. Verbal communications, however, are highly prone to misunderstandings, errors in reproduction, and can be easily ignored.
2. *To record.* Never trust memory. No memory is perfect. Exact amounts, costs, dates, times, and similar data are easily forgotten unless recorded.
3. *To demonstrate alertness.* By recording incidents, the security officer makes both supervisor and client aware of the job being done. It is very easy for people to get the impression that security officers do little but stand around. One way of avoiding this type of image is to conscientiously document all incidents.
4. *To protect yourself.* There may come a time when it becomes necessary for a security officer to prove to have witnessed an event, accomplished a certain action, or notified the proper authorities of an incident. The reports will accomplish all four of these goals.

The report should be clear and concise. A good report answers five basic questions:

1. *What?* The report must state what happened as accurately as possible.
2. *Where?* The exact location of an occurrence can have great bearing in establishing guilt, innocence, or liability.
3. *Who?* When writing a report, the officer should

answer as many whos as possible; for example, who did it and who was notified?

4. *When?* The when of an incident may establish an alibi, or help to prevent damage, theft, or injury.

5. *Why?* The why involves judgment and opinion and may not be easily proven, but it may be very important in judgment of guilt or liability.

In addition to answering these questions, there are simple guidelines to follow when preparing a report to assure that the final result is clearly written and well organized.

1. Use simple language which anyone can understand. When using technical words and phrases, be sure the meaning is clear. Avoid using slang terms or words that have multiple meanings.

2. Be sure that you use the proper spellings and addresses of the individuals involved in the report.

3. Prepare the report in such a manner that the happenings are in logical sequence and, when possible, show the approximate time of the occurrence.

4. Do not ramble. It is preferable to use short paragraphs, with each covering one particular point.

5. Do not use vague descriptions. Write only specific observations.

6. When descriptions of individuals are obtained, list all the usual manners of description such as height, weight, color of hair, etc., but also include unusual details such as presence of a mustache, sideburns, eyeglasses, and any peculiarities of walk of speech. Notice and report all information possible on types and color of dress.

7. Avoid contradictory statements that would tend to discredit the overall information.

8. Facts, not fiction, are important. If you include your opinion, label it as your opinion, not as a fact.

Any problem, from a missing light bulb to a major safety hazard, should be reported. The security officer should continue to provide written reports on any incident until appropriate action is taken to correct the situation. In this way, you can demonstrate your importance to the client.

Weapons Safety

No part of the training of a security officer is more critical than firearms training. Your life, as well as the lives of others, depends upon your skill with a revolver and knowledge of its proper and safe use.

Safety is the basic reason for the existence of security personnel. They are employed to assure the safety of persons and property and should always reflect this concept.

Weapons safety, unlike any other aspect of a security officer's job, places a great demand upon skills, knowledge, and the judgment necessary to best use both. Judgment can be exercised only when the factual basis for making such judgment is present. In this case, the principles of firearms safety must be well understood by security officers before any judgment can be made.

The first principle of weapons safety is control. The officer must control the firearm when wearing, storing, and firing it.

Wearing a Firearm

When on duty, the officer's weapon must be readily available for immediate use. It should be worn in a manner that permits swift access while also offering maximum safety. To satisfy this requirement, the weapon should be worn at the belt line and on the same side as the strong shooting hand.

The weapon should always be carried in its holster. Any other method, such as tucked in the belt, is hazardous and has contributed to self-inflicted gunshot wounds. The holster strap or flap should be kept securely snapped over the gun. This prevents the weapon from accidentally falling or being jarred out of the holster. It will also prevent someone from grabbing the revolver.

The weapon must always be loaded when worn on duty. An unloaded revolver is a hazard to the wearer. Drawing an unloaded gun in an invitation to be shot.

When the shifts change and the revolver must be transferred from one officer to his relief, the weapon should be empty. Never transfer a loaded weapon. More accidents occur at this time than at any other time of duty.

When transferring a weapon, unload the gun and hand it to the person receiving it with the breach open. The cartridges should be transferred separately. An additional benefit is derived from this procedure. The relief officer must check and load the weapon prior to assuming the duties of the post.

Storing a Weapon

Common sense demands that all firearms be kept out of the reach of children and irresponsible adults.

Unloaded weapons should be locked up at all times and cartridges should be secured separately from the weapon. Never store a loaded weapon.

Firing a Weapon

The security officer must keep the weapon under control while firing it. This statement may seem obvious, but it is often misunderstood. Control, in this case, refers to the mental discipline required to know when not to fire as well as the physical control necessary to hit the target. Consider these situations:

1. An armed intruder is firing at you. There is a crowd of bystanders behind. Do you return fire?
2. A saboteur is on a four-story rooftop in a crowded facility, well silhouetted against the sky. Do you shoot?
3. An arsonist is standing in front of a light frame building. You do not know if anyone is inside. Do you shoot?

The answer to all three questions is "no." In the first situation, returning fire would most assuredly endanger the bystanders. In the second case, the path of the bullet, after passing the target, could injure or kill a person several blocks away. In the third instance, the bullet could penetrate the frame building and kill an occupant, even after passing through the target. Never underestimate the penetrating power of a gun.

Control in firing also means having the mental discipline to never draw a weapon unless there is the intention to kill the target to protect life itself.

The Guard and the Revolver

No publication can describe all the cases in which a guard should and should not use a firearm. It is possible, however, to present some general guidelines and some specific examples. The guard who considers these carefully, and discusses them with the supervisor and fellow guards, should be able to develop good judgment in the use of a firearm.

The first thing an armed security officer should keep in mind is the fact that an error in the use of a firearm will probably have a long lasting, perhaps permanent, effect. It is necessary therefore to give long and careful consideration of the answers to the questions: "Why do I have a firearm?" "When should I use it?" "When should I not use it?"

While a private security officer, like a police officer, is armed, you should not confuse your rights and responsibilities concerning firearms with those of your public counterpart. There are specific and definite laws governing the police officer and the use of a firearm. There are laws, just as specific and just as definite regarding a private officer's use of a weapon.

A firearm is a symbol of a guard's authority and duty to carry out specific tasks as ordered by your employer. The police officer's duties and responsibilities are obviously much broader. The police officer can arrest suspects, a security guard cannot. A police officer can use a gun to stop a speeding automobile; a guard cannot. A police officer can use a weapon to protect property and, again, a guard cannot.

To simplify matters a bit, the security officer may use a firearm to protect a life, and only to protect a life. That life may be your own or that of a bystander. In any case, your use the gun only to protect a life.

When *not* to use a firearm? Fortunately, there are many more of these instances. Do not use a weapon:

- to prevent a theft
- to stop a fleeing suspect
- to stop a speeding automobile
- to stop someone from bothering or harassing.
- on someone who would like to harm you but cannot; for example, a knife wielder or club wielder who is restrained by a fence or gate, or by other people
- to fire warning shots at a fleeing criminal
- to attempt to frighten people

Safety

Accident prevention is said to be everybody's job, but, as everybody's job, no one does too much about it. It does, however, fall well within the domain of security personnel. It is the security officer's responsibility to observe all unsafe conditions and to warn people of potential hazards. It is also your responsibility to report any violations of safety rules and to set a good example by your own behavior.

Far too many accidents happen due to unsafe conditions which were not noted, reported, or corrected. After finding an unsafe condition, the officer must do one of two things: correct the condition or report it to someone who can make the correction. If a storm blows a power line down, the security officer should report it. If, on the other hand, you find a bag of oil rags in the corner, you would simply place them in a metal covered container and report it later. Safety is purely a matter of common sense.

Corrective action should be taken when possible, or the proper authority should be called to handle the situation.

It is important that the security officer undertake the sometimes thankless task of safety. It is important both to the client and to the people he is protecting from injuries due to careless safety practices.

Safety Checklist

1. Are the floors kept clean and free of dirt and debris?
2. Are rough, splintered, uneven or other floor defects repaired or the hazards suitably marked?
3. Are nonskid waxes used to polish floors?
4. During bad weather, are storm mats placed near entrances and floors mopped frequently?
5. Are stairways equipped with handrails?
6. Are steps equipped with handrails?
7. Are stairways well lighted?
8. Are electric fan or heater extension cords tripping hazards?
9. Are cords of electric fans or heaters disconnected from the power source when not in use and at the end of each working day?
10. Are electric fans or heaters adequately grounded?
11. Are cigarette or cigar stubs placed in suitable ashtrays or containers?
12. Are grounds free of debris, etc.?
13. Are sufficient containers provided for trash, ashes, etc.?
14. Are floors free of oil spills, grease or other substances which create a slipping hazard?
15. Are windows clean?
16. Is broken glass in evidence?
17. Are the aisles clearly defined and free of obstruction?
18. Is material neatly stacked and readily reached?
19. Does piled material project into aisles or passageways?
20. Are tools lefts on overhead ledges or platforms?
21. Is the lighting adequate?
22. Are materials stored under or piled against buildings, doors, exits or stairways?
23. Are walks kept clear of obstructions, slipping and tripping hazards, broken glass, snow and ice?

Bomb Threats

Bomb threats are a serious concern to all security personnel. Fortunately, most bomb threats turn out to be false alarms, but the next encounter with such a threat may turn out to be real, so none should be taken lightly. All bomb threats should be treated with quick, calm, steady professional action.

Normally, local police authorities will be notified by client management when a bomb threat occurs. Upon receiving a bomb threat, a security officer's first duty is to notify the client immediately and to take the action ordered. If ordered to call the police, you should do so and then evacuate anyone in or near the facility. The handling of bombs and bomb disposal are police duties. The security force's job is to assist the police in finding the bomb and in evacuation proceedings.

The security officer should *NOT* attempt to examine a bomb, regardless of any previous experience you may have had in the world of explosives. Many bombs are extremely complicated and designed to explode when any attempt is made for deactivation. Only trained demolition experts are qualified to safely handle a bomb.

Bomb Search

The number of locations where a bomb may be hidden are innumerable, and only the most obvious places can be searched in a reasonable amount of time. However, most facilities have areas which are generally more vulnerable than others and should be checked first. The following thoughts should be kept in mind when searching for a bomb:

1. Do not touch anything that does not have to be disturbed. If lights are off, do not turn them on. If fuse panels are turned off, do not activate them. These may be wired to detonate explosives.
2. Most bombs which have actually been found were of the time-mechanism variety. The timing devices are usually cheap alarm clocks which can be heard ticking at surprising distances. Be on the alert for ticking sounds.
3. Bombs found in searches were usually found near an exit. Look closely in areas near doorways.
4. Be alert for objects which look out of place, or are of unusual size or shape.
5. Thoroughly check any areas which are accessible to the public. Rest rooms and janitors' closets are frequently used as hiding places.
6. A bomb search should be conducted for a period of twenty to thirty minutes. This should provide ample time for a reasonable search, without creating unnecessary danger to the searchers.
7. A methodical search technique is necessary to ensure that no areas are overlooked. An orderly

investigation of all rooms within the facility is mandatory. It is wise to prepare a checklist of places to be searched in advance so that a thorough search can be conducted.

8. As you search, be alert to:

- freshly plastered or painted places
- disturbed dirt in potted plants
- pictures or other hanging objects not straight
- ceiling tiles that have been disturbed
- torn furniture coverings
- broken cabinets or objects recently moved
- trash cans, air conditioning ducts, water fountains
- elevator shafts, phone booths

Precautions

A security officer can assist police by observing the following precautions:

Don't:

- Touch a bomb.
- Smoke in the immediate vicinity of a suspected bomb.
- Expose the bomb to sun. Direct rays of the sun or light of any kind may cause detonation.
- Accept identification makeup as legitimate. Don't take for granted the identification markings on packages and boxes as they may have been forged. Keep in mind that bombs are usually camouflaged in order to throw the recipient off guard. Don't take for granted that the package is bona fide because of its having been sent through the mail. Many bombs are forwarded in this manner. Others are sent through express agencies, while some are delivered by individual messengers.
- Take for granted that it is a high explosive bomb. Be prepared in the event that it is of the incendiary type. Have sand and extinguishers on hand.
- Use two-way radios as transmitting could detonate a bomb.
- Have unnecessary personnel in the immediate area of the suspected bomb or explosive.

Do:

- Evacuate the building or area around the suspected bomb, only if the client orders it. In large cities, this function is usually performed by the fire department. Only vital and necessary personnel should be allowed within 100 yards of the package.

- Remove all valuable equipment, important files, computer tapes, etc. at least 100 yards away from the package.
- Open all windows and doors in the immediate vicinity of the suspected devices. This allows the blast to escape, thereby reducing pressure on the walls and interiors. It will also reduce window breakage and the hazards caused by flying glass and debris.
- Shut off all power services to the area *immediately*. This reduces the possibility of gas explosion or electrical fires.

Types of Explosives

Blasting caps or detonators are:

- Metallic cylinders approximately 2 inches long, $3/16$ inches in diameter closed at one end (may be larger or smaller).
- Partially filled with a small amount of relatively easily fired or detonated compound.
- When fired, the resultant shock or blow is sufficient to detonate explosives.
- *Very* dangerous to handle, as they can be detonated by heat, friction, or a relatively slight blow.

Nitroglycerin is:

- Colorless to yellow liquid with a heavy, oily consistency.
- Highly dangerous—extremely sensitive to heat, flame, shock or friction.

Dynamite is:

- High explosive, usually cylinderical in shape, size: 1¼ inches diameter and approximately 8 inches long, (may be up to 12 inches diameter, and 30 inches long).
- Outer wrapper often covered in parafin and *usually* marked "DANGEROUS—HIGH EXPLOSIVE."
- Shock sensitive—needs a blasting cap for detonation.

Fire Protection

Of the many jobs a security officer performs, one of the most important is that of fire protection. To do the job effectively, you must be familiar with fire fighting equipment and know how and when to use it.

Fire is comprised of three elements: heat, fuel and oxygen. Remove any one of these three and the fire will go out.

If a fire should break out the following directions will most effectively safeguard persons and property against harm and damage:

1. Call the fire department first.
2. Direct all employees out of the burning building and keep them out after evacuation.
3. Notify and enlist the help of the company fire brigade if one exists.
4. Check and close fire doors.
5. Shut off machinery, power and gas.
6. Check to see if gate valves are in working condition, if a sprinkler system exists.
7. Now and only now, attempt to control the fire by means of an extinguisher.
8. Post someone to direct the firefighters to the fire.
9. Remove motor vehicles from the area.
10. Once the fire has been contained, keep a close watch on the area to see that the fire does not start again.
11. Be sure all extinguishers used are immediately recharged.
12. Complete a written report covering all of the information about the fire.

Fire Prevention

The best way to fight a fire is to prevent a fire from starting. Following is a list of things that you should be alert for while on patrol to eliminate sources of fire and obstructions that might lead to fire spreading:

1. Look for violations of no-smoking regulations.
2. Investigate any unusual odors, especially smoke and gas. Don't be satisfied until you have found the cause and action has been taken.
3. Check for obstructed passageways and fire doors.
4. Look for obstructions in front of fire-alarm boxes, extinguishers and fire hydrants.
5. On every patrol, check all gas or electric heaters, coal and kerosene stoves to see that they do not overheat.
6. Check to see that boxes, rubbish or hazardous materials are not left close to stoves, boilers, steam or smoke pipes.
7. Check to see that all gas or electric appliances not in use are disconnected.
8. Check to see that all discarded and disposable

materials have been placed in their proper containers.

Emergency Medical Assistance

It is possible that a security officer will be present when someone needs medical assistance. The first reaction should be to summon help. If this is not possible, the officer should be prepared to assist the victim. Guards should be trained in emergency medical assistance (EMA) procedures in the event a severe accident occurs. Someone's life may depend on your knowledge of EMA.

At the Scene

People at the scene of an accident will be excited. A security officer must remain calm, dealing with the most serious injury or condition first. The most urgent medical emergencies which require prompt action to save a life are: severe bleeding, stoppage of breathing, and poisoning. Shock may accompany any of these, depressing the body functions and keeping the heart, lungs and other organs from functioning normally.

What to Do First

1. Don't move the injured person, unless it is absolutely necessary to save the victim from danger. If the victim has been injured internally, or if the spine is broken, unnecessary movement may kill or cripple him.
2. Act fast if the victim is bleeding severely, has swallowed poison or has stopped breathing because of drowning, gas poisoning or electric shock. Every second counts. A person may, for example, die within three minutes of the time breathing stops, unless given artificial respiration.
3. Because life-and-death emergencies are rare, in most cases a guard can start EMA with these steps: Keep the patient lying down quietly. If she or he has vomited and there is no danger that the neck is broken, turn the head to one side to prevent choking. Keep the victim warm with blankets or coats, but don't overheat or apply external heat.
4. Summon medical help. The doctor should be told the nature of the emergency, and asked what should be done.
5. Examine the patient gently. Cut clothing, if

necessary, to avoid movement or added pain. Don't pull clothing away from burns.

6. Reassure the patient, and try to remain calm. Calmness will convince the patient that everything is under control.
7. Always be prepared to treat shock.
8. Do not force fluids on an unconscious or semi-conscious person. Fluids may enter the windpipe and cause strangulation. Do not try to arouse an unconscious person by slapping, shaking or shouting. Do not give alcohol to any victim.
9. Following any incident where EMA would be rendered, a detailed written report should be made covering all of the circumstances. Be sure to include the treatment given.

Controlling Bleeding

The adult human body contains approximately six quarts of blood. Although an adult can readily withstand the loss of a pint, the amount usually taken for transfusion purposes, that same loss by a child may have disastrous results. In an adult, lack of consciousness may occur from the rapid loss of as little as a quart of blood. Because a victim can bleed to death in a very short period of time, immediate stoppage of any large, rapid loss of blood is necessary.

Direct Pressure

The preferred method for control of severe bleeding is direct pressure by pressing a hand over a dressing. This method prevents loss of blood from the body without interfering with normal circulation.

Apply direct pressure by placing the palm of the hand on a dressing directly over the entire area of an open wound on any surface part of the body. In the absence of compresses, the fingers or bare hand may be used, but only until a compress can be obtained and applied.

Do not disturb blood clots after they have formed within the cloth. If blood soaks through the entire compress without clotting, do not remove, but add additional layers of padding and continue direct hand pressure, even more firmly.

On most parts of the body, a pressure bandage can be placed to hold pads of cloth over a wound. Properly applied, the bandage will free the hands for another EMA.

To apply the bandage, place and hold the center directly over the pad on the wound. Maintain a steady pull on the bandage to keep the pad firmly in place while wrapping the ends around the body part. Finish by tying a knot over the pad.

Elevation

If there is no evidence of a fracture, a severely bleeding hand, arm or leg should be elevated above the level of the victim's heart. Once elevated, the force of gravity will reduce blood pressure at the site of the wound and slow the loss of blood. Elevation is used in addition to direct pressure.

The combination of pressure and elevation will stop severe bleeding in most cases; however, there are times when additional techniques are required. One additional technique is pressure on the supplying artery.

Pressure on the Supplying Artery

If severe bleeding from an open wound of the arm or leg does not stop after the application of direct pressure plus elevation, the use of pressure points may be required. Use of the pressure point technique temporarily compresses the main artery which supplies blood to the affected limb against the underlying bone and tissues.

If the use of a pressure point is necessary, do not substitute its use for direct pressure and elevation, but use the pressure point in addition to those techniques. Do not use a pressure point in conjunction with direct pressure any longer than necessary to stop the bleeding. However, if bleeding recurs, reapply pressure at a pressure point.

Pressure Point: Open Arm Wound

Apply pressure over the brachial artery, forcing it against the arm bone. The pressure point is located on the inside of the arm in the groove between the biceps and the triceps, about midway between the armpit and the elbow.

To apply pressure on the brachial artery, grasp the middle of the victim's upper arm, your thumb on the outside of the victim's arm and your other fingers on the inside. Press your fingers toward your thumb to create an inward force from opposite sides of the arm. The inward pressure holds and closes the artery by compressing it against the arm bone.

Pressure Point: Open Leg Wound

Apply pressure on the femoral artery by forcing the artery against the pelvic bone: The pressure point is located on the front center part of the diagonally slanted *hinge* of the leg, in the crease of the groin area, where the artery crosses the pelvic bone on its way to the leg.

To apply pressure to the femoral artery, position the victim flat on the back, if possible, and place the heel of your hand directly over the pressure point. Then lean forward over your straightened arm to apply the small amount of pressure needed to close the artery. To prevent arm tension and muscular strain, keep your arm straight while applying the technique.

Call for Assistance

Whenever possible, get medical assistance as soon as you have made the victim comfortable and are sure the person's life is not in immediate danger. Often you can do more harm than good if you don't summon proper help immediately.

If in doubt as to a victim's well-being, keep the person quiet, preferably lying down and covered. Sometimes a concussion victim will appear perfectly normal and insist upon returning to work only to collapse later. In any case, do not allow the victim to move around. Remember, your greatest contribution to a victim's well-being may be to restrain efforts to move the person in a mistaken belief that such efforts are helpful. It is usually best to let the victim remain calm and relaxed before transporting to the medical station. Obtain professional help whenever possible.

Reporting a Medical Case

When reporting a medical case, the following information must be given clearly so that the necessary equipment and medical assistance can reach the victim in the shortest possible time:

- Exact location and phone number from which you are reporting
- Type of injury, if evident
- Seriousness of injury
- Number of persons involved
- Visible symptoms, such as heavy bleeding, poison stains, etc.
- Cause of injury, if known, so that adequate per-

sonnel may be sent to the area to handle such dangerous conditions as leaking gas, flowing chemicals, etc.

Guard Supervision

In every business organization, different management levels exist that are responsible for various tasks. At the top of the structure are people who must decide the organizational goals and policies. At the opposite end of the operational spectrum are those who are immediately responsible for the accomplishment of established goals. Between top management and these workers are the people who must explain management's objectives to all employees. These people give guidance and leadership. They represent top management to the workers by setting standards, developing work schedules, training employees, and exercising necessary controls to insure quality performance. A guard supervisor is one of these important people.

The Supervisor

A supervisor, the person in the middle, is the key to success. The greater your ability to carry out your responsibilities, the more efficiently the company will operate.

In addition to job skills, a modern supervisor must be familiar with up-to-date personnel practices and the legal requirements that affect the jobs of your personnel. You must also know how to deal with the day-to-day problems of a security department.

One of the most important ways a supervisor can get the best results from the people is to let them know they have your full support. You can reinforce this knowledge by giving the employees the necessary authority to do their jobs, and by seeing that this authority is respected. You should step in to share responsibilities and, if things go wrong, help to clear up the problem without condemnation. As happens on occasion, a good worker may run into controversy. When this occurs, it is comforting to know that the boss will stand by. This does not mean insisting someone is right when clearly he or she is not, but rather it is accepting some of the responsibility for a poor plan and helping someone to carry the blame. All these steps will demonstrate a supervisor's support of the crew, and people support a leader who supports them.

Another important trait of a good supervisor is

willingness to accept suggestions from the workers. In fact, encourage such comments. It is natural for people to offer suggestions. A supervisor who makes it clear that you are not interested in such input cuts off an important flow of communication between yourself and your staff. Once the employees realize their supervisor is not interested in their ideas, maybe even resents them, they will not take the time to devise a better system of doing things.

Making the mistake of ignoring the thoughts and ideas of another person will hinder working relationships within the company. One person cannot think of everything. Those employees most knowledgeable in a specific area could be of assistance and should not be overlooked. The people who handle the day-to-day situations are in the best position to suggest changes in the organization's policies and operations.

The best way to get more suggestions from the staff is to simply ask for them. Whenever a problem arises, the supervisor should discuss the situation with the people involved to further encourage input. By offering them the chance to do some of the thinking, the manager is openly demonstrating interest in their ideas. Most employees would love to do some brainwork.

Keep Communications Open

While not every idea submitted will be a workable one, no suggestion deserves the fifteen-second brush-off. The supervisor must be appreciative of all suggestions, regardless of caliber. Each and every idea merits consideration. The employee should be thanked for the time and interest and encouraged to keep trying, on the premise that the next idea could be a winner.

Leadership

The guard supervisor sets the example of professional quality for the staff. The subordinates are a mirror of the management. If a guard appears sloppy, unshaven, in need of a haircut and a shoeshine, his supervisor probably needs to take a good look at her own appearance. If a guard speaks sharply to the client's customers or employees, it may be a reflection of the woman who is in charge. Perhaps the supervisor should pay careful attention to her own manner. The guard force reflects the company's image and the supervisor should ensure that the proper appearance is being projected.

Techniques for Setting the Example

1. Be physically fit, well-groomed and correctly dressed.
2. Master your emotions. Erratic behavior, ranging from anger to depression, is noneffective.
3. Maintain an optimistic outlook. Excel in difficult situations by learning to capitalize on your own capabilities.
4. Conduct yourself so that your own personal habits are not open to censure.
5. Exercise initiative and promote the spirit of initiative in your subordinates.
6. Be loyal to those with whom you work and those who work with you. Loyalty is a two-way street.
7. Avoid playing favorites.
8. Be morally courageous. Establish principles and stand by them.
9. Share hardships with your people to demonstrate your willingness to assume your share of the difficulties.

The Professional Security Supervisor

Today's security work requires a person with an exceptionally high degree of skill, training, and information. The person who demonstrates these qualities is recognized by others as a professional. You exude the confidence and skill to make it possible for the rest of the community to have faith in your ability to act in their interest. The security officer who meets these standards is a professional in the fullest meaning of the word, and is respected as such.

A professional person has:

Education. By virtue of having completed certain education programs and having passed official examinations, professional people are recognized as possessing distinctive kinds and amounts of knowledge and skill. These are types of knowledge and skill in which the average citizen feels deficient, and therefore, turns to professionally trained people for help, in the form of advice or other services.

Standards of Performance. Professional people are expected to be dedicated to high ideals. They are assumed to operate under a superior code of ethics. To this end, the professional organizations establish standards of ethical performance, as well as standards of competence. Professional people take pride in these standards and expect members of their profession to meet them. Because of the continuous flow of social and economic changes in our world, training and the improvement of standards is a continuing problem for every security authority.

It is the understanding of fundamental principles which distinguishes the competent professional person from the mere technician. This is as true in security work as it is in medicine, law, and other professional fields.

A security supervisor is personally judged by the general public. The client, as well, looks upon you as the contact with the organization and will measure the company by the supervisor. The security personnel, as well, look to the supervisor to set an example. As in other areas, therefore, the leader must maintain a professional code of ethics. Professionalism is vital to any position of authority and this fact is no less true for the security supervisor.

Train Personnel Effectively

The responsibilities of a guard supervisor include providing sound, effective training to the staff. An understanding of every operational requirement of the security officers will give the supervisor more awareness of the difficult facets of their work, areas where you may be able to offer assistance when and where it is needed.

The supervisor can facilitate this aspect of your job by determining the duties of each security officer and establishing a master training plan that will teach the new employees their respective tasks. This plan will also serve as refresher training for other personnel who have been on the force for a long period of time.

Treat Employees Courteously

Mutual respect is essential to an efficient working relationship. Employees should not be treated as natural enemies; nor should they be made to feel inferior. You must in turn report to your bosses; you should treat staff in the same courteous manner you expects from *your* superiors.

Consideration is a key word. A demand should be accompanied by an explanation. Advance notice of any situations that might alter an employee's plans, such as overtime, post reassignments, or special orders, is a simple courtesy that will prevent unnecessary ill will. Reprimands or criticisms made in private, away from the watchful eyes of one's peers, precludes humiliation of a staff member.

Develop Loyalty

An effective supervisor is loyal to the employees, the company, and the client. Constant criticism of the company and management is destructive to employee morale. While criticism is a necessary and unavoidable part of any activity, it must be offered constructively to resolve a problem, improve a system, lower costs, and other worthwhile purposes. Criticism for the sake of criticism has no worth and no place in business.

A responsible supervisor does not indulge or pass on gossip or rumors about other employees. A supervisor who is loyal to the personnel is usually repaid with loyalty from the unit.

When You Must Criticize

"To err is mortal; to forgive, divine." The supervisor is sitting on the semicolon of this statement. Not only must you recognize errors, see that they are corrected, and discourage further mistakes, but you are also expected to maintain composure while doing so.

It is a fact of life that most people resent being told that they have done something wrong, especially if the person who does the criticizing is tactless and forceful. Harsh criticism can hurt a person's morale, damage the ego, and create lasting antagonisms. When faced with the job of criticizing an employee, the supervisor should try to follow these seven simple rules:

1. *Be sure of the facts.* Ask the right people the right questions, and do so objectively. Only when you are sufficiently satisfied that an error has been made should you call in the employee. If being criticized for something you *did* can cause resentment, being criticized for something you *didn't* do will really breed antagonism.

2. If the mistake is important and has upset you, *cool off before you talk to the employee.* When you are angry, you are more likely to say something personal. Avoid personal criticism; address your comments to correcting the mistake, not to punishing the security officer.

3. *Discuss the situation in private.* Nothing embarrasses a person more than being reprimanded before one's peers or, worse yet, one's subordinates. Take time to move away from inquisitive eyes and ears. Your criticism will be better and lasting resentment may be avoided.

4. *Ask questions first—don't accuse.* This fits in neatly with the "Be sure of your facts" rule.

Don't come into the discussion with your mind made up. Ask for the employee's side of the story. Everyone appreciates being heard, especially when a mistake has been made.

5. *Before you criticize*, let your worker know that you appreciate some of the good work produced. Medicine is easier to swallow if you mix it with sugar!

6. When the situation dictates that an oral reprimand be given, *explain to the employee the reasoning behind your actions.* An employee deserves to know why there is criticism and how this will affect the future. For example, if a security officer is being criticized for the first tardiness, the officer should not be made to feel that the job is in jeopardy. However, if the reprimand is for continual absences or latenesses, and the job *is* on the line, the employee should know this as well.

7. If at all possible, *leave a good impression* with your employee at the end of the discussion. This does not mean you should make light of mistakes. Rather, it will remove some of the tension and embarassment if, when the employee returns to work, you pat the person on the back or say something like, "At least we know you're human."

These seven rules will help the supervisor to deal tactfully with the situation when you *must* criticize. You should remember that the goal of criticism is to leave the person with the feeling of having been helped.

Personnel Counseling

Every supervisor must be prepared to discuss an employee's personal problems when asked to do so, but only to the extent that the individual desires, and within limits carefully set by the supervisor.

The biggest problem for the manager, in a counseling situation, is to steer a proper course between practical and constructive advice, and particularly to stay clear of amateur psychiatry. When an employee seeks personal counseling, the supervisor should consider these guidelines:

1. *Watch your general attitude.* Always show a continuing sincere interest in your people as individuals with homes and families and not simply as subordinates. If there is sickness at home, remember to ask about progress. If someone's daughter is graduating from high school, show some interest in that also.

2. *Make yourself available.* If someone indicates a desire to talk to you about a matter that has come up, answer by saying that if it is important to the employee, you'll be glad to take whatever time is necessary. The employee will probably agree to have the interview after hours, when nobody else is around. In any case, it is obvious that you should make it possible to have the employee talk to you in private. Hold the meeting as soon as possible after the request.

3. *Some meetings you will have to initiate.* This can occur, for example, when a usually competent and reliable person shows a marked falling off in interest or quality of work, or is unusually tardy or frequently absent, all indicating that some personal situation is interfering with efficiency. Don't keep putting the meeting off ... it will never be any easier than at the present moment.

4. *Be as prepared as possible.* If you have initiated the meeting, be sure of your facts with specific examples of the kinds of behavior that are giving you concern. If the employee has asked for the meeting, refresh your memory about any personal situations that may previously have come to light about the employee.

5. *Put the employee at ease.* You will already have achieved part of this by arranging for a private meeting. Maybe a cup of coffee or a soft drink is indicated.

6. *Be a good listener.* Whether the problem is real or imagined, give the employee a chance to explain the situation without interruption.

7. *Be wary of advice on personal matters.* On emotional and personal problems, your best contribution will be to serve as a sounding board. You can, of course, give advice on any company policy that may be involved, avenues of financial assistance available through the company, and other matters where you are sure of your ground. But with a personal problem, your main function as a counselor should be to help the individual recognize what the problem is, and to explore possible alternate solutions, with final decisions left to the individual. Always remember, when you are dealing with personal and emotional problems, you will rarely be in possession of enough facts to take the responsibility for recommending specific solutions.

8. *Avoid assuming the psychiatrist's function.* If you have reason to believe that the employee has more than the normal kinds of anxiety, suggest professional counsel.*

*Excerpts taken from "How To Communicate Better With Workers" by Carl Heyel.

Chapter 13

Fire and Safety Protection

Fire Detection and Alarm*

DON T. CHERRY

Fire protection is a team effort involving those charged with planning and installing the system and those safety and security personnel who are responsible for monitoring and testing the system. Should a fire occur, the company fire brigade, local fire department, security staff, and employees are all involved.

The building owner bears the ultimate responsibility for the installation and continued effectiveness of the fire system. A building that "meets the codes" is seldom truly adequate.

Fire protection begins in the planning stage. The services of an architect are essential in the fire design for new construction, and are sometimes required for a fire system retrofit. Consulting engineers must ensure that all systems work in harmony and are mutually supportive. The system design team also includes the building owner, key operational chiefs, and the insurance underwriter.

The wise owner will have the underwriter check with the Insurance Services Office (ISO) for design and construction guidelines. The ISO establishes building rating criteria for underwriters' use in setting premiums on specific buildings. Construction materials, number and size of exit points, and occupancy factors are only three of the many criteria considered in establishing insurance credits for the owner.

In planning for fire protection, the design team must prepare for all possibilities. The fire system layout should consider all protective aspects of the personnel and property to be protected. The fire system hardware must include the equipment neces-

sary to cope with potential problems. Building and fire system expansion are also key elements in long-range planning for a fire protection system. Last, review of facility fire protection requirements, continual testing, and system maintenance and updating must continue after installation.

There is no such thing as a fire-proof building. Fire codes are generally nothing more than minimum requirements. A few communities have improved their fire codes, but they should be still more stringent. There is also a need for stricter enforcement of existing fire codes.

Meeting Codes and Standards

Fire protective systems must operate in a legislated arena. There are a great many codes and standards that determine what equipment can and what equipment cannot be used in connection with fire alarm systems. These codes and standards also dictate how that equipment will be installed and how it should operate. While these codes vary from locality to locality and are governed by rules laid down by the authority having jurisdiction, every facility management team must be aware of and conform to any number of these codes and standards.

Fire protective systems are generally subject to local building codes, state building codes, National Fire Protection Association (NFPA) codes and standards, and a requirement for UL (Underwriters Laboratories) listing and/or FM (Factory Mutual) approval.

State and local municipalities, under the *authority having jurisdiction* provision, add their requirements

* From *Total Facility Control*, by Don T. Cherry (Stoneham, MA: Butterworths, 1986).

to the nationally accepted codes and standards. More recently, the state fire marshall's approval is being required under force of law. In some regions this approval must be granted in advance of even offering the sale of fire alarm equipment, much less installing or using it. When owners add extra requirements, a nonstandard system can result. This may call for approval by the *authority having jurisdiction* prior to construction or installation.

Fire Safety Techniques

Construction techniques such as fire walls, fire doors, and ventilation system closures by fire dampers have done much to contain fires to limited areas. They cannot, by themselves, solve the problem. There must also be some indication that a fire door is closed and that the fire dampers on a ventilation closure order have been activated. If the system does not provide this sort of information, it is not properly protecting the facility.

No building is immune to a hot fire—a fire so intense that even steel may warp. Almost all materials used in the construction and furnishing of a building have a combustion point. There are fire retardant materials available, but they give off explosive vapors and toxic fumes when heated. Most synthetic materials burn twice as hot and emit fumes 500 times more toxic than natural materials. It is important to remember that smoke and gas are the

real killers. Synthetic fibers give off deadly chlorine and cyanide-based gases when burned.

It is essential that fires be detected as quickly as possible so that danger can be kept to a minimum. The location of an explosive fire must rapidly be identified and brought under control to minimize the threat to life and property. If the fire alarm system is well designed with an efficient detection system and early initiation of alarm, such a rapid response is possible.

Fire Alarm Systems

To be intelligently conversant about fire systems, one must know what the various systems are and which National Fire Protection Association (NFPA) standard applies to each.

The Local Fire Alarm System is a system in which the operation of an automatic or manual initiating device will cause alarm-indicating devices to alert individuals on the premises to evacuate or investigate. Generally speaking, this type of system provides no record of any activity by the alarm system. It is important to note that the local alarm system does not provide for alarm information to be transmitted off the premises. Figure 13–1 illustrates the simplicity of a local fire alarm system. The building has a fire system that rings a bell on an outside wall. The expectation is that someone will hear the bell and call the fire department.

Figure 13–1. Local fire alarm system.

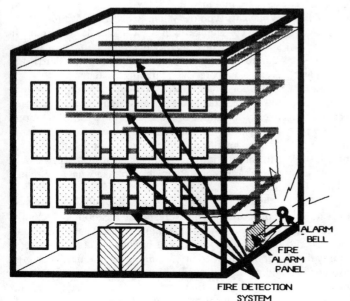

FIRE DETECTION
SYSTEM

ALARM
BELL

FIRE
ALARM
PANEL

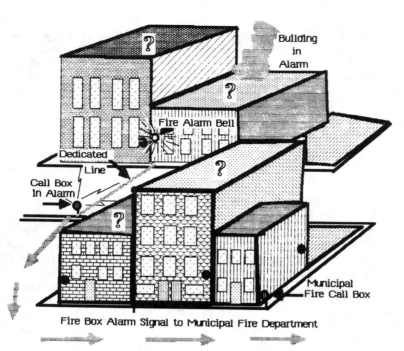

Figure 13–2. Auxiliary fire alarm system.

Local systems offer little peace of mind, since only people present at the time of the alarm are alerted. When the building is unattended, the system is simply an alarm that sounds in the night in hopes that someone will hear and report the signal. NFPA 72A, *Local Protective Signaling Systems*, should be read closely and the system's limitations understood before recommending or installing this type of fire alarm system. An *Auxiliary Fire Alarm System* is only one rung up the alarm ladder. This is basically a local system with a connection to the municipal fire alarm system (i.e., street fire box) to transmit a fire signal to the municipal communication center. Here signals from an auxiliary fire alarm system are received on the same equipment and by the same alerting methods as alarms transmitted from the municipal fire boxes located on the streets. Permission must be obtained from the local *authority having jurisdiction* before any linkup with a municipal system can be made. NFPA 72B sets forth the criteria for this system.

Figure 13–2 graphically displays the problem. The building with smoke rising from it is in alarm. This fact is transmitted to the municipal call box on the street. The municipal communications center cannot generally distinguish between the street municipal fire box and the signal generated by the auxiliary fire alarm system. Therefore, the initial response by the municipal fire department will be to the location of the street fire box, not to the facility using the au-

xiliary system. Upon arrival at the street fire box, firefighters must actually look for smoke or fire to locate the source of the alarm. This task is difficult enough on a summer night, but given a cold winter night with snow, sleet, or rain, the source of the fire alarm might not be discovered until the blaze is out of control.

Auxiliary fire systems may work in some instances, but in others they are practically useless. While this type of system provides a bit more balm to the conscience than a local fire alarm system, it still fails to furnish real fire protection in a timely manner. NFPA 72B provides the standards for Auxiliary Protective Signaling Systems.

Remote–Station Fire Systems are really nothing more than local fire alarm systems connected to a twenty-four-hour operation. Typical remote stations are a sheriff's dispatcher, volunteer fire department, or even an all-night filling station. Individuals at the central location must be trained to recognize emergency signals and competent to take whatever action is required.

Figure 13–3 illustrates how the building's fire system is connected to a response location—a local fire department—via telephone lines. These lines may be dedicated leased lines or merely the standard telephone line with an automatic telephone dialer providing a prerecorded alarm message.

Remote station operations are a major step up from the local or auxiliary fire alarm systems and,

Figure 13–4 Remote station fire system.

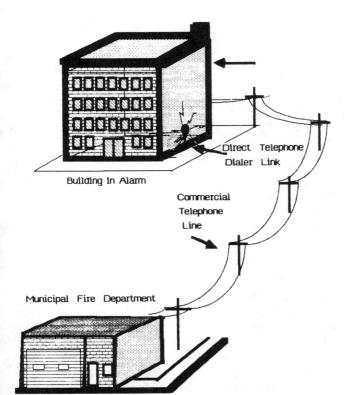

Direct Telephone
Dialer Link

Building in Alarm

Commercial
Telephone
Line

Municipal Fire Department

short of going to the expense of a central station operation, are a viable alternative in certain circumstances. NFPA 72C describes remote station protective signaling systems. The cost-effectiveness must be rationally considered before any system is chosen.

Central Station Operation is a system, or a group of systems, in which the initiation of certain sensors and various devices at a remote location are signaled automatically to an appropriately equipped central alarm-monitoring facility. These signals are supervised, recorded, and maintained through the services of the central station operator. Figure 13–4 illustrates how various client locations can tie into the central station via dedicated telephone lines, buried cable, or radio.

In a well-managed central station operation, trained personnel take the action required by the alarm indication. This action includes, but is not limited to, any or all of the following: (1) notifying the nearest fire department; (2) alerting the building management; (3) dispatching a "runner" who will act as the owner's agent on the scene pending the arrival of the owner's de facto representative.

As there are a wide variety of central station operations and operators, generally the *authority having jurisdiction* recommends reliance on an *Underwriters Laboratories approved* central station service only. These UL-approved central station facilities are subjected to annual no-notice inspections to ensure reasonable and timely response actions.

Good central station operators maintain a staff of skilled installation technicians as well as competent personnel at the central station around the clock. While practices vary with geographic location, it is generally preferable to have the central station operator provide a turn-key installation. This protects the owner by having a complete professional installation performed. The central station operator will not have to rely on an outsider's installation and sensors. Complete definition and information concerning this type of protective system in found in NFPA 71, *Central Station Signaling Systems*.

A *Proprietary Fire Alarm System* is the on-site installation of protective signaling systems which serve a single property or multiple properties under a single ownership. Ideally, this system is staffed continuously by trained and competent personnel, but it could also operate untended, if properly designed. A proprietary fire detection and alarm system is an intregal part of a total facility control protective system.

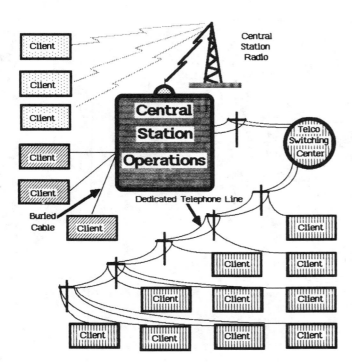

Figure 13–4. Central station operation fire alarm and security monitoring.

Figure 13–5 illustrates how the company owned and operated proprietary system can use direct hardwire connection to local buildings; reach across the city or state via commercial telephone lines; use microwave transmission across freeways or rivers where dedicated telephone lines might be prohibitively costly to monitor and control nearby facilities; and even reach across oceans to monitor foreign operations.

For small, single-location operations with up to about 50,000 square feet, a hard-wired system will probably be more cost-effective. Depending upon the use of the building's space, somewhere between 50,000 and 100,000 square feet is generally the break-even point for adoption of a proprietary multiplex fire detection and alarm system. In a multiplex system the majority of the system data is transmitted by a single twisted pair of wires or possibly by fiber optics. This data transmission bus connects the central processing unit (CPU) and intelligent control panels (ICPs) at appropriate locations throughout the building. Short runs of typical copper wire connect the various sensors, actuators, controllers, and building control devices to the ICPs.

For most facilities in excess of 100,000 square feet, a complex of buildings, numerous remote locations, or multiple buildings at separate locations, a multiplex system will generally be the most cost-effective approach. Many options are available

within the field of multiplexing. Upward mobility of the system can allow for future facility expansion, yet permit management to maintain continued close control of local and remote building systems.

Proprietary systems normally require a greater initial outlay of funds. However, like most capital expenditures, they pay for themselves in a relatively short period of time, usually in three to five years.

Before selecting either a hardwire or multiplex system NFPA 72D, *Proprietary Protective Signaling Systems*, should be read. It is also helpful to visit and investigate proprietary systems already in operation at other facilities. With this knowledge, the right decisions can be made.

Proprietary Fire Alarm Systems provide complete coverage when staffed by trained operators. The operators usually work out of a supervising office located on the property to be protected. The central operating location includes equipment and a control console that permit the operators to maintain, test, and operate the system. Upon receipt of an alarm signal or trouble signal, the operators can take local action as required under the guidance provided by management, as well as the rules of response established by the insurance rating organizations having jurisdiction over the facility.

State-of-the-art proprietary systems based on a microprocessor/multiplex arrangement are capable of supervising proprietary fire alarm and security

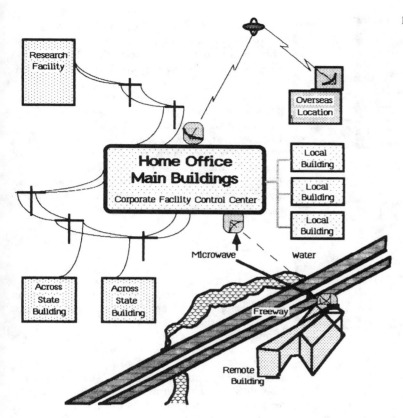

Figure 13–5. Total facility control
proprietary fire alarm system.

systems over a large number of buildings at multiple geographic locations. Large system applications of multibuildings and multiple locations are extremely cost-effective.

Proprietary systems are available that incorporate other systems in addition to fire detection and alarm. These include full energy management, security, access control, closed-circuit television (CCTV), and patrol tour management. They readily can pay for themselves if normal building management systems are totally integrated. By including security, access control, CCTV, energy management techniques, lighting control, equipment monitoring, and preventive maintenance schedules with a proprietary fire alarm system, operating budget savings will immediately become evident.

The threat presented by fire depends upon whether a fire develops slowly or erupts quickly. The critical first few minutes will generally determine how destructive the fire will be. There are four stages of fire: incipient, smoldering (smoke and gas), visible flame, and intense heat. (See Figure 13–6).

Building Fire Zoning

The key to rapid fire detection and alarm is finite zoning. The smaller the individual zones, the quicker the actual fire location can be determined. Great care must be taken to ensure that fire zoning takes into consideration the physical construction around and within the zone, the human factor being protected, cost of material protected, suppression systems concerned, and emergency response elements.

Zoning must be specifically designed to provide effective physical compartmentalization of the building. Provisions need to be made for use of the building's heating, ventilating, and air-conditioning (HVAC) system in containing the smoke and fire by zone. Careful planning is required for the design of venting and smoke evacuation. Selection of specialized suppression systems may call for expert consultation. Building codes determine the number and size of emergency exit points by zone, but these requirements should be viewed as minimal. Finally, the indication of a zone in alarm should be rapid and easily understood.

a

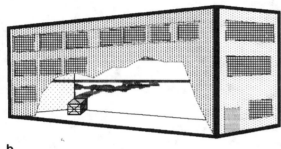

b

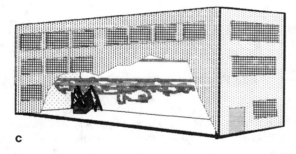

c

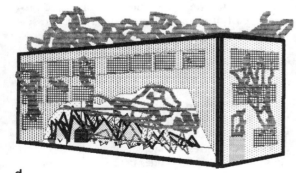

d

Figure 13–6. Four stages of fire: (a) incipient stage, (b) smoldering stage, (c) visible flame stage, (d) intense heat stage.

The selection of fire detection devices and their proper application is necessary to ensure that the zone is adequately protected. Knowledge of the various devices, where they can and cannot be used, the effects of air currents, physical placement of the devices, device reaction time, and many other variables are important considerations in the development of a zoning scheme. There are no hard and fast rules for correct zoning. There are minimum requirements as established by local fire and building codes, the National Fire Protection Association (NFPA), and the authority having jurisdiction. In the final analysis, proper zoning, like proper protection, is the responsibility of the owner.

Classes of Fires

Fires are classified into four groups. These groups and what these designations mean are important in the development of any fire suppression system, from fire extinguishers to large industrial, stand-alone systems. The type of extinguishment used is dependent upon the type, or class, of fire (see Figure 13–7).

Class A fires are fires that are fueled by ordinary combustibles. These fires can normally be brought under control with water or water fog. In a Class A fire the water or water fog is used to cool the mass below the ignition point to stop the fire.

Class B fires are fueled by petroleum, oil, lubricant (POL), and volatile fluids that are present practically everywhere. Only the volume or amount of POL fuel base seems to change. Class B fires are usually smothered with carbon dioxide (CO_2) or water fog, which is excellent because it cools the fire without spreading the flame. A stream of water sprayed on a petroleum-based fire can be disastrous. This action spreads the combustible fluids and with it the flames.

Class C fires are those concerned with live electrical equipment, including transformers, generators, and electrical motors. Automatic action to shut down such equipment in the event of fire is prudent, and this possibility should be investigated.

Class D fires are fueled by combustible metals such as magnesium, sodium, and potassium. The best extinguishing agent in the case of Class D fires is usually a dry powder. In many cases this may be the only method of suppression. This type of fire occurs only when the combustibles are in use. Thus they are rare, but nevertheless dangerous. The use of water or other extinguishing agents could result in an explosive chemical reaction. Care must be exer-

Kind of fire	Approved type of extinguisher							
Decide the class of fire you are fighting . . .	Foam Solution of Aluminum Sulphate and Bicarbonate of Soda	Carbon Dioxide Carbon Dioxide Gas under pressure	Soda-Acid Bicarbonate of Soda solution and Sulfuric Acid	Pump Tank Plain water	Gas Cartridge Water expelled by Carbon Dioxide Gas	Multi-Purpose Dry Chemical	Ordinary Dry Chemical	Dry Powder
Class A Fires Ordinary combustibles • Wood • Paper • Cloth etc.	●		●	●	●	●		
Class B Fires Flammable liquids, grease • Gasoline • Paints • Oils, etc.	●	●				●	●	
Class C Fires Electrical equipment • Motors • Switches etc.		●				●	●	
Class D Fires Combustible metals • Magnesium • Sodium • Potassium etc.								●

How to Operate

Foam: Don't spray stream into the burning liquid. Allow foam to fall lightly on fire.

Carbon Dioxide: Direct discharge as close to fire as possible, first at edge of flames and gradually forward and upward.

Soda-Acid, Gas Cartridge: Direct stream at base of flame.

Pump Tank: Place foot on footrest and direct stream at base of flames.

Dry Chemical: Direct at the base of the flames. In the case of Class A fires, follow up by directing the dry chemicals at the material that is burning.

Figure 13–7. Use of fire extinguishers.

cised against storing combustible metals in areas covered by automatic sprinkler systems.

Fire Detection Devices

All elements of a fire system are essential, but none more so than the individual detection sensors. These devices include manual stations. When properly zoned, a manual pull station will indicate that a human being initiated an alarm and also the location of the alarm.

An even more efficient detection device is the ionization smoke detector (Figure 13–8), which is designed to detect microscopic particles of combustion too small for the eye to see. These devices are adept at providing early warning of smoldering fires, and their unit cost is relatively low. Ionization smoke detectors can readily be used indoors, but they are easily contaminated, and care must be taken concerning the environment where they are installed. They are effective at rapid detection of Class A, C, and D fires.

A similar smoke detection device is the photoelectric smoke detector (Figure 13–9), which works on a principle of smoke reflectance or obscuration.

It goes into alarm when smoke reflects light into a receiving element or obscures a beam of light. It provides relatively early warning of smoldering fires and has a low unit cost. This device is limited to indoor use and the smoke must be contained within the unit to trigger the alarm. Photoelectric detectors are also effective in office space and commercial buildings. Their best response is against Class A fires.

Infrared (IR) heat detectors are high-speed detectors sensitive to heat. They have a moderate sensitivity and cost. There is usually a manual self-test capability through the sensor's window. IR detectors are affected by temperature and subject to a false alarm due to the myriad of infrared emissions in the industrial environment. Applications for the IR detectors are indoors, in plenums and in air ducts. They respond best to Class A or B fires.

Dual infrared (IR/IR) detectors provide moderate speed and sensitivity and a low false alarm rate. However, this dual device has a limited operational temperature range and self-testing capability. The dual sensor makes this a relatively expensive device. It can bee used both indoors and out and is effective against Class A and B fires.

At the other end of the visible spectrum are *ultra-*

Figure 13–8. Ionization smoke detector.

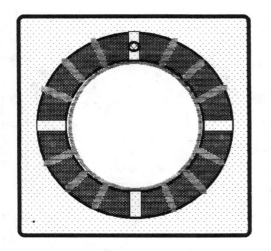

DUAL CHAMBER, IONIZATION SMOKE DETECTOR FOR
SENSING OF PARTICLES OF COMBUSTION

Sensing Chamber

Smoke

Source

Decreasing Current

Reference Chamber

Alarm

NORMAL CONDITION

ALARM CONDITION

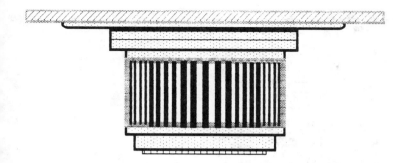

Figure 13–9. Photoelectric smoke detector.

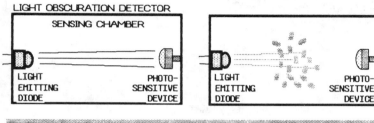

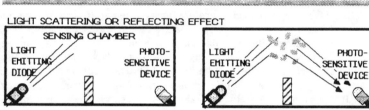

violet (UV) flame detectors. In addition to their high speed, they also have a high sensitivity and automatic self-test. Considering the moderate cost per unit, the UV flame detector is a viable sensor in many industrial situations. It is subject to false alarms, but these are generally from readily identifiable sources. This device is subject to being blinded by thick smoke and, if faced with that sort of situation, should be used in conjunction with an appropriate type of smoke detector. The ultraviolet detector can be used indoors and out and is effective against Class A, B, and D fires.

The *dual infrared and ultraviolet (IR/UV) detector* is a very effective device. It incorporates high speed with high sensitivity and has a low false alarm rate. A wide operational temperature range and automatic self-testing are incorporated into this device. It is an expensive unit and thick smoke will reduce the range, but it can be used both indoors and out and is effective against Class A, B, and C fires.

Among the less expensive and sophisticated devices are *thermal detectors*. They work on the principle of the fusible element and need no electricity to activate. They are low cost and highly reliable, but are very slow, as heat must impinge

upon the fusible link itself. This type of device should only be used as a backup working in conjunction with a fully supervised system. Most common uses are in commercial and industrial buildings or sites subject to explosive heat situations requiring immediate deluge activation. Thermal fusible link devices are usually targeted against Class A, B, and C fires.

Another reliable and simple sensor is called a *fixed temperature, heat-activated device*. It is effective indoors and is a low-cost unit; however, it is slow and can be affected by the wind. The normal application is indoors in an enclosed area. It is used to detect Class A, B, and D fires.

The *fixed temperature, rate-of-rise detector* is self-adjusting to temperature, day and night, summer and winter. It can detect a rapidly growing fire more rapidly than the fixed temperature device. This device is activated by heat riding on convection currents, and the heat must actually impinge on the sensor. The device is affected by the wind. Its normal application is indoors in an enclosed area. Properly installed, it is effective against Class A, B, and D fires.

A proprietary *heat-detecting cable* (Figure 13–10) is available for a wide variety of industrial fire detec-

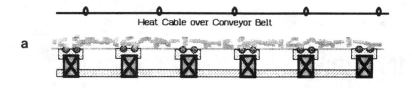

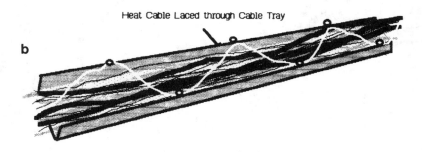

Figure 13–10. Heat-detecting cable: (a) Conveyor system protection. (b) Cable tray protection.

tion applications. According to UL tests, this heat-detecting cable responds at least thirty seconds faster than a sprinkler-head rated at the same temperature, even when the cable is installed 50 percent further away from the fire. Normally, heat-detecting wire is installed in direct contact or at least in very close proximity to the equipment being protected. Its normal application is to shut down equipment and activate fire suppression systems. It is designed to be installed in close proximity to virtually any conveyor system or monorail in open manufacturing areas. It is also used to protect cable trays, power distribution apparatus, dust collectors, cooling towers, pipelines, fuel distribution terminals, piers, mine shafts, offshore platforms, tank farms, refrigerated warehouses, and a wide variety of unusual industrial equipment operations.

Alarm Initiating Techniques

Fire detection devices, regardless of whether they are designed to sense smoke, fire, flame, or heat, can easily be hardwired to one of the intelligent control panels of a multiplex system. Fire detection is initiated by the sensors, with a signal being transmitted over the system's transmission bus to the central system. It is up to the central system to provide the occupants of the building with the indication of the alarm.

Fire Indication and Reporting

All the best fire sensors in the world are worthless unless there is also some method to warn of impending fire danger. There are many devices available that provide audible signals indicating a fire.

There are fire horns designed for indoor and outside use. A sonalert buzzer has been designed for indoor alerting. Fire bells generally come in two versions, a rapidly vibrating alarm bell and a single-stroke alarm bell. While designed for either indoor or outdoor application, the single-stroke bell is more suitable for indoor use where a horn or vibrating bell would be undesirable.

Next up the line in fire annunciation devices are a series of felt-paper cone speakers, usually about 8 inches in diameter. Most of these speakers are suitable for tone or voice transmission and a wide variety of general-purpose communications and public address applications.

For use in noisy industrial areas there are some UL-listed speakers that conform to section 2531 of NFPA 72A. They are highly efficient and applicable to life safety and communications systems providing high intelligibility reproduction and transmission of audible fire alarm signals and voice messages. This type of fire annunciation device can be found under the heading of 15-watt reentrant speakers in most speaker catalogs. These loudspeakers are equipped with enclosed wiring and a vandal-deterring cover.

The newest innovations in fire signaling devices include *visual alarm signals*. These devices offer a high-intensity xenon flash tube that operates like a multiple-ray flashing strobe light. Some of these visual alarm signals come equipped with an audible horn or speaker. The better ones are designed to flash below the cycle-threshold that might trigger latent epileptics.

Latest in the speaker line are *voice communication and alarm system speakers*. The compression driver/horn provides greater sound pressure levels than other devices of similar size. They are highly efficient in the voice and signaling range and may be equipped with a visual alarm signal.

To provide additional visual indication of the alarm, there are a wide variety of standard annunciator panels. In addition, individual custom annunciators may be locally manufactured and used as an additional visual indication of the alarm. Since annunciators are not usually electrically supervised, they may *not* be used as a primary source of fire annunciation and still meet NFPA and UL standards.

The most efficient and effective approach for coordinating fire-alarm indicating, initiation, and reporting is via the multiplex system. Finite zoning is the key to determining the location of the alarm in the most efficient, precise manner.

Safety and Loss Control*

Safety consciousness in business and industry did not begin with the passage of OSHA—the Occupational Safety and Health Act—in 1970, but it is largely a product of the twentieth century. Prior to the Industrial Revolution, the worker was an independent craftsman. If he suffered economic loss because of an accident or because of illness rising out of his prolonged exposure to a particular work environment, the problem was his, not the employer's. This attitude generally prevailed during the rapid expansion of the factory system in America throughout the nineteenth century. Only toward the latter part of this century did it begin to become obvious that factories were far superior in terms of production to the small handicraft shops, yet they often were inferior in terms of human values, health, and safety.

The atmosphere of reform which gained impetus after the turn of the century resulted in, among other new laws, the first effective Workmen's Compensation Act in Wisconsin in 1911. Compulsory laws on workmen's compensation followed in many states after the Supreme Court upheld their constitutionality in 1916. Even the most hard-headed employers found that their costs dictated compliance with the spirit of the law.

*From *Introduction to Security*, 4th ed, by Gion Green, revised by Robert J. Fischer (Stoneham, MA: Butterworths, 1987).

As a result of this growing concern for industrial safety, there followed a long downward curve in work-connected accidents and injuries that lasted through the period between the two world wars and continued into the 1950s. By 1958 this trend had leveled off, and by 1968, for the first time in over fifty years, the curve began to rise again.

Fourteen thousand occupational fatalities and over two million disabling work-connected injuries each year seemed to be considerably more than the number that might one day be arrived at as the irreducible minimum. The result, through the 1960s, was increasing federal concern with establishing standards of occupational safety and health. Prior to that decade, only a few federal laws, such as the Walsh-Healey Public Contracts Act, had been enacted, with most legislation in this area being left to the states. During the 1960s, a number of laws were passed—the McNamara-O'Hara Service Contracts Act, the Federal Construction Safety Act, the Federal Coal Mine Health and Safety Act, among others—all dealing with safety and health standards in specific fields and under specific circumstances. Public Law 91–596, known as OSHA, which was signed into law on December 29, 1970, was the first legislation which attempted to apply standards to virtually every employer and employee in the country.

OSHA Standards

Generally speaking, OSHA requires that an employer provide a safe and healthful place for employees to work. This is spelled out in great detail in the act to avoid leaving the thrust of the legislation in any doubt.

Though much of the language in the act is technical in nature and largely couched in legalese, the thrust of the legislation is absolutely clear and unambiguous in what is known as the "General Duty" clause which states that each employer "shall furnish to each of his employees . . . a place of employment . . . free from recognized hazards that are causing or likely to cause death or serious physical harm to his employees" and that, further, he "shall comply with all occupational safety and health standards promulgated under this Act."[1] Much of the rest of the act deals with procedures and standards of safety and is, in places, difficult to follow.

It speaks of free and accessible means of egress, of aisles and working areas free of debris, of floors free from hazards. It gives specific requirements for machines and equipment, materials, and power sources. It specifies fire protection by fixed or portable systems, clean lunch rooms, environmental health controls, and adequate sanitation facilities. Whereas, in past years, employers might contend in all sincerity that their facilities met community standards for safety and cleanliness, with the enactment of OSHA these standards have been formalized to describe minimum levels of acceptability. They might also contend that some specific demands of the act were unclear, but there is no mistaking what the act is getting at. "The Congress declares to be its purpose and policy . . . to assure so far as possible every working man and woman in the nation safe and healthful working conditions and to preserve our human resources."

Perhaps the strongest resistance to OSHA in its first years has been the complaint that some of the basic standards went too far or were unnecessary. Recent emphasis by the OSHA administration has been upon the elimination of "Mickey Mouse" standards that have no direct bearing on improving safety in the workplace.

Setting Up the Safety Program

H.W. Heinrich, an outstanding pioneer in safety studies, held that unsafe acts caused eighty-five percent of all accidents; unsafe conditions caused the remaining fifteen percent. Therefore, if these acts could be modified, the accidents would be sharply reduced. Today, safety supervisors agree that unsafe acts are the principal villain and that the system's approach to safety is the only way to really control losses. It is necessary, however, for management to get the system together and implement a strong, active program for it to be effective. Safety problems are caused, they don't just happen, and each one of these problems can be identified and controlled.

In setting up a loss control program, it is important to look at the concept of loss in the broadest sense. While the effort is thought of purely as a safety program, the conclusion is that it concerns itself only with accidents, or even more narrowly, with accidents resulting in injury to a person or persons. To limit the program in this way would be to lose much of its value. Frank E. Bird, Jr., in his informative book, *Management Guide to Loss Control*[2] refers to any undesired or unwanted event that degrades (or could degrade) the efficiency of the business operation as an "incident." Thus, the field of view is

broadened immeasurably. Incidents could be anything from production problems to bad inventory control; from serious injury to a breakdown in quality control. An accident, on the other hand, is an undesired event resulting in physical harm to a person or damage to property. Thus, an accident is an incident, but an incident is not always an accident. The distinction is important, especially in view of a 1969 study of industrial accidents undertaken by the Insurance Company of North America. In this study, 1,753,498 accidents reported by 297 cooperating companies were analyzed. These companies represented 21 different industrial groups, employing 1,750,000 employees who worked over three billion man-hours during the period under the study. This massive study indicated a ratio of 600 no-damage or near-miss incidents to 30 damage-to-property, to 10 minor injuries, to 1 serious or disabling injury. As Bird points out, property damage accidents cost billions of dollars a year, and yet they are frequently reported erroneously as near-miss accidents. Even though property damage resulted, the absence of any personal injury in the case removed it from the category of accident in the view of the reporting agency. This is a throwback to earlier attitudes which related the term *accident* to injury only.

Accidents, by our definition, refer to property damage as well, and in aggregate, can amount to substantial costs for the company that fails to keep these accidents under control. In fact, an effective loss control program can be an organization's best money-maker when it can be seen that the actual cost of accidents may be anywhere from six to fifty times as much as the money recovered from insurance. Uninsured costs in building damage, production damage, wages to the injured for lost time, clerical costs, cost of training new workers, supervisors, extra time, all mount up. By controlling such incidents, the profit picture is immeasurably improved. In a company operating at a 4 percent profit margin, the sales department would have to generate sales of $1,250,000 just to compensate for an annual loss of $50,000 in incidents.

Assessment

In order to set up for acceptable performance or to take action to bring a facility up to an acceptable level of loss control effectivness, an assessment of the situation is necessary. This can be done in two parts and, preferably, by one well-qualified person.

The team approach may be used, but it is usually not as effective in the long run as is the individual approach.

The first order of business is an attitude survey. This consists of a private, one-on-one interview with all line supervisors from the facility manager to various first-line supervisors or foremen. Questions directed at each individual should elicit attitudes about current safety conditions, the need for a safety program, attitudes about safety management, generally, and feelings about some of the techniques (or absence of techniques) in the loss control effort. Questions might be along the lines of:

1. Who do you think is responsible for safety?
2. Does a sloppy loss control program affect your job? How?
3. How would you improve the safety record of this facility?
4. How can top management inprove the safety record of this facility?
5. Have you done everything in the past six months to improve the safety of the facility? Your crew?
6. How much authority do you have to correct unsafe conditions?
7. What supervisory safety training have you had?

After the questionnaire has been drawn up and the interviews have been conducted with supervisors, a tabulation of responses should be very revealing. They should indicate the management levels where deficiencies exist, and they should point up existing problems both in plant safety and in the program in general.

After the attitude survey, the assessment should undertake a review of all accident-incident records of the past three years. This should be classified by type such as burns, bruises, broken bones. From this, it will be easy to see the types of accidents that have been occurring and perhaps pinpoint an area or process or condition that is particularly unsafe. When this list has been drawn up, it will be necessary to assign cause and responsibility to each accident. There will usually be several causes in each case. In developing the accident-case correlation chart, assign causes as: management responsibility, supervisor responsibility, employee error, mechanical design, mechanical failure.

The next step in the assessment is to determine those accidents caused by lack of personal protective equipment. These accidents are eye injuries and foot injuries. It must be determined whether the problems arise from lack of protective equipment or

an unwillingness to use it, and corrective action must be taken.

Next determine accidents by job title.

Finally, list accidents under each supervisor.

These last two categories should immediately suggest corrective action, whether it be changing job specifications or educating supervisors.

Finding the Causes of Accidents

The causes of accidents should be determined before they occur. Since accidents are caused, the conditions that cause can be known and controlled. It is, therefore, of the greatest importance that management deal vigorously with what can cause an accident. Unsafe acts and unsafe conditions will ultimately cause accidents if they are allowed to continue.

Unsafe acts will be discovered and corrected only when immediate supervisors are alert to the problem. They must set up systems for closely observing all workers, especially those in hazardous jobs, in operation. To do this, they must have a job safety analysis at their disposal. This analysis breaks each job down into component parts, and each part is studied for the hazards it may present.

Unsafe conditions are uncovered by constant inspections. Such conditions do not disappear entirely because they were taken care of once. Unsafe conditions are continuously created by the operation of the facility. Normal wear and tear, careless housekeeping, initial bad design, or simply the deterioration that results from inadequate maintenance caused by a cost-cutting management all create unsafe conditions which have a high potential loss factor. Early discovery of unsafe conditions is essential to good loss control, and the procedure is simply inspections, inspections, inspections.

Identification and Control of Hazards

OSHA standards (or equivalent state standards) provide the baseline for the company safety program. A bewildering catalog of standards has already developed (Cal/OSHA, in California, has more than 6,000 standards), and new ones are constantly being added. Checklists (available from OSHA, the National Safety Council and other sources) can provide the starting point for detailed inspections designed to identify hazards. The confusion that might accompany a consideration of all the standards begins to

Monthly Safety Check

Dept. _____ Date _____

Supervisor _____

Indicate discrepancy by ⊠

General area	
Floor condition	
Special purpose flooring	
Aisle, clearance/markings	
Floor openings, require safeguards	
Railings, stairs temp./perm.	
Dock board (bridge plates)	
Piping (water-steam-air)	
Wall damage	
Ventilation	
Other	
Illumination—wiring	
Unnecessary/improper use	
Lights on during shutdown	
Frayed/defective wiring	
Overloading circuits	
Machinery not grounded	
Hazardous location	
Other	
Housekeeping	
Floors	
Machines	
Break area/latrines	
Waste disposal	
Vending machines/food protection	
Rodent, insect, vermin control	
Vehicles	
Unauthorized use	
Operating defective vehicle	
Reckless/speeding operation	
Failure to obey traffic rules	
Other	
Tools	
Power tool wiring	
Condition of hand tools	
Safe storage	
Other	

First aid	
First aid kits	
Stretchers, fire blankets, oxygen	
Fire protection	
Fire hoses hung properly	
Extinguisher charged/proper location	
Access to fire equipment	
Exit lights/doors/signs	
Other	
Security	
Doors/windows, etc. secured when required	
Alarm operation	
Department shut down security	
Equipment secured	
Unauthorized personnel	
Other	
Machinery	
Unattended machines operating	
Emergency stops not operational	
Platforms/ladders/catwalks	
Instructions to operate/stop posted	
Maintenance being performed on machines in operation	
Guards in place	
Pinch points	
Material storage	
Hazardous & flammable material not stored properly	
Improper stacking/loading/securing	
Improper lighting, warning signs, ventilation	
Other	

Figure 13–11. Monthly safety checklist.

sort itself out when inspections zero in only on those that apply to specific operations and conditions.

A safety program should include periodic inspections scheduled at regular intervals. Figure 13–11 is an example of a monthly checklist for inspection. In addition, looking for safety hazards and violations should be part of the day-to-day activity of both safety professionals and security personnel. Some hazards which might be present in any business facility are shown in Table 13–1.

A Hazardous Materials Program

In addition to the seven steps in safety planning, particular types of businesses dealing with hazardous substances should have a hazardous materials program. As a minimum, it is necessary to:

1. Identify what hazardous materials you have and where.
2. Know how to respond to an accident involving

Table 13–1. Common Safety Hazards

Floors, aisles, stairs, and walkways

Oil spills or other slippery substances which might result in an injury-producing fall.

Litter, obscuring hazards such as electrical floor plugs, projecting material, or material which might contribute to the fueling of a fire.

Electrical wire, cable, pipes, or other objects, crossing aisles which are not clearly marked nor properly covered.

Stairways which are too steep, have no nonskid floor covering, inadequate or nonexistent railings, or those which are in a poor state of repair.

Overhead walkways which have inadequate railings, are not covered with nonskid material, or which are in a poor state of repair.

Walks and aisles which are exposed to the elements and have not been cleared of snow or ice, which are slippery when wet or which are in a poor state of repair.

Doors and emergency exits

Doors that are ill-fitting, stick, and which might cause a slowdown during emergency evacuation.

Panic-type hardware which is inoperative or in a poor state of repair.

Doors which have been designated for emergency exit but which are locked and not equipped with panic-type hardware.

Doors which have been designated for emergency exit but which are blocked by equipment or by debris.

Missing or burned-out emergency exit lights.

Nonexistent or poorly marked routes leading to emergency exit doors.

Flammable and other dangerous materials

Flammable gases and liquids which are uncontrolled, in areas in which they might constitute a serious threat.

Radioactive material not properly stored or handled.

Paint or painting areas which are not properly secured or which are in areas that are poorly ventilated.

Gasoline pumping areas located dangerously close to operations which are spark producing or in which open flame is being used.

Protective equipment or clothing

Workmen in areas where toxic fumes are present who are not equipped with or who are not using respiratory protective apparatus.

Workmen involved in welding, drilling, sawing, and other eye-endangering occupations who have not been provided or who are not wearing protective eye covering.

Workmen in areas requiring the wearing of protective clothing, due to exposure to radiation or toxic chemicals, who are not using such protection.

Workmen engaged in the movement of heavy equipment or materials who are not wearing protective footwear.

Workmen who require prescription eyeglasses who are not provided or are not wearing safety lenses.

Vehicle operation and parking

Forklifts which are not equipped with audible and visual warning devices when backing.

Trucks which are not provided with a guide when backing into a dock or which are not properly chocked while parked.

Speed violations by cars, trucks, lifts, and other vehicles being operated within the protected area.

Vehicles which are operated with broken, insufficient, or nonexistent lights during the hours of darkness.

Vehicles which constitute a hazard due to poor maintenance procedures on brakes and other safety-related equipment.

Vehicles which are parked in fire lanes, blocking fire lanes, or blocking emergency exits.

Machinery maintenance and operation

Frayed electrical wiring which might result in a short circuit or malfunction of the equipment.

Workers who operate presses, work near or on belts, conveyors, and other moving equipment who are wearing loose fitting clothing which might be caught and drag them into the equipment.

Presses and other dangerous machinery which are not equipped with the required hand guards or with automatic shut-off devices or dead man controls.

Welding and other flame- or spark-producing equipment

Welding torches and spark-producing equipment being used near flammable liquid or gas storage areas or being used in the vicinity where such products are dispensed or are part of the productive process.

The use of flame- or spark-producing equipment near wood shavings, oily machinery, or where they might damage electrical wiring.

Table 13–1. *Continued*

Miscellaneous hazards

Medical and first aid supplies not properly stored, marked, or maintaiined.

Color coding of hazardous areas or materials not being accomplished or which is not uniform.

Broken or unsafe equipment and machinery not being properly tagged with a warning of its condition.

Electrical boxes and wiring not properly inspected or maintained, permitting them to become a hazard.

Emergency evacuation routes and staging areas not properly marked or identified.

Adapted from Eugene Finneran, *Security Supervision: A Handbook for Supervisors and Managers* (Stoneham, Mass.: Butterworth Publishers, 1981).

hazardous materials.

3. Know how to deal with spills.
4. Set up appropriate safeguards.
5. Train employees in dealing with hazardous materials.

Materials Safety Data Sheets are designed specifically to help identify the nature of potential hazards. These data sheets, obtainable from vendors of hazardous materials or equipment, include such information as chemical composition, health hazard rating, protective gear needed, reactivity data, fire data (such as flash point), disposal procedures, and Threshold Limit Value (or TLV, which is the amount of exposure an individual can have to a specific chemical).

Managing the Safety Operation

Whatever the overall integration of safety and the security operation, the safety function can operate in any one of three modes:

1. In a staff capacity, where its experts offer advice, make recommendations to upper echelon management and develop policy for management approval. Line supervisors bear full responsibility for safety in their areas.
2. The safety department is both staff and line in that it performs all staff functions as above and it will also help out on especially hazardous jobs. It will hold some safety meetings and training sessions.
3. The department holds all safety meetings, training sessions, and accident investigations, and actively performs in all areas of safety. A good case can be made for operating in any one of the three methods, though it would appear that the combination of staff and line method is generally the most effective.

Management Leadership

Management's attitude toward safety filters down through the entire company. Top management's concern will be reflected in that of the supervisors; in turn, the supervisor's attention to safety will affect the individual employee's attitude.

Management is responsible not only for basic policy of providing a work environment free of hazards—which should be embodied in an executive policy statement—but also for active leadership. This can be expressed by holding subordinates responsible for accident prevention, and in such visible ways as plant tours, letters to employees, safety meetings, posters, prompt accident investigations, and personal example. (In a hard hat area, the president of the company should also put on a hard hat.)

General safety rules must be established and published, as in the employee handbook or manual. Safety rules should be continually reviewed and updated.

Assignment of Responsibility

Responsibility for the safety program should be clear and personal. In the small company it may rest on the owner if he or she is the acting supervisor. Otherwise, it will generally be an added responsibility of the supervisors in companies with fewer than 100 employees.

In larger companies, safety should be an assigned responsibility of a ranking member of management. He or she may delegate the authority to oversee the program to a safety director (who may be called the safety professional, safety engineer, or safety supervisor, depending on the qualifications and the nature of the operation). In many companies safety is a responsibility of the security director, who will often have a safety specialist as a subordinate. (In virtually all circumstances, there is a close relationship between safety and security.)

Training

All employees must be initially and periodically trained both in general safety principles and in safe work practices in their specific jobs. Safety rules, such as the wearing of protective clothing (gloves, headgear, respirators, shoes, eye protection) should be clearly explained and promptly enforced. The importance the company attaches to safety should particularly be emphasized in new employee training, but it is also important to pay attention to regular employees—including the "old timers" who did not grow up with safety awareness as part of their conditioning.

In addition to the above, there are specific training requirements in the OSHA standards (such as those involving the operation of certain types of equipment). Employer and employees should be aware of those standards that apply in the specific workplace.

Emergency Care

Under OSHA, all businesses are required, in the absence of an infirmary or hospital in the immediate vicinity, to have a person or persons trained in first aid available, along with first aid supplies. Where employees are exposed to corrosive materials, procedures for drenching or flushing of the eyes and body should be provided in the work area.

Procedures should be established for handling injury accidents without confusion or delay. The extent of these preparations will, of course, depend on the nature of the business and the type of hazards.

Employee Awareness and Participation

Developing safety and health awareness is one of the primary goals of OSHA. Active steps by management, such as those suggested above, are essential to involve all employees in the need to create a safe work environment.

Safety awareness has an added benefit for both employer and employees in that it tends to carry over into a concern for off-the-job safety. Accidents away from the work environment account for more than half of all injuries, and the ratio of deaths is three-to-one higher in off-the-job accidents. Carrying over safety practices from the job to activities away from it is an aspect of safety training that is receiving increasing emphasis from today's safety professionals.

Appendix 13a
Fire Prevention Survey*

LAWRENCE J. FENNELLY

Security safety and protection go hand in hand with fire safety and protection. Recently a fire occurred in a warehouse which caused the company a financial loss of three million dollars. If an assault on the

*From the Boston Fire Prevention Unit, Survey Checklist, published with Assets Protection, Vol. 4, No. 3, July/August, 1979. Article titled "Security Surveys," by Lawrence J. Fennelly.

building was committed by six thieves, the company losses wouldn't have reached three million dollars. The following checklist was prepared by the Boston Fire Prevention Division. It will aid you by pointing out fire vulnerabilities, which if corrected, may have an effect on your clients insurance policy and overall security.

I.   Fire Vulnerabilities
       A. Construction type (Check)

1. Fireproof
2. Semi-fireproof
3. Heavy timber and masonry
4. Light wood and masonry
5. Metal frame
6. Wood frame
B. Number of stories
C. Height
D. Width
E. Depth
F. Number of guest rooms or occupants
G. Certificate of occupancy
H. Certificate for places of assembly (List location and approved capacity)
I. Fire department licenses, permits, or flameproofing certificates (List) (Are they up to date?)
   1. Other
J. Maintenance contracts (name and address of contractor)
   1. For cleaning range hoods, ducts, etc.
   2. For maintaining fire alarm system

II. Fire Alarm System
A. Type (local, etc.)
B. Was it tested at this inspection?
C. Did it operate properly?
D. Is there a municipal, automatic, A.D.T., etc., alarm box on the premises?
E. Is it connected to the local alarm system?
F. Are there any features to this system that should be noted? (pre-alert, manual wound, etc.)
G. What means are provided for notifying Fire Department of fire?
H. Will a responsible person be available 24 hours a day to transmit an alarm?

III. Emergency Lighting
A. Type of system
B. Are all units operational?
C. Are all areas covered by system?
D. Is system regularly inspected and tested as required by law?
   1. By whom?
   2. Are records maintained of such tests?
E. Are fire drills held for employees?
F. Are competent watchmen assigned and on duty from 9:00 P.M. to 6:00 A.M. as required by Chapter 143? (Two men required for 100 or more sleeping rooms in buildings 4 or more stories high, one man required for 50 or more

sleeping rooms in buildings 3 stories high)

IV. Sprinkler System
A. Is it complete or partial?
B. Are there any areas that should be sprinklered?
C. What supervisory features are provided?
D. Are sprinkler valves open?
E. Gauges registering properly?
F. Sprinkler heads free and unobstructed?
G. Where does sprinkler alarm sound?

V. Standpipe and Hose System
A. Condition of hose and nozzle?
B. Location of first aid standpipe
C. Locations of Fire Department standpipes

VI. Fire Extinguishers
A. Sufficient in number? (One for every 1,500 sq. ft. floor area?)
B. Is the type provided suitable for the hazards?
C. Condition of extinguishers
   1. Have they been recharged as required? (yearly)
   2. Are they accessible?

VII. Exits
A. Are there two independent exits from each floor?
B. Any obstructions to, or in, doors, stairs, landings, corridors?
C. Do exit doors open OUT?
D. Fire doors kept closed? (Remove any wedges or other obstructions)
E. Is there any location where additional exits are necessary?
F. Exit and directional signs (natural or artificial lighting)
G. Are there barred windows or locked doors? (Clarify if answer is YES)
H. Are enclosed stairs or fire towers available?
   1. Location of same
   2. Self-closing doors?
   3. Proper lighting; type of emergency lighting
   4. Hand rails
I. Are there any transoms over room doors?
   1. Locations of same

VIII. Interior Finishes of Floors, Walls, and Ceilings
A. Is any acoustical ceiling tile used?
   1. Location of use

B. Is any questionable wall covering used?
    (wood paneling, tile, fabric, etc.)
    1. Location of use
C. What type of floor covering is used?
D. Note: Samples of above should be ob-
    tained if possible and submitted for
    testing. Burden of proof is on occupant.

IX. General Check—Any Area
A. Accumulation of waste paper, rubbish,
    furniture, etc.
    1. Where?
B. Housekeeping deficiencies
C. Stairs, ramps, elevators, vent, dumb-
    waiter and other shafts
    1. Are they enclosed?
    2. Are doors self-closing?
    3. What type of interior covering?
        (must be noncombustible)
D. All chutes, including *rubbish* and
    laundry
    1. Do they have self-closing doors?
    2. Are there noncombustible linings?
        (Building code requires 1 hour fire
        resistant rating)
    3. Is there an automatic sprinkler in-
        stallation in the chute?
    4. Is there a fire detection unit pro-
        vided?
    5. Are venting facilities provided which
        extent through roof?
        (a) Are they adequate?
E. Are there instances of temporary
    wiring, extension cords, or the use of
    electrical equipment which should be
    corrected?
F. Are covered metal containers pro-
    vided for rubbish, oily waste, and other
    materials?
G. What methods are used to dispose of
    rubbish?
H. Is rubbish removed daily?
I. Note: Plastic baskets and barrels cannot
    be used for rubbish.

X. Maintenance Shops
A. Indicate violations found, corrections
    made
    1. Carpentry
    2. Plumbing
    3. Electrical
    4. Upholstery
    5. Paint

XI. Incinerator
A. Location
B. How cut off from rest of building?

C. Is it an approved type?
D. Do feed hoppers close tightly?
E. Has it a spark arrestor?
F. How is rubbish handled in transfer from
    chute?

XII. Heating Equipment
A. Location
B. How cut off from rest of building?
C. Are all openings thereto kept closed?
D. Type of fuel used?
E. Where and how fuel stored?
F. Individual responsible for this equip-
    ment
G. What defects were noted?

XIII. Kitchen
A. Location
B. Type of fuel for cooking
C. Condition of ranges, hoods, ducts, etc.
D. Fire protection equipment available
    1. Can personnel use properly?
E. Refrigerating equipment used
    1. Does it have separate enclosure?
        (a) If answer is "no," should it
             have?
    2. Refrigerant used
    3. Condition of motors, etc.
F. Is area vented?
    1. How?
    2. To where?

XIV. Laundry
A. Location
B. How cut off from rest of building?
C. Are dryers and controls properly in-
    stalled?
D. Are vents kept free and clear?
E. Do electric devices including irons
    have automatic controls and are they
    operating properly?
F. Do pilot lights operate OK?

XV. Emergency Electrical Service
A. Type
B. Location
C. How and when placed in operation?

XVI. Utility Gas Service
A. Location
B. Size
C. Shut-off location

XVII. Electrical Service
A. Location
B. Shut-off location

XVIII. Heavy Fuel Oil Shut-Off
A. Location
B. Is it operable?

XIX. Outside Means of Egress

A. Number and type
B. Location
C. Condition
D. Do they open out?

XX. Outside Entrances to Basements
A. Location
B. Do they open out?

XXI. Steamer Connections
A. Location
B. What do the supply?
C. Are they accessible?

XXII. Air Conditioning
A. Complete or partial
B. Location of intake
C. Shut-off control
D. Dampers (automatic where passing through walls, floor, etc.)
E. Refrigerant used

XXIII. Inspector Check Following from Outside Building
A. Location of nearest city fire alarm box number and location of hydrants in relation to building
1. City hydrants

2. Private hydrants
B. Condition, width, and grade of streets
1. Drives or approaches to hotels
2. Can apparatus approach for emergency evacuation, etc. (clarify)
3. Building areas that are accessible
4. Building areas not accessible
C. Factors or obstructions influencing or hampering accessibility for department operations (such as narrow drives, tunnels, grades, overhead wires, fences, walls, gates, parked cars, building set back, etc.)
D. Exposures to this building
1. Adjacent buildings
2. Grass, rubbish, brush, etc.
3. Combustible sheds, other
E. Buildings that this building might expose
F. Remarks
G. Recommendations
H. Note: Briefly describe the existing stairways including the number, type enclosure, their termination point, etc.

Appendix 13b

Safety Attitude Development*

JOHN A. WANAT, et al.

Security supervisors often have the responsibility of instilling safety consciousness into their subordinates. The ideal time to begin this process is as soon as a new person is hired. If people are trained to have a positive safety attitude early, they will think and act safely.

*From *Supervisory Techniques for the Security Professional*, by John A. Wanat et al. (Stoneham, MA: Butterworths, 1981).

Merely telling people to behave safely will not motivate them to change their unsafe behavior patterns. An example is the automotive industry where seat belts are required to be installed in all new cars. Even though the general public is informed of the advantages of using seat belts, the majority of drivers neglect to "buckle up for safety." Adding warning lights and ignition lock-out devices to automobiles did not substantially change things. People simply found ways to disengage these safety precaution devices.

The airline industry requires its passengers to fasten their seat belts during take-off and landing in rough weather and during emergency situations. Most people, as a matter of habit, fasten their seat belts when they board an airplane. This is especially true of those who are accustomed to flying. The commercial airline industry introduced the seat belt safety habit early to its passengers while the automobile industry apparently introduced the safety device much too late for it to be widely accepted. This analogy supports the theory that habits formed early, good or bad, are hard to break.

An important aspect of teaching safety awareness to subordinates is for the supervisor to demonstrate, by constant example, proper safety procedures in carrying out assignments. You cannot expect subordinates to conform to positive safety standards when you neglect to behave safely. A subordinate cannot take a supervisor's *No Smoking* order seriously if the supervisor smokes in unauthorized areas.

Instilling safety consciousness into subordinates is no simple task. It takes time, effort and constant positive reinforcement. The subject of safety is not something that can be discussed today and forgotten tomorrow. Building positive safety attitudes in your subordinates requires constant attention and repetition. Constant reminders will assist subordinates in thinking, acting and working safely.

Warnings alone appear to be of little value in instilling safety awareness in our subordinates. Warnings certainly do prevent illness, accident, or injury. Does the warning on a pack of cigarettes, "Warning: The Surgeon General Has Determined That Cigarette Smoking is Dangerous To Your Health," keep many people from smoking? Does the warning sign above the mechanic's garage door, "Do not enter this work area," keep customers from entering the area where mechanics have cars on lifts? Do we like to be told, "Drive carefully, now," as we enter a car to go somewhere? Do people react positively to warnings such as "Watch yourself"? Such admonitions may even cause some people to react negatively.

A valid safety program can help prevent accidents. It requires, however, that every person, from the highest ranking individual of the management team to the newest employee within the organization, think safety. It is a fallacy to believe that an establishment is safe because it has complied with existing state or federal government safety regulations. Warning signs and machine safety guards are not effective if the employees do not have the proper safety attitude and training.

Safety Training

Safety training, through a well-planned safety program, appears to be an essential element in developing safe working habits. Security supervisors should provide their subordinates with on-the-job safety training, formal safety tranining programs, safety demonstrations, individualized safety talks, bulletin board displays, and employee safety meetings.

It is your responsibility to insure that all new subordinates are given proper safety training on the job. Accompany new security officers on routine patrol, pointing out safety hazards that should be reported, such as smoking violations, cracked walking surfaces, defective electrical wiring, broken glass and items on floors that can cause slips and falls, blocked exits, or faulty fire extinguishers and equipment. Explain the proper procedures for reporting unsafe conditions in detail.

Formal Safety Training Programs

The responsibility for arranging formal in-house training programs for subordinates rests with the training supervisor. Formal training programs should consist of a combination of lectures, demonstrations, films, and reading material which thoroughly acquaints the new security officer with all safety aspects associated with their position.

In addition to regularly scheduled in-house training programs, formal training programs can take place through association workshops and college programs. Formal training programs should be used to introduce employees to management's safety regulations and procedures, to instill safety awareness as a habit, to identify proper safety methods of working, and to acquaint employees with new equipment and techniques.

Safety Demonstrations

There are a host of individuals and groups who are willing to demonstrate the proper safety techniques associated with their line of work or with their line of products.

For fire safety, the local fire department is usually more than eager to demonstrate the safety procedures for extinguishing small fires, using the appropriate fire extinguisher on a fire, evacuating a building, and conducting a fire safety inspection.

Manufacturers usually have trained technicians who are equally eager to demonstrate the safety features of their products.

First-aid squads and organizations such as the American Red Cross Association provide safety demonstrations and classes on how to administer emergency first aid, transport injured victims, and provide emergency disaster assistance.

Individualized Safety Talks

Since safety is a subject that should be given constant attention, it is wise to schedule individual safety talks with subordinates on a routine basis. This procedure provides the security supervisor with the opportunity to review the subordinate's accident record. It affords both parties the opportunity to ask questions that might not be brought out in the open during a group meeting. Individual problems relating to poor safety habits can be discussed while solutions for positive safety behavior can be found.

Bulletin Board Displays

A positive reinforcement to all of the preceding approaches is to place appropriate safety posters on employee bulletin boards as well as in other conspicuous places. Simple, right to the point, posters and safety displays act as nonthreatening constant reminders to think, talk, and practice safety. A specific safety theme can be highlighted each month. For example, October is Fire Safety Month; November can be devoted to Good Housekeeping for Safety; December can stress Electrical Safety; January could be devoted to Positive Safety Attitude Modification. The National Safety Council has hundreds of inexpensive posters that the supervisor can order throughout the year.

Staff Safety Meetings

Periodic safety meetings should be conducted to discuss a specific safety topic. Meetings of this nature should be routinely scheduled well in advance, so the staff can come prepared to discuss intelligently the scheduled topic. In this regard, the supervisor should come prepared with a statement of purpose, hand-out materials on the subject, and a determination to limit discussion to the specific topic of the day. Provide ample time for questions and answers. Plans for future meetings should be made before the staff safety meeting is brought to a conclusion. The supervisor should appoint a recorder who will maintain a record of these meetings. Figure 13b–1 is an example of a brief form which summarizes the most important points discussed at a safety meeting. A copy should be distributed to those who attended the meeting as well as to other interested parties.

```
                    RECORD OF SAFETY MEETING

   Date: _____
   Topic:_____
   Short description of topic outcomes: _____
   _____
   _____

   List hand-out materials:_____
   _____
   _____

   Staff Attending:
   _____    _____
   _____    _____
   _____    _____

   Date of next meeting: _____
   Topic(s) to be discussed _____
   _____
```

Figure 13b–1. Record of safety meeting.

Safety Inspections

Since safe conditions depend on diligent vigilance for possible hazards and on immediate remedial action, routine inspections are one of the most important aspects of a successful safety program.

A checklist becomes an essential tool in performing a self-inspection of your facility. Keep in mind that although standardized checklists are useful, a customized list that meets your particular facility's needs is essential.

Using the checklist, you or a designated representative make periodic walk-through inspections to identify problem areas so that appropriate corrective action may be taken.

Sidewalks, Steps and Parking Areas   Yes No N.A.
■ Are all areas free of conditions which will cause slipping and falling?   ☐ ☐ ☐
■ Is there adequate exterior lighting at night?   ☐ ☐ ☐
■ Are all steps and ramps provided with securely fastened handrails?   ☐ ☐ ☐

Exits
■ Are all exits:
a. free of obstructions and readily accessible?   ☐ ☐ ☐
b. properly marked with exit signs and lighted?   ☐ ☐ ☐
c. equipped with an emergency lighting system in good operating condition?   ☐ ☐ ☐
■ Are all exit doors:
a. arranged to open outwards?   ☐ ☐ ☐
b. easily operated?   ☐ ☐ ☐
c. provided with anti-panic hardware in all public rooms and exits?   ☐ ☐ ☐
■ Are all fire escapes in good condition?   ☐ ☐ ☐

Stairs and Doors
■ Are all stairs covered with anti-slip surfaces?   ☐ ☐ ☐
■ Are all handrails securely fastened?   ☐ ☐ ☐
■ Are full-length clear glass doors and windows marked to avoid persons walking into them?   ☐ ☐ ☐
■ Are all stairway doors kept closed when not in use?   ☐ ☐ ☐

Corridors, Meeting Rooms and Public Areas
■ Are floor surfaces free of slipping and tripping conditions?   ☐ ☐ ☐
■ Are emergency lighting units in good operating condition?   ☐ ☐ ☐

Elevators
■ Are elevators maintained and serviced on a regular schedule?   ☐ ☐ ☐
  Date of last inspection _____

Deliveries
■ Are all delivery trucks inspected and maintained on a regular schedule?   ☐ ☐ ☐
■ Are all drivers experienced and trained in safe driving techniques?   ☐ ☐ ☐

Housekeeping
■ Are adequate ash trays and metal wastebaskets provided in each room?   ☐ ☐ ☐
■ Is combustible trash and rubbish:
a. collected at frequent intervals?   ☐ ☐ ☐
b. stored in covered metal containers?   ☐ ☐ ☐
c. disposed of frequently and not accumulated?   ☐ ☐ ☐
■ Are storage rooms neat and orderly?   ☐ ☐ ☐
■ Are flammable paints and liquids:
a. kept to an absolute minimum?   ☐ ☐ ☐
b. kept in sealed metal containers?   ☐ ☐ ☐
c. stored in vented metal cabinets?   ☐ ☐ ☐

a

Figure 13b–2. Safety inspection checklist. (Reproduced with the permission of the Insurance Company of North America and Pacific Employers Insurance Company.)

Safety Inspection Guidelines

An effective safety inspection depends on several factors. The individual or safety surveillance team must[3]:

1. Be selective. Coverage of all safety aspects in one tour of a department is difficult, if not impossible. Therefore, an inspector might check for basic safety the first time, for improvement of operations the second time, for training needs the third, and so on.

2. Know what to look for. The more a supervisor or safety committee member knows about a job and

	Yes	No	N.A.
■ Are all public areas thoroughly checked for fire hazards after closing?	☐	☐	☐
■ Are only non-flammable cleaning fluids used?	☐	☐	☐
■ Are all closets free of oil mops and flammable materials?	☐	☐	☐

Heat, Light, Power and Appliances

■ Is all heating equipment (including flues and pipes):

	Yes	No	N.A.
a. properly insulated from combustible materials?	☐	☐	☐
b. cleaned and serviced at least annually by a competent heating contractor? Date _____	☐	☐	☐

■ Are electrical, heating and air conditioning rooms:

	Yes	No	N.A.
a. restricted to only authorized personnel?	☐	☐	☐
b. free of combustible storage?	☐	☐	☐
■ Are there indications of frequent replacement of fuses and/or resetting of circuit breakers which would indicate overloading of electrical circuits?	☐	☐	☐
■ Are electrical cabinets kept closed?	☐	☐	☐
■ Are electrical extension and appliance cords in good condition?	☐	☐	☐
■ Has the electrical system been checked and serviced by a competent electrician within the past year? Date _____	☐	☐	☐
■ Is air conditioning equipment cleaned and serviced annually by a competent serviceman? Date of last service _____	☐	☐	☐
■ Are all motors kept clean, and adequately ventilated to reduce over-heating?	☐	☐	☐
■ Are all electrical appliances properly grounded?	☐	☐	☐

Rest Rooms

	Yes	No	N.A.
■ Are rest rooms cleaned regularly and well maintained?	☐	☐	☐

Kitchens

	Yes	No	N.A.
■ Are hoods, ducts, ovens, ranges and filters cleaned on a regular schedule?	☐	☐	☐
■ Is the automatic fire extinguishing system inspected and maintained by contract? Date _____	☐	☐	☐

Fire Protection

■ Are all fire extinguishers:

	Yes	No	N.A.
a. serviced annually?	☐	☐	☐
b. tagged with the date of last service? Date _____	☐	☐	☐
c. conspicuously located and easily accessible?	☐	☐	☐
d. hung within 75 feet of any point on each floor except where a lesser distance is required for a more hazardous area?	☐	☐	☐
e. protected against freezing?	☐	☐	☐

■ Are periodic tests and inspections made of the following to ensure their proper operation:

	Yes	No	N.A.
a. fire hoses? Date _____	☐	☐	☐

b

Figure 13b–2. Continued

each worker's responsibilities, the better an observer she or he will be.

3. Practice observing. The more often a person makes a conscious effort to observe, the more she or he will see each time. Like all skills, observation improves with practice.

4. Keep an open mind. The inspector must avoid judging facts in advance. The inspector must not deny a fact, no matter what conclusion it may seem to force. The inspector must keep his mind open until all the facts are in, then act accordingly.

5. Go beyond general impressions. A clean laboratory or pharmacy, or a careful routine, may still contain hidden hazards.

6. Guard against habit and familiarity. Asking the basic questions who, what, where, when, why, and how often will uncover the real meaning of a situation.

7. Record observations systematically. All notes should be dated, with space for comment on the action taken and its results. The notebook can serve both as a reminder and as a record of progress.

8. Prepare a checklist. A systematic check for litter, obstructions, handling of flammables, condition of fire-fighting equipment, and so forth, will uncover tangible problems that can be corrected.

9. Most important, set a good example.

Figure 13b–2 shows an inspection checklist that can be used as a guide in preparing a customized checklist for your institution and operation.

	Yes	No	N.A.
b. automatic sprinkler system? Date _____	☐	☐	☐
c. fire alarm system? Date _____	☐	☐	☐
■ Is the fire alarm system:			
a. tested periodically? Date _____	☐	☐	☐
b. If manual, marked and accessible?	☐	☐	☐
■ Has fire dept. phone number been conspicuously placed at the switchboard and maintenance shop?	☐	☐	☐
■ Is at least 18″ clearance maintained between sprinklers and high-piled stock in storage?	☐	☐	☐

Employees
■ Are all employees:

	Yes	No	N.A.
a. instructed to call the fire department immediately in case of fire?	☐	☐	☐
b. instructed in evacuation procedures?	☐	☐	☐
c. instructed in the use of fire extinguishing equipment?	☐	☐	☐
d. instructed on what to do in case of a bomb threat?	☐	☐	☐
■ Are signs displayed on each floor instructing employees and tenants where the emergency exits are located?	☐	☐	☐

Burglary and Theft — Money and Valuables

	Yes	No	N.A.
■ Are all windows, doors, and transoms protected against burglary?	☐	☐	☐
■ Is the cash on hand kept in a burglar-resistive safe which is kept in a well-lighted area visible from the street?	☐	☐	☐
■ Are all outside entrances to the basement kept locked when not in use?	☐	☐	☐
■ Do the delivery trucks have good locks on the merchandise compartments?	☐	☐	☐
■ Is the money on the premises kept near the minimum needed to operate on?	☐	☐	☐
■ Are money collections:			
a. deposited the same day in a bank night depository, or	☐	☐	☐
b. stored in a burglar-resistive safe until deposited?	☐	☐	☐
■ Are valuable items and equipment stored in a safe or vault when not in use?	☐	☐	☐

c

Figure 13b–2. Continued

Safety Training for Subordinates

A safety training program is needed for new and existing employees. The supervisor who is responsible for providing the in-service safety training should tailor the program to the audience's needs, based on clearly defined objectives. These objectives should be determined after reviewing the duties and responsibilities of the trainees.

Security personnel job descriptions, although varied, have many common duties and responsibilities. The safety outline in this appendix indicates the subjects that should be covered in a safety program for security personnel.

The security supervisor should supplement each session with appropriate hand-out materials and audio-visual aids. An up-to-date listing of films and other safety teaching aids may be secured from the National Safety Council and from other organizations listed at the end of this appendix.

Safety Training Outline

Session I
Safety and the Security Officer:
Team Effort; Accidents Affect Morale and Public Relations; Safety—Everyone's Responsibility; Accidents are Costly; Company Safety Rules and Regulations; Think Safety.
Session II
General Safety Practices:
Proper Lifting Procedures; Slips and Falls; Ladders; Machine Guards; Skin Protection; Falling Objects; Materials Handling; Personal Protection Clothing.
Session III
Identifying Accident Problems:
OSHA Regulations; Electric Hazards; Safety Inspections; Unsafe Conditions; Unsafe Acts; Accident Investigations; Accident Reports.
Session IV
Housekeeping:
Benefits of Good Housekeeping; Security's Responsibility; Sources for Help; Physical Plant—Floors and Aisles; Storage Yards and Grounds; Machines and Equipment.
Session V
Fire Prevention and Control:
Identifying Fire Hazards; Causes of Fires; Alarms, Equipment and Evacuation; Fire Drills; Fire Extinguishers; Special Fire Protection Problems.

Session VI
First Aid:
First Aid Procedures—Fire Blankets, Stretchers, Telephone Communications; General Medications; First Aid Supplies; Bleeding; Shock; Resuscitation; Breaks and Fractures; Open Wounds; Chemical Burns; Fire Burns; Convulsions.
Session VII
Firearm Safety:
Firearm Training; Safe Handling; Loading and Unloading; Maintenance; Control; Horseplay; Storage.

Accident Investigation

Supervisors have a responsibility to investigate accidents in an effort to control tomorrow's potential losses as well as to help prevent similar accidents in the future. Proper investigation of an accident can lead to the real or basic cause of the accident so that corrective action can be taken to avoid future mishaps (see Figure 13b–3).

Not all accidents result in major injuries requiring medical attention. There are those instances commonly known as *near misses*, where individuals often escape with minor injuries or no injuries at all. These near misses should also be investigated. Today's near miss may be tomorrow's tragedy. Look on accident investigation as accident prevention.

Every accident should be investigated as soon as possible. The sooner an accident is investigated, the better the opportunity to obtain all of the facts. The greater the time span between the accident and the investigation, the greater the chance for information and evidence to be lost, forgotten, or destroyed.

Make every effort to investigate the accident at the scene. Make clear to everyone involved that the purpose of the investigation is to obtain the facts and not to place blame. The investigation may uncover human error or negligence, or it may uncover an unsafe condition. The investigation itself, however, should be concerned only with the facts.

The investigation, based on accumulated facts, should determine the cause of the accident. Most accidents have multiple causes or contributing factors. The investigator should endeavor to identify all the causes and contributing factors to determine the overriding cause of the accident. Once the major cause of the accident is determined, make a recommendation to correct the cause of the accident.

MORE EFFECTIVE ACCIDENT CONTROL

THROUGH GOOD

INVESTIGATION   AND   REMEDIAL ACTION

BY APPLYING THESE OBJECTIVES

1. To determine all contributing causal factors.
2. To determine the fundamental or basic reason for the existence of each contributing factor.

1. To eliminate or control each contributing cause.
2. To eliminate or control the reason for the existence of each contributing cause.

AND FOLLOWING THESE GUIDEPOSTS

- In case of injury, make sure worker is properly cared for before doing anything else
- When practical, have scene kept as undisturbed as possible
- Investigate as promptly as possible
- Whenever possible, go to scene of accident for initial investigation
- As applicable, have someone else get photographs; make drawings or measurements
- Interview all witnesses, one at a time and separately
- Reassure each witness of investigation's real purpose
- Get witnesses' initial version with minimal interruption; ask for complete version step by step; have them describe and point without doing
- Apply empathy in interviews; make no attempt to fix blame or find fault
- Be objective; don't have fixed opinion in advance
- When witness finishes initial explanation, ask questions to fill in gaps
- Avoid questions that lead witness or imply answers wanted or unwanted
- Summarize your understanding with witness after interview
- Express sincere appreciation to anyone who helped in the investigation
- Record data accurately

(Select appropriate actions)
- Institute formal training program
- Give personal reinstruction
- Institute proper job instruction program
- Institute a safety tipping program
- Temporarily or permanently reassign person/s
- Institute a job analysis program
- Order job analysis on specific job/s
- Revise existing job analysis
- Institute a job observation program
- Order job observation on specific job/s
- Institute new or improve existing inspection program
- Institute pre-use checkout of equipment
- Establish or revise indoctrination for new or transferred employees
- Repair or replace equipment
- Improve biomechanic design of equipment
- Establish biomechanic requirements for new equipment
- Improve basic design or establish design standards
- Improve identification or color code for safety
- Install or improve safeguards
- Eliminate unnecessary material in area
- Institute program of order or improve clean-up
- Institute mandatory protective equipment program or improve existing coverage or design
- Use safer material
- Estabish purchasing standard/s or controls
- Institute incident recall program
- Create safety incentive program
- Improve physical examination program

WILL REDUCE

INJURIES & DAMAGE	DEFECTS & DELAYS
REJECTS & REWORK	MISTAKES & WASTE

. . . . Adequate time spent today on proper investigation and effective remedial action is cost reduction effort on tomorrow's losses.

Figure 13b–3. More effective accident control. (Reproduced with permission of the Insurance Company of North America.)

SUPERVISOR'S ACCIDENT INVESTIGATION REPORT

COMPANY OR BRANCH _Eastern Packing Company_		DEPARTMENT _Shipping_		
EXACT LOCATION _Bldg A. South side, west loading dock_	DATE OF OCCURRENCE _3-7-69_	TIME _2:45_ ☒ AM ☐ PM	DATE REPORTED _3-7-69_	

PERSONAL INJURY		PROPERTY DAMAGE	
INJURED'S NAME _Paul S. Riley_		PROPERTY DAMAGED _Lift truck_	
OCCUPATION _Lift truck operator_	INJURED PART OF BODY _right arm_	ESTIMATED COSTS $ _650._	ACTUAL COSTS $ _785.90_
NATURE OF INJURY _Fracture of upper arm_		NATURE OF DAMAGE _mast and steering column bent_	
OBJECT/EQUIPMENT/SUBSTANCE/INFLICTING INJURY _lift truck_		OBJECT/EQUIPMENT/SUBSTANCE/INFLICTING DAMAGE _ground_	
PERSON WITH MOST CONTROL OF OBJECT/EQUIPMENT/SUBSTANCE _Paul S. Riley_		PERSON WITH MOST CONTROL OF OBJECT/EQUIPMENT/SUBSTANCE _Paul S. Riley_	

DESCRIPTION

DESCRIBE CLEARLY HOW THE ACCIDENT OCCURRED: ATTACH ACCIDENT DIAGRAM FOR ALL MOTOR VEHICLE ACCIDENTS.

Paul was backing lift truck #26 North to clear aisleway in order for truck #22 to pass. He backed into bumping block without applying brakes causing block to break off dock resulting in his truck moving backward off dock to ground 6 ft. below on North side 35 feet from East end. Riley struck arm on truck as he attempted to jump free. He landed clear of truck on ground 6 ft. below dock.

ANALYSIS

WHAT ACTS, FAILURES TO ACT AND/OR CONDITIONS CONTRIBUTED MOST DIRECTLY TO THIS ACCIDENT?

Riley reported defective brake on Operators Report form at start of turn on 3-7-69. He removed truck from garage and operated it from 11 A.M. with defective brake. Operator was using bumping block as stopping mechanism for truck. The bumping block on the dock was in unsafe condition. Condition of block was reported on inspection reports of 1-5-69 and 2-20-69.

WHAT ARE THE BASIC OR FUNDAMENTAL REASONS FOR THE EXISTENCE OF THESE ACTS AND/OR CONDITIONS?

Employee was not properly motivated to recognize seriousness of unsafe brake condition. Garage personnel did not properly follow-up condition on Operators report form. Maintenance control failed to effect prompt corrective action to bumper block. Area supervisor failed to properly follow-up unsafe bumper condition.

LOSS SEVERITY POTENTIAL			PROBABLE RECURRENCE RATE		
☒ Major	☐ Serious	☐ Minor	☒ Frequent	☐ Occasional	☐ Rare

PREVENTION

WHAT ACTION HAS OR WILL BE TAKEN TO PREVENT RECURRENCE? PLACE X BY ITEMS COMPLETED.

X Personnel dept. has been requested to assist in establishing lift truck operators training course. Lift truck rules will be reviewed with all operators by 10-6-69. Riley will be included in both programs when he returns to work. X A statement of policy on handling of safety work orders has been issued by Vice President Matthews. X Maintenance control has issued a hazard classification coding system for use on all safety work orders. X All operators have been properly instructed not to operate equipment considered to be unsafe. X A follow-up system for inspection report items is being developed by Ad Hoc Committee headed by Investigator.

INVESTIGATED BY _Ralph B. Jones_	DATE _3-7-69_	REVIEWED BY _Frank K. Roberts_	DATE _3-8-69_

Figure 13b–4. Supervisor's accident investigation report. (Reproduced with permission of the Insurance Company of North America.)

Submit a report to management indicating the cause and recommended corrective action.

Accident Investigation Report

A written report of an accident investigation should list the facts uncovered during the investigation (See Figure 13b–4). It also should include any action taken or recommendations to management. As with all reports, forms differ with each company or organization. A survey of accident reports lists the following essential questions:

- Who was involved in the accident?
- When did it happen?
- Where did it happen?
- What was the cause of the accident?
- What action was taken?

Service Organizations and Associations

The following list will provide you with an idea of the types of services available. A more complete list of possible sources can be found in the National Safety Council publication titled "Accident Prevention Manual for Industrial Operations."

American Chemical Society
1155 16th Street, N.W.
Washington, D.C. 20036

American Industrial Hygiene Association
210 Haddon Avenue
Westmont, New Jersey 08108

American Medical Association
Department of Occupational Health
535 North Dearborn Street
Chicago, Illinois 60610

American National Standards Institute
1430 Broadway
New York, New York 10018

American National Red Cross
Safety Services
17th and D Streets, N.W.
Washington, D.C. 20006

American Public Health Association
1740 Broadway
New York, New York 10019

American Society for Testing and Materials
1916 Race Street
Philadelphia, Pennsylvania 19103

American Society of Safety Engineers
850 Busse Highway
Park Ridge, Illinois 60068

Human Factors Society
P.O. Box 1369
Santa Monica, California 90406

Industrial Hygiene Foundation of America, Inc.
5231 Centre Avenue
Pittsburgh, Pennsylvania 15232

Industrial Medical Association
55 East Washington Street
Chicago, Illinois 60602

Industrial Safety Equipment Association, Inc.
60 E. 42nd Street
New York, New York 10017

The National Fire Protection Association
60 Batterymarch Street
Boston, Massachusetts 02110

The National Safety Council
452 North Michigan Avenue
Chicago, Illinois 60611

National Society for the Prevention of Blindness, Inc.
79 Madison Avenue
New York, New York 10016

Underwriters Laboratories, Inc.
207 East Ohio Street
Chicago, Illinois 60611

References

1. *General Industry: Safety and Health Regulations, Part 1910* (U.S. Department of Labor, OSHA, 1974).
2. Frank E. Bird, Jr., *Management Guide to Loss Control* (Lexington, Mass.: Lexington Books, 1983), p. 4.
3. Safety Guide for Health Care Institutes, a Joint Publication of the American Hospital Association and the National Safety Council, pp 109–110.

Index